# THE KNIGHTS OF COLUMBUS
## AN ILLUSTRATED HISTORY

# ANDREW T. WALTHER
# MAUREEN H. WALTHER

## FOREWORD BY CARL A. ANDERSON

SQUAREONE
PUBLISHERS

**Cover Photo Images:**

*Front cover photos:* Top row (left to right): Supreme Officers' meeting with Calvin Coolidge, 1926; August 1925 *Columbia* cover; K of C field secretaries ("Caseys") giving aid to American troops. Second row: Father Michael McGivney.

Third row (left to right): St. Mary's Church; Knights' Tower at the National Shrine; Pope John Paul II at Aqueduct Mass, 1995.

Bottom row (left to right): K of C field secretaries in 1918; sheet music *Casey*; Iraqi Christians raising cross in 2017.

*Back cover photos* (left to right): Father Michael McGivney; George Herman "Babe" Ruth; John F. Kennedy; Mother Teresa; Floyd Patterson.

COVER DESIGNER AND TYPESETTER: Jeannie Rosado
IN-HOUSE EDITORS: Marie Caratozzolo and Joanne Abrams

**Square One Publishers**
115 Herricks Road
Garden City Park, NY 11040
(516) 535-2010
(877) 900-BOOK
www.squareonepublishers.com

**Library of Congress Cataloging-in-Publication Data**
Names: Walther, Andrew T., author. | Walther, Maureen H., author.
Title: The Knights of Columbus : an illustrated history / Andrew T. Walther,
  Maureen H. Walther.
Description: Garden City Park, NY : Square One Publishers, [2020] | Includes
  index.
Identifiers: LCCN 2018051750| ISBN 9780757002243 (pbk.) | ISBN 9780757003080
  (hardback) | ISBN 9780757053085 (ebook)
Subjects: LCSH: Knights of Columbus. | Fraternal organizations—United
  States—History. | Catholic Church—Societies, etc.
Classification: LCC HS1538.C73 W35 2020 | DDC 267/.24273—dc23
LC record available at https://lccn.loc.gov/2018051750

Printed in India

10   9   8   7   6   5   4   3   2   1

# Contents

*Acknowledgments*, v

*Foreword by Carl A. Anderson*, ix

Introduction, 1

**1.** In the Beginning, 5

**2.** The Early Years *1881 to 1896*, 11

**3.** Taking Root, Expansion, and the War Effort *1897 to 1919*, 39

**4.** In Search of Liberty *1920 to 1929*, 67

**5.** Helping Our Neighbors—The Great Depression *1930 to 1939*, 91

**6.** War and Peace *1940 to 1950*, 113

**7.** "One Nation Under God" *1951 to 1964*, 135

**8.** Balancing Modernization with Preservation *1964 to 1977*, 157

**9.** One Christian Family *1978 to 1999*, 177

**10.** Into the New Millennium *2000 to Present*, 207

The Path Ahead, 259

*About the Authors*, 261

*Index*, 262

*Image Permissions and Credits*, 269

# Acknowledgments

During the 125th anniversary of the Order, many long-forgotten photographs were brought forward to contribute to the context of the celebration by then-photo archivist Bob Murphy. Embracing this visual history, Supreme Knight Carl Anderson saw a need for a book that would bring to life the story of the Order with both pictures and words.

Over the years, the Knights of Columbus had commissioned a number of works related to its history. There were formal histories like *Knights of Columbus in Peace and War* (1920), and *Faith and Fraternalism* (1982, with an update in 1992). There were also books that dealt with various aspects of the Order's past, including *By their Works* (2005) and *Parish Priest* (2006). There have been other histories as well—including state council histories, regionally known, but little known nationally—which were also incredibly helpful in stitching together more than a century of dynamic stories and unearthing hidden gems that bring life to the past. Critical, too, were the past issues of *Columbia* magazine and its predecessor *Columbiad*, which documented the Knights' history in real time, month by month.

Until his death in 2018, Christopher Kauffman served as the dean of Knights of Columbus history. His many books and articles, most notably *Faith and Fraternalism,* provided an indispensable service to those interested in the Order's past.

This book, *The Knights of Columbus: An Illustrated History*, is in some ways the third—illustrated and updated—edition of *Faith and Fraternalism,* building upon and incorporating key facts from that work. It also draws upon and synthesizes other contributions to the organization's history from the other books mentioned above, as well as from the Order's magazine, newsletters, website, archives, museum, etc. In short, this new book was designed to be a window into the fascinating story of the Knights' past— some aspects of which were already known, some of which had been forgotten, and many of which have increasing relevance today.

As the project progressed, we soon discovered that the richness of the Order's history included elements that had never before been treated. So in addition to building upon and synthesizing past efforts, this book breaks substantial new ground, tying together important threads and introducing the reader to aspects of the Knights' history that have remained hidden for decades.

Of course, the archives did not give forth their secrets without help, and this book is the work of many hands, many minds, and many friends.

Particular thanks goes to Anne Ostendarp, the Knights of Columbus' multimedia archivist, who made this project a top priority, assisting with both the text and the photos with supreme energy and enthusiasm. Her professionalism, tireless help, and countless hours on this project were a *sine qua non* for its successful completion.

VivianLea Solek, the Order's archivist, opened the archives to us and spent many hours helping with invaluable research, finding critical historical documents and artifacts, and offering important feedback on the text itself. Bethany Sheffer, the Knights of Columbus Museum curator, also provided significant help with the text and with needed elements from the museum's collection. Special thanks also to Stephen Feiler, who always seemed to have the answer no one else could find; to Luis Guevarra, whose knowledge of the Order's past and present work in Mexico was irreplaceable; and to Brian Caulfield, whose careful review produced fact-checks and edits that substantially improved the text. Evan Holguin, too, has our sincere gratitude. He helped us bring the project together in the home stretch by running down missing items and securing needed photos, and helping in myriad ways, large and small, without which the book would still be a work in progress.

Also noteworthy was the effort of so many of the staff of the Knights of Columbus' communications department. Between 2010 and 2017, many had roles in researching and editing this book. Particular thanks go to Rose Wagner, Michele Nuzzo-Naglieri, Kaitlyn Landgraf Bartley, Liz Hansen, Matt St. John, Kyle Montgomery, Tom Serafin, Chuck Lindberg, Andrew Butler, and Rebecca Devine. From outside New Haven, the editing support provided by Gerald Korson deserves special mention, as does the work of Professor Charles Mercier, who helped us in the early stages of the project and whose love of history is profound and contagious. Alton Pelowski, Andrew Matt, and the rest of the *Columbia* magazine staff provided assistance as well, most notably access to the digital archive of the magazine, which facilitated the research process enormously.

Some friends who worked on this project have since retired, but their contributions were nonetheless substantial. They include MaryLou Cummings (former curator at the Knights of Columbus Museum), Sue Brosnan (the Order's former archivist), and, of course, the previously mentioned Bob Murphy, who reintroduced us to the many great photographs of the past, and who inspired this book as a result.

An important contribution was also made by the late Patrick Korten, former spokesman for the Knights of Columbus, who did substantial work on the drafts of the early chapters of this book. While he is no longer with us, he is missed, and this book is a testament to his hard work and his love for the Order. John Cummings, former director of the graphics department and a font of interesting historical detail, also holds a special place in our hearts and memory.

Warm thanks go to Supreme Knight Carl Anderson, for his overall vision in leading the Knights of Columbus as well as for his deep appreciation of the Order's history and future, which led to the commissioning of this book, giving us a chance to both update the Order's history and tell the story visually as well as verbally. His interest in maintaining the vision and mission of Father McGivney has been an example to millions of Knights around the world.

The other supreme officers and their staffs also have our deep appreciation: Supreme Chaplain Archbishop William Lori of Baltimore, for his contributions to the Catholic identity of the Order. Deputy Supreme Knight Patrick Kelly and his staff in Corporate Communications under the leadership of Kevin Shinkle, and those at the Knights of Columbus Museum and the Saint John Paul II National Shrine—especially Maxime Nogier. Supreme Secretary Michael O'Connor and his staff—especially Kevin Brady and the membership records department for their aid in questions of membership and logistics, respectively. Supreme Advocate John Marrella and the legal department, including Rick St. Hilaire, Matt McGrath, Mike Votto, Szymon Czyszek, and Cheryl Cocchiola, who helped us navigate the various issues related to the rights to photographs and works of art that inevitably arise in a project of this type. Supreme Treasurer Ron Schwartz and his staff—especially Dana Cirillo in procurement and the untiring Evan Holguin, whom Ron was kind enough to loan to this effort for several critical weeks. Supreme Master Dennis Stoddard for his expert input on the sections of the book related to the Fourth Degree.

Supreme Director Tony Minopoli and William Murray, Senior Vice President of Agency and Marketing, always made time to answer questions about the business aspects of the Knights of Columbus and its related history and future. Gary Nolan, Vice President for Fraternal Education, Training and Ceremonials, also helped ensure the accuracy of the sections on local council organization and the Order's degree ceremonies; while Colonel Chuck Gallina, the Order's Advisor for Military and Veterans Affairs, assisted with details related to the Order's history with the military and in Korea. In Rome, Enrico Demajo helped us relate the history of the Knights of Columbus there, and also helped us secure critical documentation and permissions. Arnaud Boutheon likewise assisted from France. The Order—and the authors—have been blessed to work with such a team.

A word of thanks also to Past Supreme Knight Virgil Dechant, who helped shape Chapters 8 and 9 of this book through our many conversations over the years and with his own recent biography, *The Fraternalist*, which is an important historical record in its own right.

Likewise, the history of the Knights of Columbus could not be written without the many heroes, whose work large and small has contributed to this great enterprise. The witnesses to faith and charity in the work of Knights on the local level have been both the lifeblood of the Order and a constant inspiration to us throughout the process, and we hope that this book is a tribute to all of them. The ingenuity of past unsung hard workers shaped not only the Order but also our appreciation of it, including that of long-serving Supreme Secretaries Daniel Colwell and William McGinley, overseas commissioner William Larkin, and board members like Supreme Master John Reddin, who all made outsized contributions to the Order.

Others from outside the Order lent important input to this project, as well. Dr. Jonathan Reyes graciously read a draft of the book and provided important contextual insights and feedback. In addition, L. Martin Nussbaum's legal research uncovered long-forgotten but immensely important documentary evidence related to the founding of the Knights of Columbus, and specifically the thinking of the founders concerning the central role of faith in the endeavor.

The team at Square One Publishers deserves particular mention and thanks. In addition to bringing in an outside researcher to assist with the project, Rudy Shur, along with Marie Caratozzolo, Joanne Abrams, Jeannie Rosado, Anthony Pomes, and Michael Weatherhead, were indispensable in keeping this project on track, and in providing excellent ideas, edits, research, feedback, encouragement, and professional insight. Their layout and graphic skills and their help with photo selection and textual edits helped make this not just a book, but a thing of beauty.

Of course, no acknowledgment would be complete without thanks to the founder himself: Father Michael McGivney. It is his timeless vision, genius, and care for his flock that this book—and those in it—celebrates most of all.

# Foreword

"**N**one of us—neither you nor me—were manufactured in a laboratory; we have a history, we have roots. And everything we do, the results we achieve, the beauty we create in the future, all comes from those roots."

As the book in your hands neared publication, Pope Francis's 2018 message to young people resonated deeply with its purpose. The Knights of Columbus often refers to itself not just as a brotherhood, but as a family. This book is both our family's chronicle and its photo album: a history of more than 100,000 words and 500 pictures, masterfully joined to tell a story so unique that neither words nor pictures alone could suffice. And as with a family's history, it is more than mere prologue to its present. As Pope John Paul II observed when visiting Japan in 1981: "To remember the past is to commit oneself to the future."

Like Pope Francis, Pope John Paul II understood that the future is built upon the past, and he believed that the embrace of the truth of the past is critical to committing to the future. In light of this idea, *The Knights of Columbus: An Illustrated History* is not simply a record of yesterday's harvest, but also contains within it the seeds of a future filled with promise. Taken comprehensively, this book provides a kind of decoding key, facilitating the type of understanding or—in the case of our members—self-understanding that is foundational to knowing what the Knights of Columbus is, why it has been able to achieve so much, and what it might be capable of achieving in the future. With that in mind, it is a joy to be able to present, for the first time since the founding of the Knights of Columbus, a history that is simultaneously accessible, comprehensive, and richly illustrated.

Considering both the quantity and quality of history-shaping endeavors that the Knights of Columbus has led since 1882, the organization has been without doubt one of the most important American associations, and certainly the most notable lay Catholic organization founded in the United States. So while this book is of obvious relevance to my brother Knights of Columbus, I am confident that the reach of the Order's good works will be of interest to and will surprise almost any reader, particularly those interested in the Catholic Church, philanthropy, religious freedom, patriotism, and race relations.

That America would give rise to such a uniquely important Catholic association is not as surprising as it might first appear, if one takes into account two observations made about Catholics and American social self-organization by Alexis de Tocqueville. Chronicling his impressions of nineteenth-century United States in his renowned work *Democracy in America*, de Tocqueville concluded that Catholics in America were uniquely patriotic. Although they were a minority, he observed that "the Catholics of the United States are at the same time the most faithful believers and the most zealous citizens." De Tocqueville also noted America's unique capacity for "associations," writing: "In no country in the world has the principle of association been more successfully used, or more unsparingly applied to a multitude of different objects, than in America." He went so far as to say that in the United States, "nothing, in my opinion, is more deserving of our attention than the intellectual and moral associations."

With de Tocqueville's commentary in mind, we might better understand that the group Father Michael McGivney would forge would be an organization uniquely suited to the United States. Indeed it would unite those seen by the French author as America's most zealous citizens (Catholics) with what he saw as the country's most notable problem-solving tool (associations). Besides the Catholic basis for its membership, the Knights of Columbus was an association based on the Catholic faith in every detail of its functioning. As events in this book illustrate, the young priest sought specifically to protect the faith of Catholic men from the caustic effects of anti-Catholic secret societies, which offered men advancement at the price of their religious beliefs.

While the Order has a charitable component in the protection of widows and orphans, it had an evangelizing component, as well. After a breadwinner died in the late nineteenth century, poor families often found themselves further shattered, as family members were often separated and sent to live with relatives or in state-run institutions. In such circumstances, the family members' practice of the faith could be become very difficult. An insurance plan that kept families together after the death of a breadwinner also helped them keep the faith with the understanding that the family that stays together, prays together.

In this, the Catholic faith brought Knights together in a unity that manifested not only in providing charity together, but also in keeping the faith together. Such emphasis on evangelization of the laity by the laity also had uniquely "American" resonance and roots. The greatest mass conversion to the Catholic faith in history was the result of a layman, Saint Juan Diego, faithfully delivering the message and image of Our Lady of Guadalupe in 1531 in the middle of the American hemisphere. Under that title, she would become patroness of the entire American hemisphere—and of the Philippines (which were under Spanish control for many years). Like Saint Juan Diego, the Knights—faithful sons of the Church—were instrumental in forming and supporting lay people in their faith. Although not a priest himself, Saint Juan Diego served as the messenger of the Catholic faith to his people, working closely with the Church's priests and bishops. The Knights' work was more diffuse, but still carried forward this tradition of the laity supporting the faith of the laity, with brother Knights supporting one another in the faith while working closely with their pastors and bishops, as well.

Although born in the immediate aftermath of the First Vatican Council, the Knights seemed to anticipate the Second Vatican Council by embracing the "universal call to holiness" and the role of the laity. While seemingly coincidental, the Order's early expansion beyond the United States paid tribute to the hemisphere's history of lay evangelization. Each of the countries to which it formally expanded in its first quarter century or so of existence claimed Our Lady of Guadalupe as a patron, including Canada (1897), Mexico (1905), the Philippines (1905), Cuba (1909), and Panama (1909). Notably, the first council in Mexico was named for Our Lady of Guadalupe.

At the same time, the Knights anticipated by a decade—and grew up alongside—Catholic Social Teaching, which formally began with Pope Leo XIII's encyclical *Rerum Novarum* (promulgated a little more than a decade after the Order's founding). The encyclical focused not only on what a just society should look like but also on the importance of the family. The Knights continued to embrace Catholic social teaching and became excellent examples of Church teaching on the twin responsibilities of subsidiarity—the idea that problems should be solved at the most local level—and solidarity towards one's neighbors, near and far.

While uniquely American in certain ways, two additional characteristics helped the Order come of age in diverse circumstances and environments. The first was an unwavering Catholic sense of the importance of evangelization. The second was a creative flexibility to meet needs as they arose. Together, these characteristics helped the Order navigate challenges and opportunities in the nineteenth and twentieth centuries—and into the twenty-first century—in thousands of communities, and in regions as diverse as North and Latin America, Europe and Asia.

In addition to helping Catholic men and their families keep the faith, since the 1880s, the Knights have sought to evangelize its membership and the broader culture. Knights today receive faith formation through the degree process itself, as well as from their chaplains, through *Columbia* magazine, and through the programs and outreach that have been added over the years. The family and parish-based Domestic Church program, Catholic Information Service, Eucharistic and Marian Congresses, books and films produced by the Order, and an Order-wide emphasis on the sacraments and the rosary further promote a solid faith. At the state and local levels, additional faith formation programs abound.

Formed with the understanding that the Catholic faith offered a positive influence within the public square, as well as within the family itself, the early Knights completely embraced Father McGivney's choice of the name Columbus—the most famous Catholic lauded as a hero in nineteenth-century American history books. In choosing this name, the fledgling group underscored the fact that from the first contact with this region by Europeans, Catholic evangelization of the Americas had occurred and had a profound impact. While staunch defenders of the rights of all faiths to have a place in America, the Knights were making clear in their name that Catholicism had just as much right as any other religion to flourish in the New World. They also understood that the Knights had a unique role to play among Catholics in uniting their co-religionists regardless of race or background. In other words, this choice of name made the same case that de Tocqueville had made: Good Catholics made great citizens.

Pope Benedict XVI had a well-known fondness for de Tocqueville and his analysis of the United States. In the Holy Father's encyclical *Deus Caritas Est*, his discussion of the need for organized action by groups of individuals—regardless of state action—has been seen as echoing de Tocqueville. He explicitly cited de Tocqueville in his 2008 speech at the United Nations headquarters. In his subsequent words at St. Patrick's Cathedral in 2008 about early-American Catholicism's "unity of vision and purpose," one can again hear an echo of the French writer's views. There, the Holy Father also explicitly placed Father McGivney's work within this unique American context, saying:

> Was not this unity of vision and purpose—rooted in faith and a spirit of constant conversion and self-sacrifice—the secret of the impressive growth of the Church in this country? We need but think of the remarkable accomplishment of that exemplary American priest, the Venerable Michael McGivney, whose vision and zeal led to the establishment of the Knights of Columbus. . . .

Not surprisingly, the commitment to evangelization meant that, in addition to the many faith resources made available to Knights, faith and freedom were inseparably joined in the Order's commitment to defend the free exercise of religion for Catholics and those of other faiths, and faith should be explained to even the most hostile non-Catholic audiences. This commitment led to the establishment of the Knights' Commission on Religious Prejudices a century ago, effectively countering anti-Catholic propaganda with the truth about Catholicism. The hospitality centers run by the Knights of Columbus before and during World War I likewise shared the faith with those defending freedom by showing the extent of the Catholic commitment to country and love of neighbor under the banner: "Everybody Welcome, Everything Free."

When the freedoms of religious groups and believers were curtailed, or populations were persecuted for their faith, the Knights spoke out and took action time and again. The Order decried anti-Catholic actions by the United States government in Cuba and the Philippines at the turn of the twentieth century. It spoke out against the secularism laws in France in 1905, the persecution of Catholics in Mexico, and the genocide against Christians in the Middle East in the 1920s (and again, more recently). Also in the 1920s, more than a decade before concentration camps revealed the most repulsive face of anti-Semitism, the Order sought to give Jews a place of honor in American history, commissioning a book on their history in the United States. A decade later, the Order spoke up for the Jews again, this time for those in Germany as well as for others persecuted by the Nazis in the 1930s and 1940s. Following the war, the Order vocally supported the civil and religious rights of those who had lost their freedom to Communism behind the Iron Curtain during the Cold War.

From its earliest days, the Knights saw itself as supporting ideals that transcended race or color and further unified Catholics. As early as the nineteenth century, the Knights invited African Americans to join and to take on leadership positions within the Order. The Knights of Columbus was also praised as unique for its running of integrated military hospitality centers during World War I—decades before the military itself was integrated. Following the war, the Knights provided education and job training for veterans, black and white alike. And when the Navy and Marines finally integrated, three decades after World War I ended, Past Supreme Knight (and then Secretary of the Navy) Francis Matthews played a key role.

In the 1920s, the Order commissioned books on the important contributions of African Americans (by W.E.B. du Bois), Jews, and German Americans to the country's history. Du Bois would go on to contrast the Knights of Columbus' work on race with the segregation still present in much of the Catholic Church. The Order showed an early concern for Hispanics and those in the Philippines, as well. In the midst of strong anti-Spanish sentiment in the United States following the Spanish-American War, the Order established itself in Cuba, Mexico, and the Philippines. During the Civil Rights Movement in the 1960s, Knights were involved at many levels, with the Supreme Council even forcing a prominent New Orleans Hotel to integrate or lose our business. As a former member of the U.S. Commission on Civil Rights, I am proud to say that this work for racial harmony has continued into the present, most recently with the Order's support for the USCCB Ad Hoc Committee Against Racism, and its work with African-American Church leaders from many faith traditions to call for an end to racism and political violence. In this work, the Knights have sought to emulate the Good Samaritan and provide for their neighbors—of any race or background.

The Knights are probably best known for charity, and that charity itself has had an important evangelizing component. The Order's embrace of Christ's great commandment—to love God completely and your neighbor as yourself—shows an implicit understanding of what Pope Francis has said: "There can be no authentic compassion for others if there is no loving passion for Jesus," and expressed itself in the Order's first principle as what Pope John Paul II called "a charity that evangelizes"—bringing an expression of faith both to the giver and the receiver.

In its work for religious freedom, inter-religious dialogue, and outreach and support of people of other faiths, the Order anticipated the calls of the Second Vatican Council on these issues specifically. At the same time, its dedication to charity—for *everyone*—fit well Pope Paul VI's description of the Catholic Church and the council, taking as its model the story of the Good Samaritan. This model was further developed by Pope Benedict XVI, who wrote:

> The Christian's program—the program of the Good Samaritan, the program of Jesus—is "a heart which sees." This heart sees where love is needed and acts accordingly. Obviously when charitable activity is carried out by the Church as a communitarian initiative, the spontaneity of individuals must be combined with planning, foresight and cooperation with other similar institutions.

Millions of Knights have had hearts that see. United with their fraternal brothers, they have acted on what they have seen. This book is their story, and the ways in which they have acted are an important part of this story. Specifically, at every level, Knights have shown an incredible creativity and flexibility in responding to a vast array of needs in a way that demonstrates both love of God and love of neighbor. The fact that around the world, love answers concrete needs, combined with the Knights' willingness to address needs as they arise, led the organization to take root in the diverse soils of the northeastern United States, French Canada, Latin America, and the Philippines—and later throughout all of North America as well as in the Caribbean, Europe, and Asia. The Order was at its best when it was creative and even prophetic, with many of its early actions punching far above their weight.

In many ways, the method and virtues of the Knights' charity—locally and globally—were encapsulated in Pope Benedict XVI's prayer for young people for the 2007 World Youth Day. After enjoining them to take Catholic Social Teaching to heart, he prayed: "May the Holy Spirit make you creative in charity, persevering in your commitments, and brave in your initiatives, so that you will be able to offer your contribution to the building up of the 'civilization of love.' The horizon of love is truly boundless: it is the whole world!"

No mere bystander, the Knights of Columbus has helped shape individual lives and major historical circumstances in profound ways through creative charity, combined perseverance, and bravery. Responding in this way, and always grounded in its Catholic faith, the Order has found itself quickly at home in many foreign lands. This is part of the genius of a local council system, which allows men in communities around the world to meet local needs while at the same time working on global or national priorities. Just as every family is unique, so every council is uniquely shaped by the faith and strengths of its members and by the needs of its parish and community. And while no book could do justice to the millions of works of brotherly love undertaken on the local level by councils and assemblies, this book gives voice to the councils' many important deeds. By thus highlighting not only the work taken on by the Knights of Columbus institutionally but also individual examples of council work conceived and carried out through local initiative, this book provides a fuller picture of the Knights of Columbus. It is a portrait of men embodying the spirit of *faith in action*—and of action in time of need.

Much has changed since 1882. The insurance and financial service aspects of the Order have been updated in keeping with industry best practices and technological advancements. New lines of business—such as K of C Asset Advisors—have been offered. With such changes in business practices and technology, the Order has taken major steps forward in better organizing itself and creating greater efficiency to ensure the long-term sustainability of its important work. However, modernization has always been informed by our values, our commitment to living the Gospel, and our understanding that the creative and flexible nature of the Knights of Columbus is critical to its ability to meet changing needs and to flourish in communities throughout the United States and around the world.

Each decade has brought its own challenges and opportunities for the Knights, and in each decade since the 1880s, they have responded with faith and creativity. Future generations of Knights will no doubt have to face some issues reminiscent of those in the past, and others that are completely new. Depending on the circumstances, some issues will be local or regional, while others will be national or global in nature. In each case, by living and witnessing to the Gospel with the sort of adaptive ingenuity that has characterized the work of the Knights of Columbus at every level for well over a century, I believe that the Order stands poised to be a force for the good in every parish, community, and country where it is located.

Carl Anderson, Supreme Knight
Knights of Columbus

# Introduction

In October 1881, a young priest named Michael McGivney gathered a small group of men from his parish in the basement of St. Mary's Church in New Haven, Connecticut. His purpose was to form a fraternal organization that would "promote the principles of unity and charity so that the members would gain strength to bestow charity on each other." In a country that was then hostile to Catholics, the organization would help protect and provide for the families of its members while keeping them strongly connected to the Catholic faith. It was understood that the organization would also make the case to their neighbors that Catholics could contribute to America's civic life in important ways as well.

This small band of dedicated men would become the Knights of Columbus—an organization that is now approximately 2 million strong. Through text and photos, this book tells the remarkable story of the organization—why it formed, how it grew, and how, through faith in action, it has demonstrated for more than a century that faithful Catholics can be good citizens in America and around the world.

The opening chapter of *The Knights of Columbus: An Illustrated History* tells the story of Catholics in America before the 1880s. Catholics had a role to play in America's founding, but—except in French or Spanish regions of North America—they were often discriminated against. Both their exclusion and their contributions are explored, providing insight into the social climate in which the Knights would be born, and explaining why its work would so often focus on faith, religious freedom, civil rights, anti-discrimination, and the promotion of patriotism.

The early years of the Order, from its founding to nearly the end of the nineteenth century, is the subject of Chapter 2. The genius of Father McGivney and the men he brought together to found the Order is described, as is the Knights' multifaceted founding mission: to protect the members' faith, to protect the financial viability of Catholic families in the event of the death of a breadwinner, and to help make the case that faithful Catholics could also be good American citizens. This chapter also explores the adoption of Christopher Columbus as the Order's namesake; the establishment of the degrees, which represent the principles of the organization; the birth of the insurance plan that would protect the financial future of the Order's members; the first years of the *Columbiad*, a monthly newspaper devoted to the interests and activities of the Knights; and the group's early growth and expansion. Special mention is made of the founder, Venerable Father Michael McGivney, and early leaders of the Order. These first members were leading Catholic men of Connecticut, many of whom also held elected office. It was they who would guide and grow the group through its fledgling years, and would, by their own example, show the important contribution Catholics could make.

As the Order expanded domestically, demand for K of C councils grew around the world. By 1909, the Knights had been established in Canada, Mexico, the Philippines, and Cuba. Chapter 3 covers the Order's rapid expansion and growth from 1897 to 1919, including the beginning of its international work. Other important topics include the Order's growing charitable work at local and national levels; its effective response to a new wave of anti-Catholic sentiment in the United States; and its embrace of providing social and moral formation to men that went even beyond its insurance component. Finally, it begins the exploration of one of the greatest chapters in the Knights' history—the establishment of Army huts, innovative recreation centers that helped meet the spiritual and practical needs of World War I troops both at home and abroad.

The Knights' charitable work during World War I impressed Catholics and non-Catholics alike. Chapter 4 looks at the post-World War I years, when the Order's membership exploded, and the Knights helped returning veterans with education and job placement. At the same time, due to the Knights' growing reputation, Pope Benedict XV invited the Order to establish centers in Rome to assist the children of that city. During this period, the Order was also active in fighting the resurgence of the Ku Klux Klan; advocating for Catholics who suffered under government persecution in Mexico; and promoting greater racial and ethnic tolerance through the publication of books that highlighted the contributions of African Americans, Jews, and Germans to American life.

The difficult period of the Great Depression is covered in Chapter 5. While helping their struggling countrymen through job placement and other charitable outreach, the Knights continued to speak out for Catholics in Mexico and, with the rise of Nazism, to urge their own government to take action in support of European Jewish refugees. As the Depression dragged on, the Knights also had to counter a continuing decrease in membership. Their answer was Mobilization for Catholic Action, a program that made members and potential members aware of "the ideals of Christian citizenship for which the Church and Knights stand." Although the Order could not completely restore its membership numbers during this economic crisis, the program established a new vision for the Knights and their councils with the twin priorities of religious freedom and Catholic charity.

Chapter 6 focuses on the period between 1941 and 1950. As World War II began, the Knights again stepped up as patriotic partners to allied servicemen. Knights in Canada ran Army huts, along the same lines as the Order had done in World War I; and Knights in the United States served as part of the United Service Organizations (USO), raising money for war bonds, running blood drives, and reaching behind enemy lines to extend charitable outreach in the Philippines and Rome. Immediately after the war, the Order began to sound the alarm about the rising threat of communism, which soon swallowed up half of Europe.

The period from 1951 to 1964 is the focus of Chapter 7. The Order's memorable achievements of this era include successfully advocating to have the words "under God" included in the Pledge of Allegiance; supporting the creation of the Vatican Film Library at St. Louis University; helping with the construction of the Basilica of the National Shrine of the Immaculate Conception in Washington, DC; developing the Catholic Information Service, which explained the faith to Catholics and non-Catholics alike; and speaking out for those persecuted for their faith behind the Iron Curtain. Of course, for most of the nation's Catholics, the most notable event of that era was the election of brother Knight John F. Kennedy to the office of the president of the United States. Chapter 6 explores the relationship between the Order and its most famous member, who for many Catholics was a sign that long-time discrimination against the Church had finally been overcome.

The late 1960s and 1970s were a turbulent time socially and religiously. Chapter 8 tells the story of this era, concentrating on the Order's important place as a leader of the laity in the post-Vatican II Church, as well as its need to confront a radically changing society, especially in terms of its approach to sexual morality. Other notable subjects include the Knights' work for racial harmony both within and outside the Order, its efforts to help the Vatican better communicate with the world via new technology, its construction of a modern new headquarters able to better serve its growing organization, its initial pro-life work, the professionalization of its insurance operation, and the establishment of its long-standing partnership with the Special Olympics.

As the Knights' one hundred-year anniversary neared, the organization had much to celebrate, including a remarkable period of growth in membership and insurance, and a deepening relationship with the Vatican. Between the years 1980 and 1999—the focus of Chapter 9—the Order would take part in the restoration of the façade of St. Peter's Basilica as well as other sections of the basilica. It would also work closely with Pope John Paul II, sponsoring his Mass in the Diocese of Brooklyn, and working with him on behalf of Catholics persecuted for their faith in Eastern Europe. It would also establish a fruitful relationship with Mother Teresa of Kolkata.

The final chapter looks at the Knights in the twenty-first century. From the Order's greatest foreign expansion in nearly a century; to the growth in charity, insurance, and membership; to an even closer working relationship with the Vatican, this period would be unique in its global outlook. Under the heading "Faith in Action," the K of C would implement a strengthening of its charitable programs, including global disaster relief and support for local families in need. The Order would also again embrace issues that had long been at its core. Religious freedom at home would become a major issue for the first time in five decades, with the Knights—as before—defending the rights of American Catholics. Persecution and genocide against Christians and others abroad would also elicit a strong response from the Knights, who made advocating for the protection of Christians in the Middle East a major priority. Faith formation and education returned to center stage, as well, with academic programs, books, documentary films, and conferences designed to reach out to Catholics and to society at large. Pro-life activities also increased, and the Knights' polling operation helped shape the national discussion of the issue.

Throughout this book, photos and images bring to life the fascinating and largely unknown story of the Knights of Columbus. "Notable Knights" insets highlight the lives and contributions of members such as baseball legend Babe Ruth, presidential candidate Al Smith, and Vietnam War hero Jeremiah Denton. "Visionary Council Initiative" insets focus on life-changing programs such as the K of C Rest Home, which offered care and shelter to the families of POWs in the Philippines during World War II. Rounding out the story of the Knights and of the Catholic experience in America and beyond, beautifully illustrated sections provide detailed looks at the Knights of Columbus Museum in New Haven, Connecticut; and the Saint John Paul II National Shrine in Washington, DC. These spiritually and historically important sites offer visitors information and inspiration, showing in depth what faith in action can do.

With a Foreword by Supreme Knight Carl Anderson, this book not only celebrates the history of this organization, but helps illuminate the future—a future filled with promise and built upon the founding principles of charity, unity, fraternity, and patriotism.

During the late 1800s, few Catholics in American history were held in high regard. Christopher Columbus—praised as a hero for his daring voyage of discovery and for bringing Christianity to the New World in 1492—was an exception.

# 1.
# In the Beginning

Committed to charity and the protection of the faith and financial viability of Catholic families, the Order of the Knights of Columbus has touched the lives of countless individuals—Catholic and non-Catholic—in communities around the world. From its 1882 founding by a handful of men from a small, predominantly Irish Catholic parish in New Haven, Connecticut, the Knights of Columbus has grown to an international brotherhood of nearly 2 million members across North America, Latin America, Asia, the Caribbean, and Europe.

For more than a century, the Knights of Columbus has been a staunch defender of religious freedom, while making the case that Catholics could be good citizens. This was necessary because the Knights were born into a country that had been steeped in prejudice against Catholics since its colonial days. From the anti-Catholic sentiment of the early Puritans to the anti-immigrant movements of the latter nineteenth century, Catholics had to overcome bigotry to define their place in the New World. At the same time, the country's Catholics were blessed at key moments with strong leaders who helped counter the prevailing bigotry and guide their fellow Catholics on the path of integration within the new nation.

With a few exceptions, the Protestant colonies did not tolerate differences in religious matters. Persons who did not adhere to the established religion of these colonies—such as Puritanism or Anglicanism—were seen as threats and often made to feel unwelcome. Laws had even been passed in an effort to keep Catholics from living in certain states or from obtaining

During the 1700s, the majority of Catholics lived in Maryland, where the Toleration Act of 1649—assuring religious freedom—stood in stark contrast to the religious intolerance of most other colonies. With a few exceptions, such as Pennsylvania and Rhode Island, the Protestant colonies did not tolerate differences of opinion in religious matters.

Father Andrew White, SJ, celebrated the first Mass in what would become Maryland. From his pen came a catechism, grammar, and dictionary of the native language. But his ministry in Maryland ended when the Protestant majority gained the upper hand and sent him back to England in chains.

This 1793 engraving by James Barry is an allegorical representation of the 1649 Maryland Act of Toleration, which was meant to ensure religious freedom for Christian settlers of diverse sects.

the full rights enjoyed by their fellow citizens. A 1647 Massachusetts law, for example, prohibited Catholics from settling anywhere in the state, while a 1719 Rhode Island law imposed a number of civil restrictions on Catholics.

The tensions and struggles played out dramatically in Maryland. Originally founded as a haven for Catholic religious freedom by Cecil Calvert, Maryland was the bastion of Catholicism among the colonies. While governed by Catholics, the colony granted freedom of worship to citizens of other Christian churches, a right enshrined for much of the seventeenth century in its flawed but progressive 1649 Act of Toleration, which assured religious freedom, in stark contrast to the religious intolerance of many of the other colonies. Still, Protestants from within and outside Maryland periodically attacked and wrested control of the colony, abolishing the Act of Toleration and outlawing the Catholic faith.

A "Protestant revolution" that began in 1689, seized Maryland, which was then declared a royal colony. Anglicanism became the official state religion. Within a few years, the practice of Catholicism was abolished, and Catholics were denied the right to vote. This state of affairs prevailed until the time of the American Revolution. Nevertheless, by 1785, Maryland had 15,800 Catholics, the most of any colony at the time. Despite its limited scope and ultimate failure, the Maryland Act of Toleration served as a model for laws concerning religious liberty in other states and would influence the framers of the Constitution and its First Amendment.

When the American colonies declared independence from Great Britain in 1776, Catholics comprised less than one percent of the 2.5 million inhabitants embroiled in war. While British leadership often faced a religious test (an oath rejecting the Catholic belief of transubstantiation of the Eucharist) in the newly forming country, Catholic patriots like Charles Carroll played a formative role. As George Washington later wrote, Catholics' "fellow-citizens will not forget the patriotic part which you [Catholics] took in the accomplishment of their Revolution, and the establishment of their Government."

Despite religious prejudice, Catholicism managed to take root in the United States. This was aided in part by the successive wave of immigrants from Catholic countries that began arriving during the mid-1800s. The acquisition by the United States of vast expanses of largely Catholic territories, such as Louisiana, California, and Texas, which had been colonized by the French and Spanish respectively, further increased the Catholic presence.

Within fifty years, the nation's Catholics more than doubled, from a mere 56 congregations in 1776 to more than 120 congregations by 1820. While this was far fewer than the thousands of Protestant congregations established by that time, such rapid growth of the Church nevertheless testified to the dedication of American Catholics to their faith.

While the British Colonies often were hostile to Catholics, missionaries like Saint Junipero Serra made great strides in Catholic evangelization in the Southwest and even offered prayers for the success of the American Revolution.

Maryland's Charles Carroll of Carrollton was the sole Roman Catholic signatory of the Declaration of Independence. When America declared independence in 1776, fewer than one percent of its 2.5 million inhabitants were Catholic.

# Archbishop John Carroll

Three Catholic men of the Carroll family—Charles, Daniel, and John—were exemplars of patriotism and civic activity in America's early years. Charles, the only Catholic signatory to the Declaration of Independence, also worked side by side with Benjamin Franklin in an attempt to recruit Canadian sympathizers to the revolutionary cause. Daniel Carroll, Charles' cousin, participated in the Constitutional Convention and eventually was a signatory to the Constitution of the United States. According to Peter Guilday's book, *The Life and Times of John Carroll,* Daniel was an articulate and powerful leader on behalf of strong protections for religious liberty in the new nation. And Daniel's brother, Father (later Bishop) John Carroll, played a pivotal role in the coalescence and stability of the Catholic Church in the United States.

Born and raised in Maryland, John Carroll had studied abroad and had been a priest for five years by the time he returned to the United States in 1774. With the presence of only a handful of priests during and after the Revolutionary War, the country was considered mission territory. Given the hostility and discrimination against Catholics at the time, there were very few Catholic churches in the country and none in Maryland, where—at this time—religious freedom laws had been abolished and replaced with laws preventing Catholics from openly practicing their faith. Carroll initially worked as a missionary in Maryland and Virginia. Ten years after his return to the United States—in part through the recommendation of Benjamin Franklin, who supported any religion that promoted morality and virtue—the dynamic and well-spoken Father Carroll was selected and confirmed by Pope Pius VI as Superior of the Missions in the thirteen United States. Having many of the responsibilities of a bishop in his new role, Carroll set about unifying Catholics and strengthening the Church throughout the country.

In 1789, Carroll was appointed by the pope as the first American bishop; later, he would be elevated to the rank of archbishop. His Baltimore-based diocese encompassed the entire nation, and included the roughly 25,000 Catholics who lived primarily in Maryland and Pennsylvania.

Among his many achievements, Carroll established a number of schools, including Georgetown University, even today one of the foremost institutions of higher education in the United States. He also worked with the leaders of the new nation to protect the religious liberty of Catholics and their Church. Such ideals, including provision for the protection and maintenance of religious liberty and the freedom to practice and teach religion, would eventually be enshrined in the First Amendment to the US Constitution.

It was largely due to Carroll's guidance and leadership that the Roman Catholic Church took such firm root in the United States despite its entrenched anti-Catholic sentiment. Because there were so few priests to serve the Catholic population, clergy often had to rely on the help of lay people. Although this was sometimes challenging, it was also an excellent way to get the laity involved in the life of their parish communities. As the country coalesced around its Constitution and Bill of Rights, American Catholics embraced the new nation and its promise of religious liberty, seeking to express their faith within the context of America's unique cultural landscape.

John Carroll's dedication to building up the Catholic Church in the United States and to training priests were hallmarks of his administration. He understood the importance of addressing the spiritual needs of the American people in ways consonant with the teachings and identity of the Church. He also actively countered anti-Catholic discrimination by stressing that Catholics were committed to the country's democratic ideals. For Carroll, and for his kinsmen Daniel and Charles, there was no necessary conflict between being a faithful Catholic and a patriotic American.

# THE FAITH GROWS IN CONNECTICUT

Connecticut, where the Knights would be founded, shared in the troubled history of Maryland and Pennsylvania. For nearly two centuries, Puritans, also known as Congregationalists, maintained all churches and essentially controlled civil authority throughout Connecticut. Church and state were closely linked, so much so that the autonomous Congregationalist churches were supported by tax revenues. Meanwhile, the Catholic community of late-eighteenth century Connecticut remained small, claiming only a few hundred followers. New Haven, the future home of the Knights, was one of the most religiously insular communities in America.

In 1818, a new Connecticut constitution declared that while it was the duty of each man to worship the Supreme Being in a manner consistent with his own conscience, no man should feel compelled to join or support any particular church or religious association. Catholics, however, were still unwelcome and still unable to own land without an act of the legislature. Nevertheless, they were able to establish Holy Trinity Church in Hartford in 1829, the first Catholic church in the state.

At the time, the entire state had roughly 700 Catholics but only a few priests. In fact, the Catholic residents of New Haven had to read the newspaper to learn when a priest would be coming to celebrate a liturgy with them. Once, when a priest was hours late to Midnight Mass, the parishioners gathered a search and rescue party and found him on foot, having encountered issues with his horse. They escorted him to New Haven, where he celebrated Mass and then promptly began his return journey.

Just after a prohibition against Catholic land ownership was lifted, Connecticut's second Catholic church, Christ Church (later St. Mary's) was established in New Haven in 1834 to hostility in the local press. While more churches followed, challenges remained, and an openly anti-Catholic governor took office in 1855. It was into this uncertain world that the Knights of Columbus would be born in the basement of St. Mary's in 1882.

# FACING EARLY ANTI-CATHOLIC SENTIMENT

The establishment of parishes in Connecticut coincided with an increase in Catholic immigration to the state, which would swell its Catholic population to nearly 5,000 by 1845. But even as the protection of religious liberty in state constitutions improved, anti-Catholic sentiment was never far off. Fits of nativism often targeted Catholics and immigrants from Catholic countries, and anti-Catholic bigotry remained socially acceptable in many quarters of American society.

Beginning in the mid-1800s, nearly 1 million Irish immigrants fled their homeland to escape the "Great Famine." They flocked to the United States,

**Holy Trinity Church**
Founded in Hartford in 1829, Holy Trinity was Connecticut's first Catholic church.

"We have no Popery in New Haven and we don't want any." This was the message to Catholics looking for space for a Mass in New Haven. Churchless and barred from owning property in Connecticut without state dispensation until the 1830s, Catholics in New Haven built what would become St. Mary's Church in 1834.

Anti-immigrant nativism closely overlapped with anti-Catholicism, and sometime turned deadly. This drawing depicts the 1844 anti-Catholic Nativist riots in Philadelphia, which killed twenty people, destroyed two churches, and ruined an Irish neighborhood.

settling largely on Manhattan's Lower East Side, and making their way to New Jersey and Connecticut where jobs were available. By 1850, New Haven was home to nearly 3,400 Irish-born Catholics. These immigrants took jobs in factories, on railroads, and just about anywhere they could find manual labor. The work was difficult, and so was the environment, as they often found themselves despised by their Protestant neighbors. On many occasions, nativists actually took to the streets to try to rid cities of immigrants. Anti-Catholic riots broke out in cities like Boston and Philadelphia. Catholic churches and schools were burned and homes were destroyed. In one such confrontation, the cathedral in New York City escaped the torches of a nativist mob only after the archbishop organized armed parishioners to defend it.

By the late 1800s, Catholic immigrants from countries including Italy, Germany, and Poland began making their way to America. Anti-immigrant sentiment and anti-Catholicism went hand in hand. Catholics were often viewed with suspicion and remained a widely despised minority in the United States, with open discrimination against Catholics continuing well into the twentieth century.

A nation that had been discovered, explored, and evangelized by many Catholics, often denied Catholics their constitutionally-guaranteed freedoms. Despite this, the Catholic population continued to grow.

The need for Catholics as soldiers in the Civil War, and the many Catholics who fought bravely in that conflict, helped reduce some anti-Catholic sentiment in the nineteenth century. However, Catholics were still often viewed with suspicion and prejudice.

What began with a surge of Irish immigrants flocking to the United States in the mid-1800s continued with a steady flow of Catholic immigrants into the twentieth century from European countries like Italy, Poland, and Germany.

Father Michael J. McGivney's vision of charity and unity
inspired the formation of the Knights of Columbus.

# 2.
# The Early Years
## 1881 to 1896

As Catholics sought their place in America, the Knights of Columbus had humble beginnings. In New Haven, Connecticut, in the basement of St. Mary's Church in October 1881, the parish's dynamic twenty-nine-year-old assistant pastor brought together a group of the city's Catholic men to discuss the possibility of forming a fraternal fellowship. This young priest was Father Michael Joseph McGivney, and the men who joined him included several of New Haven's civic leaders.

## BIRTH OF THE KNIGHTS OF COLUMBUS

Even before becoming a parish priest at St. Mary's, Father McGivney was quite aware of the challenges for Catholics who were trying to live their faith. A small minority, American Catholics could not count on support from the broader community or the dominant culture. Given the climate of anti-Catholicism that surrounded them, Father McGivney and the men of his parish had their work cut out for them.

St. Mary's Church itself, which was rebuilt in a new location after fire destroyed the original church, had been the subject of controversy and concern among the people of New Haven. Although most of the Protestant

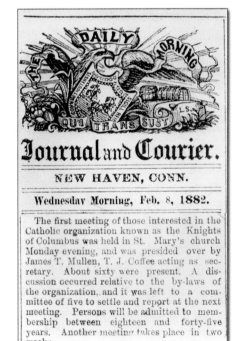

*Journal and Courier* article reporting the first meeting of the Knights of Columbus in February 1882.

In the mid 1800s, only 5 percent of Americans were Catholic. Waves of immigrants from Europe would change US religious demographics substantially. In just over fifty years, at the turn of the twentieth century, the population had grown to 17 percent—making Catholics the country's largest religious group.

The power of the so-called Know Nothing Party—whose real name was the American Party—was obvious in Connecticut. In 1855, Know Nothing candidate William T. Minor was elected governor after running a campaign that attacked Catholics and immigrants.

## PRICE FOUR CENTS.

### AN UNPROFITABLE CHURCH

#### ROMAN CATHOLIC TROUBLES IN NEW-HAVEN.

HOW AN ARISTOCRATIC AVENUE WAS BLEM-
ISHED BY A ROMAN CHURCH EDIFICE—
THE PARISH BADLY IN DEBT—EFFORTS
TO DISPOSE OF THE VALUABLE PROPERTY.

NEW-HAVEN, July 27.—The most aristocratic street in this city is Hillhouse-avenue;
its length is only two blocks, and it extends
from Wall-street to Sachem-street. At its
northern end lies the old Hillhouse property—a
large private park, finely wooded, with the Hillhouse mansion near its centre. The avenue is
broad, and it has been made beautiful by the
residents on each side. It is paved with asphalt,
and there are wide stretches of well-kept lawn
between the yard fences and the road-way,
shaded by noble elm trees. Among those who
live on the avenue are President Porter, of
Yale College; Joseph E. Sheffield, the founder
of the Yale Scientific School; Prof. Benjamin Silliman, Prof. Dana, the geolo-
gist; Prof. Fisher, of the Yale Theological
School; Mr. Farnam, a millionaire, and other
representatives of this City's best society. Several years ago, an inventor who suddenly ac-
quired wealth bought the only vacant lot on
the avenue, and intended to build a house for
himself there. But his money did not hold out,
and he had to sell. He offered the lot to residents of the avenue, but they would not give
him his price. Intimations that he might sell
to undesirable persons did not cause them to
raise their figures. He then offered the lot to
the Roman Catholics, and it was bought by St.
Mary's Parish, then worshiping in a cheap
building on Church-street.

When the residents of this aristocratic avenue discovered that they were in danger of
seeing a Roman Catholic church spring up
among them, with all that the establishment of

*New York Times* article objecting to the rebuilding of St. Mary's Church on New Haven's fashionable Hillhouse Avenue.

churches were built on the town green in the center of the city, St. Mary's was controversially situated on fashionable Hillhouse Avenue, which was dotted with stately mansions. *The New York Times* published a hostile article about St. Mary's in 1879 complaining about, "How an Aristocratic Avenue Was Blemished by a Roman Church Edifice." The article derided the church for its large debt and its community as a parish of "servant-girls." Despite such attacks, St. Mary's would become a key Catholic center.

The push for removing Catholicism from the public life affected the personal lives of many Catholic men, some of whom began losing interest both in attending Mass and joining religious associations. "It was not that the men were exactly neglected," wrote Father Joseph Gordian Daley in *Columbiad* in 1900, "but the task of inducing laymen in any considerable number to join an association which involved religious requirements seemed too great a problem for anyone up to that time to respond to. Father McGivney with sanguine faith made the attempt by bringing into being the Knights of Columbus."

Providing for one's family—in life, sickness, or in the case of death—tempted men to join other associations: secret societies. With poverty often only a breadwinner's death away, many Catholic men also began turning to these societies, which helped them meet their financial needs by advancing their careers through a fraternal network or providing some kind of life insurance options. Unfortunately, many of these groups were anti-Catholic—to such a degree that the Catholic Church prohibited membership in them.

But without assistance, Catholic families faced unappealing alternatives. Upon the death of a parent, children were often taken from their families and placed in secular orphanages, risking not only the breakup of families, but the loss of faith as well. At that time, the dean of the Yale Law School noted, "In chronic cases of absolute poverty or serious sickness, the woman and her family had to go into the almshouse." The conditions there were poor; an 1877 report stated, "At the New Haven almshouse, there were fifty-four insane persons, some of them lying upon loose hay, without much clothing, and sorely in need of care."

This was the landscape in which newly ordained Father Michael McGivney found himself. He was in a church that was singled out and publicly ridiculed for its poor immigrant parishioners; in a community where employers were known to force men out of their jobs because of their faith; in a city in which a judge had, but a few decades earlier, prosecuted his childhood parish priest for administering last rites.

Father McGivney was greatly concerned about Catholic men joining these secret fraternal societies, but he also realized their motivation for

The first native-born American citizen to be canonized, Elizabeth Ann Seton was born an Episcopalian. She converted to Catholicism in 1805, after the death of her husband, and dedicated her life to caring for others. Mother Seton is credited with opening the country's first parochial school and first religious order—the Sisters of Charity.

According to the 1880 United States Census, 1 out of every 758 people in the nation lived in an almshouse. A number of hardships, including poverty, homelessness, alcoholism, and mental illness, might force a person or an entire family into a house for the poor, which offered food and shelter, often in exchange for hard labor.

doing so. He understood that these men needed to protect the financial future of their families, as well as enjoy the bonds of fellowship with their peers. Through the death of his own father, McGivney knew all too well the burdens a family faced when the breadwinner became ill or died. Against this backdrop, he gave Catholic men an alternative to anti-Catholic societies that would not violate their consciences, would help keep Catholic families together when a breadwinner died, and would make the case—even in its name—that Catholics could be patriotic citizens, entitled to the same rights as every other American.

The men who joined Father McGivney in starting the Knights of Columbus were well suited to the task. The group collectively combined fraternal experience with the ability to navigate the times and move others to action despite anti-Catholic sentiment. Living proof that Catholics could be good citizens, several of the men were prominent public servants and some could even win elections (as alderman, mayor, state legislator, etc.) without compromising their Catholic faith.

In October of 1881, Father McGivney presented his idea of forming a fraternal organization to the leading men of his parish. The core of his vision was simple: ". . . to promote the principles of unity and charity, so that the members would gain the strength to bestow charity on each other." The group would collectively protect the families of its members, providing charity to those in need while offering fraternal connections and activities for those who were involved. In its fundamental character, this group would also help keep its members strongly connected to their Catholic faith. It was Father McGivney's desire that these Catholic laymen would have the opportunity to grow in holiness, while contributing to their parishes, to their communities, and to their country.

It would soon be clear that the organization Father McGivney proposed that evening would also serve an important role in defending Catholics and their place in American life. At that time, the nation was still recovering from the effects of the Civil War, and adjusting to the massive influx of European immigrants arriving on its shores. Immigrant families and their children were trying to assimilate in a country that was not particularly welcoming to them.

**St. Mary's Church**
Birthplace of the
Knights of Columbus.

The Knights, however, would soon provide significant national leadership for Catholics. Within a few decades, the Order became an important force

As women filled church pews, male-majority atheist groups like the "Freethinkers" labeled religion unmasculine and irrational. One priest noted that uniting men with spiritual requirements was "too great a problem" until Father McGivney: "No one took the trouble to pursue the layman into the paths of his everyday social life and animate him . . . with Catholic principle."

The increased presence of Irish-Catholic immigrants in the United States began in the mid-1800s with the start of Ireland's potato famine. They fled their homeland, settling largely on Manhattan's Lower East Side, and then began making their way to New Jersey and Connecticut, where jobs were available. By 1850, New Haven was home to nearly 3,400 Irish-born Catholics.

# Sowing the Seeds of Distrust

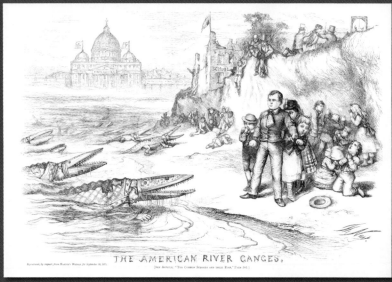

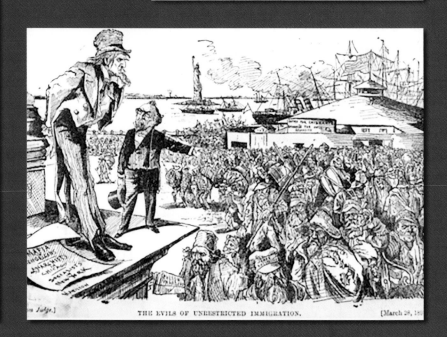

in its charitable initiatives and a strong voice on the issues of the day—including Catholic rights. It would also prove a catalyst for bringing about positive change in the country's conversation about the contribution of Catholics in America.

The men in attendance at that first meeting were inspired by the concept of this new organization and gave it their wholehearted support. A number of the men had experience in other organizations and even public office. Cornelius T. Driscoll, for example, had served as president of the Connecticut Catholic Temperance Society and was also a state legislator and future New Haven mayor. Others, too, were public servants and/or had belonged to the National Guard's Irish-Catholic militia unit known as the Sarsfield Guard and its fraternal off-shoot, the Red Knights. Such experienced leadership among the men would help in forming a strong foundation for the organization.

At the end of that initial meeting, the men remained focused on ways to organize themselves. As documented in the minutes recorded during that meeting, a committee of ten was chosen to draft a constitution and create bylaws. Regularly scheduled meetings followed. By the fifth meeting in December 1881, officers were elected to serve six-month terms. Notably, although the men had wanted Father McGivney to be its leader, he insisted that the organization be run by laymen. Cornelius T. Driscoll was elected the first president, while Father McGivney agreed to be the financial secretary responsible for the group's business activities.

Initially, it was unclear whether the organization was going to be independent or affiliated with another Catholic fraternal group. Father McGivney met with a number of priests throughout the Northeast to discuss his mission and to get their ideas and feedback. He also met with leaders of other Catholic fraternal groups to gain a better understanding of their structure. He visited the Catholic Benevolent Legion in Brooklyn, New York, as well as the Massachusetts Catholic Order of Foresters. The latter fraternal benefits society shared Irish Catholic immigrant heritage similar to the men at St. Mary's, and although but three years old, the Boston-based society already boasted more than a dozen courts. Father McGivney initially considered the possibility of his new organization becoming the Connecticut branch of that society, but at a meeting on February 2, 1882, the group agreed to found an entirely independent organization.

A few days later, on February 6, Father McGivney and the men of St. Mary's would gather again in what is generally regarded as the first official meeting of the Knights of Columbus.

**Cornelius T. Driscoll**

Irish-born Cornelius T. Driscoll was elected the first president of the newly formed organization that would soon become known as the Knights of Columbus.

On March 15, 1875, John McCloskey, Archbishop of New York, was appointed by Pope Pius IX as the first cardinal in the United States. During his tenure as New York's archbishop, the Brooklyn-born son of Irish immigrants established eighty-eight parishes, including the first parish for African-American Catholics.

In February 1882, the men of St. Mary's Church adopted Christopher Columbus as the patron of their new fraternal organization. The great explorer was selected because he was one of the few Catholics who was highly regarded in late-nineteenth-century America.

# Venerable Servant of God

The McGivney home in Waterbury, Connecticut.

Father McGivney may have chosen the vocation of a simple parish priest, but the life he lived was anything but ordinary. Throughout his life, people praised him for "his depth of piety and his fund of good humor" and appreciated his active concern and involvement in their daily lives. He managed to build a strong community of parishioners and inspire the birth of a fraternal organization that would serve not only New Haven, but also, in time, the rest of the country, the continent, and the world.

Michael Joseph McGivney, the son of Irish immigrants, was born on August 12, 1852 in Waterbury, Connecticut, where he was baptized and raised. The oldest of thirteen children, Michael was no stranger to hardship and struggle. As a young boy, he faced a number of tragic heartbreaks, including the deaths of six of his younger siblings. He was a bright student, but had to set his schooling aside to take a job in a local brass factory to help support his family. But God was calling Michael to the priesthood, and at the age of sixteen, he left his home to enter a seminary in Canada.

At seminary, Michael excelled as a student. He earned a number of academic awards both at the College of St. Hyacinthe in Montreal, and then at Our Lady of Angels Seminary in Niagara Falls, New York. When Michael was twenty-one and attending the Jesuit-run St. Mary's College in Montreal, his father died. Had the Bishop of Hartford not intervened to help with his education, Michael would have had to leave the seminary. Thankfully, he was able to complete his studies for the priesthood at St. Mary's Seminary in Baltimore, Maryland.

A few days before Christmas in 1877, Michael was ordained a priest by Archbishop (later Cardinal) James Gibbons, the most prominent American churchman of his day. Returning home, Father McGivney celebrated the birth of Christ with the first Mass of his priesthood before taking up his first assignment as an assistant parish priest at the newly rebuilt St. Mary's Church in New Haven.

At St. Mary's, Father McGivney distinguished himself through his passionate outreach and charitable dealings with parishioners. To help foster a sense of community, he was active in organizing parish events, from staging full-scale theatrical productions to planning outings for the youth of the parish to arranging children's entertainment at church picnics. Encouraging such social events also helped keep his parishioners—particularly young adults—off the streets and out of trouble. According to his biographer, Julie Fenster, "He could play baseball and have a laugh with his young parishioners—in other words, he had a way of mixing into the secular lives of parishioners without forsaking his spiritual responsibilities to them. . . . Judging by his actions, he didn't want people to leave their religious lives in church. . . . Father McGivney did have a graceful way of proving that Catholic teachings could be a part of everything, all the time."

Throughout his ministry at St. Mary's and later at St. Thomas Church in Thomaston, Connecticut, Father McGivney touched the lives of countless individuals. His personal interest in his parishioners also led him to help alleviate their financial struggles when possible, and even serve as a guardian when necessary. The Downes family, for example, came to know Father's generosity personally. Mr. Downes was a hard-working, devoted family man. When he died, his wife became solely responsible for her children, stepchildren, and family debts. Given their bleak financial state, the family faced the threat of being torn apart by the courts. Fortunately, between the oldest

Young Michael McGivney (first row, far left) appears at graduation with his classmates.

# Father Michael Joseph McGivney

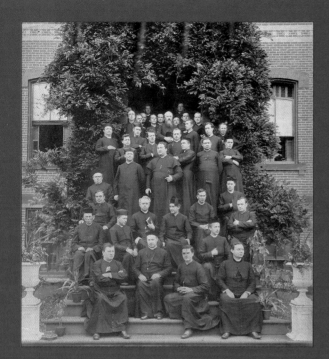

Father McGivney (third from left, bottom row) with fellow priests.

When Father Michael J. McGivney died at age thirty-eight, those who knew him described him as a saint. The incredible effect of his short life was apparent at his funeral, which brought together a vast crowd that included dozens of Connecticut's Catholic priests, the Bishop of Hartford, numerous civic leaders, and hundreds of Knights.

As family acquaintance Father Joseph Daley wrote of him in 1900: "To meet him was at once to trust him; children actually loved him; and the very old people of the neighborhood, whom he hunted up and who got part of his time even on busiest days, called him a positive saint and meant it."

A kind and gentle spirit who labored tirelessly for his flock, Father McGivney was truly beloved. He cared for his flock's physical and spiritual needs, and showed a real genius in meeting the needs of his community in an attractive way. His insightfulness was revealed again in the choice not only of the organization's name, but also of the kind of leading men who could personally make the case that Catholics could be good citizens, and could stand up for their rights when appropriate.

A testament to his holiness, hard work, and insight is the fact that Father McGivney would very much recognize the founding principles at work in the Knights of Columbus today.

son taking over his father's store and relatives scraping together enough money for two expensive guardianship bonds, the court was convinced the family could stay together—except for young Alfred. When no guardian and bond could be arranged for him, Father McGivney stepped in to serve as his guardian and arranged for the required bond that allowed Alfred to remain with his family. Despite the tragic loss of his father, Alfred was blessed with a true father figure in Father McGivney—who believed in him. Alfred would graduate from Yale Law School, write for *The New York Times*, and become a top assistant to New York City's mayor.

Father McGivney's prison-ministry duties reached a new level of demands when he befriended and undertook the spiritual care of "Chip" Smith, a young man condemned to death for killing a police officer during a drunken altercation. This undertaking was what he called "the most trying ordeal of my life." The young priest ministered to Smith for over a year and visited him almost daily. The local newspapers credited Smith's great change of heart and demeanor to Father McGivney's involvement. As his execution day neared, Smith told Father, "Your saintly ministrations have enabled me to meet death without a tremor." McGivney accompanied him even to the scaffold; blessed him; led him in the Acts of Faith, Hope and Love; and embraced him tearfully before the execution. Close friends of the priest noted that he did not recover from the strain of the experience for some time.

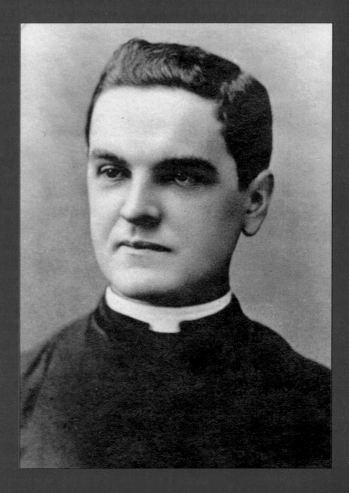

## ESTABLISHING THE ORDER

In February 1882, when the decision was made among the men of St. Mary's to establish an independent fraternal organization, they adopted Christopher Columbus as their patron. It was a well-conceived choice. During the late 1800s, few Catholics in American history were held in high regard. Columbus—praised as a hero for his voyage of discovery and for bringing Christianity to the New World in 1492—was an exception.

Father McGivney proposed the name "Sons of Columbus." Another organizer, also seeking to honor Columbus, suggested "The Columbian Order." In the end, the founding members chose the name "Knights of Columbus." During the Victorian era, knighthood and chivalry were held in high esteem for their code of ethics and aspiration to virtue. While every man was born a son, knighthood brought to mind an honorable choice and a way of life dedicated to principle. "Columbus" highlighted Catholicism's place in America. So did McGivney's choice of incorporators: faithful Catholics who had achieved the status of leading men of the community, including a state legislator, and the constable and fire commissioner of New Haven. They were the epitome of Catholic citizenship, and would prove strong leaders for the incipient group. The Order's first four leaders were men who also held elected public office—at least three while simultaneously leading McGivney's young organization.

A few days later, the first official meeting of the Knights of Columbus was held at St. Mary's Church with sixty attendees. Presiding over the meeting was James T. Mullen, a New Haven native, Civil War veteran, and former supreme knight of the Red Knights.

On March 29, 1882, the Order of Knights of Columbus was legally incorporated by the State of Connecticut. But getting approval proved no smooth task. Early in March 1882, the group submitted for approval a draft containing both reference to its Christian faith and a detailed explanation of its vision of service to widows, orphans, and its members:

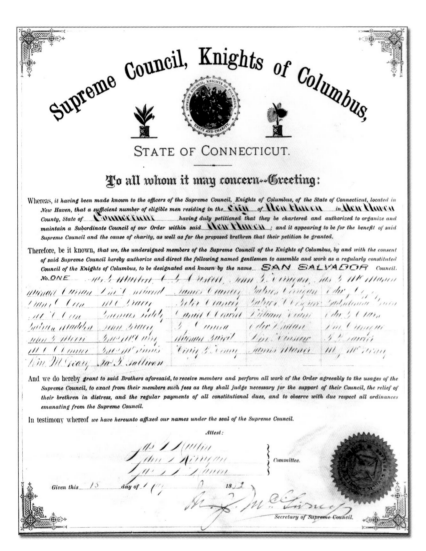

With this charter signed by Father McGivney and other members of the newly incorporated Order, the first Knights of Columbus council was established in May 1882, bearing the name of the first New World island encountered by Christopher Columbus: San Salvador.

On March 29, 1882, the Knights of Columbus was legally incorporated by the State of Connecticut. The charter would be amended periodically to include more details of its functions as well as its purpose, including relief work and religious, educational, and charitable welfare.

The first official convention of the Knights of Columbus took place in New Haven, Connecticut, in May 1884. At the time, the Order was showing significant growth. It had five councils throughout the state and over 450 members. Groups from outside Connecticut were also requesting information about the Order.

. . . having for its objects Fraternity, Unity and true Christian Charity amongst its members. And for the purpose of raising and maintaining a fund so as to enable us to give substantial assistance in time of sickness and distress, and to make suitable provision for their decent burial in Case of Death, and to make further provision for the widows and orphans, and to do all in our power to further the interests of our fellow members.

When the state rejected their proposal, revised articles of incorporation—with a much pared-down explanation of its purpose— were adopted on March 29, 1882.

On May 15, 1882, the first council was formed. It was named the San Salvador Council after the first New World island discovered by Christopher Columbus. Father McGivney, along with the other members of the Order, signed the first charter.

Mullen's previous fraternal experience with the Red Knights and his familiarity with ceremonials made him a good candidate for grand knight of the San Salvador Council. Many fraternal organizations never made it out of the early stages, and disbanded, but Mullen helped guide the fledgling new organization through its infancy.

Members of San Salvador Council No. 1 were both enthusiastic about moving forward with their own council and anxious for the organization to grow. With the help of Father McGivney, they began looking outward for places to establish new councils. As supreme knight for four years, Mullen would oversee the early expansion of the Order.

Initially, growth was slow, but Father McGivney remained a persistent advocate for a robust, developing organization. Once expansion began, it quickly continued. In 1883, the Order's second council was formed in Meriden. The council was named Silver City, as Meriden was home to a number of businesses and manufacturers that worked with the precious metal. Councils 3, 4, and 5 soon followed in Middletown, Meriden, and Wallingford, respectively. Within the next two years, the number of councils in the towns and cities throughout Connecticut grew to two dozen.

The need for the Order was clear. One member from Chicago, Charles Conley, later reflected, "At this first meeting of Chicago Council, I realized the establishment of the Knights of Columbus, with the sanction of the Church, was a long step forward, and must tend to promote a fraternal spirit among the Church militant, which for so long was lacking."

**James T. Mullen**
First supreme knight
and grand knight
of San Salvador Council.

A Yale professor's 1882 report on New Haven and Meriden found "many widows with from three to nine children each, who are struggling along in the hopeless endeavor to properly support themselves and families." Shortly after, New Haven and Meriden became the first two towns with K of C councils.

The First and Second Degrees, or principles, of the Knights of Columbus—charity and unity—were established at the founding of the Order. Then in 1885, fraternity was added as the Third Degree. When a member reaches Third Degree status, he is granted full knighthood.

# Christopher Columbus

Columbus had an honorable reputation in Victorian-era America. He was one of the only Catholics popularly lauded at that time for his role in American history. His popularity was easily seen by the many institutions and cities that bear his name, including the nation's capital, the District of Columbia. Choosing him as the namesake for an order of Catholic men was designed to show directly that Catholics had had a role in "American" history from its very beginning. The early Knights embraced Columbus, extolling among other things his deep faith, his role (as a layman) in beginning the evangelization of the hemisphere, his bravery in the face of adversity, and his skill as a navigator.

In keeping with the important place in American history that Columbus had secured for Catholics, the Order strongly—and successfully—advocated for the adoption of Columbus Day at the state and national level. Not everyone, however, shared the Order's enthusiasm for the explorer.

Opposition to Columbus in the United States began in earnest in the 1920s with the Ku Klux Klan. Because of Columbus' Catholicism, the anti-Catholic Klan objected to honoring him. The Klan disrupted Columbus Day celebrations, and opposed the commemorations of the explorer, which the Order promoted vigorously. Various political movements also sometimes viewed Columbus with suspicion. Frederick Engels, for instance, saw him as a father of class differences and the market economy. And modern opposition to Columbus from groups like "Antifa" often tends to be along political lines.

Columbus has become, in some circles, shorthand for every negative instance of colonialism and every abuse of Native Americans. While the names of those who actually engaged in campaigns to exterminate Native Americans are

often forgotten, Columbus is blamed in some circles for any atrocity that occurred after 1492—regardless of his personal involvement.

The explorer, however, also continues to have his defenders. Professor Carol Delaney—who taught at Stanford and Brown Universities—has argued that the historical record does not support seeing Columbus as motivated by greed or animus toward the Native Americans. Her work, particularly the 2011 book *Columbus and the Quest for Jerusalem,* is an important contribution to the modern understanding of Columbus.

Delaney didn't start out a Columbus defender. She notes:

*Columbus has become a symbol for everything that went wrong. But the more I read of his own writings and that of his contemporaries, my understanding of him totally changed. His relations with the natives tended to be benign. He liked the natives and found them to be very intelligent. He also described them as "natural Christians" because they had no other "sect," or false faith, and believed that they could easily become Christians if they had instruction. Columbus strictly told the crew not to do things like maraud or rape, and instead to treat the native people with respect. There are many examples in his writings where he gave instructions to this effect. Most of the time when injustices occurred, Columbus wasn't even there.*

With little immunity to Western diseases, many Native Americans did perish in the years immediately after Columbus' voyages, but Delaney says that it is unfair to blame him for that. At his time, concepts such as immunity and even the causes of disease were poorly understood.

One of his contemporaries, Dominican friar Bartolomé de las Casas, who was among the first missionaries to the Americas, also affirmed Columbus' honorable intentions, writing: "Truly, I would not dare blame the admiral's intentions, for I knew him well and I know his intentions are good."

**Emblem of
the Knights
of Columbus**

## THE CREATION OF AN EMBLEM

A year after the organization was incorporated, an emblem was created for the order by Supreme Knight Mullen. The Order's description of the emblem reflects the symbolism of its heraldic components, including a shield mounted on a formée cross, as well as the anchor, sword, and *fasces*—an ax surrounded by vertical rods that are bound together.

- The *cross* represents the cross upon which Christ was crucified.
- The *shield* evokes Catholic knighthood and the protection of those in need.
- The *anchor* symbolizes Christopher Columbus, the great navigator.
- The *sword* is the weapon used by knights during errands of mercy.
- The *fasces* represents strength through unity. (A single rod is weak, but many rods bundled together are strong.) An ancient Roman symbol, fasces were carried by a special group of attendants called *lictors,* who accompanied and guarded Roman magistrates. Often used as symbols for the Roman Republic, fasces stood for power and jurisdiction.

Also mounted on the shield are the letters "K of C," the initials of the Knights of Columbus. Finally, the emblem prominently includes the colors red, white, and blue—the colors of the flag of the United States, where the Order was founded. The colors themselves are also meaningful. Red is symbolic of courage, faith, and devotion. Blue is a sign of hope and tranquility under God. White represents nobility of purpose and purity.

In 1896, in one of the first major articles introducing the Knights to a national audience, Thomas Cummings (the Order's National Organizer and *Columbiad* founder) presented the Order in terms of its commitment to civil and religious liberty, its vision of modern-day knighthood, its unity transcending race, and its charity-oriented benefits. He summed up the organization, saying, "Human needs, human love, human sorrow—in these all men are one, and the Order of Columbus is in the world to seek and to serve that which is common to all men."

McGivney's ledger of early parish duties reflects how he often shouldered the work of two priests. At St. Mary's, the pastors he assisted were often absent with ill health. Later, he was assigned to St. Thomas parish in Thomaston. On Sundays, he commuted by horse and carriage between the churches for morning Masses.

Founded in 1887, the American Protective Association (APA) was openly anti-Catholic. Restricting Catholic immigration, removing Catholic teachers from public schools, and banning Catholics from public offices were its primary goals. Despite its efforts, the society had limited political influence. By the early 1900s, it had essentially disappeared.

# The Officers & Members of the Organization

The Order's constitution was amended several times during its first fifteen years. Nonetheless, the organization's general authority structure has remained since it was first established.

## THE SUPREME COUNCIL

*The Supreme Council is composed of supreme officers, state and territorial deputies, the most recent former state deputy of each jurisdiction, and elected representatives from each state. They include:*

### Supreme Officers

| | |
|---|---|
| Supreme Knight | Supreme Treasurer |
| Supreme Chaplain | Supreme Advocate |
| Deputy Supreme Knight | Supreme Physician |
| Supreme Secretary | Supreme Warden |

### Deputies

| | | |
|---|---|---|
| State Deputy (Supreme Knight) | Territorial Deputy (Supreme Knight) | District Deputy (Supreme Knight) |

## LOCAL COUNCILS

*Each local council includes the following officers:*

### Local Council Officers

| | | |
|---|---|---|
| Grand Knight | Chancellor | Financial Secretary |
| Chaplain | Recorder | Warden |
| Deputy Grand Knight | Treasurer | Guards |
| | Advocate | Board of Trustees |

◄ Depicting the Virgin Mary and Christ, Columbus, and sacraments for a dying man, this turn-of-the-century membership record illustrates the centrality of faith to membership in the Order.

"There is no man, however humble his lot or calling, but can be the means, the cause of good," wrote original incorporator William Geary in 1884, extolling the Knights as an opportunity for love of neighbor. Geary (on that train for the 1905 Supreme Convention) helped shape the Order's first four decades, alongside Daniel Colwell.

# THE FOUR DEGREES

The principles of the Knights of Columbus are exemplified in the form of four degrees. Each degree is dedicated to one of the four important principles of charity, unity, fraternity, and patriotism.

The First and Second Degrees were established at the founding of the Order under the tenure of Supreme Knight Mullen, with the Third Degree being added shortly after. Mullen had also proposed the idea of adding an optional Fourth Degree of patriotism. In 1900, shortly after Edward Hearn had been elected as the Order's fifth supreme knight, this Fourth Degree was instituted.

When a member is admitted to the Third Degree, he is granted full knighthood and is eligible to become a council officer. He also has the option of becoming a Fourth Degree Knight, whose encouragement of the spirit of patriotism can include service as a member of the honor guard—a highly visible representative of the Order. (See "The Fourth Degree" on page 40.)

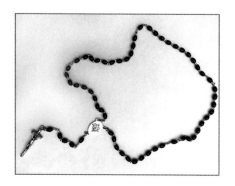

As a sign of devotion to Our Lady of the Rosary, the Order's twelfth supreme knight, Virgil Dechant, began the practice of distributing a special Knights of Columbus rosary to each new member of the Order.

| NUMBER | DEGREE | VIRTUE |
|--------|--------|--------|
| First | Admission | Charity |
| Second | Formation | Unity |
| Third | Knighthood | Fraternity |
| Fourth | Patriotic | Patriotism |

For Knights, degrees began with a ceremonial initiation. Solemn and significant, these ceremonials were designed to teach key lessons regarding the virtues that formed the Order's principles and highlighted the importance of embracing these principles as members of the Knights of Columbus. As described by Christopher Kauffman in *Columbianism and the Knights of Columbus: A Quincentenary History:*

> The initiation ceremonies were like rites of passage as the journey to knighthood was in a sense a dramatic rendition of the principles of the Order: charity, unity, and fraternity, and after 1900, patriotism. The ceremonial portrayed the lessons of Columbianism: Americanization of the immigrants' loyalty grounded in the Catholic component of the Catholic heritage, defense of the faith in a society characterized by fits of anti-Catholic hysteria, reverence for the priesthood, and a concern for the economic integrity of the family through the Order's insurance program.

After the founding of the Knights of Columbus in New Haven, the first few councils were established in Connecticut. But on July 11, 1888, the Order officially expanded outside of Connecticut with the formation of the Tyler Council in Providence, Rhode Island.

Amid American fears of anti-Catholic immigration, perhaps the only immigrant arriving in 1889 at papal urging was Saint Frances Cabrini. Caring for the poor, hungry, orphaned, and uneducated, including many immigrants, the foundress of the Sisters of the Sacred Heart of Jesus made the journey two dozen times in support of this work.

The degrees, which have been updated from time to time to better communicate the principles of the Knights in contemporary society, are typically bestowed in person by a team of Knights. The First Degree, however, is sometimes conferred via video presentation, enabling potential members with scheduling issues to join at a time that is convenient for them. Becoming a Knight took a twenty-first century turn in 2017 when online e-membership became available.

## "PASSING THE HAT"
## ESTABLISHING AN INSURANCE PROGRAM

A few years into the Order's existence, Father McGivney praised the practical results of the members' acts of charity, writing, "Although but a few years organized, the Order has effected incalculable good in many households. Not only in sickness, but when death takes the support of the family away, the Knights of Columbus comes to the relief of the widow and the orphan in a very substantial manner."

Protecting the financial future of members' families was one of the primary reasons Father McGivney had formed the Knights of Columbus. Like the organization itself, the assistance to Catholic families that one day would grow into a top-rated insurance operation had humble beginnings. And yet,

Father McGivney took a keen interest in encouraging the arts in parish life. He took liturgical music seriously, recruiting musicians (including his sister) to ensure organists for St. Mary's and St. Thomas and to improve the choir of the latter. At both parishes, he also played an active role in helping to organize and even direct theatrical productions. In addition to raising money for the churches, these plays helped build a wholesome social life for his parishioners, both young and old.

# The Concept of Catholic Knighthood

Drawing from the chivalry and code of conduct that characterized the knights of the Middle Ages, the Knights of Columbus forged a new type of knighthood—one that was suited to modern times.

Initially, knights fulfilled secular rather than religious roles. However, spirituality and fidelity to the Church soon became increasingly important. Knighthood became overtly religious with the founding of monastic orders of knighthood, promoted by Saint Bernard of Clairvaux. The ideals of non-monastic Catholic knights also received significant attention in a treatise on knighthood by Blessed Ramon Llull, who also devoted his life to evangelization in the Middle East. Although the works of knights varied and evolved over centuries, these holy men urged knights to settle for nothing less than the pinnacle of virtue and fidelity.

The concept of knighthood enjoyed a resurgent popularity in the Victorian Era, which extolled its code of chivalric conduct, its defense of others, and its fraternal brotherhood.

August 1925 issue.

As Nigel Saul wrote in *Chivalry in Medieval England*, "Its roots lay in an idealized view of the medieval past which grew up in reaction to the horrors of the grim industrialization of the time."

But while other groups adopted knightly themes or names devoid of faith, the founders of the Knights of Columbus placed the Catholic faith and Christian values and virtue at the center of its conception of knighthood. At the same time, the Order did away with the requirements of social status, money, and physical ability that had been a part of knighthood historically. Writing in his 1898 *Columbiad* article "True Knighthood," future supreme knight Edward Hearn explicitly embraced the idea of the Knights recapturing knighthood for the modern day: ". . . it was to bring back into our hurried and restless American life some of the characteristics of ancient knighthood that the society of the Knights of Columbus was established."

as the second supreme knight would often express, even though insurance was an essential element, it was not the "motive for the Order's existence, apart from its spiritual influence."

The initial program began with what is commonly known as a "pass-the-hat" system, in which a $1 per-capita assessment was made upon the death of a member. The idea was that the system would work especially well when the Order reached 1,000 members, making it possible to pay a $1,000 death benefit to the surviving family of a deceased member. (A death benefit of $1,000 in 1882 would be equivalent to around $25,000 today.)

Initially, membership into the Order was open to men between the ages of eighteen and fifty. An eighteen-year-old paid $3.25 to join, and an additional 25 cents was added for each year from that point. This meant a nineteen-year-old paid $3.50 to join, a twenty-year-old paid $3.75, and so on.

Along with the $1,000 death benefit (provided there were 1,000 members), the Order also provided financial aid—$5 per week—to members who were ill and unable to work and earn a salary. In 1885, the Order paid the first death benefit from the insurance fund. Three more deaths followed that same year, which raised concern about running out of funds in the event of additional deaths or illnesses. As a result, the maximum age for membership was lowered to forty-five, even though all three of the deaths were of men under age forty. Existing members who were over forty-five could remain, but no one over that age could join. At the Knights of Columbus annual convention in 1885, the membership fees were increased to help assure that there would be enough money available to cover additional death benefit payments.

Over time, the insurance system was formalized and updated. Still providing coverage exclusively to members and their immediate families, the Knights of Columbus has now grown to become one of the country's largest—and most highly rated—life insurers. The remarkable growth, from its modest beginnings to the current multi-billion dollar enterprise it has become, was made possible because the Order has always maintained its mission of protecting families. It treats each brother knight it insures as a member of its own Knights of Columbus family, and follows a code of ethics based on Catholic principles.

Death-benefit payment given to the widow of Supreme Knight James T. Mullen.

The consequences of a breadwinner's death were clearly understood by the Knights of Columbus' founding members and by the organization's early officers. Several served on the board of St. Francis Orphanage (left), while another served at the Probate Court and another as an undertaker.

Like Father McGivney, Pope Leo XIII expressed concern over the social issues surrounding poverty. His 1891 encyclical *Rerum Novarum*, written to address the grinding poverty of many workers, included a condemnation of socialism and would form the basis of Catholic school teachings in the modern era.

# Transcending Racial Division
## Visionary Council Initiative

Although its original members were Catholics of Irish heritage, the leadership of the Knights of Columbus quickly saw the need to include Catholics of other backgrounds. When original member and the Order's second supreme secretary, Daniel Colwell, later described the organization's purpose, he stated:

> It was designed to unify American Catholic citizens of every national and racial origin in a social and fraternal organization, giving scope and purpose to their aims as Catholics and as Americans, whether in developing the social and fraternal spirit that should exist among those who are sons of the same Church and citizens of the same republic, or in furthering great educational and religious enterprises undertaken by the Church in America.

The idea quickly transcended color as well. The Order's first recorded African-American member, Samuel F. Williams, was welcomed in 1895. Williams, along with members of the literary club to which he belonged, founded Philip Sheridan Council 119 in Southborough, Massachusetts.

They had wanted to belong to an organization with a charitable focus, not a purely social one.

After deciding on the Knights of Columbus, the men founded a new council with Williams holding the office of chancellor. A year later, he took to the stage addressing the Massachusetts State Convention, an occurrence that was written up and disseminated in *Columbiad*.

Also in Massachusetts, Congressman Joseph O'Neill laid out the Order's vision on Columbus Day in 1895, stating that it would strive:

> Under the constitution, which guarantees to all the citizens of the country civil and religious liberty, to join with all other citizens in maintaining a high standard of citizenship regardless of race or color.

In future years, the Knights would often find themselves working to overcome racial or religious intolerance. Long before the Civil Rights Movement, it was the Knights of Columbus who took the initiative to ensure that neither race nor creed meant exclusion from American history books, from charity, or from other key aspects of American life.

This 1918 photo of a multi-racial group of K of C secretaries—"Caseys"—reflects the Order's commitment to racial integration.

# The Columbiad.

## A Monthly Paper Devoted to the Interests of the Knights of Columbus.

Vol. 1. No. 1.    NOVEMBER, 1893.    Price 10 Cents.

PUBLISHED EVERY MONTH BY

### THE COLUMBIAD PUBLISHING COMPANY

**258 Washington Street, Boston, Mass.**

THOMAS H. CUMMINGS, President.    C. I. FITZGERALD, Treasurer.

*Subscription per annum, in advance, $1.00.*

WITH this number we begin the publication of THE COLUMBIAD. In doing this we are yielding to the earnest entreaties of the membership, in different parts of Connecticut, Rhode Island, and Massachusetts, to give them a monthly paper, by which they might learn what is being done in the Order outside their several local Councils.

In accordance with these views, we propose to set before our members such information as in our judgment will best tend to excite interest and arouse enthusiasm through the Order at large for the aims and purposes of this organization.

The moral and social uplifting of our members —helping them to grasp the large possibilities of t h e Order — enabling them to comprehend the principles as laid down in the original act of incorporation — these are some of the objects we propose to accomplish. Under the inspiration of him whose name we bear, and with the story of Columbus' life, as exemplified in our beautiful Ritual, we have the broadest kind of basis for patriotism and true love of country. Our Order knows no state, lines, or sections, but only a whole and undivided people. We take the men of all races, traditions and language, and weld them into a homogeneous whole.

Like the multitude who gathered around the Apostles on the wonderful day of Pentecost, or, still better, like the members of the crew who sailed with Columbus on the first voyage to America, we have men of various races and languages. But, by drawing close the bonds of brotherhood, we produce the best type of American citizenship.

For the best American is he who best exemplifies in his own life that this is not a Protestant country, nor a Catholic country, nor a *Hebrew country*, any more than it is an Anglo-Saxon, or a Latin country, but a country of all races and creeds, with one great, broad, unalterable creed of fair play and equal rights for all.

It is our purpose to publish matters relating to Columbus and the e a r l y discoveries of America, to collect news of the Order from different quarters, to publish the official financial statements, c i r c u l a r s, decisions, etc., promulgated by the Supreme Body ; also a list of the new Councils to be instituted during t h e month, besides editorial discussion and corre spondence on questions that are agitating the minds of the members.

In fact, in all that pertains to making this a first-class paper, no expense will be spared by the management. No single influence can possibly be more powerful in promoting the interests of our noble Order than this.

WE urge upon the Secretaries of Councils to send us all the information they can about the order in their immediate locality. Give us any item of interest you have. Remember that if it is interesting to you, that it will also prove so to other members.

MINISTRY OF MARINE PORTRAIT OF COLUMBUS.

First issue of *The Columbiad*, November 1893.

The Voice of the Knights of Columbus Through the Years

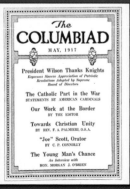

# Spreading the Word

In November 1893, the Columbiad Publishing Company in Boston printed the first issue of a monthly newspaper called *The Columbiad*. The paper was dedicated to providing information about the interests and activities of the Knights of Columbus. Thomas H. Cummings, who from 1893 to 1895 served the Order as the National Director of Ceremonies and later served as National Organizer, was named the first editor. Well-known Catholic lecturer Christopher I. Fitzgerald was appointed the business manager. An annual subscription to *The Columbiad* was $1.

In 1898, magazine publisher Daniel Toomey purchased *The Columbiad*. Within five years he had established the publication as the official magazine of the Order. It provided communication from the national council, the board of directors, and various committees to the membership.

In August 1921, the Knights took over the publication and changed its name to *Columbia*. From that point, the magazine was managed entirely by the staff of the Supreme Office. A printing press was installed in the building to facilitate production. While maintaining its Catholic nature, the magazine expanded its focus to become more than a simple news service for the Order. Along with newsworthy articles, it began including items like short stories and interviews with notable personalities, all to appeal to a broader audience—members as well as non-members, and men as well as women.

In 1955, over thirty years and several editors later, *Columbia* underwent a format change. The magazine's page count doubled, while its dimensions were reduced from a large-size format to that of a standard magazine. With a circulation of 900,000, *Columbia* rivaled major publications of its time. A new plant was built to accommodate its steadily growing circulation. When news of the forthcoming inaugural issue of the revamped *Columbia* was announced, it was greeted by a letter from the Vatican Secretary of State. The letter extended the personal good wishes of the Holy Father, Pope Pius XII, who was chosen to appear on the cover of the newly formatted magazine's first issue.

Today, with a circulation of 1.7 million, *Columbia* continues to be the leading source of information about the Knights of Columbus. It is distributed in the United States, Canada, Mexico, Poland, the Philippines, Puerto Rico, and countries in the Caribbean and along the Pacific Rim.

In addition to its English edition, the magazine is published in French and Spanish with an abbreviated Polish version. Although *Columbia's* readership consists mainly of members and their families, it is geared toward a general Catholic audience.

First issue of *Columbia*, August 1921.

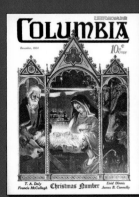
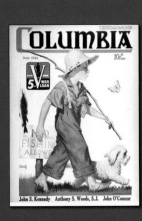

# AN EYE FOR RELEVANCE

By 1885, a requirement for any sustainable fraternal benefits association was reached: a body of members large enough to be able to bestow charity on one another's families in time of need. Public and visual proof of this came in August with a parade of more than 1,000 Knights from twenty-one councils led by Father McGivney himself—a scene that impressed bystanders, according to contemporary newspaper accounts. The parade's invitation to councils also exuded hopeful determination about its future noting: "The enthusiasm that has cradled the young organization must not slumber till the prophesy of its founder has been fulfilled, and the glorious pennant of Columbus waves over all who are worthy to have its beneficial fruits."

**John J. Phelan**
Second supreme knight.

The event underscored that many Catholic laymen in Connecticut were already reaping these "beneficial fruits." Supreme Knight Mullen was honored at a clambake following the parade and accepted a gold watch "in recognition of his eminent services and untiring efforts in establishing the order."

But a year later, the 1886 convention might have been the Order's last. Mullen declined re-election due to other business responsibilities, instead accepting the new title of director general of ceremonies. Facing the logistical challenges posed to its fraternal and insurance structures, delegates found themselves at odds about solutions, including those proposed in a revised constitution. Only a full, detailed explanation could avert what some considered an existential crisis.

A pivotal voice was that of John Phelan, an Irish immigrant and Bridgeport lawyer. Although a Knight for just over a year, Phelan served as Grand Knight of Park City Council 16, and was an author of the proposed constitution. Speaking at length, he laid out a vision for the Order and the need for it in both the Church and society. As a result, he was elected as the organization's second supreme knight, and re-elected for the next eleven years.

A visionary and natural mediator, Phelan also brought experience—and a personal mission—which dovetailed with the Order's founding concerns. As a young man eager to show by example that Catholics could contribute greatly as citizens, he attended law school part time while working as a stonecutter. While serving as supreme knight, he was also elected Connecticut's secretary of the state, an incredible achievement for anyone, let alone a nineteenth-century Catholic.

Phelan's ideas dramatically shaped the Order's future. Believing the organization's benefits eclipsed financial security alone, he urged opening the fraternity to non-insurance members as well; so every Knight who has not held insurance has Phelan to thank. He also saw the Order's relevance beyond New England Catholics, and urged expansion—an idea that proved sound as the Knights extended into ten states and Montreal during his tenure.

In 1892, the 400th anniversary of Columbus' voyage drew celebrations worldwide. President Harrison declared October 21 an unofficial national holiday, while Pope Leo praised Columbus for "join[ing] to the study of nature the study of religion" and called for Solemn Masses to be celebrated in every cathedral in the Americas, Italy, and Spain.

The first Pledge of Allegiance appeared on September 8, 1892 in a popular publication called *The Youth Companion.* In 1954, as a result of Knights of Columbus' efforts, the words "under God" would be added, making it the pledge that is known today.

## Members of the Order of Knights

| NAME. | Age. | Council. | No. | Location. | Nativity. | Occupation. | Initi |
|---|---|---|---|---|---|---|---|
| McGivney M.J. Rev. | 30 | San Salvador *Dead aug 14 90* | 1 | New Haven | Waterbury | Clergyman | Feb. 2 |
| Mullen Jas. T. | 31 | *Dead 7/6-1891* | " | " | New Haven | Merchant | " |
| Colwell Daniel | 36 | | " | " | Massachusetts | | " |
| Kerrigan John T. | 28 | *Withdrawn Apr. 16/91* | " | " | New Haven | Postal Clerk | " |
| Geary Wm. M. | 31 | " | " | " | " | " | Clerk | " |
| McMahon Jas. T. | 29 | " | " | " | " | " | " | Carriage Mkr | " |
| Driscoll Cornelius T. | 35 | " | " | " | " | Ireland | Lawyer | " |
| Curran Michael | 37 | *Died May 7/85* | " | " | " | Undertaker | " |
| O'Connor Matthew C. | 33 | " | " | " | " | Physician | " |
| Tracy John | 40 | " | " | " | " | | |
| " Michael | 37 | " | " | " | " | | |
| Kenney Henry P. | 44 | " | " | " | " | Providence | Packer | " |

This page from the early insurance books of the Order lists Father M.J. McGivney and other charter members and states each member's age, occupation, and other information.

## Daniel Colwell
### Notable Knight

It is doubtful that the Knights of Columbus would be the successful organization that it became without the collective efforts of its founding members. One of these unsung heroes, Daniel Colwell, played an especially important role. Praised for his optimism and profound faith, Colwell served not only as the new Order's long-time supreme secretary, but also as a great contributor to its initial success.

An officer of the Superior Court of Connecticut, "Uncle Dan" Colwell had always shown great interest in Catholic fraternal organizations. Before his involvement with the Knights, he had been active with other such groups, including the Red Knights and the Knights of Saint Patrick, for which he was an officer. He also helped form the Sarsfield Guard, an Irish-Catholic militia unit of the National Guard. When the Knights of Columbus was being formed, Colwell's past experience, skills, and vision were put to work immediately. From his pen came the petition to the State of Connecticut for approval of the charter. He also drafted the articles of incorporation, chaired the committee to file the constitution, and assisted with the ceremonials.

Along with his organizational skills, Colwell was also a man of great kindness and character. For instance, as a constable and court officer of the state's Superior Criminal Court, he became involved in the case of Chip Smith, who was executed for the murder of a policeman. Colwell took special interest in Smith, offering him friendship, comfort, and compassion. While in prison, Smith was also under the spiritual care of Father McGivney (see "Venerable Servant of God," page 16). Together with Father McGivney, Colwell helped give Smith strength and support during his final days.

When the board of directors sought to increase his salary due to his excellent management of the Order's finances, Colwell declined. For him, his work with the Knights was a labor of love, not a job. The legacy he left behind was not wealth, but rather a vibrant organization that he had helped shape.

# DEATH OF THE FOUNDER

In June 1889, the Knights honored its founder, Father McGivney, with a gift of $1,000 as a "testimony of gratitude of the Order for his past services on its behalf." Father McGivney was only thirty-seven years old, but he had become the spiritual father of an organization that would never forget him.

During the late nineteenth century, parish priests rarely lived into their forties. This was largely due to their hard work and dedicated ministries, which typically included frequent visits to the sick. Father McGivney was no exception. Just six months after the Knights honored him that June, he developed pneumonia. Although he had dealt with various illnesses in the past, this time the battle to regain his health was unusually long and difficult. On August 14, two days after his thirty-eighth birthday, he passed away.

*St. Thomas Church in Thomaston, Connecticut, where Father McGivney served as a parish priest after leaving St. Mary's until his death.*

One of the Order's earliest recorded fundraisers was an 1895 concert and lecture held by Everett Council of Massachusetts. Funds were raised for a hospital bed free to brother Knights at Carney Hospital, run by the Sisters of Charity. Everett Council soon appealed to other councils, noting "the time is opportune to make our charity and brotherly love practical."

Front of an early Memorial Card for Father McGivney, using English, Spanish, and French (languages used by Knights in the first countries where the Order was established) as well as Italian. The back of the card appears on page 34.

# LA RÉDEMPTRICE
## DU GENRE HUMAIN.

Sin la Cruz no hay salvacion; ella es camino
verdad y vida.

Senz'essa non vi è salute; essa è la Via,
essa la Verità, essa la Vita!..

OF YOUR ✝ CHARITY

PRAY FOR THE SOUL OF

# Rev. Michael J. McGivney,

**Priest of Hartford Diocese,**

**Who Died in Thomaston, August 14, 1890,
in the 38th year of his Age.**

———

"Being made perfect in a short space, he fulfilled a long time; for his soul pleased God, therefore He hastened to bring him out of the midst of iniquity."

*Wisdom*, iv. 13, 14.

———

## LET US PRAY.

"O most merciful Jesus, saviour of souls, grant, I beseech Thee, by the merits of Thy precious blood, a place of eternal rest to the soul of Thy dear servant MICHAEL, that he may glorify Thee forever." Amen.

Father McGivney's death was met with great sorrow. More than 250 knights—representing all fifty-seven councils—were in attendance at his funeral in Thomaston, Connecticut. More than seventy priests, numerous civic leaders, and the Bishop of Hartford attended. No funeral of its size had ever been seen before in Thomaston. Father McGivney was interred in the family plot at St. Joseph's Cemetery in Waterbury, Connecticut.

The next year, Alfred Downes' brother Edward (New Haven's town clerk, future US consul to Amsterdam, and later a priest) eulogized Father McGivney:

> He was a man of the people. He was ever zealous for the people's welfare, and all the kindliness of his priestly soul asserted itself more strongly in his unceasing efforts for the betterment of their condition. . . . Oh, Reverend Founder if [naught] else in all thy holy priestly career merited for thy heavenly rest, that act alone of thine, which gave life to the Knights of Columbus, has surely secured for thee everlasting joy and eternal peace.

Downes also praised McGivney's wisdom in embracing Columbus, saying:

> Comfort and help are not the only fruits of our organization, its province is more far reaching. . . . The very name of our Order, bespeaking the wisdom of our founder, necessarily inspires our members with renewed patriotism and makes us better citizens. The name stands as a beacon light reminding us of the duties we owe our country, and reminding us that unrivaled civil liberty on the one side and unrivaled religious liberty on the other demand of us cultivation and exercise of the most ardent patriotism.

In 1997, Archbishop Daniel A. Cronin of Hartford opened Father McGivney's cause for canonization. Following three years of work by the archdiocese and the Knights, in 2000, Father McGivney's cause for sainthood was presented to the Vatican.

In March 2008, Pope Benedict XVI approved a decree recognizing Father McGivney's heroic virtue, recognizing him as a "Venerable Servant of God." If he is canonized, Father McGivney could become the first American-born priest to be named as a saint. (See "Father Michael Joseph McGivney's Cause for Canonization" on page 203.)

A man of foresight, wisdom, and compassion, Father McGivney touched the lives of many during his short time on earth. He recognized the spiritual as well as the material needs of those around him. With the founding of the Knights of Columbus, his vision of charity and fraternity continues to live on.

The Knights' proposition that faithful Catholics could also be good citizens spurred the Order's efforts to ensure that religious freedom rights were extended to Catholics, as well as to those of other faiths. This theme appeared early—in Edward Downes' eulogy of Father McGivney—and often thereafter. In 1895 at a banquet in Massachusetts, Congressman Joseph O'Neill laid out the Order's vision, stating that it would not "proscribe any man on account of his faith." He added: "We believe that the better Catholics we are, the better citizens we are also. Inspired by this spirit, we are tolerant of the opinions of others, and demand like toleration from others." The next year, the Order's National Organizer Thomas Cummings wrote in *Donahoe's Magazine* that Catholics had first planted religious freedom on the continent and that "with true American patriotism," the Knights of Columbus "ask that no man's social and civil rights be affected by his religious beliefs."

Reflecting the spiritual work of mercy to pray for the living and the dead, the first memorial liturgies for deceased members of the Order drew more than 450 Knights, filling St. Joseph's Cathedral in Hartford, Connecticut for music-enriched vespers and for a memorial Mass the following morning.

At the 1896 Olympic Games in Athens, Greece, James B. Connolly, of Boston's Back Bay Council 331, became the first American to win a gold medal. The twenty-nine-year-old son of Irish immigrants took first place in the "triple jump" track and field event. Along with winning for the US, he desired to bring home the gold for both Irish Americans and the "Catholicism that had nurtured him since birth."

## APPROACHING THE NEW CENTURY
## EXPANSION LEADS THE WAY

**Thomas Cummings**
National organizer
for the Order.

Within a decade of that first meeting in the basement of St. Mary's Church, nearly sixty councils were formed throughout Connecticut, as well as Westerly, Rhode Island. The council was formed in 1885 as a result of problems encountered at a planned location nearby in Connecticut. Further expansion was inevitable for an organization of this nature, despite the initial indications that the Order would limit itself to its home state. The expansion was due to two major factors. The first was that the Knights of Columbus so clearly met the needs of Catholic men; the second was the passionate enthusiasm of existing members, who were quick to invite other men to join them in their fraternal mission of providing charity while protecting faith, family, and Catholic honor.

Against the backdrop of an America that was still often hostile to Catholics, membership in the Knights of Columbus meant a commitment to the Catholic faith, to charity, to fellowship, and to the protection of the financial resources of families. This unique and attractive combination soon had its own name: *Columbianism.* Desiring to spread Columbianism far beyond the Connecticut border, delegates to the 1890 convention approved a new governance system for a national organization. Within a year, Supreme Knight Phelan traveled to Brooklyn, New York, to meet with twenty-nine men who wanted to become Knights. Although Brooklyn Catholics already had several means of obtaining insurance through groups like the Catholic Benevolent Legion, Royal Arcanum, and Legion of Honors, the Knights of Columbus took root there, establishing Brooklyn Council 60. Meanwhile, local organizers continued to promote the Order state by state. Within four years, councils were chartered in New York, Massachusetts, and New Hampshire.

The success of the Knights in these areas was due in part to the continued support of local priests and bishops, but primarily, it was the result of the uniqueness of the Order itself. The group encouraged policies and practices that were different from those found in other Catholic fraternal organizations. In the early 1890s, for example, a new system was created allowing for non-insured members to benefit from the fraternal and social aspects as associate members, while insured members had the option of various insurance policies. Later, those who were insured also benefited from the Order's use of actuarial tables and other modern tools of commercial insurers.

Thomas H. Cummings, who was elected in 1893 into the newly established position of national organizer for the Order, also helped accelerate the Order's increase in membership. Cummings, who served as a curator at the Boston Public Library, had emerged as a lecturer and photographer, often speaking on the life of Christopher Columbus. He also helped expand on the

The El Paso Council degree team traveled throughout Texas to institute councils in other parts of the state. Around the country, such events were sometimes large fraternal celebrations. Lawrence Council 67's installation, for instance, received 1,250 Knights and visitors, forcing the event to the town hall.

As the turn of the century approached, membership in the Knights of Columbus had grown exponentially, with 16,651 men in the Order. This was more than 250 times larger than the K of C had been at its birth only twelve years before.

already mainstream concept of Columbianism, which had originated during the era of the Revolutionary War. As described in *Columbianism and the Knights of Columbus*, the notion was born during a time "when patriotic poets, eager to assert the distinctive character of the American experience, focused on Columbianism as a symbol of the new nation. This form of Columbianism was later influenced by Italian-American immigrants and Catholics of all nationalities who came to see Columbus as the integrating symbol of Catholic presence at the foundation of the 'New World.'" Expounding on Columbianism through his lectures and articles, the well-spoken Cummings helped lay the foundation for the Order across the nation, particularly in Vermont, Maine, Pennsylvania, Delaware, and Illinois.

Supreme Knight Phelan himself was a talented visionary and a catalyst for the Order's growth—geographically and numerically. He led the Order's expansion beyond Connecticut and also instituted "associate" (non-insurance) membership, having a vision for the Order that went far beyond insurance. He said: "The growth and anticipated greatness of this society lies in and through the development, for Catholics, of the great moral and social forces, with the insurance or other pecuniary features as a vital appendage." Phelan also professed the belief that "The Order is destined to become in the near future the ideal of its founders, as well as a powerful factor in the elevation of the social and moral status of the Catholic people in this and neighboring states." He insisted that "Our laws design us to be Catholics pure and simple," and he went to great lengths to ensure its Catholic reputation

Some worried that the Knights' sense of fraternalism was simply Catholic deference to Masonic brotherhood. This raised concerns since Catholic membership in the Masonic Orders had been forbidden—on theological grounds—for a century and a half. So Phelan sought the Order's official approval from Archbishop Francesco Satolli, the Apostolic Delegate to the United States. On July 24, 1895, the archbishop responded, "We gladly grant to the Knights of Columbus our warm approbation and apostolic benediction." Having learned about the Order, he expressed great pleasure that "there exists a society for practical advancement of insurance, benevolence, and fraternity, proffered by the most popular secular societies without any of the disadvantages of prohibited companionship."

From the time Phelan had become supreme knight in 1886 to the end of his tenure in 1897, the Knights of Columbus had not only received the blessing of the Vatican, but also expanded to have a presence in ten states. The number of councils had grown from 38 to 210 and membership had increased from 2,700 to 17,000—and it was only the beginning.

"Solicitude to participate in developing dormant sympathy of love of Catholics for each other's sake and welfare, seems to have supplanted the indifference, jealousy, and distrust of the past. It seems destined in the providence of God that through the medium of this society will the kindliness of the Catholic heart find consolation to the fullness of content in loving his neighbor as himself and in divinely sharing his joys and sorrows."
–Supreme Knight Phelan

**K of C**
***Every Body Welcome***

Formed by officers, men, and camp activity
workers at Camp Wheeler, Georgia, 1918.

# 3.
# Taking Root, Expansion, and the War Effort
## 1897 to 1919

W hen Massachusetts politician James E. Hayes took office as the new supreme knight in 1897, it was during an era of great expansion for the Order. A Boston College graduate, Hayes had already been elected a state legislator and state senator, and was chairman of the state's Democratic caucus. A decade after its founding in Connecticut, the Order came to neighboring Massachusetts. Hayes was one of the first men to join, becoming a charter member of Bunker Hill Council 62—the state's first council. He served as his council's first deputy grand knight and Massachusetts's first state deputy. Massachusetts was fertile ground, and had in Hayes a talented leader. Under his leadership, membership and councils there grew exponentially, so that by the time he was elected supreme knight, one in three councils and one in two members Order-wide called Massachusetts home. Overseeing the foundation of seventy-five new councils in just three years, Hayes' zeal and record led to his victory over John Phelan as supreme knight.

When Hayes died unexpectedly less than a year after taking the position in 1898, he was succeeded by John J. Cone, a founding member of Jersey City Council 137, and the Commissioner of Public works in Jersey City. Cone's short-lived tenure as supreme knight ended in 1899.

Despite their brief tenures, during the years that Hayes and Cone served as supreme knights, the 42,000-member Order continued to expand further from its New England epicenter, into the southern and western United States and north into Canada. The rapidly expanding Order needed a strong leader with

"The Knights of Columbus . . . has no purpose other than to encourage its members to be and remain good Catholics, good citizens, good men."

–Joseph J. Thompson, past state deputy of Illinois, in *Knights of Columbus in Illinois*

In 1897, James E. Hayes became the Order's third supreme knight. The Massachusetts politician had served as state deputy, leading his state to become the membership powerhouse of the Order. Hayes died unexpectedly less than a year after becoming supreme knight.

A founding member of Jersey City Council 137, and the city's fire commissioner, John Cone served as deputy supreme knight before becoming supreme knight following the death of James Hayes. Cone was the only supreme knight never elected to the position, and he had been a knight for less than three years when he took office.

a unifying vision of the future at that point in time—perhaps more than any other point since its founding. And in 1899, the Knights elected just such a man: Edward L. Hearn. Hearn had succeeded Hayes as state deputy, had attended his funeral, and after Cone's brief tenure, succeeded him as supreme knight.

Born in Framingham, Massachusetts, Hearn joined the Knights in 1894, becoming a member of Coeur de Leon Council 87 in South Framingham. Unlike previous supreme knights, the young state deputy was a businessman, not a public servant or political office holder. With the Order's insurance operation in a critical state, Supreme Convention delegates sought him out at midnight to convince him to accept the role of supreme knight if elected. Although reluctant initially, Hearn would oversee a successful term by improving insurance benefits, expanding further internationally, and prioritizing patriotism a prescient decade and a half before the Great War would boost and depend on citizen support. Even after retirement, the once-hesitant candidate would continue to lead key Order initiatives.

**Edward L. Hearn**
Fifth supreme knight.

## THE FOURTH DEGREE

The embrace of patriotism was the natural outgrowth of the Knights' foundational conviction that Catholics could be good citizens. Adding the virtue of patriotism to charity, unity, and fraternity as a Fourth Degree had been proposed by Supreme Knight James T. Mullen in the 1880s. The Fourth Degree was formally added under newly elected Supreme Knight Edward L. Hearn. On February 22, 1900, nearly 1,100 knights participated in the first exemplification of the Fourth Degree in New York City. Three months later, another 750 members took the degree in Boston.

Any Third Degree Knight in good standing who had been a member of the Order for at least six months was eligible for this optional degree. Fourth Degree Knights earn the title of "Sir" and become members of special groups called assemblies while remaining members of their local councils. The main purpose of the Fourth Degree is to "foster the spirit of patriotism by promoting responsible citizenship and a love of loyalty to the Knights' respective countries . . ."

Nearly 1,100 members participated in the first grand exemplification of the Fourth Degree, which took place on February 22, 1900 in New York City. Pictured here are members of New York's Charles Carroll Assembly.

An early uniform of
the Fourth Degree.

Feathered chapeau and
cape over tuxedo.

Blue blazer and grey pants
with military guard beret.

Sir Knights of the Fourth Degree have the option of joining the Color Corps—the most visible arm of the Order. These members take part in a number of religious and civic gatherings, including liturgical processions, funerals, and parades, as well as events like wreath-laying ceremonies (such as the one performed at the Tomb of the Unknown Soldier in Arlington National Cemetery).

Members of the Fourth Degree are visible reminders of community service, and easily recognized by their distinctive uniform, which has evolved over time. The early uniform, which included a top hat and white bow tie, was replaced in 1940 with a white-feathered chapeau and cape that was worn over a tuxedo. Later, the chapeaux took on a variety of colors and were worn with matching capes. In 2017, the uniform was updated once again. This modernized version includes a blue blazer and gray slacks worn with a military guard beret. The sword and baldric—the most timeless elements of the uniform—have remained.

The images above show some of the versions of the Fourth Degree Knight uniform as it has evolved over time. Climate as well as time has also altered the uniforms worn. For example, in the warm Philippines, light-weight white attire was long worn.

In 1897, the Knights of Columbus became an international organization when Montreal Council 284 was formed in Quebec. Among the first members were two Montreal Catholics who had joined in New York while studying abroad, and a local politician—and future mayor of Montreal—J.J. Guerin, who served as the council's first grand knight.

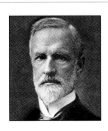

Considered by many to be the "dean" of the actuarial profession in the United States, David Parks Fackler was hired by the Knights in 1898 to be its first actuary. Fackler successfully helped reform the insurance arm of the Order to make it more financially sustainable.

# John H. Reddin
## Notable Knight

One of the most successful organizers of the Order, John Reddin played an important role in helping the Knights establish councils throughout the western states. He was appointed Territorial Director of the Far West and served as a supreme director for more than thirty years.

In 1903, Reddin composed the Ritual for the Patriotic Degree of the Knights of Columbus, and became the supreme master of the Fourth Degree, holding that position until his death on December 30, 1940 at age eighty-two. Reddin saw the Fourth Degree as the intellectual and patriotic arm of the Order. He also helped launch a lecture series and the Order's Historical Commission.

Fourth Degree assemblies are separate from councils and have a separate set of officers and a separate emblem.

The Triad Emblem of the Fourth Degree (see page 43) features a white dove, a blue globe, and a red cross. The dove, a symbol of peace, is flying above the globe. Both are mounted on a cross in the same style of those worn on the clothing of knights of the Middle Ages. The three items on the emblem are also representative of the Blessed Trinity:

- The globe represents God the Father, Creator of the Universe.

- The cross represents God the Son, Redeemer of Mankind.

- The dove represents the Holy Spirit, Sanctifier of Humanity.

The patriotic red, white, and blue colors on the emblem are those of the flag of the United States, where the Knights of Columbus originated.

The year 2000 marked the 100-year anniversary of the Fourth Degree. Launched with 1,100 members, it has grown to include more than 368,000 Sir Knights and 3,500 assemblies.

In 1905, France's secularism law put new restrictions on the Catholic Church. The Order protested in *Columbiad*, and also took public issue with other anti-Catholic policies, including those of the American government in Cuba and the Philippines in the wake of the Spanish-American War.

Concerned that Native Americans in some government schools were prevented from attending Mass or religious instruction, the Order established its Bureau for Indian Affairs to coordinate with the Catholic Indian Bureau so "that the rights of the Catholic Indians and the rights of the Church [would] be protected."

**Emblem of the Fourth Degree**
The Triad Emblem of the Fourth Degree was designed in 1900.

"[The Fourth Degree] is the highest or ultimate degree in the Knights of Columbus. . . . Its principle is patriotism. It appeals to the highest intelligence in the Order. It is a factor of great educational and moral value to both Church and country. . . . Its patriotism is virile. Its Catholicity is militant. It seeks by the spread of intelligence and of the knowledge of the moral code of the Catholic Church to make a lasting foundation for civil society and civil government."

–John Reddin, 1913

## Officers of the Fourth Degree

### Supreme Assembly Officers

Supreme Master      Supreme Secretary

Supreme Knight      Vice Supreme Master
of the Fourth Degree

### Provincial Assembly Officers

Vice Supreme Master

### District Assembly Officers

Master of the District

### Local Assembly Officers

*Each local assembly includes the following officers:*

Faithful Navigator      Faithful Scribe

Faithful Friar      Faithful Purser

Faithful Captain      Faithful Inner and
Outer Sentinels

Faithful Pilot

Faithful Admiral
Faithful
Comptroller      Trustee

In 1903, Kansas experienced the most destructive flood in its history, with widespread devastation throughout the state. The Knights quickly raised thousands of dollars for the Kansas Flood Relief Fund, which offered grants and loans to the area's many councils and churches.

Surrounded by patriotic bunting and a crowd of onlookers, in 1904, the Knights provided The Catholic University of America with more than $55,000 to endow a chair of American History. Provided by Knights nationwide, the gift reflected the Order's commitment to education and to rectifying the public's view of Catholics.

# EXPANSION IN THE NEW CENTURY

Wives and children join Knights of Columbus delegates at the 1908 Supreme Convention in St. Louis, Missouri—home to one of the first councils established west of the Mississippi River (Council 453, established in 1899).

In 1897, the Knights of Columbus became an international organization. This happened when J.P. Kavanaugh and Charles F. Smith—two young Canadian expatriates who had joined the Order while in Plattsburgh, New York—took it upon themselves to start a new council in Montreal after repatriating. They did so with the help of the pastor of St. Patrick's Church in Montreal and James J. Guerin, the city's future mayor. Father McGivney had studied in Quebec at St. Hyacinthe College near Montreal and at St. Mary's College in the city itself, making Montreal a fitting city for the Order's first international establishment.

Catholics in Canada, like those in the United States, had also faced marginalization, prejudice, and discrimination. As grand knight of Montreal Council 284, Guerin joined with council leaders in an effort to establish new councils to fight this discrimination. Within two years of the formation of the Montreal council, two more councils were founded in Quebec City and Montreal. Soon, councils had spread beyond the Province of Quebec to Ottawa, New Brunswick, Nova Scotia, Ontario, and Prince Edward Island.

While Catholics were a minority facing discrimination in much of North America, they were a majority being undermined in places like Cuba and the Philippines. The American government had taken control of these territories from Spain after the Spanish-American War, and had adopted policies seen by the Order as anti-Catholic.

Following the war, hundreds of American servicemen were stationed in the Philippines. Many of these servicemen were drawn to the Cathedral Parish. Some were already members of the Knights of Columbus, and their efforts led to the development of the Knights' 1,000th council in 1905. Although the council was initially composed of American members, Filipinos soon began to join. That same year, the Order began in Mexico—a feat of unity that went against contemporary cultural clashes. In many European countries as well as the United States, anti-Spanish sentiment demonized Spanish and Latin American culture and their people as cruel, lazy, uncouth, and inferior. This resulted from pro-British and anti-Spanish propaganda known as the "Black Legend." These stereotypes persisted for centuries, peaking during the Spanish-American War and recurring subsequently from time to time. In contrast, the Knights reached out to Latin America and established councils there—first in Mexico, then in Cuba—building on the Catholic faith, which served as a source of unity in North and Latin America alike.

Leading the Knights' expansion in Mexico was John B. Frisbie Jr. With a father who had served as a general in the Mexican-American War, Frisbie had a unique connection to Mexico. He recognized the need for Catholic organizations there, and after considering the possibility of forming groups for both English-speaking Catholics in Mexico and the Spanish-speaking Mexicans themselves, Frisbie attended the Order's 1905 national convention

By the end of 1905, the Knights of Columbus had councils in every state of the Union, as well as in Mexico, the Philippines, Newfoundland, and five of Canada's nine provinces. The last state to establish a council was Nevada, where the Order formed the Reno Council on April 9, 1905.

In 1906, the Knights of Columbus moved into its new headquarters at 956 Chapel Street in New Haven, Connecticut. Designed by architect Lyman Faxon, it was the first building specifically constructed to serve as the Order's home office. It remained there until 1922.

in Los Angeles. The Knights, impressed by Frisbie's plans to spread the Order south of the American border, appointed him territorial deputy for Mexico to oversee the establishment of a new state council.

By the fall of 1905, a contingent of American knights—including Father Patrick J. McGivney, the brother of the founder—journeyed to Mexico for the First Degree exemplification, forming Guadalupe Council 1050, with Judge Ignacio Sepulveda, a Mexican-American expatriate, as grand knight. Mexican Knights soon developed their own Spanish-language ceremonials, and began integrating the K of C into the life of the Church there. Significantly, while local and cultural needs led each council and territory to address certain specific issues, the Catholic heritage of Columbianism gave an international character and universal appeal to the organization that allowed it to thrive. Mexico would prove to be both a natural next step and a challenging one. Although it was an overwhelmingly Catholic country, it would soon be enveloped in civil wars marked by anti-Catholic sentiment. As dictatorial governments periodically opposed the clergy and confiscated most Church property, the Order became a strong voice of defense for the Church there.

Cuba was another challenging place for the Order's growth in the early 1900s. By the time Cuba had won independence from Spain after the Spanish-American War in 1898, the Catholic Church there had lost credibility because many Cubans associated it with the former Spanish colonial government. However, Augustinian Father Patrick Edward Moynihan of St. Augustine's College in Havana believed the Knights of Columbus could bring Catholics to a better understanding and practice of the faith. In November 1908, he wrote to Supreme Knight Hearn: "I believe it would be a very great good for the Church, and I might say absolutely necessary at present as our people are not Catholic by practice, [but] simply in name . . ." Strongly supporting the idea, Hearn sent a team under the direction of Alabama State Deputy M. Mahorner Jr. to lay the groundwork.

By the time San Agustín Council 1390 was instituted in Havana on March 28, 1909, it was clear that the presence of the Knights could deeply influence the culture in which the Order was established. The US government controlled Cuba as it did the Philippines, and the Order also took a stand against anti-Catholic US policies there. The Knights in Havana also offered a visible witness of putting faith into practice from the start. As the Bishop of Havana noted when seeing the candidates together at Mass, "It was the first time in the history of the island that a communion rail had been filled by a body of men." Although all members of this first council spoke English, Spanish-speaking Cubans would comprise the majority of the council by the 1920s.

**Father Patrick J. McGivney**
Brother of the founder, Patrick McGivney served as supreme chaplain from 1901 to 1928. He traveled to Mexico for the First Degree exemplification, forming the country's first council.

In 1905, the expansion into Mexico was momentous for the Order. Supreme Knight Hearn travelled personally to install Guadalupe Council 1050, and met with President Porfirio Díaz. Its first grand knight was Judge Ignacio Sepulveda, and the degree ceremony was held in the home of General John Frisbie Sr., a Mexican-American War veteran.

Knights from Alabama established the Order in Cuba in 1909, only a few years after Cuba had won independence from Spain. The San Augustin Council helped renew Cubans' practice of their faith.

Residents of San Francisco
watch the fires caused by
the 1906 earthquake.

# HOPE IN ACTION

During this time, the Order began to experience greater public visibility due to its charitable works on both the local and national levels. Its continued growth allowed it to not only better protect its members, but also come to the aid of others who were in need. This commitment was put into action in 1903 when Kansas experienced the most destructive flood in its history. Several days of heavy rain coupled with overflowing rivers caused widespread devastation throughout the state. Thousands of lives were lost, houses and buildings were swept away, bridges were destroyed, and railways were submerged. The Knights immediately raised nearly $5,000 (a value equivalent to over $100,000 today) to create grants and loans for the area's Catholic churches and for local councils that had been affected.

Two years later, when San Francisco was rocked by one of the most destructive earthquakes on record on April 18, 1906, the Knights were again on hand to help. The earthquake and the resulting fires throughout the city left thousands dead and hundreds of thousands homeless. Knights from various councils traveled to the affected areas to help those in need, finding them shelter in homes and public facilities in nearby cities that had sustained less damage. They also collected over $100,000 to aid in disaster relief.

Rose J. Quinn, a woman from San Francisco who lost her home in a fire, wrote of her experience with the Knights in an article that appeared in the *Vallejo Daily Times* on April 27, 1906. In the following excerpt, Rose recalls the occasion:

> . . . we knew not where to go when my brother, who had been searching for his fellow Knights of Columbus, returned and informed us that a home awaited us in Vallejo. These noble, generous, brave hearted Knights of Columbus came to our aid, and to them do we owe our present safety. They have provided everything for us and for our comfort. How can we, homeless wanderers, ever repay them? Oh, who can realize the anguish, the sorrow that is ours? . . . but now God has been with us. He will not desert us now.
>
> We have naught to offer now but our thankful hearts and fond prayers. May every kindness you have shown us, oh, Knights of Columbus, be showered a hundred fold on you and yours, and may your deeds of charity be sparkling jewels added to that crown of eternal life, which our God has promised His faithful followers.

The new century also saw the Knights of Columbus rally in response to the considerable financial difficulties being experienced by other Catholic institutions. In the early 1900s, the newly established Catholic University of America took root. Established by the US Catholic bishops with the support

In 1910, President William Howard Taft declared October 12, Columbus Day, a legal US holiday. By that time, a growing number of cities had been celebrating the day with parades and other festivities, while an increasing number of schools began teaching students about Columbus and his historic journey.

Notre Dame Council 1477, the first college council, was established in 1910. Other colleges followed suit and in 1920, graduate students from Harvard, led by African American Pedro Albizu y Campos, founded the Harvard Knights of Columbus Club. It was a group similar in aim, though not in form, to other college councils.

of Pope Leo XIII, the Washington, DC institution found itself in dire need of monetary assistance. Knowing the Order's commitment to intellectual faith formation, the university turned to the Knights for help.

Initially, the Knights provided the university with more than $55,000 to endow a chair of American History there. Supreme Knight Hearn and the K of C leadership saw this as both a symbol of the Order's fidelity to the Church and an important means of correcting the historical record concerning Catholics in the United States. Soon afterward, the Knights raised an additional $500,000 for the university at the urging of Archbishop John J. Glennon of St. Louis. The educational gift was one of the first and most prominent causes promoted, adopted and funded Order-wide, with Knights contributing a voluntary assessment of $1 per year for five years, which was placed into the Knights of Columbus Catholic University Endowment Fund. Within five years, by December 1913, the $500,000 goal had been met.

The fund was presented to the university in 1914. For every $10,000 contributed, the university agreed to provide a fellowship for graduate studies leading to a master's or doctoral degree. Knights and their families were granted a preference for these fellowships. The awards, which covered tuition and liv-

# Homes of Faith
## Visionary Council Initiative

Concern for orphans had been one of the main motivations for founding the Order. It was a concern that became a personal challenge for the Knights in Illinois.

At the 1911 state convention in Dixon, State Chaplain Bishop P. J. Muldoon gave an impassioned plea regarding the fate of older children who were being discharged from state institutions. Along with their basic welfare, he noted the particular need for providing Catholic children with an environment supportive of their faith—namely, Catholic homes. Moved by the bishop's words, the Knights founded the Catholic Home Finding Association to locate suitable homes for these children. Members supported the initiative with yearly contributions of ten cents.

Chartered in 1914, the association—reminiscent of a modern adoption agency—placed more than 700 children in the first eight years. As the *History of the Knights of Columbus in Illinois* reported: "Childless homes are opening their doors to the poor little ones, there to find love and affection, and an opportunity for that religious training and education that will equip them to take their place in the world as good Catholic men and women."

By giving "careful and thorough investigation" of both applicants and homes, its placements proved "eminently satisfactory to all concerned." It also nurtured the unique interplay of charity, love, and faith in a home.

Christmas 1905 began an Order-wide cause when Baltimore councils sought to brighten the holiday for all 600 children in the city's Catholic orphanages. With presents and entertainment, the Santa Claus Party became a yearly tradition and so impressed future Supreme Knight Flaherty that he encouraged other councils to follow suit, which many did for decades.

In the early 1900s, from Boston to San Antonio, councils formed baseball teams and developed a K of C league, with great sportsmanship and not a little rivalry. Here, future Baseball Hall of Famer Ross Youngs (on right) poses in his K of C baseball uniform in Rockport, Texas in 1916.

ing expenses, were designed primarily to prepare the graduate students to become teachers in both Catholic and public institutions of higher education.

Along with lending support at both the local and the national levels, the Order was involved with humanitarian relief abroad. In 1915, the Ottoman Empire began what was considered the first modern genocide with its persecution of Armenians and other Christians. This slaughter continued through World War I with the killing of about 1.5 million Armenians and as many as half a million other Christians in the Middle East. Through a combination of public and private efforts and funding coordinated by Near East Relief, the American people launched one of the greatest humanitarian responses in history. Into the 1920s, America contributed more than $100 million to care for the victims and ensure the continued survival of the Christian communities that had been targeted for extermination. The K of C was among the organizations that helped support this important work through grassroots charitable activities and by raising both awareness and funds. It would take up this work again a century later as ISIS swept through Iraq and Syria, devastating Christian and other religious minority communities there.

Campaigns like these expanded the Order's charitable mission beyond councils' local communities to touch lives around the world. They also laid the essential foundation of fraternal coordination needed in the national and international efforts for which the Knights would soon be known.

Following World War I, in response to the persecution of Armenians and other Christians in the Middle East, the Knights of Columbus council in Rochester, New York, collected a mountain of clothes for Near East Relief.

# Connie Mack
## Notable Knight

Cornelius Alexander McGillicuddy, better known as Connie Mack, was born into a large Irish Catholic immigrant family on December 22, 1862. The third of seven children, Connie was active in the Church, and his religious upbringing would shape the course of his life. His love of baseball began at a very young age, and his passion and ability for the game grew as the sport itself was gaining popularity.

Mack became the owner and manager of the Philadelphia Athletics in 1901. The fledgling team was inexperienced and truly awful—it was considered a joke among the other teams. When a rival team manager called the team a white elephant—a team that nobody wanted to be associated with—Mack considered it a personal challenge and committed himself to making the team a winner. As a reminder of his mission, he had the image of an elephant put on the team uniforms (a symbol that is still worn by the now-Oakland Athletics).

Mack had a reputation for treating everyone with fairness and respect. He managed the team for an amazing fifty seasons and became the first manager to lead his team to three World Series wins.

In 1937, Connie Mack's name was added to the Baseball Hall of Fame in Cooperstown, New York. In 1953, Philadelphia's Shibe Park was renamed Connie Mack Stadium.

# Columbus Day
## The Making of an American Holiday

During the early years of the twentieth century, Columbus Day celebrations were elevated to a grand level, with strong support from the Knights of Columbus.

In 1892, the quadricentennial of Columbus' historic journey generated great fanfare under President Benjamin Harrison. The president issued a proclamation encouraging Americans to mark this 400th anniversary of the voyage of Columbus with patriotic festivities. Harrison wrote:

> On that day, let the people, so far as possible, cease from toil and devote themselves to such exercises as may best express honor to the discoverer and their appreciation of the great achievements of the four completed centuries of American life.

The patriotism and loyalty to the nation that was exemplified at this 1892 celebration continued in subsequent years. Then, in 1906, Colorado became the first state to make Columbus Day an annual holiday. As the Knights of Columbus grew and continued to spread the spirit of Columbianism throughout the nation, it was only fitting that they would expand upon the opportunity to celebrate the voyage of discovery by the esteemed Catholic navigator.

By 1907, at the encouragement of the Knights of Columbus, a number of cities—including Chicago, San Francisco (which had unofficially celebrated Columbus Day since the early nineteenth century), and even smaller towns like Poughkeepsie, New York—began such celebrations. Observing this special day gave schools the opportunity to include Catholics in American history as they discussed Columbus and his faith.

By 1910, more and more cities were celebrating the day with parades and other festivities. That year, President William Howard Taft officially established October 12 as Columbus Day, although it would take nearly three more decades for it to become a federal holiday.

In the years that followed, the holiday would be opposed by nativists and the Ku Klux Klan on the basis that it celebrated a man who was Catholic and a non-Anglo. In Kentucky, for instance, the Ministerial Association of Louisville opposed the holiday as "to all

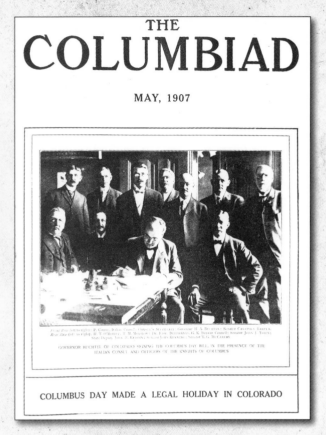

THE **COLUMBIAD**

MAY, 1907

COLUMBUS DAY MADE A LEGAL HOLIDAY IN COLORADO

Governor Buchtel of Colorado
signing Columbus Day Bill.

effects and purposes a Roman Catholic holiday." But the lion's share of outrage came from the Klan, who formally opposed the holiday in an article entitled "Columbus Day: A Papal Fraud," which appeared in its periodical *The American Standard*.

In Colorado, as the Klan took increasing political control of the state in the 1920s, Italians were targeted and the Columbus Day parade was stopped. In Oregon, where the Klan also had considerable political power, the group attempted to remove Columbus Day as a state holiday. On the other side of the country, in Pennsylvania, the Klan burnt a cross to disrupt the Columbus Day festivities in Nanty Glo, while in Richmond, Virginia, the group nearly succeeded in blocking a statue of Columbus that had been proposed by an Italian group.

Despite attempts to remove Columbus Day as a state holiday, the navigator's accomplishments continued to be celebrated. In 1937, this day was established as one of the country's national holidays.

▲ The memorial above bears the following inscription:

TO THE MEMORY OF CHRISTOPHER COLUMBUS
WHOSE HIGH FAITH AND INDOMINATABLE
COURAGE GAVE TO MANKIND A NEW WORLD

BORN  MCDXXXVI
DIED  MDIV

The unveiling of the Columbus fountain at Washington, DC's Union Station took place on June 8, 1912. The ceremony was attended by a huge parade composed of detachments of soldiers and marines, and of members of the Knights of Columbus, who came from all parts of the country for the unveiling.

# THE COLUMBUS MEMORIAL

The Knights of Columbus soon contributed to American celebrations of Columbus in an even more public way. Largely as a result of the Order's lobbying efforts, Congress approved the building of a memorial in honor of Christopher Columbus in the nation's capital and appropriated $100,000 for its construction. A commission was formed to oversee the project. It included the secretaries of State and War, the leadership of the House and Senate, and Supreme Knight Hearn.

The result of the commission's work was unveiled in the plaza in front of Washington, DC's Union Station on June 8, 1912. A huge globe, signifying the Western Hemisphere, sits atop the forty-five-foot-tall shaft in the center of a magnificent marble fountain. Four eagles connected by garland surround the globe as a sign of protection. A full-length statue of Columbus, standing on the prow of a ship, appears in front of the shaft. On either side of Columbus are statues of two figures—an elderly man, representing the Old World, and a Native American, representing the New World. A medallion with images of Ferdinand and Isabella of Spain, who made Columbus' voyage possible, appears on the back of the shaft. The monument includes three flagpoles, representing the three ships that carried the discovery party to the New World. Both sides of the fountain are flanked by lions as a symbol of protection.

In his speech at the statue's unveiling, President Taft praised the navigator's courage and daring. Following his remarks, more than 2,500 soldiers and sailors and nearly 20,000 members of the Knights of Columbus paraded past the reviewing stand, where dignitaries from the federal government and leaders of the Order sat side by side.

From the parade to this program for the banquet following the Columbus Memorial dedication, patriotic imagery figured prominently in every detail.

That evening, just thirty years after the Order's founding, the Knights of Columbus gathered in the heart of the nation's capital to conclude the festivities. Twelve hundred individuals attended the banquet sponsored by the Order, including Supreme Knight Hearn's successor, James Flaherty, along with Cardinal James Gibbons, who had ordained Father McGivney in 1877. Also present were members of the House of Representatives and many other prominent political leaders, ambassadors, and clergymen. Those who gathered for this national celebration would have been acutely aware of the Order's rise to prominence in the United States.

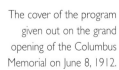

The cover of the program given out on the grand opening of the Columbus Memorial on June 8, 1912.

The July 1912 issue of *The Columbiad* was dedicated to the unveiling of the Columbus Memorial.

# The Continued Targeting of Catholics

A priest-taught people are never versed in scripture.

Romanism and civil liberty will not mix any more than oil and water.

Cultivate common sense and you lessen Peter's pence.

Jesuitism is the incarnation of political hypocrisy.

Romanism is a menace to any country and America's worst enemy.

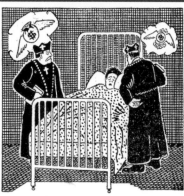

## DYING LIKE CHRIST

A man whose life and home had been wrecked like hundreds of others (by an agent of the Foreign, Pagan, Hierachy) was told by his Doctor that he was dying, so he sent for two priests. These holy vultures, thinking there would be some rich leavings, came posthaste and were requested to stand one on each side of the bed, when they asked him if he wished to confess and receive the last hokus-pokus. The priests were told he did not. "Why, then, did you send for us?" they asked. "Because," said the dying man, "I want to die like Christ did—between two thieves."

**Postal Cards, 15c per dozen, assorted.**
LIBERTY PRINTING CO, Flint, Mich,

## When Al Smith is President

When the jackass learns to sing tenor
And the rattlesnake walks on legs;
When the razorback shoats grow feathers
And the milch cow sets on eggs.

When the bluebird mates with the peckerwood
And the hoot owl mates with the wrens;
When the bull frog sails on snowy wings
And the sapsucker chums with the hens.

A CATHOLIC PRIEST SAYS "THE PILGRIM FATHERS WERE CONCEITED ASSES". ASSES DON'T MARRY, BUT THE PILGRIM FATHERS DID.

When cotton grows on the fig tree
And alfalfa hangs from the rose,
When the Catholic's rule the U. S. A.
And the dagoes all grow a straight nose.

When Pope Pius is praised by every one
In the land of Uncle Sam, and when;
Al Smith is elected president
Our country won't be worth a damn.

# An Alledged Oath Taken By Knights of Columbus

## A Secret Organization of Roman Catholics

## This Is On Record In The Congressional Record
### February 15th 1913, Page 3215

I, _____ now in the presence of Almighty God, the Blessed Virgin Mary, the blessed St. John the Baptist, the holy Apostles St. Peter and St. Paul, and all the Saints, sacred host of Heaven, and to you, my Ghostly Father, the Superior General of the Society of Jesus, founded by St. Ignatius Loyla, in the pontification of Paul the III, and continued to the present, do by the womb of Virgin, the matrix of God, and the rod of Jesus Christ declare and swear, that his Holiness, the Pope, is Christ's vice-regent and is the true and only head of the Catholic or Universal Church throuout the earth; and that by virtue of the keys of binding and loosing given his holiness by my Saviour, Jesus Christ, he hath power to depose heretical or Protestant authority whatever, especially the Lutheran Church of Germany, Holland, Sweden, and Norway, and the now pretended authority and churches of England and Scotland, and the branches of some now established in Ireland, and on the continent of America and elsewhere and all adherents in regard that they may be usurped and heretical, opposing the sacred Mother Church of Rome.

"I do now denounce and disown any allegiance as due to any heretical king, prince, or state named Protestant or Liberals, or obedience to any of the laws, magistrates or officers."

"I do further declare that the doctrine of the Churches of England and Scotland of the Calvinists, Hugenots and others of the Protestants or Masons, to be damnable, and they themselves to be damned who will not forsake the same.

"I do further declare, that I will help, assist and will advise all or any of his Holiness agents, in any place where I should be, in Switzerland, Germany, Holland, Ireland or America, or in any other kingdom or territory I shall come to, and do my utmost to exirpate the heretical Protestant or Masonic Doctrines, and to destroy all their pretended powers, legal or otherwise.

"I do further promise and declare that, notwithstanding I am disposed with to assume any religion heretical for the propagation of the mother church's interest! to secret and private all her agents counsels from time to time, as they entrust me, and not divulge, directly or indirectly, by word, writing or circumstances whatever, but to execute all that should be proposed, given in charge or discovered unto me, by you my Ghostly Father, or any of this sacred order.

"I do further promise and declare that I will have no opinion or will of my own or any mental reservation whatsoever, even as a corpse or cadaver (perinde ac cadaver), but will unhesitatingly obey each and every command that I may receive from my superiors in the militia of the Pope of Jesus Christ.

"That I will go to any part of the world whithersoever I may be sent, to the frozen regions of the North, to the burning sands of the desert of Africa, or the Jungles of India, to the centers of civilization of Europe, or to the wild haunts of the barbarous savages of America without murmuring or repining, and will be submissive in all things whatsoever is communicated to me.

"I will further promise and declare that I will, when opportunity present, make and wage relentless war, secretly and openly, against all heretics, Protestants and Masons, as I am directed to do, to extirpate them from the face of the whole earth; and that I will spare neither age, sex or condition, and that I will burn, hang, waste, boil, flay, strangle, and bury alive these infamous heretics, rip up the stomachs and wombs of the women and crush their infants' heads against the walls, in order to annihilate their exterorable race. That when the same cannot be done openly, I will secretly use the poisonous cup, the strangulation cord, the steel of the poiniard, or the leaden bullet, regardless of the honor, rank, dignity or authority of the persons, whatsoever may be their condition in life, either public or private, as I at any time may be directed to do so, by agent of the pope or Superior of the Brotherhood of the Holy Father of the Society of Jesus.

"In confirmation of which I hereby dedicate my life, soul and all corporal powers, and with the dagger which I now receive I will subscribe my name, written in my blood in testimony thereof; and should I prove false or weaken in my determination, may my brethren and fellow soldiers of the militia of the Pope, cut off my hands and feet and my throat from ear to ear, my belly opened and sulphur burned therein with all the punishment that can be inflicted upon me on earth and my soul shall be tortured by demons in eternal hell forever.

"That I will in voting always vote for a K. of C. in preference to a Protestant—especially a Mason, and that I will leave my party so to do; that if two Catholics are on the ticket I will satisfy myself which is the better supporter of Mother Church and vote accordingly.

"That I will not deal with or employ a Protestant if in my power to deal with or employ a Catholic. That I will place Catholic girls in Protestant families that a weekly report may be made of the movement of heretics.

"That I will provide myself with arms and ammunition that I may be in rediness when the word is passed, or I am commanded to defend the church either as an individual or with the militia of the Pope."

"All of which I, _____ do swear by the blessed Trinity and the blessed Sacrament which I am now to receive, to perform and on my part to keep this my oath.

"In testimony thereof, I take this most holy and blessed Sacrament of the Eucharist, and witness the same further, with my name written with the point of this dagger, dipped in my own blood, and seal, in the face of this Holy Sacrament."

FROM "THE TRUTH SEEKER," NEW YORK, N. Y.

### THE COILS ARE TIGHTENING

Subscribe for the world's greatest Anti-Catholic paper. Single subscriptions, 50c; in clubs of four or more, 40c; sample copy and circulars, 10c. Get the dope and whip the Pope. Address The Rail Splitter, Milan, Illinois.

# RELIGIOUS PREJUDICE AND THE BOGUS OATH

Supreme Knight James A. Flaherty, who succeeded Edward Hearn, proved to be a dauntless trailblazer and visionary, leading the Order through a turbulent era that included World War I, a resurgent Ku Klux Klan, and the persecution of Mexican Catholics south of the border. He also established a close working relationship with the Vatican that continues to this day. A successful lawyer, Flaherty joined the Knights in 1896 and rose quickly in the ranks from serving as grand knight in Philadelphia to becoming deputy supreme knight in 1905. By the time he was unanimously elected as supreme knight at the 1909 national convention in Mobile, Alabama, he was already well loved.

In the United States during this period, bigoted writings and publications targeted Catholicism in general and the Knights of Columbus specifically due to its growing prominence as a Catholic organization. In his weekly Missouri-based newspaper, *The Menace,* progressive William Franklin Phelps vented his wrath against Catholics. The Knights, as a large organization with a high public profile, became a growing target for anti-Catholic voices. In 1911, for example, politician Thomas Edward Watson, who had run for vice president on the Populist Party ticket with William Jennings Bryan in 1896, characterized the Knights as part of a papal conspiracy in his bigoted journal, *Watson's Magazine.*

Unfortunately, attacks were also sometimes launched by certain Catholics. Perhaps the most notable was a vocal opponent of the Knights named Arthur Preuss, a German Catholic journalist and theologian, who published the journal *Fortnightly Review.* Focused on the fraternal ceremonial elements, and seeing the Knights as corrupted by American ideals, including secularism, Preuss seemed unconvinced by either the Knights' approval by the Church or by its record, and his journal ran pieces that sought to stir controversy. Against the backdrop of an America still wary of Catholics, these "friendly fire" incidents were doubly harmful since they tended to propagate inaccuracies and sow seeds of confusion precisely when Catholics most needed unity. Thankfully, such incidents were rare, and the Order enjoyed broad Catholic support.

The attacks against the Knights from outside the Church soon became more aggressive. In 1912, a false version of the Fourth Degree oath was written, printed, and widely circulated by anti-Catholic groups to newspapers

**James A. Flaherty**
Sixth supreme knight.

The nuance of how anti-Catholicism was changing was not lost on Supreme Knight Flaherty, who noted in 1913: "In the future we will have to fight the enemies of our Church in connection with great questions touching taxation, education, divorce, and socialism. We will be fair, always fair, and our enemies will find us in the open ... but, as counsellor, I can give no better advice, to every council in our Order, than is conveyed by the word 'Prepare.'"

Founded in 1911, *The Menace*—a publication with 1.5 million weekly readers—attacked Catholics, including the Knights of Columbus specifically. Although it faded in popularity during World War I and ceased publication in 1919, its anti-Catholic writings provoked bigotry and helped fuel the Ku Klux Klan's resurgence.

The 1915 release of D.W. Griffith's profoundly bigoted film *The Birth of a Nation* sparked renewed interest in the Ku Klux Klan. The Klan's subsequent meteoric rise would capitalize on both racism and anti-Catholic sentiment—and would target the Order, which countered both racism and religious bigotry in its Historical Commission.

throughout the country and overseas. This "Bogus Oath," as it became known, vilified the Order—and, by extension, Catholics—by claiming that the Knights swore to commit violence against non-Catholics. This was not only false, but also ironic since Catholics in early twentieth-century America were often the targets of violence by anti-Catholic elements. Although the Knights eventually prevailed in legal action taken against publishers of the oath for disparaging the organization's good name, they knew that the damage had been done. Many who had read the Bogus Oath would continue to have misconceptions about Catholics and the Order. That anti-Catholic bigots would resort to such smear tactics showed just how much of a force the Knights had become.

Established to stop publications that promoted bigotry against Catholics, the Knights' Commission on Religious Prejudices combined ecumenical outreach, public opposition, and the education of journalists and publishers. Within three years, it reported more than 90 percent of such prejudicial publications had ceased production.

To investigate the sources of such prejudicial materials and to educate editors, publishers, and journalists on these issues, the Knights established the Commission on Religious Prejudices in 1914. Commission members met personally with anti-Catholic publishers, and built important bridges between the Catholic and Protestant communities. The commission also worked with the Department of Justice. By the time it ended its work in 1917, the commission had helped reduce by more than 90 percent the country's anti-Cathloic publications. The "huts" program in World War I would be seen as an important postscript to this work.

Religious opposition to Catholicism was one threat. Socialist opposition was another. Some socialists were promoting anti-Catholic views and virulent propaganda against the Church. The Knights responded with a nationwide lecture tour featuring two expert speakers to combat both socialism and these anti-Catholic attacks. Former socialist David Goldstein, a Jewish convert to Catholicism and member of Mt. Pleasant Council 98 in Boston, and Peter W. Collins, former general secretary of the Brotherhood of Electrical Workers and member of Newton Council 167, embarked on an extensive 27,000-mile lecture tour throughout North America in 1914. Goldstein traveled to the Midwest, Northwest, and into Canada, while Collins made his way to the South and Southwest. These 148 free lectures drew large and sometimes hostile crowds. When speaking of this initiative at that year's Supreme Council meeting in St. Paul, Minnesota, Supreme Knight Flaherty said it was "a most unprecedented success, and must certainly bring its full share of glory to the Order as it will bring its benefit to the country."

In a 1915 Columbus Day speech at New York's famed Carnegie Hall to an audience of Knights, former President Theodore Roosevelt told the packed house that there was no room in this country for "hyphenated Americanism." He argued that Irish-Americans, German-Americans, and so on should regard themselves simply as Americans.

The Knights' membership grew from roughly 230,000 in 1910 to over 340,000 by 1915. But even that impressive growth was eclipsed by the surge that occurred after the popular Army hut program was established during World War I. Nearly 400,000 men joined the Order between 1917 and 1923—roughly 67,000 a year.

# THE KNIGHTS AND WORLD WAR I

One of the most effective ways in which the Knights of Columbus overcame the bigotry it faced was by preaching the faith not through words, but through actions. Few actions spoke as loudly, or to as large an audience as the aid given by the Order to US servicemen during World War I.

By 1914, the horrors of that war had already spread throughout Europe, but the United States remained neutral during the first years of the conflict. Pressure to enter the war increased in 1915, when a German U-boat sank the RMS *Lusitania*, a British passenger ship carrying 128 US citizens. Not long after Congress declared war on Germany in April of 1917, American soldiers, including many Knights, were engaged in battle on the European front.

Supreme Knight Flaherty wrote to President Woodrow Wilson offering the Knights' assistance by "establishing centers for the large body of men who would be concentrated in training and mobilization camps." President Wilson gratefully accepted. To fulfill this offer, the Order established a War Activities Committee, which, in turn, devised a plan for hospitality centers to serve the troops. This became known as the "K of C Hut Program." Under the banner "Everybody Welcome," the Knights provided soldiers with a wide range of amenities. Unlike some of the other service organizations, everything the Knights provided was free, and the slogan soon reflected that with the words "Everybody Welcome, Everything Free." The Order also served troops regardless of the soldier's faith, and even operated integrated facilities.

The huts—typically, one-story wooden buildings—were first set up at military training camps in the United States, and soon expanded overseas to more than 100 locations in Europe and Asia. A precursor to the United Service Organization (USO) recreational centers that were first established

"Of all the organizations that took part in the winning of the war, with the exception of the military itself, there was none so efficiently and ably administered as the Knights of Columbus."

–General John J. Pershing, Commander-in-Chief of the American Expeditionary Forces

During World War I, the K of C established recreation centers ("huts") in Europe based on those used in the United States during the 1916 Mexican Expedition against "Pancho" Villa. This center at Fort McIntosh in Laredo, Texas, was one of the models for the WWI huts.

# One Soldier's Remembrance

The following article appeared in the September 1967 issue of *Columbia*. It recounts one soldier's experience with a Casey during World War I while stationed in Russia.

## One Soldier's Remembrance

Here I was alone in a strange land and walking an eerie post, not knowing at what moment an instant attack on our thinly held line would be launched by the crafty Reds. I had not been walking the post very long when my ear caught the faint sound of crunching footsteps on the snow-crusted ground ahead in the inky blackness. Forcing myself into instant alert, I snapped my Springfield down from my shoulder and shouted into the black night, "Stoy!" This ringing challenge in Russian was familiar to all Allied troops, the equivalent to "Halt! Who's there?"

Instead of the reassuring response "Karasha . . . Amerikanski" ("All right . . . American") I distinctly heard a chuckle, immediately followed by a deep bass voice with a New England twang, "OK, soldier, it's just Marty!"

Naturally I came back with, "Marty who?"

And there stepped forward a tall, smiling man of mature years, clad in a sheepskin coat and fur cap and boots, with his identification, "You know, soldier— Marty, the 'Casey' man here in Vladdy. Got some smokes and chewing gum for you!"

The word "Casey" together with the well-remembered Knights of Columbus emblem on his fur cap was enough. Though this was my first encounter with a K of C man in Siberia, I had many happy personal contacts with his brother secretaries in my prior wartime service in France and Germany. My mind still conjures up memories of those dedicated, devoted men of mature years and ready wit.

I am a Methodist of the old-school Protestant stock. Yet in all my associations with the Knights of Columbus secretaries overseas, never once was I asked my religious faith or whether I possessed any religious affiliation at all. The same held true of my buddies serving "over there." My experience was shared by Protestants, Jews, and others.

At no time was there any charge for any K of C items handed out. Cigarettes, tobacco, candy, toilet articles— all were distributed free, with no strings attached. One beastly, rainy dawn, my outfit was relieved of duty in a front line sector along the Marne. Dog tired, we trudged slowly back to a reserve line. Every step was an effort as we pulled our heavy, mud-clogged brogans out of the slimy, thick mud. Suddenly, out of the chilly mists, a figure pulled up beside with a welcome word: "Here, soldier . . . let me carry your pack awhile!" The Good Samaritan was a Casey.

At a so-called "rest camp," just back of the blazing front, we temporarily had pulled up in a brief, week-long bivouac to pick up replacements to fill the gaps inflicted by casualties. We had barely pitched our tents—under potential barrages from the German "Big Bertha" artillery pieces—when a K of C man came on a sidecar motorcycle, carrying smokes, chewing gum, and—one of the most appreciated gifts of all—individual sewing kits with which we were able to mend torn clothing.

I never heard a K of C secretary address us by any other title than "soldier." There was no condescending "my dear boys" routine or anything but a fine, adult, man-to-man association. Enlisted men loved the Caseys for, among other things, their use of the doughboy chow lines. They could have gone to the shorter mess lines of the commissioned officers' field kitchens. But with battered mess gear in hand and wide grins on dirty, unshaven faces, they fell in chow line with the doughboys.

*Born in New York, Sergeant Smith enlisted in the Army "at a youthful age" and retired in 1947 after service in both WWI and WWII.*

Serving everybody, regardless of race or creed, the K of C was designated by the War Department "the official agency for all Catholic activity [for troops]." The Caseys also arranged religious events, such as the Good Friday services celebrated by Cardinal Léon-Adolphe Amette of Paris, which drew 10,000 American troops at Notre Dame Cathedral.

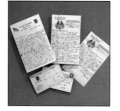

Stationery was only one way Caseys made soldiers feel connected to home. As noted in *The Knights of Columbus in Peace and War*, more powerful than the gifts was "the manner of giving," by which Caseys "were the visible examples of the interest and affection of the people at home, more vivid than the written word."

during World War II, the huts offered soldiers such amenities as food, candy, cigarettes, reading material, and stationery to write letters home, as well as forms of entertainment like music and sports activities. The Order's chaplains were also on hand to minister to the spiritual needs of Catholic men in uniform, who often had little or no access to the sacraments. Essentially, the K of C huts created a temporal and spiritual refuge for the servicemen who were fighting for their country far from home.

Running the huts were the Knights of Columbus "secretaries"—volunteers from the United States to serve the troops. Nicknamed "Caseys" for the Order's "KC" initials, these secretaries performed innumerable acts of charitable service. Suffering the same deprivations and hardships faced by the American soldiers, the Caseys still managed to find ways to ease the situations of their fellow servicemen. Along with staffing and running the army huts at bases, embarkation centers, and at the front, they also went far beyond the huts themselves to serve the troops. They made their way through the woods to bring food to units that had been cut off from the mess kitchens. They helped with the wounded in first-aid stations, served drinks to soldiers under fire, acted as stretcher bearers, and buried the dead. Determined Caseys even delivered airdropped supplies to isolated units on patrol. (For one soldier's personal account, see the inset at left.)

The Knights also set up huts away from the front lines—on both sides of the Atlantic. There were facilities in Paris, in London, and in New York's Times Square. Some included boxing rings and areas that had been cleared for baseball fields. Playing ball or sparring in the ring helped the soldiers take their minds off the rigors of war and gave them a sense of home and normalcy, if only temporarily. The Knights also organized entertainment, setting up sporting events and arranging for popular performers to travel overseas and entertain the troops, even in remote areas. Well-known members of the Order, such as major league baseball star Johnny Evers and silent film actor Garry McGarry, journeyed across the Atlantic as Caseys. These men and many others helped to bring recreation and enjoyment—a touch of home—to the troops.

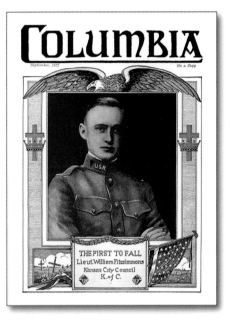

The first American casualty of World War I was Lt. William Fitzsimmons, a Knight of Columbus.

Before sailing for France, Baseball Hall of Famer Johnny Evers and forty-five fellow K of C secretaries, often referred to as "Caseys," are seen here in front of the New York Public Library in July 1918.

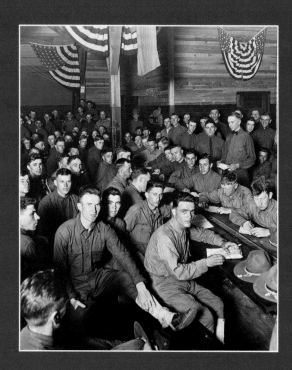

# The Caseys

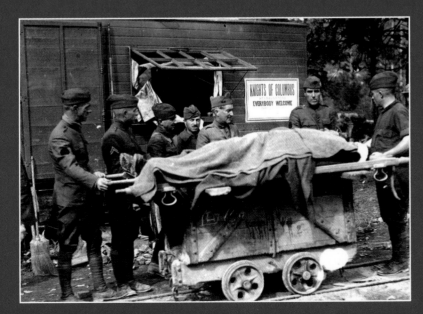

The K of C Secretaries—or "Caseys," as they were called—were excellent ambassadors for both the Order and the Church. Through the Caseys and the Army huts, American troops received food, reading material, and stationery for writing letters home. Generally, each hut had both a chapel and Catholic literature, providing a welcome home for Catholic troops. But support was offered regardless of the soldiers' race and creed, and for many troops of other faiths, this encounter with Catholicism left a positive life-long impression.

The financial support for the huts came from a combination of K of C resources and fundraising, and from participation in the US government-organized nationwide fund drive. The Knights' initial June 1917 campaign quickly surpassed its $1 million goal, and the bar was raised to $10 million. It earned council and parish support as well as ecumenical support and large gifts, including some from the Carnegie and Rockefeller Foundations. An additional $25 million was allocated for the Knights' work from the combined campaign for all service organizations proposed by the US government.

The overwhelming need for chaplains during the war was also evident. In response, the Knights both assisted Catholic military chaplains and provided additional chaplains of their own. Independent of the Army's chaplain corps and officially recognized as volunteers, eighty-four K of C chaplains served at military bases at home, while fifty-four traveled overseas, reaching France in October 1917. While serving abroad, these priests ministered to the spiritual and physical needs of soldiers while surrounded by the destruction and violence of war. They celebrated Mass, heard confessions, and anointed the sick on boats, in trenches, and on battlefields. They transported supplies, cared for the injured, presided over burials, and recovered the wounded and fallen. Many soldiers, even those who were not Catholic or even Christian, sought the attention of the Knights of Columbus chaplains for words of encouragement or a simple blessing. The strength and support provided by these priests was an immeasurable asset to the troops.

During their first month alone overseas, K of C Army hut secretaries distributed 37,719 cartons of chocolate, 25,250 cartons of chewing gum, 14,772 baseballs, 2,286 sets of boxing gloves, 1,687 footballs, 10 million sheets of writing paper, and 8 million envelopes.

Posters for the Knights of Columbus War Camp Fund were distributed nationwide. The fund supported the initial cost of the hut program.

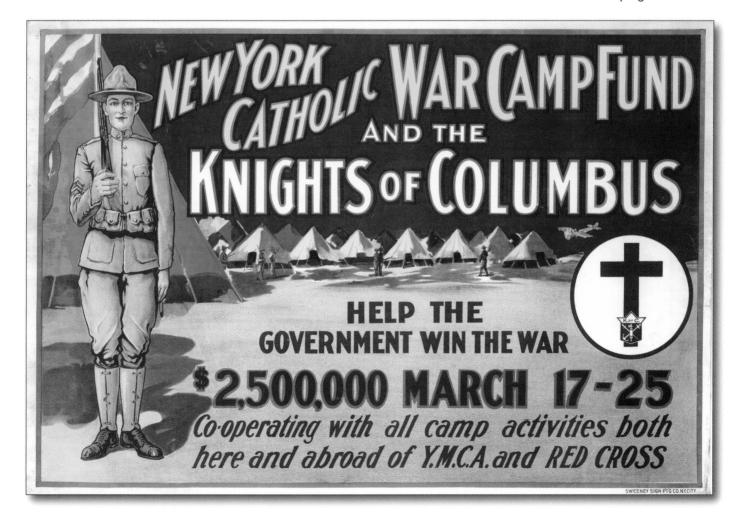

# Joyce Kilmer
## Notable Knight

Although best known as a poet, particularly for his beloved poem "Trees," Joyce Kilmer was also a journalist, a lecturer on the Catholic faith, and a soldier. After his conversion to Catholicism, Kilmer developed a rich spiritual life, and often spoke and wrote of his Catholic faith. His deep respect for God and nature is apparent in his writing, particularly his poetry. As noted American writer Robert Cortes Holliday wrote of Kilmer, "And, once a

Catholic, there never was any possibility of mistaking Kilmer's point of view: in all matters of religion, art, economics and politics, as well as in all matters of faith and morals, his point of view was obviously and unhesitatingly Catholic."

Joyce Kilmer also enjoyed a loving family life. The father of five, he often wrote with the help of his wife, who took dictation from him while he paced the floor, trying to lull a crying child to sleep in his arms.

After enlisting in the military during World War I, he asked to be sent to the front lines, where he volunteered as a scout and assistant to "Wild Bill" Donovan—one of the Army's most notable wartime leaders and founding father of the CIA. While undertaking a reconnaissance mission, Sergeant Kilmer was killed by a sniper's bullet. For his bravery, he was awarded France's prestigious Croix de Guerre.

Kilmer was a member of New Rochelle Council 339. Previously, he had been a member of Council 1177 in Suffern, New York, which was renamed in his honor. During his deployment, his brother Knights sent the writer a fitting gift: a fountain pen.

Although hostilities had ceased in November 1918, World War I officially ended on June 28, 1919 with the Treaty of Versailles. After its conclusion, US General John J. Pershing said, "Of all the organizations that took part in the winning of the war, with the exception of the military itself, there was none so efficiently and ably administered as the Knights of Columbus." At the 1918 Victory Convention of the Supreme Council in New York City, French High Commissioner Marcel Knecht likewise commented that "the devoted secretaries in khaki, wearing on their arms the well-known KC, have always been ready to give their complete services, not only to the Catholics but to all the soldiers of democracy." In 1919, Supreme Knight Flaherty was decorated by Secretary of War Newton D. Baker with the Distinguished Service Medal in recognition of the work performed by the Order during the war.

Cherokee brass musician, performer, and actors' rights pioneer Cora Youngblood Corson and her female troupe of instrumentalists brought music and theatrical acts to homesick troops under the auspices of the Knights in Europe. After the war, the troupe was sometimes advertised as the "K of C Octet" or "K of C Instrumentalists."

In Coblenz, Germany, pastries proved the way to warm soldiers' hearts. Joe Gramling, the Order's Director of War Kitchens, and up to forty-five workers manufactured 27,000 donuts per day, a figure raised to 50,000 to provide troops returning home with 10 donuts each to brighten their transatlantic voyage.

Praise came too from the African-American community. In the 1919 publication of *The American Negro in the Great War*, African-American author Emmet J. Scott—who served as special adjutant to the US Secretary of War—singled out the Knights for their wartime service to African Americans. He wrote: "Another organization was of much service in making Negro (sic) soldiers comfortable at the front. This was the Knights of Columbus, a Catholic society, which has to its credit that, unlike the other social welfare organizations operating in the war, it never drew the color line." A contemporary newspaper account also reported on the K of C's integrated acceptance of African Americans. While it could not do so in every case, for the Order to have a color blind policy was the more remarkable since it occurred nearly five decades before the Civil Rights Movement began, and before the military itself was integrated.

Secretary of War Newton Baker presents Supreme Knight Flaherty with the Distinguished Service Medal in recognition of the Order's contributions during the war.

Whether arranging Masses or walking fourteen miles to bring a priest for a doughboy's confession, Caseys were praised for making spiritual opportunities available while not proselytizing. As the war waned, K of C huts near religious sites facilitated soldiers' visits to pilgrimage locations like the Marian shrine in Lourdes.

Caseys had to undertake a long journey to reach American soldiers fighting in Siberia's bleak countryside. In addition to bringing goods by foot, motorcycle, or air-drop, Caseys used "rolling kitchens" such as this mule-drawn wagon to serve troops located in remote posts.

# Father William F. Davitt
## Notable Knight

A diocesan priest in Lenox, Massachusetts, Father William F. Davitt was also a Knights of Columbus chaplain who volunteered to serve with the American Expeditionary Forces in France during the First World War. Throughout the war, he frequently risked his life to rescue wounded soldiers and to provide proper burials for the fallen. In one operation, he led a rescue party to help forty American soldiers who were trapped in a ravine. Through a barrage of enemy bullets, he helped guide the group to safety without any injuries. For his heroic actions in battle, soldier-priest First Lieutenant William F. Davitt received the American Distinguished Service Cross and France's Croix de Guerre.

On the morning of November 11, 1918, a little more than an hour before the signing of the armistice ending hostilities was to take place, Davitt climbed a tree near the Argonne Forest and hung an American flag in celebration. When he climbed down, a shell from a German battery exploded nearby, killing him instantly. He was the last commissioned officer to be killed during World War I. Father Davitt's name is listed on a memorial for Army Chaplains at Arlington National Cemetery.

## POST-WAR INITIATIVES

After the war, the Knights of Columbus' service continued—briefly in Poland in an attempt to help American volunteers there; and then substantively in Siberia, where American troops were deployed as part of the allied North Russia intervention; in Europe, as troops remained to finish work before returning home; and back in the United States, helping the returning veterans adjust to civilian life. Unused funds from the Order's wartime efforts were redirected to establish a variety of vocational, occupational, and educational programs for them.

For these veterans, employment was a key concern. Working with the US Employment Service of the Department of Labor, the Knights began a national occupational campaign in conjunction with local councils to help the veterans find employment. Initially, because of the recession that followed World War I, helping them find jobs was quite difficult. But Peter W. Collins, a noted anti-Communist lecturer, former head of the Electrical Workers of America, and member of the Order, stepped up to assume the leadership role

Early in the war, German troops attacked and devastated much of the Belgian city of Louvain, including its famous Catholic University. In 1919, the Knights of Columbus gave $35,000 to Belgium's Cardinal Désiré-Joseph Mercier (shown here with Chairman of the K of C War Activities, William Mulligan) for the university's restoration.

Praise for the Knights' World War I hut program stimulated enormous interest in the Order, with membership growing to more than 500,000 men from the 16,000 two decades prior. The improved insurance program was earning a good reputation, and recorded $74 million of insurance in force in 1919.

in the employment program. Within a year under his guidance, the program became a great success. By the time it was discontinued in 1921, the Knights had found over 300,000 jobs for veterans of all religious affiliations.

In addition to directly helping soldiers enter or re-enter the civilian job market, the Knights established educational and vocational classes to help veterans transition back to the workforce. Evening programs provided more than 50,000 returning soldiers with free vocational classes in over 100 schools around the country. Through the administration of the Supreme Council office, thousands more were able to register for correspondence school and more than 400 college scholarships were awarded to veterans.

During the World War I era, most US soldiers—like most Americans— had been exposed to anti-Catholic propaganda. Some had never even met a Catholic. By welcoming everyone to their army huts, the Knights preached their Catholic faith through their charitable actions. Those who were skeptical of Catholics, or even hostile toward them, had to consider that the much loved and respected K of C huts and their Caseys were the extension of Catholic ideals and Catholic charity. During and after the war, through their charitable outreach, the Knights—and Catholics in general—began to grow in the esteem of their fellow Americans.

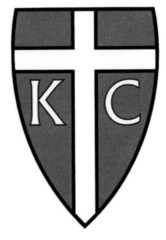

**War Emblem of the Order**
Used in conjunction with the Knights' World War I activities.

"We have served men and women of all colors and creeds in these schools; we have been enabled to better the lives of white and colored, Protestant, Jew, and Catholic alike— and it is my hope ... that we may always provide these opportunities for our fellow citizens, for in providing them we are adding immeasurably to the quality of citizenship."

–Supreme Knight Flaherty on K of C educational initiatives for veterans

Representatives of various branches of the armed services surround a field secretary as they consider job openings in front of the Order's Longacre Hut on Broadway in New York City.

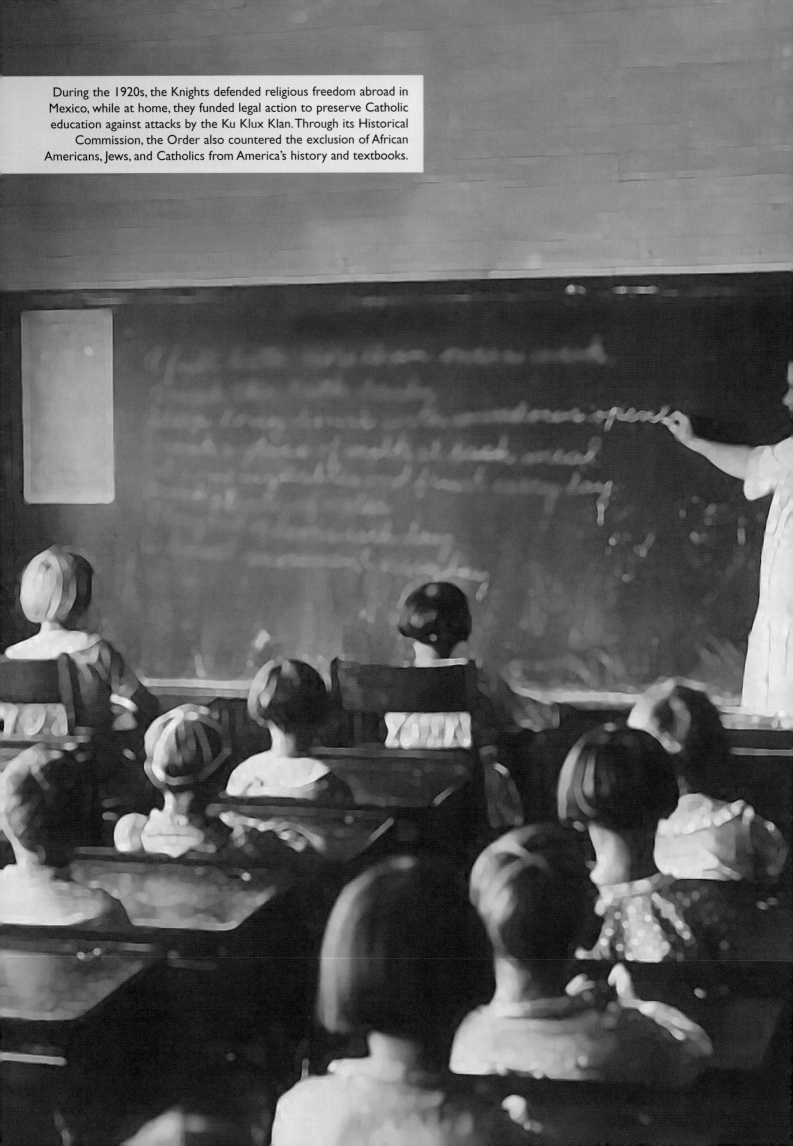

During the 1920s, the Knights defended religious freedom abroad in Mexico, while at home, they funded legal action to preserve Catholic education against attacks by the Ku Klux Klan. Through its Historical Commission, the Order also countered the exclusion of African Americans, Jews, and Catholics from America's history and textbooks.

# 4.

# In Search of Liberty

## 1920 to 1929

When the Great War began, many Americans had questioned whether Catholics could be good patriotic citizens. Both the wartime outreach of the Knights in support of *all* servicemen and the courageous military service of so many Catholics went a long way in putting that question to rest. The Order's patriotic and charitable efforts firmly established it as an integral leader among American Catholics and solidified its role in American society. These activities also revealed the Order's new and permanent ability to do great things, both domestically and internationally. For the greater part of the following decade, Supreme Knight James A. Flaherty would continue to lead the Knights to grow in charity, advocacy, and dedication to a diverse vision of America's past and present.

### FOR THE YOUTH IN ROME

In 1920, Supreme Knight Flaherty and a delegation from the Order made a post-war tour of Europe. Their trip was organized around a visit to Metz, France, where, on August 21, they attended the dedication of a statue of the Marquis de Lafayette. The Knights had given the statue to the people of his hometown in honor of the French patriot for his involvement in the American War of Independence. Lafayette was seen as a symbol of the long-standing bond of unity between the French and the Americans.

The delegation's tour continued in Rome, where they met with Pope Benedict XV. It was a meeting that would be the beginning of many fruit-

Perched atop a destroyed tank, past Supreme Knight Hearn reviews war devastation with fellow huts program coordinator William Larkin (at right). Even after retiring as supreme knight, Hearn continued to serve the Order, helping lead its hut program and its postwar activities in Rome as European Commissioner.

After WWI the Knights opened more than 100 evening schools for the education of veterans. Lasting until 1926, the program served more than 50,000 students. The Order also began a correspondence school and awarded more than 400 college scholarships to veterans. This scholarship program is seen as a precursor of the GI Bill.

ful collaborations between the Knights and the Holy See on projects to benefit all people, not only the faithful.

Even before the delegation arrived, the pope was well aware of the Order's war efforts. The army hut established by the Knights at Rome's Hotel Minerva had become legendary within the Eternal City among allied troops and Romans alike. Through audiences arranged by the K of C secretaries, Pope Benedict had met with many American troops and celebrated Mass for them. As a result of what Italians saw as slights against the country in the end-of-war agreements, antipathy towards America boiled over in Italy. However, the Knights' positive reputation in Rome was such that when anti-American sentiment resulted in the removal of American flags everywhere—even at the US Embassy—the one place the flag continued to fly in Rome was at the K of C hut at the Hotel Minerva.

During his meeting with the Knights, the Holy Father presented a problem and asked for their help. He was becoming increasingly concerned that the local Catholic youth were being drawn toward the city's non-Catholic groups because of the sports programs they offered. Calling it "another field of competition before you," the pope urged the Knights to expand their presence in Rome, to counter the anti-Catholic "propaganda, which to our sorrow we see so widely spread in this dear city." The idea of remaining in Italy in some capacity after the war appealed to the Knights. In response to their willingness to help, the pope said, "An old principle teaches that good spreads itself, and it is not surprising therefore, that, while still doing so much fruitful work in their beloved country, the Knights of Columbus have thought of

A delegation of Knights poses with French officials, military leaders, and Metz citizens beneath the unveiled statue of Lafayette given by the Knights to Metz, France, 1920.

extending their action to Italy, too, and in a special manner to this city of Rome, dear above all cities to our hearts."

At the October board meeting of the Supreme Council in 1922, Past Supreme Knight Hearn, who had led the Order's work in Europe during the war, was given the task of determining the best way to help fulfill the pope's request. It was decided that the Knights would assist the Catholic youth through the funding of athletic recreation facilities throughout the city. Between 1922 and 1927, under the expertise of Italian architect and engineer Enrico Pietro Galeazzi (who would later become the Knights' representative in Rome), five centers were built, each designed in the architectural style of the surrounding neighborhood. Although they became known as the K of C "playgrounds" (from the Italian *campi sportivi*—"playing field"), these sites were more like sports and recreation centers. Each had an outdoor soccer field, as well as a clubhouse with an indoor gymnasium.

Pope Benedict XV's successor, Pope Pius XI, was as enthusiastic about the project as was his predecessor, calling the Knights' work "very fitting . . . for it is no less important than any other level of relief work." To aid the cause, he donated some property that was adjacent to St. Peter's Basilica for the first center—historical land that marked the center of Nero's Circus, where Christians had been martyred. During construction, the Holy Father noted happily that "I can see for myself from my study window what progress they are making here in the heart of Rome."

**Count Enrico Pietro Galeazzi**

Pope Pius XI himself was responsible for naming this first facility, calling it St. Peter's Oratory. Its clubhouse was a two-story building where, in addition to recreational programs, the children were given catechetical and educational instruction. The Holy Father appointed priests to supervise the activities of the boys, while members of the Daughters of Charity—a religious community of Catholic women—oversaw the girls.

Following the dedication of St. Peter's Oratory on April 9, 1924, Pope Pius XI asked Edward Hearn to convey his "expression of true paternal recognition" to the Knights. To further display his gratitude, he ordered the design of a medal commemorating the establishment of this first playground and, in acknowledgment of Supreme Knight Flaherty's meritorious service to the Church, the Holy Father elevated him to the papal rank of the Grand Cross of St. Gregory. Papal honors were also conferred upon Commissioner Hearn, Supreme Secretary William McGinley, Supreme Chaplain Patrick McGivney, and Count Enrico Galeazzi.

The other recreation centers included the Pius XI Playground on Gelsomino Hill, the highest hill in Rome; the Benedict XV Playground, located in one of the neediest neighborhoods of the San Lorenzo district (and attended by more than 100,000 in the first year alone); the Polverini (Tiber

**Pope Pius XI**

As part of its pilgrimage to Europe, the Knights of Columbus delegation met with Pope Benedict XV, who invited them to establish a permanent presence in Rome to aid the city's children. Here, the pope prays in the Vatican Gardens with Supreme Knight James Flaherty, Edward Hearn, and the rest of the delegation.

The first of the Knights of Columbus playgrounds in Rome—St. Peter's Oratory—was dedicated on April 9, 1924. Four more playgrounds, which were more like recreation centers, complete with soccer fields and indoor gymnasiums, opened throughout Rome.

River) Playground, later relocated upriver and renamed Pastor Angelicus; and the Valle Giulia Playground, located near one of city's largest parks, and later renamed for Count Galeazzi, the Knights' representative in Rome. Dedication of a final facility—the Pius XII Playground—took place on June 7, 1952 in the residential district of Primavalle.

During the 1960s, as the number of pilgrims to the Vatican grew, Pope Paul VI expressed his desire for a larger audience hall to accommodate them. In response, the Knights donated the land of their first playground, St. Peter's Oratory, and this became the eventual site of the new Paul VI Audience Hall. In turn, the Holy See built a new playground—also called St. Peter's Oratory—on Gelsomino Hill.

To this day, all of the Knights' playgrounds continue to serve as active sporting sites, outreach stations, and meeting places for the greater community. Over the years, they have been staging grounds for numerous charitable activities, including—and perhaps most notably—food distribution centers for the people of Rome during and after World War II. They have hosted soccer tournaments and Special Olympics events, and have even hosted visitors to Rome. In 2014, for instance, they housed Polish pilgrims who had traveled to Rome for the canonization of Saint John Paul II.

In the century since the Knights' playgrounds were established, their presence has served as just one of the many ways in which the Order has contributed to the Eternal City.

One of the five Knights of Columbus playgrounds/recreation centers built for the youth in Rome at the request of Pope Benedict XV.

# FOR THE YOUTH AT HOME

Shortly after work began on the first recreation center in Rome, the Order turned its attention to a new area for evangelization and service: the Catholic youth in America. In 1923, a committee headed by future Supreme Knight Martin Carmody was formed. Its purpose was to encourage member involvement with youth guidance. From this effort came the idea for the formation of a "junior" order to help young boys gain a clear understanding of their religious as well as patriotic obligations. After a few years of planning, the Columbian Squires was brought to life.

Formed under the direction of De La Salle Christian Brother Barnabas McDonald and Supreme Director Daniel A. Tobin, the Columbian Squires fostered a sense of fraternity among its members and followed the same values and principles that guided the Knights. Brother Barnabas, who was known for his work with orphans and troubled youth, had also assisted with the formation of some of the earliest Catholic Boy Scout troops. He believed that the Columbian Squires would help cultivate the "spiritual, intellectual, civic, social, and physical improvement of its members, as well as the development of their leadership qualities." At the 1925 Supreme Convention in Duluth, Minnesota, the delegates in attendance proudly witnessed the institution of Duluth Circle 1, the first Columbian Squires group.

**Brother Barnabas McDonald**

Officers of Duluth Circle 1—the first circle of the Columbian Squires.

In 1921, Supreme Master John Reddin formed the K of C Historical Commission to investigate historical inaccuracies in textbooks. This led to the revision or retirement of a large number of texts. The commission also published a series of books featuring the contributions of Blacks, Jews, and Germans in the making of America.

In the 1910s, Catholic scouting began developing through collaboration between Catholic churches, the Boy Scouts of America, and the National Catholic War Council. Within a few years, a number of councils operated Boy Scout troops. In 1923, the Supreme Council formally praised scouting as a "fruitful activity for the Order."

In 1924, the University of Notre Dame established a two-year graduate program in cooperation with Brother Barnabas McDonald, FSC. The Boy Guidance program was designed to teach the principles of service-oriented youth programs through such areas of study as the Psychology of Adolescence and Religion for Adolescents. It also offered a training course to men working as volunteers in youth organizations, for which the Order awarded a $1,000 scholarship to eligible Knights.

The emblem for the Columbian Squires, which is circular in shape, presents a Maltese cross, layered with three sets of letters, each representing a key element of the youth program. On the arms of the cross, four letters represent areas of personal development that squires aim to achieve: "S" for spiritual growth, "C" for citizenship and civic life, "P" for physical fitness, and "I" for intellectual development. Atop this, two large red letters entwine: "C" representing Christ and "S" representing Squires. Centered on these is a small "K," for the Knights of Columbus. The motto of the Squires encircles the entirety: *"Esto Dignus"* (Latin for "Be Worthy").

Even before the Squires was established, a number of local councils had recognized the need for mentoring Catholic youth and had turned to scouting in response. During the 1910s, individual Catholic churches and the National Catholic War Council were developing Catholic scouting and coordinating the extension of the Boy Scouts of America to the Catholic population. In 1913, Monroe Council 1337 was chartered to operate Boy Scout Troop 1 in Monroe, Louisiana. Soon, councils throughout the country followed suit. In 1923, the Supreme Council formally commended scouting as a "fruitful activity for the Order."

In recent years, the Knights' efforts supporting Catholic youth developed further in response to its 2015 Domestic Church initiative—a project focused on strengthening Catholic families through joint involvements with their parishes. To help reinforce this integration, councils began shifting their focus away from the Squires' model toward one in which youth activities—including Catholic scouting—were more integrated with local parish programs.

Whether through involvement with Squires, Catholic scouting, or any other youth-supported initiative, councils have always focused on helping youth build up their faith, virtue, skills, and service.

Instructors at a 1925 Boy Leadership training class in South Bend, Indiana, demonstrate knot-tying skills. Brother Barnabus is seen at far right.

In 1924, the two-year graduate program in Boy Guidance began at Notre Dame, under the leadership of Brother Barnabas McDonald. Among the first graduates was Charles Ducey, who would go on to lead fraternal services, reverse a decade-long membership crisis, revise the Order's ceremonials, and become deputy supreme knight.

The 1920s saw a resurgent Ku Klux Klan, after new leadership, clever marketing, and aggressive campaigning swept 8 million Americans into its fold. Capitalizing on bigotry anonymized by hoods, the emboldened Klan widened its message of hate to target Blacks, Catholics, Jews, and foreigners. Throughout this era, *Columbia's* pages regularly denounced the Klan.

# "The Babe"
# George Herman Ruth Jr.
## Notable Knight

One of America's most legendary athletes, George Herman "Babe" Ruth Jr. joined the Knights of Columbus in 1919. At the time, he was just entering the prime of his major league baseball career with the Boston Red Sox. In 1920, he was traded to the Yankees and spent most of his career with the New York team. He became the game's first power hitter, setting home run records while leading the Yankees to one World Series title after another. The original Yankee Stadium soon became popularly known as "The House That Ruth Built."

Ruth, who grew up in Baltimore, had a difficult life. His mother suffered from poor health and his father, who was busy running a saloon, had little time for him. As a very young boy, Ruth spent most of his time on the streets. He stole, skipped school, and had multiple run-ins with the law. By the time he was just seven years old, his behavioral problems landed him in St. Mary's Industrial School for Boys—a reform school run by the Xaverian Brothers. He was there for the next twelve years.

As an adult, Ruth was quite aware of how difficult life was for children growing up without their families. He was also aware of the positive impact a mentor could have on a child. For him, that mentor was St. Mary's disciplinarian Brother Matthias, who became a father figure and kept him out of trouble while instructing him in both sports and religion.

"The Babe" had a genuine love for children. Never forgetting his own troubled youth, he always made it a point to visit orphans and children who were sick or disadvantaged while traveling with the Yankees. Wherever the team went, he would stop at local hospitals and even reform schools to meet with the kids. At the end of his career, he established the Babe Ruth Foundation for destitute children.

The celebrated stature of Babe Ruth and his impact upon the sports world served as an inspiration to many. During his twenty-nine years as a member of the Order, Ruth's charitable contributions and work with youngsters exemplified his generosity, which is at the very heart of the Knights of Columbus.

Babe Ruth and Yankee teammate Lou Gehrig flank Father Edward J. Flanagan, founder of Boys Town, during a 1927 visit to the school.

# BATTLING AN INVISIBLE EMPIRE

During the Great War, American servicemen, although challenged by foreign surroundings and unfamiliar language, were able to spot German soldiers largely by the uniforms they wore. Upon returning home, they discovered the presence of yet another type of enemy—one that was practically undetectable. Disguised as patriotic citizens whose intentions were to uphold law and order, this hidden enemy promoted hatred and prejudice against minorities nationwide. This "Invisible Empire," as it named itself, was the Ku Klux Klan, a group that became notorious for its bigotry, particularly against Blacks, Catholics, Jews, and immigrants.

With its portrayal of Klansmen as patriotic American citizens, *The Birth of a Nation* helped embolden bigotry, particularly against Blacks, Jews, Catholics, and immigrants.

Commonly known simply as the Klan or the KKK, the group was originally formed in 1866 in opposition to the post-Civil War Reconstruction policies aimed at establishing political and economic equality for former slaves. The members of this bigoted group secretly planned violent attacks against Black Americans and those who supported their freedom. Murder, lynching, arson, cross burning, and other vicious assaults were carried out by Klansmen, who concealed themselves in white robes and hoods during these attacks.

The activities of the Klan had quieted down considerably by the late 1800s, but in 1915, former Methodist Episcopalian preacher William J. Simmons began rallying like-minded individuals in an attempt to revive the group. Simmons' inspiration came from D.W. Griffith's epic film *The Birth of a Nation*, which provided a disingenuous fable of the Reconstruction years from the Klan's perspective. The film depicted the KKK as a heroic group that upheld law and order in the post-Civil War South. Knowing that many people disagreed with the violent tactics that had been associated with the Klan in the past, Simmons used the film as propaganda to present the group as having more subtle, nonviolent principles.

Propaganda targeting Catholicism and the Knights of Columbus specifically—as seen with these cartoons published by Rail Splitter Press—was not uncommon during the 1920s.

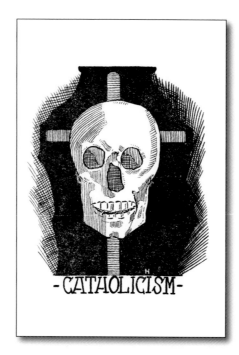

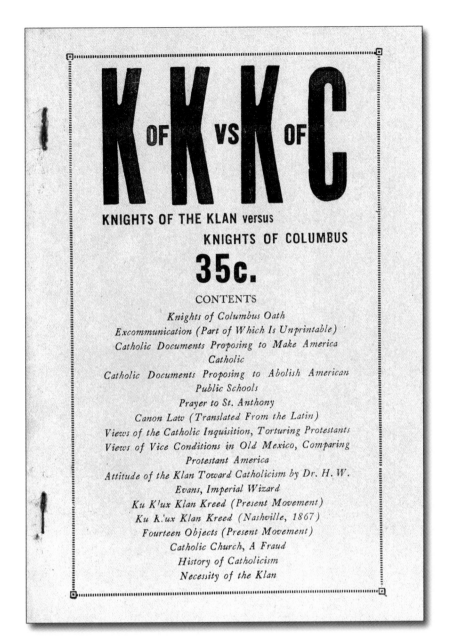

A pamphlet glorifying the Klan while instilling fear and suspicion against the Knights of Columbus and Catholicism in general.

To bolster membership beyond the southern states, Simmons hired publicists Edward Young Clarke and Elizabeth Tyler. In their recruitment campaign, Clarke and Tyler focused on the so-called Americanism of the Klan. They knew that the anti-German sentiment caused by World War I would be instrumental in spreading the fear of all foreigners and minority groups. Throughout the nation, Blacks, Jews, Catholics, and foreigners were viewed by many with suspicion, and even by some as forces of evil. As hatred and fear of certain ethnic and religious groups spread, so too did interest in the Klan. A little more than a year after Clarke and Tyler began their recruitment effort, membership reached nearly one million.

Pope Pius XI, born Ambrogio Damiano Achille Ratti, succeeded Pope Benedict XV in 1922 and served until his death in 1939. A strong opponent of political systems that infringed on human rights, including communism and fascism, Pius XI strove to increase missionary presence throughout the world.

In 1923, through the urging of Maryland State Deputy William Aumen, the Knights provided $35,000 for the Gibbons Institute, a Catholic school for African Americans. Run by Victor and Constance Daniels, the school offered an innovative blend of vocational and liberal studies, drawing on the African-American literary tradition.

## Standing Up to the Klan

The Knights were major opponents of the KKK throughout the 1920s. As Thomas Pegram wrote in his 2011 history of the Klan, "The Knights of Columbus embarked on an active, public defense of Catholicism during the Klan era. Stressing the patriotism of American Catholics, promoting Catholic contributions to the formation of American history and institutions, and displaying a willingness to answer anti-Catholic critics directly, the Columbians openly contradicted the Invisible Empire's claim to the Protestant character of American identity." The pages of *Columbia* regularly countered and denounced the Klan and its ideology. The Supreme Office established a historical commission to support research and projects that shed light not only on anti-Catholic bigotry, but on all religious, racial, and cultural prejudice as well.

The Knights also acted locally to stand up to the Klan. The New York Knights, for example, sent out a force of lecturers to speak in defense of Catholicism. Local Knights in Anaheim, California, found that exposing Klan membership was a most effective and direct manner of attack. Obtaining and publishing a copy of the Klan membership roster fueled the removal of Klansmen from the city council and caused the subsequent decline of the organization there. In places where the Klan threatened priests or religious buildings, local councils would often stand guard to protect them. And because of the Order's reputation for opposing the Klan, in a number of places like Helper, Utah, and Bemidji, Minnesota, groups of men formed councils specifically in response to the local Klan. Maryland historian John Bauernschub credits the Knights' staunch opposition to the rise of bigotry as a key factor in the success of that state's K of C membership recruitment.

For its part, the Klan targeted the Knights—both the organization and individual members. One Klansman reportedly claimed that the Klan hated the Knights of Columbus more than the Catholic Church itself. Around the country, acts of Klan-related violence against the Knights included a cross burning outside a state council convention, as well as the beating of one member and the killing of another. (See the story of Father James Coyle on page 78.) In Houston, Texas, where the Klan controlled the police department, members tapped the telephones of the local Knights of Columbus hall as well as the rectories of nearby Catholic parishes.

The Klan already objected to the Order's namesake for being Catholic and an immigrant, and attacked the navigator's reputation nationwide. But the group also manifested its particular hatred of the Knights and of Catholics by disrupting Columbus Day events.

The Klan further targeted the Knights in the political arena. The group's imperial wizard himself urged Klansmen to place bills before a state legis-

The 1920s Klan sought to undermine Columbus' reputation and legacy. It tried to prevent the erection of statues of the Catholic explorer, and disrupted Columbus Day celebrations. The Klan also worked to diminish the significance of Columbus' historic voyage by promoting the histories of Nordic explorers.

After the Great Kanto Earthquake in 1923, 48 percent of Tokyo homes were destroyed or uninhabitable, leaving 1.38 million people homeless and 140,000 dead. The international response to the disaster was strong, with Americans providing 70 percent of the total aid. The Knights of Columbus did their part by donating $25,000.

lature outlawing membership in both the Catholic Church and the Knights of Columbus. In one instance, a Pennsylvania legislator promoted a bill that carried a ten-year prison term for simply being a member of the K of C. (The bill failed.) In another case, a number of southern congressmen threatened to demand a congressional investigation of the Knights of Columbus if a special congressional committee was appointed to investigate the Klan.

In a nationwide effort to discredit the Knights, the Klan began redistributing the infamous Bogus Oath. This inaccurate account of the oath taken by Fourth Degree Knights had been distributed a decade earlier by anti-Catholic groups in an effort to question the Order's loyalty to the nation. (See page 53.) The Order responded to this latest Klan tactic by offering a sizable monetary reward to anyone who could provide actual authentication of the distributed oath. No one, of course, claimed the reward. Afterward, in a widely published advertisement, the Order stated: "Ignorance, after such a widespread denial and a generous offer for the truth, can no longer be an excuse for anyone who would use it [the bogus oath] again."

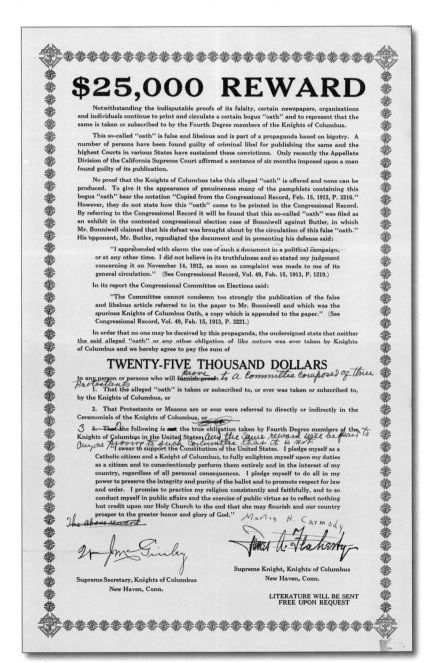

When the Klan began redistributing the fake oath, known as the "Bogus Oath," the Order offered a monetary reward to anyone who could prove its authenticity. This is a working draft of the Order's challenge.

# Father James Edwin Coyle
## Notable Knight

When Irish-born Father James Coyle volunteered to serve his priestly ministry in the United States, he was heading into what would become a hotbed of anti-Catholic hostility. Ordained in Rome in 1896, Father Coyle began his priestly work in Mobile, Alabama, before becoming pastor of the Cathedral of St. Paul in Birmingham. Over the next two decades, he witnessed Alabama grow in Klan membership and its related bigotry, as it followed what was a growing regional and even national trend.

A man of unwavering faith and humility, Father Coyle was staunch in his resistance to the prejudice around him, writing prolifically and speaking out in defense of the Church. He wrote numerous articles that appeared in the Birmingham newspapers. He urged Catholics to also raise their voices in defense, and expressed a hope that "this persecution will ... give Catholics up here some backbone."

As a result of his visible public support of the Church, Father Coyle became a target himself. In addition to death threats, he was warned of plans to burn St. Paul's to the ground.

On August 21, 1921, Father Coyle performed a marriage between Ruth Stephenson, a young Catholic convert, and Pedro Gussman, a Catholic of Puerto Rican heritage. Within a few hours, the bride's father—Edwin Stephenson, a Methodist minister and Catholic-hating Klansman—walked onto the porch of St. Paul's rectory, raised a loaded pistol, and shot and killed Father Coyle.

The murder was followed by a Klan-filled manipulation of the justice system. More than a murder case, the trial became a chance to air radical fears about Catholics and race. The Klan raised funds to hire Stephenson's defense team. The judge and jury were Klansmen as were three of his lawyers; a fourth lawyer (future Supreme Court Justice Hugo Black) later also joined the Klan.

During his trial, Stephenson accused the Catholics of seducing his daughter away from her Protestant faith. He claimed that when he learned of her marriage, he lost his mind and wasn't responsible for his actions. The defense also tried to make the groom's ethnic and racial heritage an issue, even manipulating the lights in the courtroom to make him appear darker. So it was no surprise that after a few hours of deliberation, the jury returned a verdict of "not guilty."

Father Coyle is remembered as a model of faith and courage. He served as the chaplain of Birmingham Council 635 and was a charter member of Mobile Council 666.

In 1924, the Order established the Texas Knights of Columbus Historical Commission to bring the region's Catholic history to light. One of the commission's greatest accomplishments would be the publication of a seven-volume series entitled *Our Catholic Heritage in Texas, 1519–1936,* written by noted American historian Carlos E. Castañeda.

At the 1925 Supreme Convention in Duluth, Minnesota, Knights of Columbus delegates proudly witnessed the institution of the first Columbian Squires group—Duluth Circle 1.

# Fighting for Religious Schools

The Klan may have failed in its attempt to discredit the Knights, but its prejudicial campaign continued—this time with an attack on the nation's religious schools. The group soon became active in the anti-Catholic political movement that was promoting compulsory public school education. Supporters argued that any child schooled outside the public system, especially those from immigrant families, represented a threat to American democracy.

In Oregon, where anti-immigrant sentiment was already especially strong, the compulsory education campaign was most successful. The area was ripe for further propaganda, including Klan literature on how foreigners threatened democracy. By 1922, nearly 14,000 Klansmen were living in Oregon. They had the support of other organizations throughout the state, including the Oregon Good Government League and the Masons. Working together, these groups supported a referendum requiring all students from age eight to sixteen to attend public school. Despite efforts on the part of several prominent individuals, including Archbishop Alexander Christie of Portland and Oregon Governor Benjamin W. Olcott, who openly criticized the Klan for its racial hatred and religious prejudice, the bill passed.

Oregon became ground zero for this fight in which the Knights of Columbus played an active role. In January 1923, after Supreme Knight Flaherty published a letter in *Columbia* explaining what this new law could mean for Catholics throughout the nation, Archbishop Christie met with the Order's board of directors. He proposed that the Knights financially support legal action challenging the constitutionality of the bill on the principles of protecting civil and religious liberties.

By 1924, two lawsuits had been filed—one by the Hill Military Academy, which had opened in 1901, and the other by the Sisters of the Holy Names of Jesus and Mary, who had operated a private school in Portland since 1859. To support their legal fees, the Supreme Council and local councils contributed nearly $25,000. In March 1924, the Federal District Court declared the law unconstitutional on the basis of the Fourteenth Amendment. The suit was then appealed all the way to the Supreme Court, where the decision was upheld in the case *Pierce v. Society of Sisters*. The right of parents and students to opt for religious education had been preserved. In fact, Pope Pius XI cited the decision in the encyclical *Divini Illius Magistri*, which set the foundation for the Second Vatican Council's reflections on Christian and Catholic education.

Although the Klan would continue to be a powerful anti-Catholic antiminority force throughout the 1920s, its bigotry proved unsustainable in a country that valued the First Amendment's guarantee of religious freedom.

While most Knights' evening schools for WWI veterans began closing in the mid-1920s, the school in Washington, DC continued, focusing on law and accounting. Supported by professors from The Catholic University of America, the school incorporated as Columbus University in 1935, and later became Columbus Law School at The Catholic University of America.

Spurred by anti-Catholic sentiment, in 1922, the State of Oregon passed a bill requiring students to attend public rather than parochial school. But in *Pierce v. Society of Sisters* (1925), the Supreme Court upheld the right of parents and students to opt for religious education.

Further contributing to the Klan's decline were disagreements within the group's leadership and reports of its growing violence in the South. By the end of the decade, membership had dropped significantly and the group's briefly prominent position in politics essentially faded. Although the Klan remains an active organization with an agenda similar to the one it had in the 1920s, since that time, its membership has declined from about 4 million to about 6,000.

# Al Smith
## Notable Knight

A member of Dr. John G. Coyle Council 163 of Manhattan, former New York governor Alfred E. Smith ran for president in 1924, and again in 1928. In the latter, he won the Democratic Party's nomination in the race against Herbert Hoover. He was the first Roman Catholic to gain a presidential nomination from a major party.

Blessed with a flair for public speaking, Smith was described by Franklin Roosevelt as the "Happy Warrior." Along with his ability to identify with common people, he had a willingness to engage in passionate debate on the issues. He enjoyed great popularity as a member of the New York State Assembly and during his four terms as governor.

Smith played a key role in the controversial 1924 Democratic National Convention, sometimes referred to as the "Klanbake Convention." He had opposed a Klan-supported candidate and attempted to add a condemnation of the Klan to the party's platform. Neither candidate won. But at the next convention in 1928, the delegates nominated Smith to represent the Democratic Party in a run for the presidency.

During the campaign, anti-Catholic groups, including the Ku Klux Klan, made Smith's religious faith an issue. They argued that a Catholic simply could not be trusted as president—that, if elected, he would take orders from the Vatican. To highlight its opposition, the Klan burned fiery crosses along Smith's campaign route. He lost the election, in no small part due to this bigotry. In 1932, he sought the nomination again, but lost to Franklin D. Roosevelt, who had supported Smith in 1928 and succeeded him as governor of New York.

Al Smith's political aspirations may have ended, but his legacy lives on as the first Catholic to become a major-party nominee for president of the United States. To this day, every October, the Archdiocese of New York hosts the Alfred E. Smith Memorial Foundation Dinner. A fundraiser for Catholic charities, the dinner is attended traditionally by both the Democratic and Republican candidates during presidential election years.

In August 1926, religious services ended in Mexico due to government persecution. Scarcely two weeks later, Supreme Knight James Flaherty (center) and Supreme Treasurer Daniel J. Callahan (left) presented resolutions to Secretary of State Frank Kellogg (right), urging the United States to help stop the oppression of Catholics in Mexico.

Babe Ruth was just one of many sports legends of the early twentieth century who were also Knights. Others included Jim Thorpe, John McGraw, Johnny Evers, and James Braddock. One article claimed that nearly the whole Chicago Cubs team had been "transformed into a branch of the Order."

# THE HISTORICAL COMMISSION AND THE FIGHT AGAINST BIASED HISTORY

Along with its significance as a decade in which the Order successfully fought on behalf of religious schools, the 1920s marked another notable turning point in American education—one that was spearheaded by the Knights of Columbus. American history textbooks of the time tended to highlight only Anglo-Saxon contributions and downplay the contributions of America's many ethnic, racial, and religious minorities. This not only misrepresented the country's history, but also played into the rising bigotry encouraged by the Klan.

The issue of false historical representation was raised by Fourth Degree Knight Edward F. McSweeney. A noted lecturer, labor leader, editor and political activist—especially with respect to Irish self-determination—McSweeney was a force to be reckoned with. He had served as assistant US Commissioner of Immigration at Ellis Island and was involved with a number of political campaigns. In 1920, he published a pamphlet in which he criticized American history textbooks for giving children a homogenized version of the truth.

In May of the following year, the Knights took action. In response to a resolution sponsored by Supreme Master John H. Reddin, the Order formed the Knights of Columbus Historical Commission. Chaired by McSweeney, the commission was organized "to investigate the facts of history as applicable to our country, to correct historical errors and omissions, to mollify and preserve our national history, to exalt and perpetuate American ideals, and to combat and counteract anti-American propaganda . . ."

Although the commission was active for fewer than five years, it brought about significant contributions to scholarship and research, inspiring critical assessment of textbooks and school curriculums. Among its notable offerings was the publication of the "Racial Contribution Series"—a collection of three monographs that highlighted the contributions of three minority groups: African Americans, Jews, and Germans. Along with experiencing societal bigotry, these groups had been excluded from American history books. The series included *The Gift of Black Folk* by W.E.B. Du Bois—leading scholar in Black history and co-founder of the NAACP; *The Jews in the Making of America* by George Cohen; and *The Germans in the Making of America* by Frederick Franklin Shrader. According to McSweeney, the three monographs were "a much needed and important contribution to national solidarity."

To assist in its investigation, the commission sponsored a contest in which monetary prizes were to be awarded for the best studies in American history based on original research. According to McSweeney, the commission

**Edward McSweeney**
Chairman of the Knights' Historical Commission.

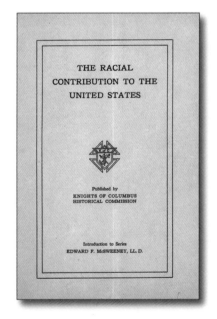

Part of the Knights' Historical Commission, this series included the contributions of Blacks, Jews, and Germans in America.

In a letter he wrote shortly after completing his book *The Gift of Black Folk*, W.E.B. Du Bois criticized the segregationist policies of much of the Catholic Church and many Catholic bishops. But he praised the Order for its "admirably conceived series of monographs for inter-racial understanding of the making of America."

The greatest athlete of the first half of the twentieth century according to the Associated Press, Jim Thorpe was a track and field Olympic medalist, and baseball, football, and basketball legend. A Knight and Native American (Sac and Fox Nations), he played baseball under manager and brother Knight John McGraw.

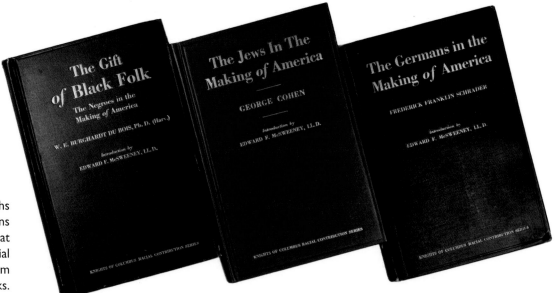

These monographs highlighted the contributions of three minority groups that had been targets of social bigotry and excluded from American history books.

**Samuel Bemis**
Winner of the Knights' sponsored contest on historical research.

hoped that the contest, whose winning submissions were to be published and then widely distributed, would provide an opportunity to correct the existing historical errors and misrepresentations. The first-prize winner of the contest was Samuel Flagg Bemis, a historian of diplomacy, who would go on to become a two-time Pulitzer Prize-winning author. Bemis' submission, *Jay's Treaty: A Study in Commerce and Diplomacy*, was later published as part of the Knights of Columbus Historical Series. Other entries by men who would become noted literary historians included *The Origins of the Propaganda Movement* by Charles Edward Russell and *The American States 1775–1789* by Allan Nevins.

By the summer of 1922, the history investigation had received a great response from college professors, high school teachers, school superintendents, and college students, particularly those who were studying American foreign relations. In the July 1922 issue of *Columbia*, John H. Reddin wrote:

> Widespread interest has been created among students of history in schools and in colleges, and among a larger number of societies and individual citizens who still adhere to the principles and ideals of the fathers of the republic. Our movement has included independent investigations of history textbooks used in the public schools and higher institutions of learning, and investigators have expressed amazement at the error, concealment, and falsification of historic facts appearing therein.

In his 1929 encyclical *Divini Illius Magistri* (That Divine Teacher), Pope Pius XI emphasized the importance of Christian education and set down its principles. He explained that in addition to providing religious instruction, Christian schools must infuse every subject with Christian piety and preserve a sacred atmosphere.

Under Supreme Knight Flaherty, significant changes were made to the insurance program in 1917. The requirement for associate membership was raised to age twenty-six, while Knights between ages nineteen and twenty-five were required to carry a $1,000 insurance policy at a cost of 80 cents or less per month. These changes paved the way for more stable and dependable growth. By 1929, the number of insured members increased by more than 20,000.

Sparking public awareness yielded positive results for the cause. Increasing numbers of Americans were becoming interested in discovering for themselves the extent of the historical inaccuracies. This included some twenty-one teachers and school principals from the New York City Department of Education who, following the Order's lead, determined that many of their school texts "fell under suspicion as being unfit for study by the youthful minds of America."

Through its historical commission, the Knights of Columbus gave a voice to American diversity, both religious and ethnic. As W.E.B. Du Bois stated, "American History has no prototype and has been developed from the various racial elements." With the Order's assistance, the contributions of Catholics and other minorities no longer remained buried, but were rightfully recognized as a valued part of America's history.

"To assert that . . . a citizen of the United States is unworthy of the right of citizenship because of color, racial descent, or religious belief is abhorrent to the spirit of the Declaration of Independence and the Constitution of the United States."

–Edward McSweeney, Chairman of the Historical Commission

# The Texas Knights of Columbus Historical Commission
## Visionary Council Initiative

In 1924, as the Klan and others fought to highlight only Anglo and Protestant elements of the nation's history, the Texas Knights of Columbus launched the most significant regional historical exploration of the Catholic (and largely Hispanic Catholic) history of the Star State.

Recognizing the rich Catholic history of the south and southwestern United States and seeking to preserve it and make it available, the Texas State Council established the Texas Knights of Columbus Historical Commission. This commission supported many projects that brought the region's Catholic history to light. There was, however, one project that dominated its efforts: the commissioning of what turned out to be a seven-volume series entitled *Our Catholic Heritage in Texas, 1519–1936*. The Texas Knights dedicated $130,000 to this massive three-decade project.

Historian Carlos Castañeda was chosen to research and write the series, which was edited by Paul Joseph Foik (who served as the commission's chairman for twenty-seven years). Under the auspices of the Texas K of C, they produced an irreplaceable, definitive, encyclopedic account of the Catholic Church in the Texas region, much of which occurred long before the famous settlements in the colonies of the eastern United States.

Through their vision and dedication, the Texas Knights made a significant contribution to Catholic American history.

"A word of very special praise is due those Catholic organizations, which during all these trying times have stood like soldiers side to side with the clergy. . . . First of all We mention the Knights of Columbus. . . . This organization promotes two types of activities which are needed now more than ever . . . the National Sodality of Fathers of Families . . . [and] the Federation for the Defense of Religious Liberty."

–Pope Pius XI,
*Iniquis Afflictisque*, 1926

# FIGHTING PERSECUTION IN MEXICO

At the same time the Order was fighting religious and cultural bigotry in the United States, Catholics in Mexico were facing their own literal battle for religious liberty. Following the Mexican Revolution, which took place between 1910 and 1920, the country's relationship between religion and politics degenerated into open conflict.

The new Mexican constitution of 1917 restricted religious education, banned worship outside of churches, and turned Church property over to the state. Religious attire was forbidden in public. Foreign priests were expelled from the country, and Mexican clergy was prohibited from voting. The new constitution also outlawed monastic orders and revoked citizenship for anyone found disobeying the constitution on religious grounds. It forbade members of the clergy to assemble and speak freely about the government, prohibited religious publications, and rescinded the right to trial by jury for any violation of the law on these issues.

These elements of the constitution were not widely applied until 1926 when Mexican President Plutarco Elías Calles publicly called for strict enforcement of its articles. The new regulations, known as "Calles Law," attached fines, imprisonment, and other penalties to the various prohibitions. As a result, both public and private worship ceased.

In opposition to the restrictions, a number of Catholic groups formed, including the National League for Defense of Religious Liberty and the Catholic Association of Mexican Youth. In an initial effort to encourage the government's reversal of the Calles Law, Catholics began staging peaceful protests by circulating petitions and forming economic boycotts. Their efforts, however, had no effect, and soon Catholics were violently stripped of their religious freedom. Parish churches were expropriated by government troops and priests were summarily executed. Having been unsuccessful through peaceful means, many Catholics throughout the country responded to the call for a unified rebellion by the National League for the Defense of Religious Liberty. They took up arms in defense of their faith, accompanied by the battle cry "¡*Viva Cristo Rey!*" ("Long Live Christ the King!").

Although the Knights of Columbus did not support the military response of these *Cristeros*, as the Catholic insurgents were called, the Knights in Mexico were known for their support of the Church and opposition to persecution, and were specifically targeted by the Calles government. Many men had joined the Order under the looming threat of religious persecution. In fact, when Venustiano Carranza drafted the constitution in 1917, there was only one council in Mexico; yet by 1923, membership had grown to nearly 6,000 with a total of forty-three councils. Due to the Order's fidelity to the Church and its ties to the United States and other countries, the Mexican government viewed the Knights with suspicion. The Knights' headquarters in Mexico City was ransacked. *Columbia* magazine, which was outspoken

The persecution of Mexican Catholics had American supporters. Margaret Sanger said: "With the yoke of medievalism thus thrown off we can anticipate a splendid development of the government work for birth control already begun in Mexico." The Klan also offered $10 million and 4 million men to stop external interference with Calles' policies.

Demonstrations such as this one in 1926 in Mexico City were designed to protest the persecution and restrictions on religious practice; however, such efforts ultimately failed to improve the situation.

# Martyred Knights of the Persecution

With the 1926 Calles Law's harsh restrictions on the clergy, Catholic priests in Mexico had to be exceptionally discreet in their ministries. Hearing confessions, administering Communion to the sick, and performing baptisms, marriages, and other sacraments were done in strict secrecy. Getting caught at a clandestine liturgy was dangerous not only for the priest, but also for those in attendance. Of the ninety priests who lost their lives during the Cristero War, twenty were members of the Knights of Columbus. On May 21, 2000, six of those twenty priests were canonized by Pope John Paul II along with nineteen other martyrs of the war.

Like the vast majority of Mexican priests at that time, these six did not take up arms or encourage violence. They were killed simply for tending to their pastoral work. For his refusal to submit to the country's anti-religious laws, Father Luis Batis Sáinz faced a firing squad. Father Rodrigo Aguilar Alemán was killed for failing to disclose the identities of seminarians. Father

Bottom, left to right: Rodrigo Aguilar Alemán, Luis Batis Sáinz, Mateo Correa Magallanes
Middle, left to right: Pedro de Jesús Maldonado Lucero, José María Robles Hurtado
Top: Miguel de la Mora de la Mora

Mateo Correa Magallanes sacrificed his life by refusing to break the seal of confession of his fellow inmates. Father Miguel de la Mora de la Mora, shot for signing a letter that spoke out against the anti-religious laws, was killed while praying the rosary. When Father Pedro de Jesús Maldonado Lucero was caught administering the sacraments, he was savagely beaten and later executed. While preparing to say Mass, Father José María Robles Hurtado, founder of the Sisters of the Sacred Heart of Guadalajara, was arrested and executed on the following day.

Another three Knights were among the thirteen martyrs of the Cristero War beatified by Pope Benedict XVI on November 20, 2005. Spanish Claretian missionary Father Andrés Solá Molist, Mexican diocesan priest Father José Trinidad Rangel Montaño, and devout layman Leonardo Pérez Larios were arrested, interrogated, and tortured. Together, on April 25, 1927, they were executed for their faith in Rancho de San Joaquin, Mexico.

Nearly 100 priests were killed by the Mexican government in the late 1920s struggle of the Mexican people against the anti-clerical policies of their government. A number of these priests were also Knights, and several were subsequently declared saints.

On September 1, 1926, President Calvin Coolidge received the Knights delegation. The group urged US involvement in the Mexican crisis. ▶

against the persecution, was banned from Mexican mail. Members were expelled from their homes. Simply being a Knight was cause for punitive measures, including physical punishment and even execution—as in the case of Yocundo Durán.

Aware of the brutalities suffered by the thousands of Catholics in Mexico, including his brother Knights, Supreme Knight Flaherty denounced the persecution of Catholics at the 1926 Supreme Council meeting. He demanded that the United States—which, under President Calvin Coolidge, had provided arms and ammunition to the Mexican army—deny recognition of the Calles government until it respected religious liberty. On September 1, 1926, President Coolidge received a delegation of Knights, whose primary agenda was to encourage the United States to help bring an end to the religious persecution through diplomatic means. Coolidge's response was positive.

Like the US bishops, the Supreme Council had withdrawn financial aid to the National League for Religious Liberty once it called for Catholics to take up arms. The Order did not, however, stay silent. Through a pledge of $1 million from its members, the Knights established the Mexican Fund, which not only provided aid directly to Catholic refugees, but also raised awareness in the US of the seriousness of the situation. The Order disseminated information through lectures and radio speeches. It publicized the conflict through the distribution of nearly 5 million pamphlets and through articles published in periodicals like *Columbia*.

Long displayed in the office of the Knights of Columbus in Mexico, this painting of Our Lady of Guadalupe had its edges (but not the image itself) bayoneted by Federal soldiers during the persecution. The Knights' Mexico office was also ransacked, and many documents were destroyed.

In 1926, as the Mexican government intensified its persecution of Catholics, the Order spoke out at its Supreme Convention. Supreme Knight Flaherty and the Supreme Officers also met with President Calvin Coolidge to urge the United States to help end the oppression of the faithful in Mexico.

# Saint Rafael Guízar Valencia
## Notable Knight

Ordained a priest in 1901, Rafael Guízar Valencia was a Mexican-born missionary who ministered to Catholics during the Mexican Revolution. He was steadfast in his defense of the Church, often disguising himself in order to serve the sick and administer the sacraments. After being declared a government enemy, who was to be "shot on sight," Father Valencia fled Mexico in 1915 and served the Church in Guatemala and Cuba. Shortly after he was ordained a bishop in 1919, he returned to Veracruz, Mexico, at the end of the revolution. There, he became a member of Knights of Columbus Council 2311.

As bishop, he gave away nearly all of his possessions to help the poor. And after the government forcibly closed the seminary in his diocese, he helped establish a clandestine seminary in Mexico City. Although he was again forced to flee Mexico in 1927 as a result of President Plutarco Calles' anti-Catholic regulations, he returned in 1929 and continued to serve the faithful of his diocese. Beatified in 1995 by Pope John Paul II, Bishop Rafael Guízar Valencia was canonized in Rome by Pope Benedict XVI on October 15, 2006. He was the seventh Knight and the first bishop/Knight to be declared a saint.

Along with raising public awareness, the Knights' campaign also maintained pressure on the United States to exert influence on Mexico to stop the persecution.

Within a year after receiving the Knights' delegation, President Coolidge sent US Ambassador Dwight W. Morrow to Mexico. Morrow helped facilitate an agreement in 1929 that promised both amnesty for the Cristeros and suspension of the Calles Law.

By this time, the Cristero War had already claimed the lives of approximately 200,000 people. Even after the peace accords were signed, peace would not last, and the Knights would once again take up the cause of religious freedom in Mexico. It was not until 1938, under the presidency of Lázaro Cárdenas, that Mexico reached a semblance of peace. A constitutional reform was finally passed in 1992, with an actual revision of the anti-Catholic laws that first prompted the Cristeros rebellion.

Supreme Knight Flaherty was a dedicated philanthropist, who also served as president of the National Santa Claus Association and Vice President of the American Society for Visiting Prisoners. When he stepped down from his position as supreme knight in 1927, the Supreme Convention created a new position for him: supreme counselor.

In 1929, the stock market crashed and the Great Depression began. The Depression would take a toll, but the Order ended the 1920s strong, with 630,000 Knights—making its work all the more effective. During this decade, the Order added more than $200 million of insurance in force, for a total of $278 million.

The conflict, lengthy and brutal, was only part of a wide-reaching suppression of religious freedom felt in many places during the twentieth century. Time and again in its history, the Knights of Columbus gave great witness to the spiritual element of its founding by supporting or leading the resolve of the faithful in their refusal to deny God or reject the Church. At the same time, the principle of charity was always present, as the Order assisted physical as well as spiritual needs of the persecuted. Such work was not an abstraction, and many made the ultimate sacrifice for God and neighbor. Numerous courageous women and men of the twentieth century—including those who died during the Mexican government's persecution of Catholics—have been declared martyrs of the Church, including six saints and three blesseds who were Knights.

## A CHANGE IN LEADERSHIP

By the time James A. Flaherty concluded his eighteen years as supreme knight in 1927, he had accomplished much. The Philadelphia lawyer had guided the Knights through the First World War, providing immeasurable support for the American troops both at home and overseas, as well as educational and employment opportunities for them after the war. He had actively supported the Catholics in Mexico during the Cristero War. Flaherty led the Order in its defense of parochial schools and in its campaign to provide an accurate assessment of American history to the nation's students. During his tenure, Flaherty received numerous honors and awards for his work, including the Croix de Guerre (Cross of War) from the French government. After stepping down as supreme knight, Flaherty, like Hearn before him, remained involved in the Knights of Columbus. At the 1927 Supreme Convention, the Supreme Council unanimously voted to create a new position for him—supreme counselor—a sure sign of the Order's esteem and respect for Flaherty and his service.

**Martin H. Carmody**
Seventh supreme knight.

Michigan attorney Martin H. Carmody assumed the role of supreme knight in 1927. Although he had very big shoes to fill, Carmody had been at Flaherty's side through much of the previous eighteen years, serving as deputy supreme knight. Twenty-five years earlier, he had joined Grand Rapids Council 389 and was quite familiar with the Order and American Catholicism. When Carmody stepped into his role as supreme knight, he was about to lead an organization of over 600,000 members into one of the darkest eras in American history—the Great Depression.

During the dark days of the Great Depression, impoverished citizens in search of a meal waited on breadlines for food. As many as one in four people was out of work.

# 5.
# Helping Our Neighbors
## The Great Depression
## 1930 to 1939

During the early decades of the 1900s, the Knights of Columbus reached out to help the oppressed and those in need both at home and throughout the world. With its volunteer work during World War I, battles against bigotry, and efforts to promote religious freedom around the globe, the Order continued to extend beyond its American roots during the 1920s.

At the end of the decade, however, the stock market crash of 1929 devastated the American economy and initiated the Great Depression. In its wake, the Order confronted similar threats and concerns faced by people not only in America but globally. Two months before the Great Depression began, the Order stood strong at 637,122 members, 40 percent of whom were insurance members. After the crash, however, membership and financial strength suffered. The Order began to lose members, who often could no longer afford dues. And although it had not been heavily invested in the stock market, the Order suffered financially as members stopped paying on their insurance policies. The Supreme Office had to minimize expenditures and make a number of budget cuts, including a reduction in the operating expenses of *Columbia* magazine. It also had to borrow from various funds to meet expenses.

When news of the 1929 stock market crash reached the public, people gathered in shock outside the New York Stock Exchange. The crash ushered in the Great Depression—the most severe economic collapse seen in the industrialized Western world. By 1935, nearly 15 million Americans were unemployed and half the country's banks were closed.

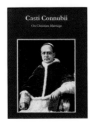

The united Christian front against artificial birth control ended at the 1930 Anglican Lambeth Conference, followed by a committee of the Federal Council of Churches. In response, Pope Pius XI issued *Casti Connubii,* his encyclical on marriage, which reaffirmed the Catholic Church's stance against artificial birth control.

Charity and protection of the financial viability of Catholic families was a founding part of the Knights mission, and the Depression made it clear that these were still much needed. It was Supreme Knight Martin H. Carmody who would lead the Order throughout this challenging period. Confident that the Knights could aid the country, Carmody was determined to lead the organization in extending help where it was most needed. As he stated at the 1930 Supreme Convention, "It is from such adverse conditions that the people of a nation rise to its full powers."

## FINDING JOBS FOR THE UNEMPLOYED

Despite its own trials, the Order turned its attention to the countless Americans for whom daily life had become a struggle. With roughly a quarter of the country's workers facing unemployment, there was no way to solve the problem overnight. No jobs meant no money. No money meant that people simply had to do without—without food, clothing, and medical care. And without money to pay mortgages, increasing numbers of families lost their homes.

As difficult as it was, finding jobs for the unemployed was a key solution. In July 1930, Supreme Knight Carmody reached out to councils throughout the nation. He urged them to appoint "strong and active employment committees" that would help local displaced workers find jobs in their cities or towns. By the following summer, councils had formed over 1,000 local committees and found jobs for 43,128 unemployed men and women. Some coun-

During the 1930s, lines of men and women desperately looking for jobs were common throughout the country. The Knights responded, creating a network of more than 1,000 council-based employment committees, which ultimately placed 100,000 people over the next two years.

Throngs of the jobless line up to begin receiving unemployment benefits.

cils worked with various civic and voluntary groups in offering similar services throughout the nation.

Energized by this success, Carmody wired President Hoover in October 1931 and offered the services of the Order's 2,600 councils for the government's newly established President's Organization on Unemployment Relief. Within a day, Hoover responded, noting the Order's "fine spirit of cooperation." Shortly after, the president appointed Carmody to a position at that organization. The supreme officers then passed a resolution to support these initiatives, contacting nearly 3,000 state and local officers to encourage cooperation with these new measures to battle unemployment.

In November 1931, the Order further expanded its outreach by establishing a central Bureau of Employment in New Haven. To head it, Carmody appointed Peter Collins, who had led the Knights' employment bureau after World War I. To create an effective nationwide plan for the new bureau, Collins began by gathering information and insight from local councils regarding regional jobs and joblessness. Learning that unemployment hit urban areas harder than rural ones, which suffered more from depressed commodity prices than actual loss of work, he urged efforts to be particularly active in city areas. Five months after the bureau was established, and just as it was beginning to make headway, Collins died. But the groundwork he had laid continued to achieve successful results. Within eighteen months, the bureau helped find full- and part-time jobs for nearly 100,000 men and women.

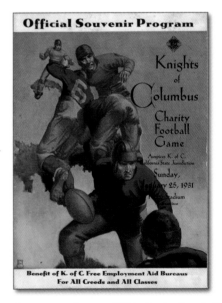

A program from a 1931 charity football game hosted by the Knights in San Francisco for the "Benefit of K. of C. Free Employment Aid Bureaus For All Creeds and All Classes." Throughout the decade, the Order hosted such games with collegiate and NFL teams.

Although the Order's postwar educational programs ended in 1926, its correspondence school continued into the 1930s. Created for "ex-service men and women regardless of creed or color, who [could not] attend K-C evening schools," courses covered nearly 100 subjects. At its peak, more than 500 pieces of curricula were mailed each day.

As families and children struggled with basic necessities, K of C councils—often struggling themselves—welcomed the opportunity to give. Maryland Mt. Savage Council 1058 noted that providing hot meals for 2,000 schoolchildren "brought glory to our Council by the exercising of the virtue of Charity."

# The Mexican Welfare Committee
## of the Colorado Knights
### Visionary Council Initiative

Unemployment was not the only job problem in the 1920s and 1930s. For some, like the Mexican migrant field laborers in Colorado, the conditions of the work itself were often deplorable. The workers—children as well as adults—faced long days of backbreaking work under the sweltering sun, often without adequate breaks, food, or water. Living arrangements were typically substandard, and working conditions were often dangerous. Wages were inadequate, compensation was withheld, and schooling was denied.

In response, at Colorado's 1923 state convention, the Colorado Knights established and funded the Mexican Welfare Committee. Through the 1920s and 1930s, this committee investigated possible abuses of the Mexican migrant field laborers, especially in the Colorado

sugar beet industry, which employed 28,000 workers. Leading the committee was Thomas F. Mahony, who proved to be an effective and passionate advocate for the cause.

"There isn't a paper in Northern Colorado that will say a thing or hardly a person who will do anything to stop this," Mahony lamented to Supreme Master John Reddin in 1930. Determined to make a change, Mahony led the Mexican Welfare Committee in investigating, documenting, and bringing about public awareness of the inherent mistreatment of the laborers. Through its diligence in exposing these injustices, the committee was credited with helping to bring about change—change that resulted in better, more adequate treatment of the migrant workers.

## CELEBRATING FIFTY YEARS

The year 1932—which marked the Order's Golden Anniversary—brought about an opportunity to help lift sinking spirits during the dark days of the Depression. Through the celebration of this landmark event, the Knights were able to highlight the organization's accomplishments while looking forward to the future. It also gave the Knights the chance to recruit new members and encourage the return of former members.

During a nationwide radio program broadcast by NBC on March 29, 1932, exactly fifty years after the granting of the Order's first charter, Supreme Knight Carmody talked about many of the Knights' achievements since its founding. He spoke of the Order's growth to 600,000 members and more than 2,500 councils; its support for families through its insurance program, which had already paid out $35 million to beneficiaries; its help for victims of floods, earthquakes, and other natural disasters; its service to soldiers and veterans of the Great War; and its fight against bigotry.

Carmody assured his listeners that the Order's work would continue to assist anyone in need, saying:

> During these trying days through which we are passing, let there be affectionate and meritorious service on behalf of our neighbor, our fellow member in the great common fraternity of mankind, who is out of employment, out of money, out of touch with his fel-

Supreme Knight Martin Carmody (center) stands with Past Supreme Knights John Cone, John Phelan, James Flaherty, and Edward Hearn at the 1932 fiftieth anniversary Supreme Convention in Washington, DC.

During a visit to Rome in 1931, Supreme Knight and Mrs. Carmody were personally introduced to Pope Pius XI, who named Carmody a papal chamberlain, one of the highest positions to be held by a Catholic layman. Traditionally an honorary position held by members of the Italian nobility, chamberlains are required to serve the pope for one week each year during official ceremonies. The Carmodys were also guests of honor at several dinners hosted by Archbishop Borongini-Duca and Vatican Undersecretary of State Giuseppe Pizzardo.

lowman, that he, like the doughboy in the trench, may know that he is not forgotten and that fraternity still lives, not merely in the handclasp of friendship, but in the supporting, sustaining, helping hands and hearts of those that generously share with others.

Accordingly, Carmody stated that during the next fifty years, the Knights intended to provide even greater service to God, the Catholic Church, the country, and to their fellow man.

The Order also drew attention to the Golden Anniversary through Commemoration Week, held from June 24 to June 30, in honor of Father McGivney. A one-act drama about the founding of the Order—originally written and staged on April 19, 1932, by members of Council 1507 in Guelph, Ontario—was performed by more than 400 councils throughout the country as part of their planned festivities. Encouraged to celebrate in any manner they saw fit, many councils marked the occasion with Pontifical High Masses, banquets, and communion breakfasts. Several councils in the northeast, including San Salvador Council 1 and the Massachusetts State Council, invited various Catholic leaders and prominent government officials to attend their celebratory banquets. Cardinal William Henry O'Connell, Bishop John J. Nilan of Hartford, Governor Wilbur L. Cross of Connecticut, and Governor Joseph P. Ely of Massachusetts were among the notable guests.

Supreme Knight Martin Carmody is honored in Rome after being named papal chamberlain by Pope Pius XI.

Aware of the Depression's impact on membership, the Order launched a special drive that reached out to new and lapsed members. This Welcome

# The Battle Over the Knights' Sporting Facilities in Rome

Not long after Benito Mussolini signed the Accords recognizing the sovereignty of the Vatican, the Fascist government attempted to sever the Church's influence from Italian public life. By 1931, Mussolini had shut down Catholic newspapers and tried to end the popular social organization called Catholic Action.

Around this time, the Knights' playgrounds/sports centers in Rome became targets as well. Italian government officials accused them of being affiliated with the group Catholic Action, with which the government had taken issue. The playgrounds were also seen by the government as athletic training centers in direct competition with Balilla, the Fascist youth program. In late May 1931, the police ordered the playgrounds shuttered. They also confiscated a number of the Order's files.

Former Supreme Knight Edward Hearn, who was then serving as the director of the Knights' activities in Rome, immediately contacted the American Embassy to protest the action, calling it "unjustified and unjustifiable." The story was picked up internationally.

Ultimately, the playgrounds were reopened and, despite the outbreak of war in which the United States and Italy fought on opposing sides, the playgrounds remained open. During and after the war, they would serve as hubs for charitable works for the people of Rome.

---

Home Program urged active members to reach out to potential newcomers and locate former members who, often due to lack of financial resources, had drifted from the Order. To make rejoining more feasible, lapsed members were reinstated for a nominal fee of five dollars. This was considered payment in full for back dues.

The program, which was in force from June until the end of October, fell far short of its lofty goal of bringing in 50,000 members. In fact, nearly 42,000 associate members and over 4,000 insurance members actually left the Order in 1932. Lack of member involvement resulted in the suspension of many local councils. However, considering the effects of the Depression, it is likely that without the Welcome Home Program and the other activities that took place during the Golden Anniversary year, the Order would have seen a far greater loss.

The Golden Anniversary was brought to a close with the celebration of Columbus Day, which had always been a special holiday for the Knights. That year, it was celebrated with great significance. Throughout the country, parades marched through the streets, while councils held parties, banquets, and other social gatherings. Dozens of notable speakers took to the airwaves, offering words of praise for both the Knights and the famous explorer who had come to symbolize the rights of Catholic immigrants.

The activities that took place on that Columbus Day—and throughout that anniversary year—boosted flagging morale while reflecting the spirit of Columbianism and the principles of the Order.

---

In 1932, the Golden Anniversary of the founding of the Knights of Columbus was celebrated by the Order. As a special feature of the observance, on March 29, Supreme Knight Carmody used a nationwide radio program to talk about the Knights' achievements, including its many charitable works and its support for families through its insurance program.

The Order's Golden Anniversary coincided with the bicentennial of George Washington's birth. Knights celebrated America's first president during the year's activities, in *Columbia's* pages, and at the annual convention held in the capital city bearing his name. There, Supreme Knight Carmody led a delegation to Washington's home, Mount Vernon.

# THE KNIGHTS AND CARDINAL JAMES GIBBONS

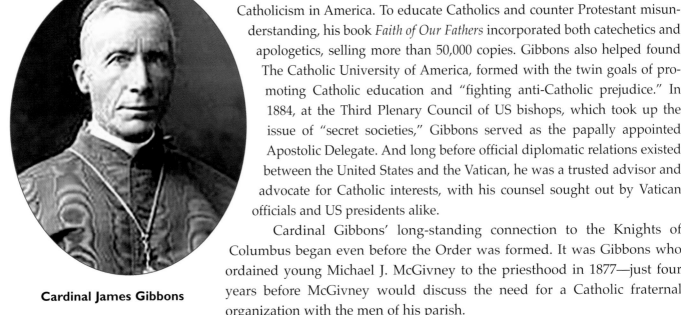

**Cardinal James Gibbons**

Another highlight of the Golden Anniversary year took place on August 14 with the unveiling of the James Cardinal Gibbons Memorial in Washington, DC. Like John Carroll, James Gibbons served as Baltimore's archbishop and helped shape Catholicism in America. To educate Catholics and counter Protestant misunderstanding, his book *Faith of Our Fathers* incorporated both catechetics and apologetics, selling more than 50,000 copies. Gibbons also helped found The Catholic University of America, formed with the twin goals of promoting Catholic education and "fighting anti-Catholic prejudice." In 1884, at the Third Plenary Council of US bishops, which took up the issue of "secret societies," Gibbons served as the papally appointed Apostolic Delegate. And long before official diplomatic relations existed between the United States and the Vatican, he was a trusted advisor and advocate for Catholic interests, with his counsel sought out by Vatican officials and US presidents alike.

Cardinal Gibbons' long-standing connection to the Knights of Columbus began even before the Order was formed. It was Gibbons who ordained young Michael J. McGivney to the priesthood in 1877—just four years before McGivney would discuss the need for a Catholic fraternal organization with the men of his parish.

Years later, in the early 1900s, when The Catholic University of America was in need of financial support, Gibbons turned to the Knights for help. The Order responded with an endowment for the university's American history

President Herbert Hoover stands behind Archbishop Fumasoni-Biondi, waiting for his turn to address the crowd at the 1932 unveiling of the Cardinal Gibbons Memorial.

In the summer of 1932, in the midst of the Depression, thousands of World War I veterans assembled in Washington, DC. There, they demanded an early payment of service certificates—sometimes called bonuses—due to be redeemed in 1945. Unfortunately, the "Bonus Army" would receive no payments until 1936.

This bronze statue of Cardinal James Gibbons was unveiled ▶ in Washington, DC, by the Knights of Columbus on August 14, 1932. A great supporter of Catholic education, Cardinal Gibbons was also notable for having ordained Michael J. McGivney to the priesthood in 1877. In 2007, the memorial was declared a historic site and added to the country's National Register of Historic Places.

"If I may single out one society without prejudice to the merits of the others, I will name in a particular manner that splendid organization, the Knights of Columbus. They are our joy and crown. 'They are the glory of Jerusalem. They are the joy of Israel; they are the honor of the people.' Wherever calumny raises its foul head, they are ever ready, like true knights, to smite the enemy. Whenever an appeal is made in the cause of religion or charity, they are always foremost in lending a helping hand."

From a speech delivered by Cardinal James Gibbons
to the American Federation of Catholic Societies, August 10, 1913

department. It would be the first of many endowments for the school. Cardinal Gibbons would declare that the Order's extensive charitable works, especially those organized during World War I, "should forever stamp the Knights of Columbus as men of practical forethought, timely patriotism, and true Christian charity."

Following Cardinal Gibbons' death in 1921, the Knights proposed the construction of a memorial in recognition of his unwavering service to Catholics in the United States. Plans for the memorial were set in motion in 1927, when District of Columbia State Deputy Charles W. Darr sought to secure a plot of land near the city's Shrine of the Sacred Heart. Although initiated on the local level, in 1930 the project became one every Knight had a hand when it was adopted Order-wide and financed through per-capita donation. The project was slated for completion in 1932, and by that summer, New York sculptor Leo Lentelli had finished the massive bronze statue.

The unveiling of the memorial on August 14, 1932, coincided with the annual Supreme Convention, which was held that year in Washington, DC. The ceremony opened with a parade through the streets of the nation's capital. Some 20,000 Knights marched with naval and civic units of the United States military, while distinguished Church officials, foreign ambassadors, and various dignitaries—including Bishop John M. McNamara of Baltimore; Apostolic Delegate Archbishop Pietro Fumasoni-Biondi; and Margaret Gibbons Burke, grandniece of Cardinal Gibbons—watched from the reviewing stands.

Although President Calvin Coolidge had signed the bill allowing the erection of the monument, the unveiling was performed by President Herbert Hoover, who spoke of the cardinal's great patriotism and pride in his American citizenship. Seventy-five years later, in February of 2007, the James Cardinal Gibbons Memorial was declared a historic site in Washington, DC. That same year, it was also added to the country's National Register of Historic Places.

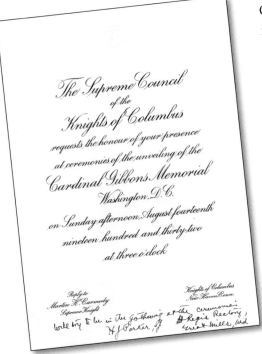

Invitation to the unveiling of the Cardinal Gibbons Memorial.

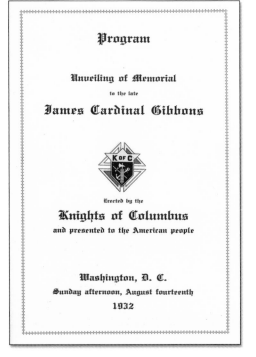

James Cardinal Gibbons
1834 ✝ 1921

# KNIGHTS FOR CATHOLIC ACTION

During the early years of the Great Depression, President Herbert Hoover worked closely with the Knights and other charitable groups who offered assistance to those in need, particularly the unemployed. His successor, President Franklin Roosevelt, however, saw such efforts as the domain of the government. By 1935, the government programs proposed by Roosevelt largely supplanted initiatives like the Knights of Columbus Bureau of Employment. The president's Works Progress Administration (later renamed the Work Projects Administration)—a relief measure created to carry out public works projects—provided millions of jobs, including the construction and repair of courthouses, schools, museums, roads, bridges, parks, and playgrounds.

Even so, the Knights would continue to conduct charitable work. They raised funds to help areas affected by droughts and other natural disasters before government agencies were able to step in. And efforts toward council-initiated outreach were, in the words of Carmody, "never ending."

But the Depression continued to drag on, and with it, the Order saw its membership continue to decrease. In 1932, membership fell 7.5 percent. The following year, it dropped 9.3 percent. And in 1934, it fell another 8.3 percent.

Despite the economic headwinds and the government's moves to de-emphasize humanitarian aid by religious groups, there was an increasing awareness among Catholics of their responsibility toward charitable outreach. They began turning their attention to their parishes and local communities. Understanding that the Order was the "logical" outlet for such charitable responsibility for Catholic men, the Knights renewed efforts to invite men to join.

Previous membership campaigns typically relied on council quotas in one form or another. They included such goals as recruiting one new member for every ten current members, or, as for the fiftieth-anniversary campaign, each officer was required to recruit one member. Although this latter campaign was presented as "the greatest membership drive in the fifty-year history of the Order," it was successful in recruitment, but failed to compensate for the larger problem of men leaving the Order during the Depression.

Carmody introduced a new program to councils. Called Mobilization for Catholic Action, its goal was to arouse members and potential members to the urgent need for active laymen who support the "ideals of Christian citizenship for which the Church and the Knights stand." Guided by new leaders, this time recruitment had a new focus, a new appreciation for the importance of each knight, and a new understanding of what the Knights of Columbus had to offer.

To help ensure its success, two proven leaders were entrusted to direct the campaign. One was William P. Larkin, former supreme director of New

In 1933, when American cinema began producing movies that many considered morally objectionable, Archbishop John Cantwell of Los Angeles formed the Catholic Legion of Decency to assess the content of newly released films. The Knights actively advocated for the cause. During Mass, Catholics pledged to stop patronizing theaters that showed movies that were deemed immoral or that glorified crime.

In 1932, Franklin Delano Roosevelt was elected president. Unlike Hoover's programs, Roosevelt's Depression-era programs did not seek the support of faith-based organizations, who thus played little role in them. The Order also clashed with Roosevelt over his response to persecution in Mexico, urging him to take a stronger stand.

York, who had overseen much of the enormously complex army hut program. The other was Al Smith, the former presidential candidate and successful businessman. Brother Knight John B. Kennedy of the National Broadcasting Company (NBC) was also part of the team as the international publicity director. And a professional fundraising group, the American City Bureau, was also hired. Headquartered at the Empire State Building in Manhattan, the movement's leadership included an internal committee to oversee the volunteer aspect of the campaign, as well as thirty-nine regional directors who organized local solicitation.

When introducing the program to councils, Supreme Knight Carmody emphasized the Knights as the "logical channel" for a Catholic layman to "make his individual contribution to the success" of "Catholic Action." He laid out the key causes at stake that needed Catholic manpower. These included a concerted effort to protest against the "invasions of civil and religious liberty, such as the current persecution of Catholics in Mexico." The program also called for "stronger support of Catholic education, social service, and community welfare work." This call had a particular resonance considering Roosevelt's push to make charitable activity, which had long been the purview of religious organizations, the realm of federal action. Carmody wanted the Knights to be held to a higher standard, noting that "there must be no such thing as passive membership." He added, "Membership for the sake of larger statistical figures means nothing. It is not membership that is needed—it is men."

Organized and strategic, Larkin provided councils with a practical vision. Noting that every campaign involves selling something—a college fundraiser sells the idea of good education; a charity sells the idea of caring for the common good—he laid out what he considered four essentials for every successful campaign:

> "There is no World War today. But there is a war for Catholic rights and Catholic righteousness, and those Catholic men who would be in the thick of the fray belong under the banner of the Knights of Columbus."
>
> –Supreme Knight Martin H. Carmody regarding Mobilization for Cathloic Action

1. There must be something worthwhile to sell.

2. The potential buyers of what is to be sold must be determined in advance.

3. There must be a definite program to create advance interest in what is being sold.

4. There must be a well-informed, enthusiastic group of persons who will personally offer to these prospective "buyers" the opportunity to invest in what is being sold.

Practically speaking, this translated into communicating the worthwhile opportunities of the Order, selectively targeting potential members, raising public awareness in advance, and tapping into enthusiastic local volunteers with an intense but short-term volunteering responsibility.

Membership in the K of C dropped precipitously in the first few years of the Depression. In response, Supreme Knight Carmody launched Mobilization for Catholic Action. Headquartered in the Empire State Building, the campaign enrolled 51,000 new members within just a few months. Former governor Al Smith served on its committee.

During the Depression and the Dust Bowl, councils conducted many innovative charitable endeavors. In 1936, Council 1128 in Chadron, Nebraska put its farming skills to use, planting and harvesting 160 acres of wheat that was sold to pay down the parish debts incurred from building a new church and parochial school.

Within a week of the campaign's launch, 9,200 applications were submitted. Within five months, the Order brought in 51,000 members. Supreme Knight Carmody hailed the effort as a "splendid success" since it had reduced the rate of membership loss.

In the middle of the campaign, the Supreme Office headquarters received a very special guest: Cardinal Eugenio Pacelli, the Secretary of State to the Vatican. (A few years later, in 1939, he would be elected Pope Pius XII.) Cardinal Pacelli endorsed the membership campaign and prayed for the success of the new membership drives, saying:

> It is my earnest and fervent prayer that this laudable endeavor to enroll the Catholic manhood of North America in the ranks of the Knights of Columbus may be a brilliant success, so that by a greatly enlarged and carefully selected membership you may be enabled, in devoted cooperation with the hierarchy, to address yourselves . . . to the social and civil life which puts to such severe tests the souls of men today.

# Myles E. Connolly
## Notable Knight

Before making his way to Hollywood as a screenwriter in the 1930s, Myles E. Connolly served as editor of *Columbia* magazine from 1924 to 1928. While still working for *Columbia*, Connolly wrote *Mr. Blue*, a best-selling novel about an idealistic man who gives away his entire fortune as he follows the Gospel message. For Connolly, though, good writing did not have to be explicitly about the Catholic faith, nor did he think that a work about the faith instantly made it good literature: "Mentioning Our Lord or Our Lady does not mean you're an artist. . . . To me, a book is Catholic if it tells in concrete terms man's relation to his God and to his soul."

After leaving *Columbia*, Connolly wrote a number of books, short stories, and movie scripts. Because he believed that it took no special talent to write about the futility of life, his work leaned toward comedy. In his words, " . . . to write comedy, you have to lift your head high into the clean, fresh air so that you can catch the wonderful tinkling sound of laughter."

As a Hollywood screenwriter, Connolly contributed to a number of major films, including *It Happened in Hollywood, Youth Takes a Fling,* and *State of the Union.* He helped write the 1939 classic *Mr. Smith Goes to Washington,* which received eleven Academy Award nominations and won for best original story. In 1945, his script for *Music for Millions* also received an Oscar nomination for original screenplay.

Connolly's stories typically included characters who were faced with a moral dilemma—and the soul-searching decisions they made involved personal sacrifice, but ultimately were for the good of others. The greater the sacrifice, the closer his characters were to God. To Connolly, these stories were true "Catholic adventures."

The campaign led the Knights to establish the Service Department in 1936. This department was dedicated to helping councils in their individual membership efforts. Whenever a council found success in an outreach program or fundraiser, it shared the information with the Service Department. In turn, the department would pass the ideas on to the other councils. In essence, by reaching out to help promote the work of the councils and encouraging them to play a greater role in both Church and civic activities, the Service Department acted as the public relations arm of the Order, helping to maintain the Knights' visibility to the community at large.

In 1936, the Order launched the "Five Points Program to Progress," providing a general strategy for council action and growth. It emphasized the importance of Catholic activity, council activity, fraternal protection, publicity, and maintenance of manpower. (See "Five Points to Progress," at right.) In implementing these five points, councils' Catholic activities were to transcend mere social ones. Councils were also to activate as many current members as possible, and thus revitalized, to attract new members.

Although the Five Points efforts did not instantly reverse the membership decline, they established a vision for the Order and its councils. Ultimately, "Five Points" would be credited with the membership turnaround in the 1940s, as the Order-wide attention to council strength would continue. Priorities for Catholic activity included focusing on religious freedom issues and also assisting the local Church in ways large and small.

Cardinal Eugenio Pacelli, who would become pope in 1939, arrives for a visit at Knights of Columbus headquarters in 1936.

## Five Points to Progress

Begun in 1936, the Five Points program provided a blueprint for councils to engage members in work beyond social activities. The councils that implemented this program helped revitalize the Order in the coming years. The Five Points were:

### 1. Catholic Activity

Encouraging involvement in Church-related events.

### 2. Council Activity

Encouraging involvement in council-related activities
(volunteer efforts, fundraisers, etc.).

### 3. Fraternal Protection

Maintaining member awareness of insurance benefits.

### 4. Publicity

Keeping the community informed of the work
of the Order and/or local councils.

### 5. Maintenance of Manpower

Maintaining memberships by doing all of the above.

## PROTESTING CONTINUED PERSECUTION IN MEXICO

Mexico's Cristero War, detailed in Chapter 3, officially ended in 1929, yet the governmental persecution of the Catholic Church continued. Pope Pius XI had written encyclicals condemning the persecutions in 1927 and again in 1932, and the Knights had long pressured the United States to take decisive action in defense of religious freedom there. Nevertheless, the Church in Mexico continued to suffer greatly under anti-clericalism. Before the war, approximately 4,500 priests had been serving Mexico, but by 1934, that number had dwindled to 334, and seventeen of the country's thirty-one states had no clergy at all. Nearly 4,200 priests had been killed or forced to leave the country. Churches were closed, religious education was forbidden, and the practice of religious faith faced legal restrictions.

"We all realize how fortunate America is, especially in these turbulent days . . . to have a strong militant body of Catholic laymen, banded together, to promote the activities of the Catholic Church, and to furnish a bulwark for the preservation of our priceless heritage of religious and civil liberty, not only in our own Nation, but throughout the American continent wherever that liberty may be assailed."

–Cardinal William O'Connell
in a letter to Supreme Knight
Carmody, January 8, 1936

As Mexican Catholics faced closed churches and persecution, the Order's leadership (here, working on a petition to US Secretary of State Hull) urged the US government to sever ties with Mexico unless its oppressive policies ended. Although the government was generally unresponsive, lobbying efforts raised public awareness of the issue.

In 1936, local Knights in the border town of Nogales, Arizona, turned an eye to the needs of those enduring persecution in Mexico. At Christmas time, the council provided those from the Mexican side of the border with necessities—including food, sweaters, and shoes—as well as Christmas trees and toys (shown here).

# John Edward "Jack" Reagan
## Notable Knight

A proud member of the Knights of Columbus, Jack Reagan was better known as the father of future Hollywood actor and fortieth President of the United States, Ronald Reagan. The grandson of Irish-Catholic immigrants from County Tipperary, Jack worked as a shoe salesman in Dixon, Illinois, where he lived with his wife, Nelle, and their two sons. Although the children would ultimately follow their mother's Presbyterian faith, Jack's deep love for his Catholic faith also made a strong impression on his boys. And while he served the Knights of Columbus without fanfare, he was responsible for instilling the values of the Order in Ronald and his brother, Neil.

John and Nelle Reagan
with sons Neil and Ronald.

During his presidency, Ronald Reagan spoke at the Order's 1986 Supreme Convention held in Chicago. He told the group, "I've had a place in my heart for the Knights of Columbus since I was a boy. You see, my father was a Knight, and he never missed an opportunity to express his pride in the K of C or join in its efforts on behalf of charity and tolerance."

The president went on to recall how his father had forbid the family from seeing D.W. Griffith's controversial and racially intolerant film *The Birth of a Nation* when it was playing in their hometown. "Dad told us that the movie portrayed the Ku Klux Klan in a favorable light, and that the Reagans were one family that wouldn't be seeing it. Even as a boy, I sensed that in taking that stand, my father had done something strong and good, something noble. To this day, I have never seen that famous movie."

John Reagan served the organization and his community quietly, without fanfare or spotlight.

As shown through his actions, he was a man of great principle, and he passed on those core values and convictions to his sons. Throughout his presidency, Reagan would continue to speak highly of the Knights of Columbus, thanks, in no small part, to the good example of his father. When the president spoke to the Knights, his words, always heartfelt and sincere, were a tribute to his dad.

Once, when addressing the members, he said, "All that you do as Knights of Columbus arises from the fundamental values you hold dear—your belief in a just and loving God, in the validity of hard work, in the central importance of the family. . . . As important as your works of charity are, however, you have also maintained individually and corporately your stalwart faith in religious and family values. Through activities such as the Catholic Information Service, you've stood unhesitatingly for these values. And that's why, for example, you were earnestly working for an end to racial and ethnic prejudice in America, fighting for justice for Blacks and Jews as well as for Catholics, and today you bring this same fervor to your work on behalf of the American family and religious values. In doing so, you provide inspiration to a world seeking desperately to find men who can make the message of the Gospel a reality in their lives . . ."

John Edward Reagan died in 1941 at the age of fifty-seven. It was at a time when Ronald was only beginning his film career and long before he entered politics. But John's proud service with the Knights made a lasting impression on his son, who is believed by many to be one of our greatest presidents.

Recognizing that the persecution in Mexico continued to occur, the Knights revived its advocacy efforts in demanding action from the US government. Along with pressuring the administration, they rallied American Catholics to do the same. As a result, the government found itself suddenly barraged with petitions, letters, and telegrams calling for defense of the beleaguered faithful in Mexico.

Supreme Knight Carmody urged President Roosevelt to get involved as well, and in July 1935, months after the request was made, Roosevelt agreed to meet with members of the Supreme Board. After hearing their concerns, the president promised to issue a public statement on the matter. When Roosevelt had not spoken out by October, Carmody wrote him a letter taking him to task. The president responded with a sharp refusal to interfere in another country's domestic affairs.

Historian Matthew Redinger notes that, although not all of their goals had been realized, the Knights "achieved the wider, unstated goals of increasing the United States government's interest in the persecution and inducing the government to formulate informal recommendations to the Mexican government."

## THE RISE OF NAZISM AND RUMORS OF WAR

Eight years before German tanks rolled into Poland in September 1939, the Knights of Columbus was already warning of the dangerous political and social ideologies growing in Europe. After World War I, the ceding of territories and the burden of reparations levied against the Central Powers in the Treaty of Versailles were exploited by Germany's National Socialist Party and its leader, Adolf Hitler. The toxic ideology of Nazism would bring the world to war and usher in the Holocaust—the systematic torture and slaughtering of 6 million European Jews. Although the Jewish population was specifically targeted, Catholics were not immune. Thousands of priests and many Catholic lay people were also killed at the hands of the Nazis.

The Order's representative in Rome, Count Enrico Galeazzi, kept Supreme Knight Carmody apprised of the situation in Germany. Particular attention was paid to the rising animosity against religion and religious people. Much like the anti-Catholic propaganda of the 1920s, the Nazis began using similar tactics to defame the Catholic Church. The year 1936 marked the beginning of such false accusations—all in an attempt to discredit the Church and reduce its influence on youth.

Joining the Jesuit journal *America* and the secular newsweekly *The Nation* in the outcry against the Nazi persecution of Catholics, the editors of *Columbia* published an editorial in July 1936 entitled "Malice in Naziland."

In 1937, President Franklin Roosevelt elevated Columbus Day to a federal holiday. Hailing the explorer, the president praised "the courage and the faith and the vision of the Genovese navigator," and cited Columbus as a symbol of future generations of immigrants and an example of perseverance.

In 1937, Pius XI issued the encyclical *Mit Brennender Sorge*, opposing Nazi ideology. Written substantially by Cardinal Pacelli (soon-to-be Pius XII), it was smuggled into Germany and read in the country's churches on Palm Sunday 1937. It defended human rights and condemned elements of Nazi ideology related to race, religion, and the state.

PUBLISHED MONTHLY BY
KNIGHTS OF COLUMBUS
MATTHEW T. BIRMINGHAM, General Manager
Executive Offices: New Haven, Conn.

Subscription: 1 Year, 60c—2 Years, $1.00

Advertising Dept.: 25 W. 43rd St., New York, N. Y.
DAVID J. GILLESPIE, Director

JOHN DONAHUE, Editor
Editorial Offices: New Haven, Conn.

Entered as second-class matter at the Post Office at New Haven, Conn., under the Act of March 3, 1879. Acceptance for mailing at special rate of postage provided for in Sec. 1103, Act of Oct. 3, 1917, authorized Aug. 19, 1922.

Manufactured in U. S. A. Copyright, 1936, by Knights of Columbus

# COLUMBIA
### The Largest Catholic Magazine in the World
(Trademark Reg. U. S. Patent Office)

## EDITORIALS

**Malice In Naziland**

IT IS never a source of great surprise for a Catholic to see his Church persecuted. The Church is the eternal stumbling block in the way of tyranny and it is natural that a stumbling block should be kicked. In Germany, the Church stands squarely across the path of the Nazi movement to establish what the *Osservatore Romano* has called "an authentic paganism." Clawing away at the Rock which is the Church, bumping their addled heads against it, the servants of the furious Fuehrer seem to have gone completely insane. It is difficult otherwise to account for the viciousness of the monstrous Nazi frame-up which has for its object the destruction of the German Catholics' faith in the moral integrity of their clergy. If it is the Nazi ambition to set a new standard of vileness in the persecution of the Church, it is being attained in the "trials" of the 276 members of the Order of St. Francis and the Congregation of Merciful Brethren, at Coblenz, on charges of immorality. The priest-hunters of Mexico and Russia can go to Berlin for postgraduate instruction in the technique of doing the dirtiest possible job in the dirtiest possible way.

News of the "trials" at Coblenz broke in the American press on May 27. It was not unexpected, for, in an interview published in *America*, March 21, Prince Lowenstein, who is living in this country because he would not live long in Germany, made this statement:

"The Nazis are now planning to launch a new assault upon the Church. There will be wholesale arrests of Catholic priests. There will be a series of trials spread out over a long period in which trumped-up—thoroughly faked—evidence of moral turpitude will be introduced against the priests. This new drive against the Church is scheduled to begin in the late summer after the Olympic games are finished. . . .

"Hundreds of faked photographs are already prepared. False witnesses are being rehearsed for their parts. Horrible charges will be lodged against many priests, and the sad part of the thing is that millions of Germans will believe the accusations, for you may be sure the clergy will not have any chance adequately to defend themselves and the German press will print only the manufactured Nazi evidence."

The prophecy is being fulfilled in every detail but one: eager for their plunge into the filth, the Nazi could not wait until after the Olympic Games. The apostate Goebbels, director of propaganda for the Nazi, probably knows by now, however, that his latest bid for sympathy in the persecution of the Church is more than merely ill-timed. Signs of backfire followed the publication of the first "trial" story almost instantly. The *Nation*, for example, said editorially in its June 10 issue:

"Germany's vicious lunge at the Roman church in the mass trial at Coblenz of 276 monks affords new evidence of the ruthless disregard of justice which characterizes the totalitarian state. Based on evidence which, as the outside world has known for some time, the Nazis have been busy faking and fabricating, wholesale charges of sexual perversion are being brought against the accused. Two have already been sentenced to four and eight years penal servitude, respectively, and in view of the fact that some witnesses for the prosecution are feeble-minded charity wards of the monasteries, there is little hope for the others.

"That the particular stick of immorality should be chosen by the authorities to beat the Catholics with bears testimony not only to their determination to break the power of the Roman church but also to discredit it in the eyes of the people. As the court proceedings are secret and the only reports which reach the public are official, the attack will be partially successful. This is the more true because the Catholic church has no weapon at hand but the courage of its leaders. In the days of the first Kulturkampf it could fight back through the powerful Centre Party, but since the dissolution of that party in 1933 and the suppression of the Catholic press the church is in no position to defeat Hitler as it did Bismarck."

This from the *Nation*, a paper which, by the way, will not feel offended if we remark that it is not inclined to give the Church more than half the road at any time.

There will be further news of "convictions" and "confessions" from the "trials" in Coblenz. It is improbable that they will have any effect other than to lower the already low regard in which the Nazi government is held by the rest of the world. The "trials" will be recognized for what they are: the most vicious phase of the campaign to destroy Christianity in Germany.

The first attack was directed against the Catholic societies in Germany, particularly against the Catholic youth organizations. It is practically obligatory for a young man today to be a member of a Hitler association if he would have any opportunity for success in the professions, commerce, or industry. The ultimatum is unveiled: "Leave your Church; abandon your Faith or live in poverty and in peril of imprisonment, torture and even death." To fight back, the Church may have, as the *Nation* says, "only the courage of its leaders," but some of the courage of Cardinal Faulhaber and the German Bishops seems to have a counterpart in the hearts of young German Catholics. In Munich, on the feast of Corpus Christi, June 11, a procession a mile and a half long, including members of Catholic youth organizations, wound its way through the main streets in a heavy downpour of rain.

Obviously unable, in the light of this and other public demonstrations of Faith, to frighten German Catholics into paganism, the Nazi gangsters are presently engaged in a campaign to persuade the people, especially the young, that their priests and nuns and brothers in religion are unworthy. The "currency trials," by which priests and nuns were thrown into jail for conscientiously paying debts contracted after the war for the construction of churches, monasteries and hospitals, were part of the same movement to discredit the shepherds in the eyes of the flock.

Said the Nazi: "See; your priests and nuns are lawless." The people said: "We see that they are honest."

At Coblenz, the Nazis say: "See; these men who guide you in your faith are immoral. We will show you the evidence."

The evidence proves something not in the minds of the Nazis when they framed up charges, photographs and witnesses: their own unspeakable vileness. In ancient times, Christians were thrown to the lions; in Naziland, anno Domini 1936, they are being thrown to the rats.

**That The Blind May Be Happy**

AMBASSADOR Francisco Castillo Najera arrived in Mexico City, June 13, to report on his mission to Washington. To reporters he distributed the standard "handout" statement that there are no problems between the United States and Mexico and that relations between the two countries have never been more cordial.

"Thanks to the spirit of understanding on the part of the American Government," said the Ambassador, "and the fact that it is converting into practice all its offers to maintain international harmony, there are no difficulties in our paths."

When we read the frequent statements, from both sides of the border, about the cordial relations officially existing between those dear old friendly neighbors, the United States and Mexico, the thought occurs to us that the late John Dillinger might still be a healthy and prosperous bandit if he had enjoyed the services of a good propagandist. If some patient instructor had taught him to lie as boldly and as gracefully as the Mexican Ambassador, he could have given out, between bank robberies, such statements as this:

"Thanks to the spirit of understanding on the part of the G-men and the fact that they are converting into practice all their offers to lay off my racket and go out to the ball game when I am shooting up bank clerks, our relations are cordial and there are no difficulties in my path."

We have had the big story about the "reopening of thousands of churches" in Mexico, which investigation showed to be one hundred percent false. We look forward to more encouraging, though faked, news about the Mexican situation, for there are those who would like to have Catholic citizens feel good at this time. Cheery words about "friendly neighbors" and soothing lies about "reopened churches," however, are just so much cologne on a dunghill—a treatment of the Mexican situation that will satisfy only the blind.

---

### Before Dawn
#### By KATHLEEN SUTTON

Within the early half-light, color is lost;
All things are sketched in pencil tones of gray,
And earth is still before its breadth is crossed
With all the bright confusions of the day.

Time moves unhurried; silence marks the hour.
The leafy boughs, concealing song and wing,
Betray no least suspicion of the power
Roused by the dawn's first startling upward swing.

Life waits; and in that strange, hushed interval
Between the lost and the not yet begun,
Peace tiptoes softly down the quiet hall,
A bird chirps sleepily—and night is done.

(See at left.) The article called attention to recent events in the ancient German city of Coblenz, where 176 Catholic priests and brothers from two religious orders had been arrested and tried on charges of "immorality" based on what the publications regarded as spurious and fabricated evidence. As the editorial noted, the evidence highlighted the "unspeakable vileness" of the Nazis.

Along with this editorial, *Columbia* published many articles expressing the Knights' growing concern over the alarming ideology and deplorable tactics of the Nazis. It was a concern that encompassed not only the Nazi's treatment of Catholics, but also their appalling actions against European Jews.

## SPEAKING OUT FOR GERMAN JEWS

During the prewar years of the late 1930s, a number of Jewish organizations urged President Roosevelt to take action in support of the European Jewish refugees. Their efforts, however, were unsuccessful. In late 1938, the Jewish War Veterans reached out to the Knights of Columbus (and Supreme Knight Carmody in particular) for help.

Carmody responded that October by writing a letter to President Roosevelt on behalf of the Jewish refugees. It read in part:

> The Order of the Knights of Columbus, embracing five hundred thousand members, moved by the same sentiments of fair play and justice that have prompted it to protest on different occasions persecution by governments and fanatical groups of peoples of various faiths who sought only the enjoyment of their God-given right to worship their Creator in accordance with the dictates of their conscience, expresses the deepest sympathy for the distressed Jews of Europe, and most respectfully urges our Government to use its influence to preserve in its full meaning, force, and intent the Palestine mandate that guarantees to the Jews, now sadly persecuted in Europe, the right unhampered to seek refuge and protection in the homeland of their forefathers. In order that the bonds that bind all peoples in human fellowship may not be destroyed, we urge in the name of humanity that prompt action be taken.

In his reply, President Roosevelt wrote to Carmody expressing his "sympathy" for the cause, but further explained that there was little he could do unless American interests were involved. While the letter did not change US policy, it demonstrated the Order's ongoing commitment to religious freedom—not just for Catholics, but for anyone facing religious persecution.

In 1938, after running successful blood drives at the local level for nearly a decade, the Knights of Columbus launched what many regard as the first blood donor program sponsored by a national organization, with hundreds of councils forming donor groups throughout the country.

World War II began when Hitler's army attacked Poland in an air and land "blitz" on September 1, 1939, quickly overrunning its defenses, but also drawing the UK and France into the war against Germany. The war between the Allies and the Axis powers would grind on until 1945.

# THE KNIGHTS AND THE GROWING THREAT OF COMMUNISM

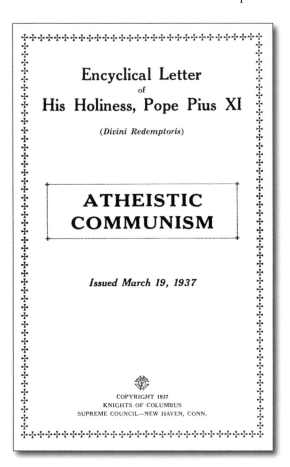

Encyclical Letter
of
**His Holiness, Pope Pius XI**

*(Divini Redemptoris)*

**ATHEISTIC COMMUNISM**

*Issued March 19, 1937*

COPYRIGHT 1937
KNIGHTS OF COLUMBUS
SUPREME COUNCIL—NEW HAVEN, CONN.

In 1937, Pope Pius XI warned of the dangers of Nazism and communism in encyclicals published days apart. He confronted Nazism with *Mit Brennender Sorge*, and communism with *Divini Redemptoris*.

As the Knights and the pope continued to speak out against Nazism, they remained cognizant of another threat as well. As the 1930s wound down, support for the Communist party had begun to spread throughout parts of Europe and even the United States. The Communist agenda was increasingly evident—a combination of hostility to religion, a brutal totalitarian regime, and the promise of equal distribution of wealth. Having confronted Nazism in *Mit Brennender Sorge* on Palm Sunday 1937, just days later, in his encyclical *Divini Redemptoris*, Pope Pius XI warned that communism took on "the most seductive trappings." He wrote:

> Bolshevistic and atheistic Communism . . . aims at upsetting the social order and at undermining the very foundations of Christian civilization. In the face of such a threat, the Catholic Church could not and does not remain silent. . . . [We have] not refrained from raising its voice, for it knows that its proper and social mission is to defend truth, justice and all those eternal values which Communism ignores or attacks.

With communism threatening to "sharpen the antagonisms which arise between the various classes of society," as well as destroy anyone or any organization that denies the importance of this "crusade for the progress of humanity," the Holy Father's encyclical called all Catholics to protect the foundation of Christianity and civilization as a whole. The Knights of Columbus would soon embark on a campaign focused on exposing the dangers of communism.

At the very least, the Knights' efforts were effective in worrying the Communist party at large. In the late 1930s, the *Daily Worker*, the official newspaper of the Communist Party USA, published a variety of articles targeting the Knights of Columbus. The attack only fueled the determination of Carmody and the Order, with several councils continuing to successfully expose Communist-dominated projects.

Carmody raised the *Daily Worker's* attacks during the 1937 Supreme Convention, and soon the Order hired George Hermann Derry to deliver a national lecture series on how the socialist ideology stood in direct opposition to Catholic social thought. Derry had been a member of the Knights of Columbus Historical Commission. He was president of Marygrove College, and had taught previously at Bryn Mawr College and Marquette University. Though anti-Communist, he was also solidly anti-Fascist. He once quipped, "If I don't like Russian caviar, that is no proof that I like Italian spaghetti." He

In response to Pope Pius XII's petition for prayers for peace, the Knights of Columbus sponsored an international Prayer-for-Peace Program on Armistice Day, November 11, 1939. The following year, the Knights sponsored a radio broadcast on May 19, again petitioning prayers for peace.

As families wrestled with the financial crisis of the Great Depression, the Order also felt its effect, losing about a third of its membership, which dropped to 419,000 in 1940. The Order's insurance service faired a little better by comparison, losing 8 percent of insurance in force, which totalled $256 million in 1940.

explained that "Communism hides behind the smokescreen of name calling. Everyone who opposes Communism is labeled a 'Fascist,'" and added that the two ideologies had much in common: "Politically, both stand for the omnipotent, totalitarian, bureaucratic state. Both contend that man exists for the State, not that the State is the servant to man."

That same year, the Knights launched another initiative—the Crusade for Social Justice. This new effort, which likewise addressed the perils of communism, proposed a solution: The application of Christian principles to private and public affairs. Paul McGuire, a noted Catholic Action lecturer from Australia, joined Derry as the primary speakers for this new campaign. The Order also continued to promote Catholic social teaching drawn from Pope Pius XI's encyclicals and to advocate programs that focused on the true social responsibilities of Christians.

## A CHANGE IN LEADERSHIP ON THE EVE OF WAR

Against the backdrop of a global depression, and with another world war looming on the horizon, the 1930s posed many challenges. However, during the twelve years Martin Carmody served as supreme knight, the Order helped the unemployed find jobs, ran charitable initiatives for those in economic distress, helped re-energize a declining membership, and consistently stood up for religious freedom at home, in Mexico, and in Europe. Carmody delivered his final address as supreme knight at the 1939 Supreme Council meeting in Seattle, Washington. In it, he looked to the future, hoping against hope for peace. Echoing Pope Pius XII's Easter address given earlier that year, he urged the following of his brother knights:

> Since external peace cannot but be a reflection of internal peace of conscience, procure it if one does not have it, guard it and cultivate it if one has it.

Carmody also referred to George Washington's farewell address to the nation, urging President Roosevelt to "observe good faith and justice toward other nations" and to "cultivate peace and harmony with all."

Peace was not to be. Germany invaded Poland less than a month later, and the world was again at war. Leading the Knights through this turbulent period would be Carmody's successor, Francis P. Matthews. An accomplished attorney, the Nebraska-born Matthews—who had served as deputy supreme knight for six years—was the first supreme knight born west of the Mississippi River. Bringing with him a mix of legal and financial experience, he would shoulder a number of additional career responsibilities during his tenure as supreme knight, including his work as a consultant for the Reconstruction Finance Corporation (a Depression-era federal lending agency), and his work as a director of the US Chamber of Commerce for the Department of Finance.

Matthews would guide the Order from the Great Depression into World War II. Although it had profoundly hoped for peace, as in World War I, the Order would support the United States and Canada in a global war, leading by example in its commitment to freedom and its support of the war effort.

**Francis P. Matthews**
Eighth supreme knight.

That even in war, we may keep clearly before us the defense of all human rights, especially the right to life, liberty, and the pursuit of happiness."

– From a "Prayer for Troops"

# 6.
# War and Peace
## 1940 to 1950

As the world headed to war and the Holocaust accelerated in Europe, the Knights were acutely aware of the stakes. In the late 1930s, the Order had spoken out about the persecution of Jews in Germany, with Supreme Knight Carmody writing President Roosevelt to express concern and urge action. Concerns about Nazism were also expressed in *Columbia* magazine, and the Knights also joined a number of Jewish organizations in protesting a speech by German Ambassador Hans Luther, whose speaking tour featured a soft-pedaling of German intentions. The Knights' concerns about Nazism were hardly surprising given the organization's long dedication to the principles of racial and religious tolerance.

As war broke out in Europe, America, behind the relative safety of the Atlantic Ocean, faced an uneasy peace, uncertain if it too would be drawn into the growing conflict overseas. The prospect of war—just a generation after the terrible toll exacted by World War I—gave many people pause. Concern was one thing, going to war another. Even after the Nazis had invaded Poland, and Japan had begun attacking its neighbors, most Catholics in the United States still hoped and prayed that America could avoid the horrors of war. In October 1939, a statement of the US Bishops noted: "The first line of defense against the involvement of our own nation in the misery of war is aloofness from emotional entanglements. Our primary duty is that of preserving the strength, stability, and sincerity of our own nation." Even weeks before Pearl Harbor, a survey found that more than nine in ten American priests opposed American involvement in the war.

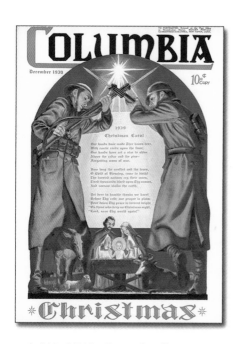

As World War II raged in Europe, *Columbia*'s December 1939 cover featured a painting of two soldiers with their bayonets crossed over the Holy Family.

Shortly after the onset of World War II, the Canadian Knights established an Army hut program for soldiers in 1939. The program was similar to the huts project run by the Order during World War I. Within a year, the group had raised nearly $250,000 to support this initiative.

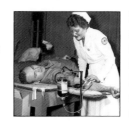

In 1940, scientific advances by Edwin Cohn and others changed the future of blood transfusions, by isolating blood components and improving usability, stability, and bottling. The practice of donating, built through programs like the Knights' blood donor groups, proved essential to combating the blood loss, which accounted for the majority of combat deaths.

During those early years of the conflict, the debate over the prospect of war overseas also generated attention within the Order. Supreme Knight Carmody hoped for peace, and a prayer program for this intention was initiated in the late 1930s. Hitler, however, was intent on conquest. The war—and all its horror—intensified, making American involvement a real possibility.

In 1940, newly elected Supreme Knight Francis Matthews led nationally broadcast prayers for peace. To Canadian Knights, already at war, he also offered praise for their Army huts work, stating that "Our respective ideals and ability to exist as free peoples will survive or perish together." Pearl Harbor soon decisively settled the matter of American involvement, and—as in WWI—the Knights' patriotism would be exemplary.

## WORLD WAR II AND THE CANADIAN KNIGHTS

**Dr. Claude Brown**
Supreme Director,
Canada.

While the United States had managed to avoid the conflict prior to the Pearl Harbor attack, Canada became involved in September of 1939 following Germany's invasion of Poland. Under the leadership of Supreme Director Dr. Claude Brown, the Knights in Canada immediately began planning war relief efforts. A committee was formed for the specific purpose of establishing an Army huts program similar to the one run by the Order during World War I.

By late 1939, the committee, along with civic and church leaders, had created its own huts program approved by the Canadian government. Then came the formation of an organization that included the Knights, the YMCA, The Salvation Army, and the Canadian Legion. Together, this coalition raised $7 million for a variety of programs, including the Canadian Army Huts. The huts program featured recreation centers in large Canadian cities and morale-boosting programs in army training camps and hostels. Troops in England, Iceland, Italy, Hong Kong, and the Middle East were also welcome to enjoy the services provided by the huts program. Thanks to a flower delivery service run by the Order, soldiers were able to send flowers to their loved ones back home. One year, over 50,000 bouquets were sent on Mother's Day alone. Nearly 200 Canadian knights volunteered for the army hut program, including Brown himself, who served as a lieutenant colonel. He was killed in 1941 as a result of a German bombing raid in England.

The huts also tended to the spiritual welfare of the servicemen, offering religious services, as well as reading material and articles. According to the 1945 annual report of the K of C Canadian Army Huts, requests for 366,101 rosaries, 4,000 missals, and 713,415 prayer books had been filled.

In 1941, a continental prayer for peace was held at the Shrine of Our Lady of Guadalupe in Mexico City. The Knights served as the honor guard of the historic event, which brought together representatives from twenty North and South American countries who prayed for Mary's "maternal protection" for the American continent.

On December 7, 1941, debates over US involvement in the war became settled when 2,300 Americans died in Japan's bombing of Pearl Harbor. The Order also lost its first American member, Ensign William Halloran, inspiring the Knights to raise $6 million in war bonds for the USS Halloran.

Perhaps the Canadian Knights' service was best summed up by Supreme Director Brown, who wrote a letter to the people of Canada in January of 1941:

*In establishing the Knights of Columbus Canadian Army Huts in order to assist in the maintenance of morale amongst the Canadian Forces in Canada and overseas, the Knights of Columbus are continuing the work carried on by them in the Great War.*

*In England at the present time, I am supervising the work of fourteen representatives of this organization. We are not operating in any of the cities or towns, but we may be found with the men in the lines and barracks, and where the soldier reads "K of C War Services" he knows irrespective of his race or creed, he will be welcomed and find everything free.*

*Some 75,000 letters a month are written in our Huts on stationery supplied free by our representative. Canadian cigarettes and other creature comforts are given gratis. Equipment for outdoor games is distributed and our supervisor directs such games as football, rugby, volleyball, horseshoes and badminton.*

*I would like to stress the fact that we are doing everything possible to cooperate with the other organizations engaged in work similar to our own. . . . I have every reason to believe that this mutual good will existing amongst the Canadian organizations working with the Canadian overseas troops will continue until victory is ours.*

Traveling from Canada on a British bomber, Supreme Knight Matthews visited England to personally review the Knights' war work there. During that time, he survived two German air raids. He visited the Canadian Army Huts operating there, and met with government officials, as well as members of the Catholic laity and hierarchy. Matthews reported in *Columbia* in April, 1943: "Everybody says that the Knights of Columbus work is indispensable to the Canadian forces." And it wasn't only the supreme knight who recognized this work. As in the United States during World War I, so impressed were the Catholic men of Canada that the pre-war number of Canadian Knights doubled shortly after the war's end.

Like the huts established by the Knights during WWI, the Canadian Army Huts were both recreational and spiritual centers for the troops.

To support troop morale, the United Service Organizations (USO) was formed in 1941. Much like the Knights' WWI huts, USO clubs nationwide provided troops with a place to gather, relax, and socialize. Supreme Knight Matthews (seen here pouring coffee for a soldier) served as Catholic representative to the USO until 1944.

On the home front, the government began food rationing in 1942. With restrictions on buying meat, dairy, sugar, and coffee, people began growing produce in what became known as "victory gardens." Massachusetts' Winchester Council 210 planted and cared for the victory garden pictured here to help the Sisters of St. Joseph.

# THE WINDS OF WAR IN THE UNITED STATES

As the war ground on in Europe, and especially after the defeat of France, Americans became increasingly concerned about the possibility of an Axis victory and looked more favorably on peacetime military recruitment. In 1940, the United States took a major step in preparedness when Congress passed the Selective Service Act. In one fell swoop, millions of men in their prime registered for the country's first peacetime draft and faced the possibility of war in their futures. Two decades after World War I, separation from families and confronting war's atrocities were experiences already deeply familiar with one generation, and were becoming generational; eventually, one in five would serve.

Seeing that American involvement in the war seemed increasingly likely, Supreme Knight Matthews met with Archbishop Samuel Stritch of Chicago—

Executive Committee of the National Catholic Community Service (NCCS), 1941. Supreme Knight Matthews appears second from left.

the Chairman of the National Catholic Welfare Conference (NCWC), which had its origins in the Catholics' response to the First World War. Made up of bishops and other members of the clergy, the NCWC conferred on matters of significance that required a national response by the Catholic Church in the United States. Matthews suggested that the Order sponsor "huts" as it had done during World War I, and as the Canadian Order was presently doing. The bishops, however, decided that this time, rather than entrusting the work to a single organization, a new entity—supported by a variety of Catholic organizations—would represent the Catholic response in the United Service Organizations (USO). This resulted in the formation of the National Catholic Community Service (NCCS).

Things sometimes moved slowly, especially in terms of the creation of programs by the NCCS, which did not want to get ahead of the government's plans. Nonetheless, the Order remained involved in the NCCS, and both Matthews and Supreme Advocate Luke Hart accepted committee positions. Matthews served as chairman of the Executive Committee and its representative in the USO, while Hart held positions on a number of other committees.

The NCCS established recreational centers throughout the country that were run by the USO with the support of several groups, including the Knights. Familiar with staging social events and entertaining the troops from their experiences during World War I, the Knights played an integral part in organizing and staffing many of these centers. And in those areas of the coun-

The 1942 fall of Bataan to the Japanese was the beginning of suffering for nearly 75,000 Filipino and American prisoners there. The prisoners' transfer to Camp O'Donnell in Capas would become known as the Bataan Death March. About 54,000 survived the march. Thousands more died at the camp itself.

During WWII, the Knights frequently denounced Nazism and anti-Semitism in *Columbia* magazine as well as in a Supreme Convention resolution. One *Columbia* article quoted Pope Pius XII, saying: "Through Christ and in Christ we are Abraham's descendants. No, it is not possible for Christians to take part in anti-Semitism. Spiritually we are Jews."

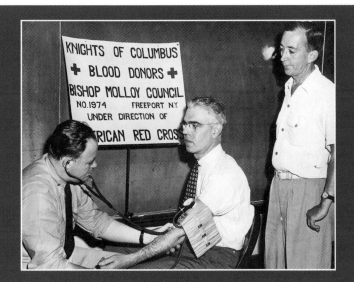

try without these centers, local councils typically formed their own—often in their meeting facilities—and sponsored activities and events for area soldiers. In some cases, they received financial support from the USO.

In addition to its active involvement as part of the NCCS, the Order also initiated a number of noteworthy programs of its own during the war, with the blood donor program among its most significant. Originating in 1938 by Minnesota's St. Paul Council 397, the service expanded throughout the nation during the war. Preceding the Red Cross's wartime blood drive by two years, the program was widely acknowledged as the first of its kind. In conjunction with local hospitals, council members actively campaigned for donors, who gave blood in centers that had been set up by the Knights. Recognizing the ongoing need for blood donations, the Order continued this valuable program after the war. Still active today, the Knights of Columbus blood drives collect an average of over 400,000 pints of blood annually.

During the war, the Knights also raised millions of dollars selling war bonds to help support military needs. Reports indicate that the members themselves bought a great number of US bonds or comparable Canadian certificates with councils averaging purchases of over $1,000. The Supreme Council also purchased a significant amount. By the end of the war, the Order

During the war, blood donations were a vital lifeline for wounded troops. Pioneered in the 1930s with council-based groups of donors ready to give at a moment's notice, the Order's blood donor program was widely adopted by councils nationwide.

Although USO staff served American troops on the warfront, on the home front, the Knights offered support by serving in USO facilities and by supplying items for the spiritual and temporal needs of troops, including portable Mass kits for chaplains and Christmas gifts for soldiers.

Posters encouraging the sale of war bonds fill the window of this store-front headquarters in Rochester, New York. Throughout the war, the Knights sold these bonds at rallies, through ads in *Columbia,* and at the many war-bond headquarters that had been set up throughout the country.

held roughly $16 million in war bonds. The money was used for a number of notable military projects. One was the building of the *William Tyler,* a Liberty ship named in honor of the first Catholic bishop of Hartford (whose diocese included Rhode Island). Sponsored by the Rhode Island Knights, who collectively sold $2 million in bonds, the *William Tyler* was launched in August 1944.

Another important program established by the Order during the war years was the Educational Trust Fund. Later renamed the Matthews & Swift Educational Trust Scholarships (named for Supreme Knights Francis P. Matthews and John E. Swift), this $1 million fund provided scholarship opportunities for the sons and daughters of members who either were killed in action during the war or died within ten years of the war's termination. At the 1944 annual convention, the Supreme Council voted in favor of the fund, for which members contributed twenty-five cents semi-annually.

Although it was established initially for the families of World War II veterans, the fund was extended in 1956, 1964, 1991, 2004, and 2007. The extensions encompassed other combat zones throughout the world, including Korea, Vietnam, Cyprus, the Persian Gulf, Iraq, Afghanistan, and Pakistan. And the scholarships were extended to children of members who were full-time law enforcement officers or firefighters killed by criminal violence while performing their duties.

The Knights' US-based initiatives benefited both the soldiers and their families during the war and even after the conflict ended. The following

The year 1943 marked the first year of positive membership growth in seventeen years, increasing by 13,000. Supreme Knight Matthews credited Charles Ducey and the Five Points Program (page 105) for this success. Council 787 in Galveston, pictured here, was one of many that recruited servicemen during the war.

One of the significant military projects financed by the Knights' war bond sales was the building of the *William Tyler,* a Liberty ship named in honor of the first Catholic bishop of Hartford (whose diocese included both Connecticut and Rhode Island). Sponsored by the Knights of Rhode Island, the ship was launched in August 1944.

excerpt from the 1942 Supreme Knight's report acknowledges a number of these efforts:

> Councils and individual members of the Order in the United States have with commendable unostentation exerted immeasurable effort to support and supplement the work of the National Catholic Community Service on behalf of the men of the Army, the Navy and the Marines. Councils in every part of the country have, with prodigal generosity, placed their club houses, equipment, revenues and man power at the disposal of the needs of men in uniform and with no official capacity or recognition are enthusiastically making a notably patriotic contribution in this vital field of national service.
>
> Likewise, our members are identified with every other movement which is promoted in support of the government's program to win the war. They are assisting in the sale of war bonds, in civilian defense efforts, in supplying blood banks through our blood donor units, in the Red Cross work and in local and national enterprises in a variety of forms, the sole purpose of which is to bring the might and power of a united citizenship to bear in defense of our liberties and in the destruction of the current tyrannical enemies of mankind.

The Knights took great pride in the work they did during World War II, just as they had done during the previous war. But the Order's greatest hope was that such war efforts would be replaced by peacetime pursuits.

Colorful posters encouraging the sale of war bonds were common sights during the war.

# THE PEACE PROGRAM

Even while supporting the war effort, the Knights laid the groundwork for a lasting peace. Here, the Order's Peace Program committee, chaired by Deputy Supreme Knight John Swift, meets with clergy in New York in 1943.

Two years before the United States became involved in World War II, Pope Pius XII issued a Christmas message in 1939 that outlined the basic principles for peace. The Knights responded immediately by organizing an international prayer for peace program and related radio broadcast. Confronting ideologies such as Nazism and communism, the Church was concerned that a purely secular approach to peace would not be successful. In November 1942, less than a year after the attack on Pearl Harbor, the American bishops issued a pastoral letter warning that "secularism cannot write a real or lasting peace."

Influenced by both the pope's message and the letter from the American bishops, the Knights set out to establish a blueprint for building a lasting peace based on Catholic principles. The Supreme Board of Directors formed a special committee in January 1943. Chaired by then-Deputy Supreme Knight John Swift, the group gathered input from the Catholic hierarchy and leading Catholic scholars, as well as theologians, philosophers, and sociologists. It was, in effect, an effort to lay the moral and ethical foundation for a "just peace" to be negotiated for all parties—victors and vanquished alike—once the present war was ended.

The prevailing concern was avoiding the mistakes of the past. The harsh war reparations and territorial divisions determined at the Treaty of Versailles after the First World War were largely punitive measures levied against Germany and the Central Powers. By contrast, the Knights proposed that lasting peace could come only "if the people of the world who become parties to the peace treaty, whole-heartedly accept the principles that embody these God-given rights."

The plan explicitly rejected Nazism, fascism, and communism for their "spurious view of the common good." It called for the rights of all nations, great and small, to exist. Against the backdrop of the Holocaust, and consistent with the Knights' long-standing support of racial equality, the plan called for "guarantees to all religious, racial, and cultural minorities, of full enjoyment of all the God-given rights of man."

The Peace Program gave war-weary Catholics a hopeful roadmap for the future. Its insightful treatment of the issue of peace also captured the attention of the Catholic press. Among these was *Catholic World,* which published the entire peace program in the magazine's October issue. The October 11, 1943 issue of the *Boston Pilot* included a story entitled "Basis on Which Peace Must Be Built." It began by stating:

In 1943, the massacre of Polish officers in the Katyn Forest, carried out three years earlier, was discovered. Initially, Soviet disinformation shifted blame onto the Nazis, limiting Allied criticism. In 1948, *Columbia* magazine denounced the Soviet perpetrators as war criminals and decried their escape from prosecution as such.

In 1944, the Order created a $1 million Catholic college scholarship fund for the children of members who died in war service. This evolved into the Matthews & Swift Scholarships. President Truman lauded the Order for being "unwearied in their labors in the cause of education, particularly [on] behalf of war orphans."

The Peace Program proposed by the Knights of Columbus is a plan which ought to be studied by every statesman in the group called the United Nations. . . .

The commentary went on to say:

The characteristic feature of this Peace Plan, its brave uniqueness, is its ringing statement of fundamental principles. Were these principles accepted, the thousand practical problems of the peace would solve themselves.

Echoing the historic perspective of the Order on issues such as race, religious freedom, and the importance of God-given rights, the Knights made clear that a peace without God would not be a real peace. As the war went on and the full extent of the Holocaust became known, and with half of Europe suffering behind the Iron Curtain following the war, the Knights' proposed program for peace proved to be prophetic.

This patriotic cover of *Columbia's* June 1942 issue featured the Knights' high-profile war bond drive to help support our fighting troops. Along with encouraging the purchase of war bonds and war stamps, the issue urged Americans to support the USO.

At the close of WWII, *Columbia* turned its attention to the return of the soldiers and their transition back to civilian life. The cover of the October 1945 issue pictures a man trying to fit back into his clothes after returning home from the war.

# UNDER FIRE IN ROME

During this wartime period, the Order's representative in Rome, Count Enrico Galeazzi, served as a liaison between the Vatican and the United States. Over the previous decades, he had not only helped build and manage the Knights of Columbus recreation centers in the city, but also became the Vatican's Special Delegate of the Pontifical Commision of Vatican City State from 1939 to 1968. In that role, he undertook a number of responsibilities related to the efforts of the Holy See. This pitted him directly against Nazi troops in Rome on at least one occasion. When Nazi forces approached the Basilica of St. Paul outside the Walls—sovereign Vatican territory that was harboring Jews—Galeazzi stood before the entrance and blocked them from entering. He made clear that invading this territory would create an international incident. The German forces turned back, and the Jewish people taking refuge inside the basilica remained safe.

The war affected the Knights in Rome, where the Order continued to run the youth recreation facilities. With the United States and Italy at war, the centers were in hostile territory. In spite of their precarious position, they rose above the trials of war through charitable outreach to the Italian people.

As the war spilled onto Italian soil, preserving Rome became a serious concern for the Holy See. It was the wish of Pope Pius XII to convince both the Axis and Allied nations to respect Rome as an "Open City" and spare it from bombings. The Allied forces did, however, bomb the city twice in 1943. The second bombing hit the San Lorenzo district, taking more than a thousand civilian lives and injuring thousands more. The Order's San Lorenzo playground was damaged and much of the surrounding neighborhood was destroyed. Joined by Count Galeazzi, the pope immediately made his way to the playground, where he joined the people of Rome in prayer.

The pope then wrote a letter to President Roosevelt asking him to spare Rome from further Allied bombing. He sent Galeazzi to Washington, DC, to deliver the letter personally. Although Roosevelt declined to see Galeazzi, the message he carried was no secret, and Rome was not bombed by the Allies again after March of 1944. In June of 1944, Allied forces were finally able to liberate the Eternal City.

Upon hearing of the bombing of Rome's San Lorenzo district, Pope Pius XII immediately made his way to the Knights' playground there. He met with the people and led them in prayer.

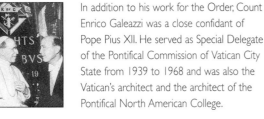

In addition to his work for the Order, Count Enrico Galeazzi was a close confidant of Pope Pius XII. He served as Special Delegate of the Pontifical Commission of Vatican City State from 1939 to 1968 and was also the Vatican's architect and the architect of the Pontifical North American College.

In 1943, famed author H.G. Wells penned an anti-Catholic screed entitled *Crux Ansata—An Indictment of the Roman Catholic Church*, which, among other things, called for the bombing of Rome. Ironically, a few months later, bombs did fall upon the city, causing death and destruction. The bomb fragments pictured here were found on the Order's property there.

Even as America and Italy battled on opposite sides of the global conflict, the Knights' recreational facilities continued to function and serve the people. The playground near St. Peter's Basilica became the headquarters for the pope's program to feed the people of Rome. Food was distributed to 400,000 people there each day. Other playgrounds also served as food and clothing distribution centers for those suffering from wartime shortages. When the war ended, the Knights' facilities continued to serve as centers for charitable outreach: the United Nations Relief and Rehabilitation Agency used the field near the Vatican as a food distribution center for the children of Rome, where thousands were fed each day.

The American bishops recognized the Knights' readiness to assist their Italian brothers and sisters in need. They praised them for their active role in war relief, as well as their part in rebuilding what had been destroyed during the war. In 2010, the mayor of Rome recognized the Order's charitable work during and after the war, and thanked them for helping "save the city."

The Knights' playground in Rome near St. Peter's Basilica served as a food distribution center by the Vatican during the war, and by the United Nations Relief and Rehabilitation Agency (UNRRA) after the war ended.

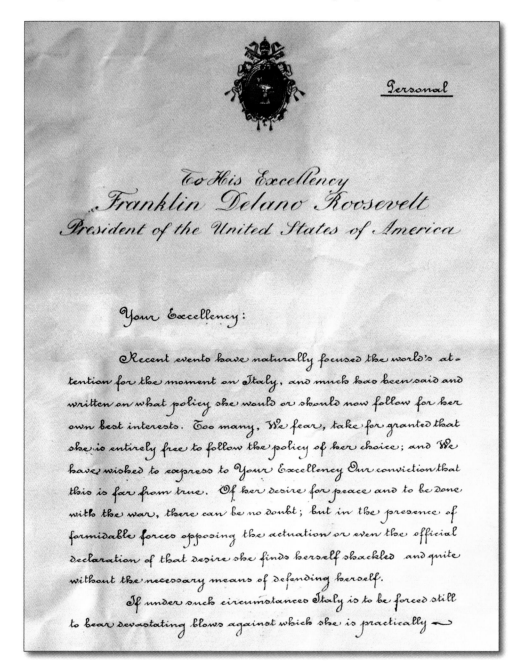

After the Allied bombing raids on Rome in 1943, Pope Pius XII wrote a letter to President Roosevelt, asking him to spare Rome from any further bombing. Enrico Galeazzi carried the letter to America, and although the president declined to meet with him, the contents of the letter were known and had an effect.

## THE KNIGHTS OF MANILA

The Knights provided charity in the Pacific theater as well. After the war, Father George Willmann recounted the K of C experience in *Columbia* magazine. He wrote:

> In mid-1941, war clouds appeared on the horizon. Remembering the glorious soldier-aid record of the Knights of Columbus in World War I, Manila Knights turned their attention to the thousands of American soldiers and sailors arriving in the Philippines. . . . Needless to say, Everybody Welcome, Everything Free was the rule.

Even after the Japanese took control of Manila and all seemed lost, Father Willmann noted:

> Our Knights of Columbus apostolic committee, however, refused to die. Just two days before the Japanese entry to Manila, the Archbishop had entrusted to the Knights the entire operation of Santa Rita Hall [which] became a haven for fire refugees from burnt–out sections of Manila, for students and other 'provincianos' unable to return to their provinces, and for marooned sailors or survivors of ships lying at the bottom of Manila Bay. At one time in 1941, it was sheltering refugees of ten nationalities. Then came April, 1942, the Fall of Bataan, and the unspeakable Death March to Camp O'Donnell. Spearheaded by our valiant, even reckless K of C Brother Enrique Albert, later executed by the Japanese, we joined the underground to smuggle medicines and other supplies into the infamous prison camp.

One night alone, 300 people, whose attempt to escape Manila by boat ended disastrously when the boat hit a mine, were sent to the K of C building. There, Father Willmann "had to supply, out of nothing, food, shelter, occupation, peace and order."

Everything changed in late 1941. On December 8, the day after the bombing of Pearl Harbor, Japanese planes attacked Clark Field on the Philippine island of Luzon. Two days later, they struck Nichols Field on the outskirts of Manila. By Christmas, Japanese forces were sweeping across the Philippine Islands, and by early March, they had captured Manila. When the Japanese military marched American prisoners "emaciated, limping, in rags," the Knights "rushed out with cooling drinks." But such acts became increasingly difficult. As a result of the Japanese occupation of the Philippines, the K of C buildings were either shut down or destroyed, and the Knights were temporarily forced to cease both their Army hut work and their outreach for the country's youth.

Nevertheless, the Knights continued their mission of charity. They reopened some clubs, offering sports, catechism, and academic pursuits like

**Father George J. Willmann**
The "Father McGivney of the Philippines"

On April 12, 1945, Vice President Harry S. Truman was sworn in as the country's thirty-third president after the sudden death of Franklin Roosevelt. He supported the Order's concern about the rise of communism. He would also appoint former Supreme Knight Matthews Secretary of the Navy.

During the war, Manila Council 1000 served soldiers, refugees, and POWs with ingenuity and bravery. After the war, the council led the Knights in the Philippines through a period of growth and charitable action. Here, council members gather before the Cebu Center for a Third Degree initiation in April 1947.

# Philippine Knights Aid the POWs
## Visionary Council Initiative

Although World War II, and especially the Japanese occupation of the Philippines, interrupted formal council functions, the Knights of Manila Council 1000 continued to work together, creatively and courageously, as Knights of Columbus. Of special note was their response to some of the war's most infamous atrocities: the notorious Bataan Death March and its internment destination, Camp O'Donnell.

The 1942 fall of Bataan led to the capture of approximately 75,000 Filipino and American prisoners by the Imperial Japanese Army. The POWs were then marched some seventy miles north to San Fernando. As they marched, the prisoners met with unrelenting cruelty, including severe physical abuse, lack of food and water, and various forms of torture. The transfer continued by rail from San Fernando to Capas in sweltering metal box cars, and finished off on foot to Camp O'Donnell.

As the prisoners marched, members of Manila Council 1000 risked their lives to try to help them. They would sneak up to the line and give the prisoners water and medical attention. While these may seem like small acts of compassion, they were true acts of bravery, for anyone caught helping the men would be punished. Take the case of brother Knight Antonio Escoda, who, along with his wife, was captured and killed for aiding the prisoners.

At Camp O'Donnell, the POWs suffered from starvation, lack of sanitation, and brutality at the hands of their captors, just as they had during their journey. Dysentery and other illnesses spread throughout the camp, and prisoners died by the hundreds each day. The Knights continued to aid the POWs and also assisted Father Willmann and brother Knight Enrique Albert, who worked to smuggle medicine into the camp.

Outside the camp's stockade, the Knights set up the "K of C Rest House." There, they offered care and shelter to prisoners' families, who would come to seek news of their loved ones. The Knights also tended those prisoners whom the Japanese guards would sometimes free due to severe illness.

In his article that appeared in *Columbia*, Father Willmann wrote of the Knights' efforts: "Braving the explicit prohibition of the [Japanese] military, many Brother Knights participated in this glorious work." Putting their own lives at risk, they proved their unwavering dedication to their fellow man and to their country.

"To me, the Knights of Columbus has never been just a mere insurance organization or a super business machine, and I have never considered it . . . a mere vehicle through which to convey honors upon individuals or to elevate persons to position of power . . . The Knights of Columbus to me has always been . . . first and before everything else, an institution of unselfish service . . . to God . . . to country, and . . . to human beings."

–Supreme Knight Francis Matthews
Supreme Knight's Report, 1943

reading and study clubs. When prisoners who had survived the torturous Bataan Death March were interned at Camp O'Donnell in Capas, the Knights cared for their families. (See "Visionary Council Initiative," page 125.)

After Manila was liberated by the US Army in 1945, under the guidance of Father Willmann, the remaining Knights set out to build a club for the American soldiers. This was no simple project as the city had been devastated by the fighting. There was no means of transportation, no phones, no supplies, no furniture, and no equipment. In the words of Father Willmann, "We started with twenty-five dollars in capital and nothing else." Starting from scratch, the group of determined Knights improvised, scrounging for items to create a makeshift oasis in the middle of the devastation. Thanks to the generosity of a local parish priest, Divine Word Missionary Father Antonio Albrecht, an empty parish hall was donated as the site for the club. And in March of that year, its doors were opened to welcome the troops. This new club was the only place for miles where battle-worn soldiers could get some rest, have a bite to eat, and sleep comfortably.

Soon, assistance for the project began to arrive from the K of C headquarters in New Haven and the US Bishops Relief Fund in Washington, DC. Generous donations from the private sector flowed in as well, including a large building space in a good location.

In this new spot, a larger club—co-sponsored by the Knights, the NCCS, and a number of local patrons—was established, while the original club was turned over to the USO as its headquarters in Manila. The new club had a game room, a portrait and photo studio, and a reading area. It offered snacks, souvenirs, and information services, as well as an office for spiritual guidance. During the first few months, from August to October of 1945, about 10,000 soldiers and sailors made use of the many conveniences featured in the new club. Those who visited were also directed to nearby Santa Cruz Church for Mass and the sacraments. And although initially the American military was dismissive of the need for such services, the vast numbers of soldiers attending proved the real need, earning not only praise from the American military, but donations from General Douglas MacArthur himself.

Word of the wartime work of Father Willmann and the Knights of Manila Council 1000 spread throughout the Philippines and became an inspiration for many. Although nothing could match the sacrifice of the brother Knights who had lost their lives in the Philippines, a number of their children were recipients of the Order's newly established educational fund. This included the children of Manuel Colayco, who died spearheading the liberation of the Santo Tomas internment camp; the children of Benito Soliven, who refused to join the Japanese puppet government in exchange for freedom from Camp O'Donnell; and the children of Enrique Albert, the

In 1945, *Columbia* defended Pius XII from stories in the Soviet press portraying him as a Fascist sympathizer. It noted that such attacks were likely caused by the pope's defense of democracy. Others, including a top-ranking Soviet-bloc defector, have similarly termed such attacks on Pius XII as "disinformation."

With the goal of maintaining international peace and security, the United Nations was formed in October of 1945. On a number of occasions, including the 1947 Supreme Convention in Boston, Supreme Knight Swift decried what he saw as an aversion to religion in the new organization.

# Father George J. Willmann, SJ
## "Father McGivney of the Philippines"

Father George J. Willmann's work in the Philippines before, during, and after WWII will be forever symbolic of how one man's dedication and steadfast determination in the face of fierce opposition can result in triumph.

Born in Brooklyn, New York, in 1897, Willmann entered the Society of Jesus on August 14, 1915 and was ordained on June 20, 1928. He was sent to the Philippines in 1936 where he taught at the Ateneo de Manila University and served there as dean. In 1938, he joined the Knights of Columbus and was appointed chaplain of Manila Council 1000.

Shortly after Father Willmann arrived in Manila, it became apparent to him that the children and youth of the city were in dire need of attention. There were no Catholic orphanages or neighborhood youth centers. He saw many young boys roam the streets, where they were exposed to lawless behavior and immorality, especially at the city's ports. As Father Willmann later wrote in the December 1947 edition of *Columbia*, "The clergy, sadly undermanned, could do very little for these children, almost untouched as they were by any religious or spiritual influence. The stark picture staring us in the face was appalling. But our Knights saw a job to do—and went to work."

In an effort to provide some type of structure for the roughly 50,000 young boys of the city, Willmann led the Knights in forming social clubs throughout the various neighborhoods. The clubs began as simple basketball leagues, but as more and more youngsters joined in, they started offering other sports activities, which included events like swimming trips and boxing programs. Religious instruction and spiritual guidance were also provided within the social atmosphere of these settings.

Although he was being closely watched by the Japanese, Father Willmann managed to rekindle some of the youth activities that had been abandoned shortly after the war began. He wrote, "We were greatly assisted at this time by Father Gregorio Tsukomoto, former Japanese parish priest of Tokyo on special duty as religious liaison for the Nipponese Army. Indeed Father Gregorio was so enthused that he expressed a desire to start similar youth work back in Tokyo."

During the war, Father Willmann also led the Knights in charitable work for soldiers, refugees, and prisoners. The Japanese view of the Knights as an "American" organization (and thus an "enemy") led to his brief capture and interrogation, after which he was released with limited privileges as a cleric.

When the bombing escalated in 1944, the situation for Father Willmann and the people of Manila went from bad to worse. In his words, "Starvation and terror reigned over the city. Untold thousands were slaughtered or died in misery or destruction during these indescribable days. Amidst such bloodshed and chaos, the Knights were scattered to the four winds, and ceased to exist as an organized body." During that time, Father Willmann was taken prisoner and held in an internment camp at Los Baños.

When the Philippines was liberated on February 23, 1945, Father Willmann was among the 2,100 prisoners—including nuns, missionaries, and clergy members of various denominations—still at Los Baños. He would emerge from the camp and restore the Order in Manila, which had been all but destroyed by the war.

In 1948, Father Willmann was appointed the first district deputy in the Philippines, and in 1962, he became the Philippines deputy, with the same rights and powers of a state deputy. He held this position until his death in 1977. For his dedication and unending loyalty to the people of Manila and the Knights of Columbus, he would always be remembered as the "Father McGivney of the Philippines."

# Father Isaias X. Edralin, SJ
## Notable Knight

A diocesan priest from Nueva Segovia in the Philippines, Father Isaias X. Edralin was one of the early members of Manila Council 1000. Although his priestly assignments often took him far from Manila, he recruited new members for the Knights of Columbus wherever his ministry took him.

To help Council 1000 extend its reach, Father Edralin established a number of local units outside Manila. Joining the Jesuits and engaging in their missionary work in Mindanao allowed him to establish one such unit in Cagayan de Oro in 1938. There, he was responsible for impressive membership growth. A past grand knight of that unit later remembered Father Edralin as "the live wire insofar as Columbianism in Mindanao was concerned. He urged and recruited as many as he could to become Knights of Columbus."

As World War II engulfed the Philippines, Father Edralin remained there to minister to his people. In 1942, he was appointed a chaplain in the US Army Forces Far East. Within two months, he was captured by the Japanese and placed in Camp Casisang, Malaybalay as a prisoner of war. He was later transferred to Cagayan, where he was placed under house arrest, which allowed him to continue his priestly duties. There, he ministered to the prisoners, often putting his own life at risk. He celebrated Mass, offered counseling and absolution, and saw to the proper burial of those killed in action. When prisoners were marked for execution, he would hear their confessions, help them prepare for death, and accompany them to the end.

Each day in the prison camp, Father Edralin bore witness to the unspeakable torture of his fellow prisoners, yet he never wavered in his mission to help them and never lost his faith. He also never cooperated with the Japanese. There were, however, times when he was forced to distribute leaflets filled with propaganda. During those times, he made sure the material made its way into the hands of the Resistance fighters to make them aware of what the Japanese were planning.

Father Edralin never stopped trying to help the Filipinos recapture their homeland. In his memoirs, he wrote of the cruelties of war that he had witnessed, along with the fervent hope that what had happened during World War II would never happen again.

In 1948, the Mindanao unit Father Edralin had founded became Council 3108, the third council in the Philippines. At that time, he began suffering from severe arthritis and rheumatism, which often left him bedridden. In spite of his physical condition, Father continued ministering as best he could. He moved to a leper colony in Palawan, where he served as superior of a Jesuit chaplaincy for thirty years.

Father Edralin suffered a heart attack and passed away on December 31, 1974 in Novaliches. His tireless work in the Philippines will always be recognized as a sign of his unrelenting love—love for his country, for his fellow man, and for the ideals of Columbianism.

"valiant, and even reckless, K of C Brother" who led Knights in ministering at the gates of Camp O'Donnell.

Father Willmann's work for the Knights and the poor in the Philippines was not over. Much like Father McGivney, Father Willmann realized the importance of both caring for men spiritually and leading them in service and camaraderie. His tireless zeal for the Order resulted in tremendous growth in membership and ministries. (For more on the life of Father Willmann, see the inset on page 127.)

## Expansion in the Philippines

Following the Second World War, the Knights of Columbus in the Philippines largely focused on recruiting members and establishing new councils. At the time, the Philippines had only a single council, Manila Council 1000. Council 1900 in San Pablo, Laguna, had been chartered in 1918 but proved to be short-lived. During a visit to the United States in 1947, Father Willmann met with Supreme Advocate Luke Hart to discuss the need for expansion and ask for assistance. He proposed the establishment of new councils, stressing that without the opportunity to join the Knights, the Filipino men who wished to belong to a fraternal organization would have no other option but the anti-Catholic groups. Realizing the importance of this proposal, Hart recommended its acceptance to the Supreme Board of Directors. His only stipulation was that Father Willmann had to serve as deputy director and supervise the new councils. In October 1947, the plan was approved.

As word spread of the Knights' accomplishments before, during, and after the war, the newly formed councils led to tremendous growth. By 1955, the Philippines would be home to more than fifty councils. By the time of the Knights' Diamond Anniversary there in 1980, membership had grown to over 40,000. Today, there are nearly 400,000 Knights in more than 3,000 councils there.

## NEW LEADERSHIP AND POSTWAR CONCERNS AT HOME

The year 1945 marked the end of World War II and the election of John E. Swift as supreme knight. Hailing from Massachusetts, Swift was sixty-five years old when he stepped into the role. A graduate of Boston College and Boston University School of Law, Swift joined Valencia Council 80 in 1912. He held numerous positions, including grand knight, district deputy, state deputy, and deputy supreme knight. Even while supreme knight, he also served as a superior court judge in his home state.

Swift, along with the Catholic Church and US government, was greatly concerned about the spread of communism. Emerging in Russia after the

When Francis Matthews stepped down as supreme knight, he would go on to serve in public life. In 1946, President Truman appointed Matthews to the president's Civil Rights Committee. He then named him Secretary of the Navy in 1949, and US Ambassador to Ireland in 1951. As Secretary of the Navy, one of Matthews' signature achievements would be the racial integration of the Navy and the Marine Corps.

In 1945, when addressing Westminster College in Fulton, Missouri, Winston Churchill memorably described an "iron curtain" being drawn across Europe, behind which Soviet-influenced nations were separated from the West. Acknowledging that communism in America was in its "infancy," he warned that "Communist . . . 'fifth columns' constitute a growing challenge and peril to Christian civilization."

In the wake of a war that saw churches bombed and priceless artwork looted, the Order funded a documentary film series for the Vatican on its cultural treasures. These films were produced by Samuel Bronston who would go on to make epic motion pictures including *El Cid* and *King of Kings*.

1917 revolution, communism had become the ideology of an increasingly powerful nation. As the USSR consolidated its control of Eastern Europe after WWII, its ideology spread quickly throughout the region. Like his predecessors had, Swift spoke out frequently against communism, noting that the USSR had "enslaved millions of our fellow Catholics all the way from Finland and Poland to Catholic Austria and Czechoslovakia and almost to the gates of Rome."

The Communist threat was a burning issue for Swift. At a testimonial dinner held for him in Boston, he gave a rousing speech on the topic that was so passionate, it generated widespread media attention. During this time, Boston was also being considered as a possible location for the United Nations. As a result of Swift's speech, the Soviets made it clear to the UN site committee that they strongly opposed Boston as the home of the newly founded international organization. Manhattan was ultimately chosen instead.

Swift denounced communism's atheistic and totalitarian ideology, contrasting it with America's values and understanding of God-given rights. Like his predecessors, he saw socialism and communism as dangers to both the American and the Catholic understandings of faith and freedom.

**John E. Swift**
Ninth supreme knight.

## ANSWERING RENEWED ANTI-CATHOLICISM

By the end of World War II, Catholics were experiencing greater acceptance in American society. They had fought bravely in two major wars, held significant roles in politics and commerce, and were greater in number than any single Protestant denomination in the country. The fact that Catholics were feeling more at home in America was a source of tension for some Protestant Americans, particularly when it came to the question of federal aid for parochial education.

The US bishops had long opposed federal aid for Catholic schools on the grounds that such funding would lead to a degree of government control over parochial education. But by the 1940s, the Catholic Church felt more at ease with federal authority and was open to the possibility of assistance. In 1947, the Supreme Court ruled in favor of allowing parochial school students to ride public school buses in *Everson v. Board of Education*. In response, sixty Protestant leaders published a manifesto opposing any use of federal funds to assist Catholic schoolchildren. This coalition, called Protestants and Other Americans United for the Separation of Church and State (POAU), resurrected old fears of Catholics answering to a foreign power (i.e. the Vatican) and taking over America's system of democracy in violation of the First Amendment.

An increased awareness of Soviet atrocities against civilian populations, coupled with concern over the growing spread of communism in Europe prompted the Truman Doctrine in 1947. Named for President Harry Truman, the doctrine was designed to counter this influence by providing aid to countries at risk of entering the Soviet orbit.

To combat the rising threat of communism, in 1947, the Knights sponsored two radio series— *Foundations of Our American Ideals* and *Safeguards of America*. Aired on hundreds of radio stations, the series covered topics ranging from the harshness of life in Communist Russia to the importance of religious freedom.

Supreme Knight Swift responded by issuing a statement characterizing the POAU position as "religious bigotry" and an insult to the patriotism of people of every faith who did not hold such views. *Columbia* editor John Donahue—who took to calling the coalition "P.U. and Co."—defended federal aid to Catholic schools in a number of subsequent editorials.

The issue was important to Swift, but also touched a nerve with the Order as a whole. Christopher Kauffman recounts that in 1949, the Supreme Council indirectly took up the issue, adopting two resolutions in direct contrast to the POAU position. The council's resolutions denounced the extreme interpretation (held by POAU) of Thomas Jefferson's "wall of separation," stating that this interpretation had misled people "into accepting a figure of speech as a principle of law." The convention also declared its support for the equal treatment of Catholics, stating that: "Catholics do not desire federal aid for parochial schools. . . . [but] Catholics insist on the right of all children to participate on an equal basis in benefits provided by the Federal Government; if such benefits are provided for school children, they should be provided for all school children without discrimination."

Fueling the fire against the Church was Paul Blanshard, a former government official who wrote two books detailing a supposed "Catholic conspiracy" that threatened democracy. His charges were laced with slurs and distorted characterizations of the pope, the Catholic faithful, and Catholic associations such as Catholic Action and the Knights of Columbus. He was highly critical of the Order's full-page advertisements in secular newspapers that sought to defend the Church, saying they "disguise the worst feature of their own faith by adroit double-talk."

The growth of Catholic influence in America was perceived by some as a threat to the status quo—a nation in which Protestant culture had been largely dominant. In response to this new surge of anti-Catholicism, John Swift and the Knights of Columbus were among those leading the charge in reminding Americans of the principles of religious freedom upon which the nation was founded.

## CRUSADING FOR AMERICAN IDEALS

In addition to domestic threats to religious freedom, Swift worried there was a global threat as well. Citing FBI reports, he raised concerns that communism was beginning to take root in the United States by infiltrating education, American labor unions, and even the UN and portions of the government. He blamed its headway largely on society's rejection of Christian values.

Playing for the Brooklyn Dodgers, Jackie Robinson broke baseball's decades-long color barrier in 1947, becoming the first African American player in the major leagues. When he retired a decade later, the Order co-sponsored an interfaith baseball game in his honor at Griffith Park Stadium in Washington, DC.

Second Lieutenant Gerry Kisters was the Army's first soldier in World War II to receive the country's two highest citations: the Congressional Medal of Honor and the Distinguished Service Cross. Kisters joined the Knights of Columbus upon his return, and is shown here signing an application for membership in Council 1096 in Bloomington, Indiana.

The Order ran full-page newspaper ads opposing communism in a dozen major American cities. It also established the Knights of Columbus Crusade for the Preservation and Promotion of American Ideals. Rather than simply opposing communism, this initiative—building on the Order's history of promoting the understanding of civil rights and religious liberty at home and abroad—would focus on American freedoms and highlight the importance of defending American principles. Swift also spoke out against Soviet-bloc persecution of the Church and its leaders and urged American condemnation of such actions.

Launched in 1946, the crusade was led by George Hermann Derry, who had also led the Order's initiatives opposing communism in the 1930s. In addition to Derry's speeches, this project encouraged local councils to discuss and promote American ideals. Within a few months, more than three hundred discussion groups were formed. To encourage these groups to remain active and grow, Derry summarized the principles of the crusade in the *Manual for Discussion Groups*, which was distributed to all councils. Derry's work proved to be very inspiring, as another thousand groups were formed by the summer of 1948. Importantly, the Knights' effort was attuned to Catholic social teaching. While critical of Marxism, it also called out the "abuses of unrestricted capitalism," noting that such abuses also generated sympathy for Marxist ideology. President Harry Truman himself endorsed the effort.

The Knights also sponsored two radio series—*Safeguards of America* and *Foundations of Our American Ideals*—that were aired on hundreds of stations throughout the country. Each series contained several short programs that ran the gamut from the harsh realities of life in the Soviet Union to the fight against communism in the United States. The prevailing theme emphasized the disparity between Communist oppression and the freedoms enjoyed by American citizens. A third radio series, *The Future of America*, was added to stress the important role of America's moral leadership in the world.

The Supreme Council's work in this area recognized the harm that was being caused by a totalitarian and atheistic system—a system that was overtly opposed to the United States and the Judeo-Christian values of the Western world. As the Cold War intensified, the Knights' concerns became more widely shared, and the Order embarked on a campaign designed, in Swift's words, to "counteract the un-American philosophies that seem to be advancing throughout the United States."

Concerns over Communist intentions were exacerbated by the famous 8,000-word *Long Telegram*, written in 1946 by George Kennan, the US Chargé d'Affaires in Moscow. Kennan wrote that the hardline policy of Stalin and the Soviets was to:

> . . . undermine the general and strategic potential of major Western powers by a host of subversive measures to destroy individual governments that might stand in the Soviet path, to do everything possible to set the major Western powers against each other.

In 1949, the North Atlantic Treaty Organization, or NATO, was created by the United States, Canada, and several Western European countries to provide security against the Soviet Union. Canadian Prime Minister and Knight Louis St. Laurent strongly supported Canada's involvement as a means of stopping the further spread of communism.

With the Depression and World War II now behind, and Catholic soldiers returning home, the Order once again grew rapidly, surpassing pre-Depression numbers and adding more than 790,000 members. Insurance also began to grow again, reaching more than $368 million of insurance in force (a more than 50-percent increase in a decade).

Sharing the Knights' concern about communism, the US government responded with its own policies that focused on containing the spread of communism abroad. An important development came in 1947 with the Truman Doctrine—a policy through which the United States government gave economic support to countries, including Greece and Turkey, to prevent them from falling under Soviet influence. It was a major step in the start of the Cold War.

As the end of the 1940s neared, the Knights, the American people, and the country's elected leaders shared concerns over the spread of communism both in this country and abroad. In 1949, a report that the Soviets had succeeded in developing an atomic bomb only intensified these concerns.

As the contest between the USA and the USSR strengthened, so did the Knights' work to alert Americans to the perils of communism, highlighting the difference in beliefs and principles between the American and Soviet systems: the former based on God-given rights, the latter based on atheistic principles. It was a contrast that the Order would continue to highlight until the fall of the Communist bloc four decades later.

## THE DECADE COMES TO A CLOSE

Throughout the 1940s, the Knights of Columbus had once again shown that one could be both a good Catholic and a good citizen. And now, even more Knights were making the case. The Five Points to Progress Program, with its strong commitment to revitalizing councils—through increased Catholic activity and activation of current members—helped the Order recover from its two-decade membership decline.

Renewed vigor and a unique blend of charity and patriotism characterized the Knights' work during and after World War II. The Order's support for troops through its "huts" in Canada and the Philippines, and through its work with the USO had again reaffirmed the Knights' patriotism and its commitment to those fighting for freedom. That patriotic commitment was also evident in the Order's sale of war bonds.

While not shying away from their wartime duties, the Knights also took time to lead prayers for peace, urging the world to embrace a peace based on rights as transcendent gifts from God. Consistent with this, throughout the 1940s, the Knights continued its strong advocacy for civil rights, religious freedom, and religious principles.

The Knights' impact was felt around the world. In Rome, the K of C playgrounds—despite being behind enemy lines—were the staging ground for the Vatican food program that helped the people of Rome survive the war. The Knights' man in Rome—Enrico Galeazzi—was instrumental not only in saving Jews who were hiding there, but also in stopping American bombardment of the city. Meanwhile, in the Pacific, the Knights provided comfort to both American troops and POWs.

The strength of these initiatives was not lost on Catholic American men. They joined. By 1950, the Knights of Columbus had more than recovered from the losses of the Great Depression. It now numbered more than three quarters of a million men, who were ready to take on the challenges of the next decade.

I pledge allegiance to the flag of the United States of America and to the Republic for which it stands, one nation *under God*, indivisible, with liberty and justice for all.

# 7.

# "One Nation Under God"

## 1951 to 1964

The Great Depression and World War II had taken a toll on the lives of everyday Americans, and the 1950s became a period of rebuilding. But while Nazism and all of its horrors had been defeated, the country was now faced with another looming threat as communism began gaining a foothold throughout the world. The global threat from one repressive, atheistic ideology was being replaced by another. Soviet communism had already consumed half of Europe and was gaining traction in Asia. The Chinese Civil War ended in 1949 with a Communist triumph, resulting in the formation of the People's Republic of China. That same year, the Soviet Union detonated its first atomic bomb. In 1950, with the backing of the Soviets, Communist-ruled North Korea attacked South Korea, drawing the United States into the Korean War. The Cold War had turned hot.

American concern over the spread of communism intensified in the 1950s—as it did in other countries as well. As Senator Joe McCarthy began his investigations, many Catholics—including the Kennedy family and the Knights—were supportive. The Order's support cooled a bit as McCarthy's campaigns became more controversial. Nor was such support unanimous among Knights; for example, although McCarthy was a Knight himself, so was his challenger in the 1952 primary, Leonard Schmitt.

Supreme Knight Swift toned down his trademark anti-Communist rhetoric during the McCarthy period. While he continued to oppose communism strongly, he also warned against "witch hunts" targeting Communists. The Order's grounding in Catholic social teaching, along with its long-standing suspicion of socialism and promotion of an American understanding of civil and religious rights, added an interesting dimension to its arguments for con-

War broke out in 1950, as Communist North Korean forces attacked both the South Korean army and the American units supporting it. The US military sent additional forces to Korea as part of the UN response. Notably, South Korea's ambassador to the US at the time—John Chang Myon—was a Knight (see page 138).

In 1951, President Truman nominated General Mark Clark—liberator of Rome in WWII—as US Ambassador to the Vatican. Due to strong opposition to US-Vatican relations by many Protestant organizations, the nomination was withdrawn. President Ronald Reagan would ultimately establish formal relations between the US and the Vatican three decades later.

# A Real Estate Success

*We all met in the Board Room at the Banker's Trust Company in Rockefeller Center.... The various documents incident to the Yankee deal were executed and I delivered a check for $2,500,000.... It was, of course, the largest check I ever signed. We then leased it back ... for an initial term of twenty-eight years at $182,000 per year and with the privilege ... of three renewable terms of fifteen years each at $125,000 per year.*

The Order owned the land until 1971, when it was purchased by the city of New York under Mayor John Lindsay. Of the eighteen real estate investments made during Hart's term, the Yankee Stadium deal was the most significant. Fittingly, the stadium itself, commonly known as "The House That Ruth Built" after legendary ballplayer Babe Ruth, is what made the land so valuable—and Babe Ruth had been a Knight.

During the 1950s, the Order's growth in membership and assets allowed it to make a number of significant investments to help support its financial strength. Supreme Knight Hart endorsed a new type of investment—real estate. The most noteworthy of these ventures took place on December 17, 1953 with the purchase of the original Yankee Stadium and the nine-acre parcel of land on which it stood.

The stadium and property were purchased from financier Arnold Johnson as part of a leaseback investment—the Knights bought the real estate and then leased it back to Johnson (who, in turn, leased the stadium to the Yankees). Supreme Knight Hart described the transaction with Johnson in his diary:

scientious economic activity, and its warnings against the excesses, lack of freedom, and atheism inherent in communism. Putting God at the center of one's life and understanding rights as coming from God rather than the state were key themes for Swift and the Knights during this period. In this way, the Knights hoped to strengthen constructively America's social and moral structure, providing a clear contrast between American and Soviet values and protecting the former.

In 1952, General Dwight Eisenhower became the first Republican elected president in twenty years. When Eisenhower signed into law legislation adding the words "under God" to the Pledge of Allegiance in 1954, it was a victory for the Order's efforts and underscored that American rights and freedoms were God-given.

CATHOLIC
PRESS COUNCIL

CARDINAL
SPELLMAN
LUNCHEON

At the 1952 Supreme Convention in Los Angeles, Cardinal Francis Spellman warned that secularism was "a corridor to Communism opening the way for the acceptance of the anti-God, anti-democratic ideologies." Spellman encouraged the Knights to embrace faith as "the only cure for the curse of secularism and Communism."

The Cold War and the Communist persecution of people of faith would remain a significant concern for the Order and the nation for the rest of the decade and beyond. Aware of the risks presented by an ideology that sought to ban God entirely from the life of its people, the Knights of Columbus remained committed to maintaining a strong and unified America "under God."

## CHANGING OF THE GUARD

In 1953, Supreme Knight John Swift's eight years of leadership came to an end and Luke Hart was elected as his successor. At age seventy-three, Hart became the Order's oldest leader.

Like supreme knights before him, Hart was a lawyer and public servant. He was also a unique bridge to the Order's past. Born in Maloy, Iowa, in 1880, Hart earned his law degree from the University of Missouri in 1905 and joined the Order three years later. An alderman and assistant city attorney in St. Louis, Hart joined the board in 1918 and became supreme advocate in 1922—a position he held until his election as supreme knight. He was involved with countering attacks by the Klan and helping steer the Order through the 1930s and World War II. He also served as a delegate to the GOP convention in 1940. Helping manage, grow, and modernize the Order's insurance program was among his signature achievements.

Hart's understanding of the Order's unique structure as an immense, growing fraternal organization, as well as a highly successful insurance operation, led to a number of significant changes. The headquarters was in New Haven, Connecticut, yet most supreme officers lived in other states. Hart relocated to New Haven and encouraged other officers to follow suit, setting a precedent for the future. Under Hart, the Order's governance was also changed. Decision making was streamlined, with the supreme knight and board taking a more leading role. For instance, the direct election of supreme officers by delegates to the Supreme Convention, was now placed in the hands of the board of directors—who were still directly elected at the convention. This resulted in a more corporate governance structure that promised more stability if less direct input from the membership.

Under Hart's tenure, strong growth in membership and insurance was also paired with centralized management in New Haven. Along with a more streamlined operation, the Order's strength showed in its priorities and projects. It promoted the teachings and practices of the Catholic faith through apologetics and support for Vatican initiatives, while also promoting a better understanding and respect for human rights by highlighting America as a nation "under God" and advocating for the rights of Catholics at home and abroad.

**Luke E. Hart**
Tenth supreme knight.

The year 1954 saw the merger of The Catholic University of America's law school and Columbus University (which developed out of the Knights' 1920s veteran education programs). This created CUA's Columbus School of Law. Prior to the merger, the schools had shared faculty and a commitment to forming generations of Catholic lawyers.

In 1954, Senator John F. Kennedy (far right) took his Fourth Degree under the direction of Master of the Fourth Degree for Massachusetts, John McDevitt (second from right). Kennedy would become the first Catholic elected president of the United States in 1960, while McDevitt would become supreme knight in 1964.

# John Chang Myon
## Notable Knight

Although later known for his active political career in South Korea, Chang Myon—or John Chang Myon, as he was known in the United States— began his professional life working for the Church. In 1925, after graduating from Manhattan College in the United States, he was employed by the Pyongyang diocese, where he translated religious terms into the Korean language and assumed other teaching and administrative duties. Chang would remain a devout Catholic throughout his life.

After World War II ended and Korea was divided into North and South, Chang entered politics, filling several positions for the Republic of Korea (South Korea). He was a member of the Constitutional Assembly; one of three representatives to the United Nations General Assembly, in which South Korea's government was recognized; and an ambassador to the United States. In his role as ambassador, from 1949 to 1951, Chang successfully appealed for international and United States military assistance against North Korea, eventually leading to US involvement.

The Knights of Columbus would not be established in Korea for another six decades, but in December 1949, Chang joined Washington Council 224 in Washington, DC. He attended the 1950 Supreme Convention, widely acclaimed as the Order's first Korean Knight.

Chang Myon's political service continued as he became deeply involved in South Korea's struggles for democracy. In 1950, he became prime minister. In 1956, he won the vice presidential election. In 1960, when he ran for reelection, he lost by such a wide margin, there was suspicion that the election had been compromised.

The government then fell and the "Second Republic" adopted a parliamentary model, shifting power from the president to the prime minister, a position to which Chang was elected in 1960. However, that arrangement was short-lived, and when a violent rebellion overthrew the government and instituted martial law, Chang was forced to take refuge in a convent.

After Chang's forced exit from the political arena, he dedicated himself to his faith and is said to have inspired the conversion of many of the people who had worked with him. He often attended daily Mass and was a Third Order Franciscan. Among his literary achievements are a dictionary of religious terms and a translation of Cardinal James Gibbons' apologetics text, *The Faith of Our Fathers*. His religious convictions also helped shape the lives of his nine children, who included Sister Benedict Chang Yi-sook and Bishop John Chang Yik.

In 1999, Chang was posthumously honored with the Order of Merit for National Foundation by the Korean government.

In 1955, the fiftieth anniversaries of the Knights in Mexico and the Philippines were celebrated. Having stood against government persecution in Mexico in the 1920s, and having provided charity despite the risk during the WWII Japanese occupation of the Philippines, the Knights in each country were rebuilding after an eventful half-century.

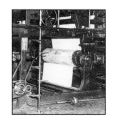

In 1956, the Order donated its retired printing press to support the efforts of the Catholic Church in Bolivia. There it was used to print flyers and leaflets to counter the growing anti-Catholic and Communist propaganda. The Apostolic Nuncio to Bolivia wrote that the equipment was a "God-send to the Church and the Catholic interests in this country."

# "UNDER GOD"

During the early 1950s, the Knights of Columbus played a key role in adding the words "under God" to the Pledge of Allegiance. This addition had both historical precedent and a growing base of support.

The original pledge, written in 1892 by Francis Bellamy, was first published in *The Youth's Companion* magazine:

> *I pledge allegiance to my flag and [to] the Republic for which it stands—*
> *one nation, indivisible, with liberty and justice for all.*

With the approval of the National Education Association, the pledge was then printed out and distributed to schools throughout the nation. Later that year, millions of students recited the pledge on Columbus Day to commemorate the 400-year anniversary of the historic voyage.

The Pledge of Allegiance remained as originally written until 1923, when it received its first change. Fearing that the children of immigrants might mistakenly consider the words "my flag" for the flag of their homeland, the words were changed to "the flag of the United States of America."

Adding the words "under God" to the pledge was the second change—one in which the Knights would play a key role. This movement to amend the pledge was initiated in 1948 by Louis Bowman, a seventy-six-year-old Illinois attorney and member of the Sons of the American Revolution. After the words "one nation," Bowman began to include the words "under God" as he led his organization in reciting the Pledge of Allegiance at meetings. He credited Abraham Lincoln's words in the Gettysburg Address, which described America as "this nation under God," for giving him the idea.

The Knights also began including "under God" as they recited the pledge. In 1951, motivated by a combination of patriotism and a desire to highlight God's important role in American society, the Knights formalized this practice. First, the board of directors passed a resolution stating that the amended pledge was to be recited by all of the country's Fourth Degree assemblies. Soon the Knights began pushing for its use even more widely.

The Knights realized the importance of the words "under God" to the entire country, not just individual organizations. Beginning with the

Supreme Knight Hart with President Eisenhower after a wreath-laying ceremony at the Columbus Memorial on Columbus Day in 1953.

Two years after President Eisenhower signed legislation adding "under God" to the country's Pledge of Allegiance, he signed a bill making "In God We Trust" the nation's official motto. Like the Pledge of Allegiance, the new motto affirmed God's role in American society—and the divine source of American rights.

Circulating information to members of the Order is done largely through *Columbia* magazine. In 1927, to extend this information further, councils began purchasing subscriptions of the magazine for their local libraries. In 1957, councils in Ohio and Illinois went one step further by donating subscriptions to all of the school libraries (public and parochial) in their states.

Declaration of Independence, the United States recognized God as the source of human rights. This also highlighted the contrast between American values and those of the Communist Soviet Union, where religion was suppressed and basic human rights were state, not God given, and thus were routinely violated. By promoting the inclusion of "under God" in the Pledge of Allegiance, the Knights of Columbus highlighted not only the United States' commitment to the concept of personal freedom, but also the recognition of the Supreme Being and Creator, who is the author and guarantor of that freedom.

At the 1952 Supreme Convention, the Supreme Council considered resolutions from several states urging that "under God" be made part of the country's official Pledge of Allegiance. Copies of the adopted resolutions were sent to the leadership of Congress and to the president and vice president.

A number of other groups joined the campaign for this official change. After several resolutions were introduced in the House of Representatives, Congressman Louis C. Rabaut of Michigan presented the bill that Congress eventually passed. Then, on Flag Day, June 14, 1954, the bill was signed by President Dwight D. Eisenhower.

On August 17, 1954, President Eisenhower sent Supreme Knight Hart the following message, which was read at the 72nd annual Supreme Convention in Louisville:

The Pledge of Allegiance with the newly added words "Under God" is proudly displayed behind the dais at the 1955 States Dinner in Philadelphia.

*We are particularly thankful to you for your part in the movement to have the words "under God" added to our Pledge of Allegiance. These words will remind Americans that despite our great physical strength, we must remain humble. They will help us to keep constantly in our minds and hearts the spiritual and moral principles which alone give dignity to man, and upon which our way of life is founded. For the contribution which your organization has made to this cause, we must be genuinely grateful.*

Adding the words "under God" to the pledge was a true victory. It not only highlighted the divine origin of American rights, it also continued to make the case that Catholics could take the lead as good, patriotic citizens.

In 1958, the Knights of Columbus Research Center was opened at the Joseph P. Kennedy Memorial Hospital (now Franciscan Children's Hospital) in Boston, enabling the hospital and local universities to partner for the care of children. Local councils, including Andover Council, contributed monthly to assist the children there.

In 1958, the Order expanded its insurance program to offer coverage to the wives and daughters of members. This decision built on the coverage for members' sons that had been extended fourteen years earlier, and made the Knights even more "family" oriented.

# Blessed Carlos M. Rodriguez
## Notable Knight

Born in 1918 in Caguas, Puerto Rico, Carlos M. Rodriguez was raised by a devoutly Catholic family. One of his sisters would become a Carmelite nun, and one of his brothers, a Benedictine monk. At the age of thirteen, Carlos was diagnosed with ulcerative colitis. But he accepted his illness gracefully, and strengthened by his beliefs, he always remained committed to Christ and the Catholic Church.

After graduating from high school, he continued to study the Catholic faith on his own and spoke openly about what he learned, teaching others the truths of the faith and making them aware of God's love for them. "Charlie," as his friends came to call him, taught about devotion to the liturgy, established discussion groups, and led high school catechism classes. His service to others in the midst of his own suffering was an inspiration to all who knew him.

Carlos had a particular love for Mass and dedicated himself to fostering appreciation for the liturgy. On his own initiative, he published the magazine *Liturgy and Christian Culture*, started liturgy circles, formed a choir, and organized Christian Life Days for students. He joined the Knights of Columbus, becoming a member of Juan XXIII Council 2033 in Caguas.

Carlos' health declined in the latter half of the 1950s. During that time, he wrote a book entitled *At That Time*, which has become a modern spiritual classic. His condition eventually developed into cancer, which took his life in 1963.

In the 1980s, the Knights of Columbus, along with Carlos' friends and family, began promoting his cause for canonization. Many who knew him came forward with testimony about his piety, faith, and virtue. In 2001, after Pope John Paul II recognized a miraculous cure attributed to his intercession, Carlos became the first Puerto Rican to be beatified. Blessed Carlos Rodriguez Council 13116 in Kissimmee, Florida, is named in his honor.

The beatification ceremony for Carlos Rodriguez took place on April 29, 2001. Thousands of people from his homeland of Puerto Rico flew to Rome to attend the ceremony.

# THE RELIGIOUS INFORMATION BUREAU AND CATHOLIC INFORMATION SERVICE

By the 1950s, although the country's Catholic population had grown dramatically since the Order's founding (one in four Americans identified as Catholic), the religion itself was still a mystery to many. To help address this issue, in the 1940s, the Knights in Missouri had launched the Religious Information Bureau. This bureau included a Catholic Advertising Program and sponsored the Confraternity Home Study Service, which was offered by Reverend Lester Fallon, a Vincentian theology professor and street preacher. Supreme Advocate Luke Hart served on the committee that launched the initiative, which was based in St. Louis under the Missouri State Council. Through Hart's advocacy, the Order officially adopted the Religious Information Bureau as its own in 1948. An initial allocation of $125,000 and a subsequent 80-cent per capita assessment funded the project.

Evangelization was a full-time job for those working at the Religious Information Bureau, answering and fulfilling the thousands of requests for free materials and courses on the Catholic faith.

Consistent with Father McGivney's vision of protecting the faith of Catholics, the bureau's mission was to better educate both Catholics in their faith and non-Catholics who wanted to learn more about the religion. It advertised in leading magazines, offering free easy-to-read publications with detailed coverage of the teachings of the Church, Catholic practices, and a variety of other topics. Within the first nine months of the Order's adoption of this program, over 12,000 pamphlets were requested and more than 300 non-Catholics had enrolled in the religious instruction program. Six years later, the continued demand for literature required a staff of thirty under Reverend Fallon's direction.

In 1969, the program was split into both Order-wide and local operations. The Order-wide unit moved to New Haven and was renamed the Catholic Information Service (CIS). The locally focused operation remained in Missouri under the original name.

To this day, the Catholic Information Service remains a valuable source of information on Catholicism and the teachings of the Church, including theological and practical aspects of the faith. Over the years, it has published millions of booklets in multiple media formats and enrolled many thousands of students in home study courses. Its outreach programs have included publications for parishes, schools, retreat houses, military installations, correctional facilities, legislatures, and the medical community. Also accessible through the Knights of Columbus website, CIS offers its database of information as well as online Catholic correspondence courses.

Elected October 20, 1958, Angelo Roncalli—John XXIII—became the first pope to visit a Knights' playground/youth center in Rome. When meeting with the Order's Board several years later, he quoted Matthew 5:16: "Let them see your good works so that they may glorify your Father who is in heaven."

Although the Religious Information Bureau was adopted by the Supreme Council at the end of Swift's tenure, Luke Hart (first as supreme advocate, then as supreme knight) was instrumental in its origination, adoption, and continuation. Ads for booklets like this one addressed common questions and suspicions, and invited readers to request more information.

# THE VATICAN FILM LIBRARY

Another major undertaking during Hart's tenure was the funding of a project that involved the microfilming of important (often irreplaceable) documents from the Vatican and making them accessible to the public. The microfilm library, which was to be housed at the Jesuit-run St. Louis University, received Vatican approval for its creation in 1951.

With assistance from both the Vatican and the St. Louis University library, Father Lowrie J. Daly led the project, which involved the arduous task of selecting, cataloging, microfilming, and indexing the documents. Over the next several years, more than 12 million manuscript pages were recorded from over 30,000 different documents and historic works. Manuscripts included documents dating as far back as 5000 BC, as well as material from the Middle Ages and the Renaissance. It was the largest micro-film project undertaken up to that time.

The Knights of Columbus Vatican Film Library opened in May of 1959 as part of the university's larger Pius XII Memorial Library, and remains open today. Currently, the collection is being digitized.

Proofing the microfilm at the Knights of Columbus Vatican Film Library located at St. Louis University.

# INTERNATIONAL CONCERNS

Hart had been supreme advocate during the Order's work to stop persecution in Mexico in the 1920s, and had supported its work opposing communism, which he continued. He also supported religious liberty abroad—especially in Eastern Europe.

The Hungarian Revolution of 1956 sought freedom from the Soviet-imposed Communist system. However, the Soviet Union was not about to give up a Communist satellite state. Soviet troops were mobilized to maintain control of Hungary and violently crushed the demonstrations, killing thousands of civilians.

Hart and Cardinal Spellman contacted President Eisenhower. The president, worried about triggering a nuclear war, was cautious and didn't take any forceful action. In the midst of the chaos, Hungary's Cardinal Josef Mindszenty fled to the US Embassy for refuge. He had been famously imprisoned by the Communists, and was freed by the protestors. The Order reimbursed the State Department monthly for the costs of his stay at the embassy.

Hungary was not the only foreign policy issue that Hart and the Knights tackled. When it was rumored that Marshal Josip Broz Tito—dictator of Communist Yugoslavia—was invited to meet with President Eisenhower in 1957, Hart once again spoke out. In a wire sent to the president, Hart firmly protested the alleged invitation, referring to Tito as the "jailer of Cardinal Stepanic, the tyrant of Yugoslavia, the persecutor of religion and the accomplice to the murders in Budapest."

Imprisoned by the Communists in 1949, Cardinal József Mindszenty was liberated by the Hungarian Revolution in 1956. When the Soviets crushed the uprising, Mindszenty fled to the U.S. Embassy in Budapest, where he received asylum for fifteen years. His expenses were paid by the Knights of Columbus, who had also previously protested his imprisonment.

HAWAII STATE
KNIGHTS
OF COLUMBUS®

Establishing the Knights of Columbus in Hawaii had been contemplated in the early 1900s, but it wasn't until 1959 that the Order took root there with the establishment of Our Lady of Peace Council 5000. A longtime US territory, Hawaii achieved another milestone that year when it became America's fiftieth state.

Along with the statue of Father McGivney in his hometown of Waterbury, Connecticut, the Order erected a memorial altar in his honor at St. Mary's Church. Contributions from members were largely responsible for funding the altar, which was dedicated on March 22, 1959.

# A Year of Publicity

In honor of its seventy-fifth anniversary, the Knights of Columbus received an impressive amount of national publicity during 1957. Among the year's notable media highlights, two of the most popular television shows of the era—the *Lawrence Welk Show* and the *Ed Sullivan Show*—recognized the Order's anniversary. (This was not entirely surprising, as both Welk and Sullivan were Knights.)

Perhaps the most exciting recognition of the Knights' Diamond Jubilee came with the May 27, 1957 issue of *Life*—the nation's treasured photographic magazine. The issue featured the K of C Honor Guard on the cover and a pictorial essay on the Order within, entitled: "Knights of Columbus in 75th Year: A Million-Member Fraternal Order is the Busy, Prosperous 'Right Arm of the Catholic Church in America.'" First covering a number of the Order's more intriguing elements, such as the Fourth Degree, the article went on to highlight the Knights' achievements, internationality, and strength, making it a memorable addition to the celebration.

Hart's strongly worded protest resulted in an invitation to meet with the Undersecretary of State for Political Affairs, Robert Murphy. Also invited to the meeting was Dan Daniel, National Commander of the American Legion, whose concerns echoed those of Hart. At the meeting, Murphy assured the men that no invitation had been sent to Mr. Tito. In an effort to further assure that Tito was not welcome by the United States, House Majority Leader and Brother Knight John W. McCormack led a public protest by sponsoring a nationwide anti-Tito petition.

The successful conclusion to this movement advocated by Hart was realized shortly thereafter, when President Eisenhower made it clear that there would be no visit to the United States by Marshall Tito of Yugoslavia.

Since 1938, up to 8,000 New York Knights and their families have come together annually for a pilgrimage to the Shrine of the North American Martyrs in Auriesville, New York. The shrine is dedicated to three Jesuit missionary saints killed by Mohawk Indians in the 1600s, as well as the Mohawk Saint Kateri Tekakwitha.

In 1959, the National Shrine of the Immaculate Conception—the largest Roman Catholic church in North America—was dedicated in Washington, DC. The massive structure was built by contractor and Brother Knight John McShain, whose work included the Pentagon, FDR Library, and Jefferson Memorial.

# THE DIAMOND JUBILEE

The year 1957 marked the seventy-fifth anniversary of the founding of the Knights of Columbus. The highlight of this Diamond Jubilee was the dedication of a statue of Father Michael McGivney by noted American sculptor Joseph A. Coletti.

Nearly 10,000 people witnessed the statue's unveiling, which took place in McGivney's hometown of Waterbury, Connecticut. A mile-long parade of Fourth Degree color guards, brother Knights, members of the Catholic hierarchy, and civic leaders preceded the dedication. His Eminence Cardinal Francis Spellman, Archbishop of New York, led the list of honored guests in attendance. Past Supreme Knight John E. Swift presided over the ceremonies, which included speeches by the Most Reverend Henry O'Brien, Archbishop of Hartford; Governor Abraham A. Ribicoff of Connecticut; and Supreme Knight Luke Hart. Also in attendance was young John William Walshe, great-grandnephew of Father McGivney, who unveiled the statue—a bronze figure of the Order's founder standing upon a base of native Connecticut granite.

Supreme Chaplain Leo Finn, Joseph Coletti (sculptor), Supreme Knight Luke Hart, and McGivney relative John Walshe stand at the base of the Father McGivney Memorial on the day of its unveiling, March 31, 1957.

The year 1959 marked the Order's fiftieth anniversary in Cuba. Celebrating around 3,000 Knights and years of spiritual and charitable initiatives, the Order there was unknowingly enjoying its last years of freedom for a long time. Two years later, Communist Castro's militia would occupy the K of C headquarters in Havana.

When Cuba's unpopular and repressive Batista government fell to Fidel Castro's revolution, many supported the change . . . initially. As Castro's Communist dictatorship emerged—with severe abuse of human rights and religious persecution, including exiling clergy and closing seminaries—reality set in. The Cuban missile crisis further cemented decades of tension.

The 1957 dedication of the bronze statue of Father McGivney was one of the highlights of the Order's seventy-fifth anniversary year.

In his speech at the dedication, Governor Ribicoff spoke of the Order's presence in Connecticut, stating:

> The Diamond Jubilee of the Knights of Columbus has a special meaning for the people of the State of Connecticut because it was here that the original charter of the Order was granted by the General Assembly. We are proud that a Waterbury-born priest, Father Michael J. McGivney, had the vision and the spirit to found the Order when he was a young curate at St. Mary's Church in New Haven. The Order's seventy-five years of religious and humanitarian work is, in itself, the greatest monument to Father McGivney's memory, and is a record of accomplishment in which Connecticut's 35,000 Knights of Columbus take justifiable pride.

The Knights of Columbus had ample reason to celebrate its seventy-fifth year. From what began as a handful of founding members, the Order had grown to a brotherhood that topped 1 million. And largely due to Supreme Knight Hart's work in expanding the insurance program, the amount of insurance in force had reached nearly $690 million.

In 1960, Squires and Knights from Monterrey "ran" a real rose to the Basilica of Our Lady of Guadalupe in Mexico City. Now known as the Silver Rose program, the tradition promotes respect for life and includes prayer services along its three-country journey through Canada, the United States, and Mexico.

In 1961, the same year Kennedy took office, South Boston native John McCormack became the first Catholic to serve as Speaker of the House. A member of Pere Marquette Council 271 since 1917, and Congressman for forty-three years, McCormack frequently cited his faith as integral to his support for civil rights.

# Care for Cuban Refugees
## Visionary Council Initiative

In 1960, Communist leader Fidel Castro ramped up hostilities against many groups, including Catholics. In a matter of just a few years, the Knights of Columbus in Cuba went from a flourishing 3,000-member body to a persecuted organization. At least sixty Knights were reported imprisoned. The fraternal periodical was shut down, and to protect the members' identities, council records and documents were destroyed.

Like other Cuban Catholics, many Knights fled to the United States, settling in Florida. Aware that English-speaking councils were not in a good position to help their brother Knights from Cuba, the Florida state deputy worked with the Supreme Council to found Our Lady of Charity Council 5110, where the refugee Knights could enjoy a spirit of fraternal fellowship.

The council established a reception center in a residential area of Miami to aid other Cuban refugees and their families. Knights met the refugees at the airport and brought them to the center, through which they could receive housing, access a food pantry, and get help obtaining visas.

# Louis St. Laurent
## Notable Knight

Born on February 1, 1882, five days before the Knights of Columbus itself, Canadian native Louis St. Laurent embodied the spirit of patriotism throughout his life. During his early career, he was one of Canada's leading lawyers, serving two terms as president of the Canadian Bar Association. But shortly after Canada's entry into World War II, as the prospect of military conscription divided the country along French-English lines, St. Laurent—who had a French-Canadian father and an Irish-Canadian mother—was recruited to serve in politics. He became Minister of Justice and then Attorney General. Later, as President of the Privy Council, his good reputation and heartfelt appeals helped unite his beloved nation.

After the war, St. Laurent served nearly a decade as Prime Minister of Canada. Stressing national unity, St. Laurent oversaw the expansion of his country's social programs, including equalization payments to the provinces, old-age pensions, and health insurance. He also promoted Canadian membership in NATO, believing that Canada should help resist Communist expansion. In 1967, several years after his return to private life, he was awarded the Order of Canada for his service to his country.

Like so many men devoted to public service, St. Laurent had a great love for the Knights, of which he was a member. In a letter commemorating the Order's seventy-fifth anniversary, he praised the group's beneficial contribution "to the social and spiritual life of Canada."

## THE KNIGHTS TOWER AT
## THE NATIONAL SHRINE

In 1959, the Order ended an eventful decade with the completion of a soaring bell tower at the new National Shrine of the Immaculate Conception in Washington, DC, a structure that had taken two years to complete. Initial plans for construction of the shrine were approved by Pope Pius X in 1913. Nicknamed "America's Church," the shrine is the largest Roman Catholic church in North America.

Early in 1957, Monsignor Thomas J. Grady, Supervisor of the National Shrine, and Archbishop Patrick Cardinal O'Boyle of Washington, DC, met with Supreme Knight Hart. They asked if the Order might consider funding the construction of the shrine's bell tower. Considering this a great privilege, Hart presented the proposal to the Knights, who agreed to be part of this significant opportunity. The Order contributed $1 million toward the construction of the 329-foot tower, which was completed in two years. A bronze tablet at its entrance bears the following inscription:

THE KNIGHTS TOWER
GIFT OF
THE KNIGHTS OF COLUMBUS
TO
THE NATIONAL SHRINE OF
THE IMMACULATE CONCEPTION

AS A PLEDGE OF THE DEVOTION OF
ITS MEMBERS TO OUR BLESSED LADY
PATRONESS OF THE UNITED STATES
1959

◀ The Knights' bell tower at the National Shrine of the Immaculate Conception was completed in 1959. In 1963, the Order donated a carillon of fifty-six bells, which were added to the tower.

During the early years of the Cold War, thousands of East Germans escaped the horrors of communism via West Berlin. In response, Communist East German authorities erected a wall in 1961 to keep their people from fleeing. The wall encircled West Berlin until it fell, together with communism, in 1989.

The 7,200-pound Mary bell is being lifted up to the top of the tower.

The Christopher bell, named in honor of Saint Christopher, is the second-largest bell in the carillon.

On November 20, 1959, with more than 1,000 Knights forming the honor guard, Cardinal Francis Spellman, Archbishop of New York, blessed and dedicated the tower.

The magnificent structure has continued to be a work in progress over the years, undergoing numerous changes in construction and beautification—and the Knights have provided ongoing support. In 1963, the Order donated a carillon of fifty-six bells, which were added to the tower. The largest of the bells, named for the Blessed Virgin Mary, features the Order's emblem, weighs 7,200 pounds, and rings every hour. The second largest bell, named for Saint Christopher (and evocative of the famed explorer named after him), strikes every quarter hour.

In 2017, the Knights of Columbus helped financially sponsor the mosaics in the Shrine's largest dome, known as the Trinity Dome. Ten years earlier, in honor of the Order's one hundred twenty-fifth anniversary, the Knights had similarly sponsored the mosaics in the Knights of Columbus Incarnation Dome depicting the Annunciation, the Nativity, the Wedding Feast at Cana, and the Transfiguration. Supreme Knight Carl Anderson, whose tenure began in 2000, said at its dedication:

> The Knights have the highest regard for the National Shrine as the preeminent Marian shrine and pilgrimage site in the United States. This gift reaffirms our long-standing relationship with the Shrine and will add to the beauty and distinction of its sacred art.

The Order continues to maintain and fund a Knights-staffed usher ministry, which it established in the 1980s. The Order also created a $1 million endowment named in honor of past Supreme Knight Luke E. Hart to promote Marian devotion and to help preserve the structure of the basilica. The Knights have also been involved in the funding of televised broadcasts from the shrine and are eager participants in many sponsored events there. In 2000, over 12,000 Knights and their families took part in a pilgrimage to the Washington site—the largest pilgrimage ever hosted by the shrine.

The Order's longstanding relationship with the National Shrine exemplifies its continued commitment, dedication, and devotion to the Blessed Mother.

---

CONCILIUM OECUMENICUM VATICANUM II

In 1962, Pope John XXIII opened the Second Vatican Council as "a special, worldwide manifestation by the Church of her teaching office, exercised in taking account of the errors, needs and opportunities of our day." The four-year council addressed issues including religious freedom, inter-faith relations, and the Church's role in the world.

On January 20, 1961, John Fitzgerald Kennedy, the country's first Catholic president, stirred the nation with an inauguration speech that continues to be a source of inspiration.

# A CATHOLIC IN THE WHITE HOUSE

At the start of the 1960s, the presidential race between Richard M. Nixon and John F. Kennedy drew the interest of the entire country, and especially Catholic Americans. Anti-Catholic sentiment had reared its ugly head when Al Smith was defeated in the 1928 presidential election, and since then, no Roman Catholic had run for the highest office in the nation.

Like many Irish-Catholic men of his age, forty-three-year-old Kennedy was a Knight, having joined Bunker Hill Council 62 in Charlestown, Massachusetts in 1946, shortly after leaving the Navy. He was an active member, having become a Fourth Degree Knight in 1952. Although the Knights had always been a non-partisan organization, there was a strong feeling among members—just as there was among American Catholics in general—that if Kennedy were elected president, it would ease the still-present anti-Catholic sentiment in the country. Supreme Knight Hart proclaimed that the election of Kennedy "would do more to eliminate bigotry in this country than anything else that has ever happened." Catholics reasoned that if Americans were to elect a Catholic, they might finally be considered full citizens and gain acceptance in American society and public life.

Although the election was close, Kennedy was victorious. On the morning of his inauguration in January of 1961, he attended Mass at Holy Trinity Catholic Church in Georgetown before making his way to the Capitol. After being sworn into office, he delivered a stirring inaugural address in which he shared his vision for the nation and for the world. Although his speech contained many notable sentiments, two in particular

"With a good conscience our only sure reward, with history the final judge of our deeds, let us go forth to lead the land we love, asking His blessing and His help, but knowing that here on earth God's work must truly be our own."

–President John F. Kennedy
Inaugural Address, 1961

# No Conflict Between Catholic Faith and the Presidency

Although by 1960, Catholics enjoyed greater acceptance in the US than they had in decades past, anti-Catholic sentiment continued to cast suspicion on Catholics in public office. While the Order had long made the case that there was no conflict between the Catholic faith and American citizenship, John F. Kennedy had to make the case personally. When he was nominated as the Democratic candidate for president, some Americans—including a group of Protestant ministers—questioned whether a Catholic could truly serve as president, or would his faith conflict with the execution of the nation's highest office.

In September 1960, weeks before the presidential election, Kennedy spoke to the Greater Houston Ministerial Association on this very issue. In a pivotal address, he made the case that no American should be disqualified from public office on the basis of faith. He made it clear that he would resign rather than violate his conscience in carrying out his duties. He said:

> But if the time should ever come ... when my office would require me to either violate my conscience or violate the national interest, then I would resign the office; and I hope any conscientious public servant would do the same.

First and foremost, he urged Americans to focus on the "real issues which should decide this campaign," specifically:

> ... the spread of Communist influence, until it now festers ninety miles off the coast of Florida; ... the hungry children I saw in West Virginia; the old people who cannot pay their doctor bills; the families forced to give up their farms; an America with too many slums, with too few schools, and too late to the moon and outer space.

Declaring that such "real issues" knew "no religious barriers," he laid out his vision for an America that valued religious freedom and tolerance:

> ... I believe in an America that is officially neither Catholic, Protestant, nor Jewish; ... where no

religious body seeks to impose its will directly or indirectly upon the general populace or the public acts of its officials; and where religious liberty is so indivisible that an act against one church is treated as an act against all. . . . I believe in an America where religious intolerance will someday end; where all men and all churches are treated as equal; where every man has the same right to attend or not attend the church of his choice; where there is no Catholic vote, no anti-Catholic vote, no bloc voting of any kind; and where Catholics, Protestants and Jews, at both the lay and pastoral level, will refrain from those attitudes of disdain and division ... and promote instead the American ideal of brotherhood. . . .

He also cautioned against letting prejudice hold sway, warning that America's history of bigotry could again be its future:

> For while this year it may be a Catholic against whom the finger of suspicion is pointed, in other years it has been, and may someday be again, a Jew—or a Quaker or a Unitarian or a Baptist. . . . Today I may be the victim, but tomorrow it may be you. . . . If this election is decided on the basis that 40 million Americans lost their chance of being President on the day they were baptized, then it is the whole nation that will be the loser, in the eyes of Catholics and non-Catholics around the world, in the eyes of history, and in the eyes of our own people.

Kennedy's successful appeal to Americans to reject the country's historical bias and bigotry against Catholics helped him win the election.

would have resonated with his brother Knights. When he stated, "The rights of man come not from generosity of the state, but from the hand of God," he expressed the importance of God as the source for the rights of all Americans. Then, in arguably his most famous words, he said, "And so my fellow Americans, ask not what your country can do for you—ask what you can do for your country." This exhortation expressed the same commitment to helping others that had always been at the heart of the Knights of Columbus. It would set the bar high for American volunteerism and service to humanity.

Later that year, Supreme Knight Hart visited President Kennedy at the White House. When they met, the president greeted Hart with the words, "Hello, Chief. You know, I'm a Fourth Degree member of the Knights of Columbus." During their visit, Hart presented Kennedy with a pin of the Fourth Degree emblem, which the president immediately placed on his lapel.

Hart also gave Kennedy a framed photo of the American flag along with the story of the Knights' role in having the words "under God" officially added to the Pledge of Allegiance.

In June 1963, Hart was invited to attend a meeting of religious leaders at the White House. The purpose of this unique gathering, headed by President Kennedy, was to consider ways to eliminate racially motivated discriminatory practices.

On November 22, 1963, when an assassin's bullets brought President Kennedy's life to an end, the entire country and much of the world felt a great sense of loss. They grieved for the man who had won their hearts and who had shown such great promise as the nation's leader. On behalf of the Knights of Columbus, the board of directors issued the following statement:

Supreme Knight Luke Hart presents President Kennedy with a framed picture of the American flag and the story of the Knights' role in having the words "under God" added to the Pledge of Allegiance.

> This horrible event brought to us and to all the world grief so profound and so personal that it will not soon subside. However heavily he was occupied with the demands of high office, there poured out of him a sympathy and concern for the least of his fellow man so genuine and so spontaneous that his death brought, throughout the world, tears that are shed only for the loss of a friend.

Born Giovanni Battista Montini, Pope Paul VI succeeded John XXIII and served from 1963 until 1978. He steered the Second Vatican Council to its conclusion, reaffirmed Church teaching on contraception, and was the first pope to visit the United States. Paul VI was canonized by Pope Francis in 2018.

As Catholics in America came into their own in the 1960s, the Knights passed two milestones—membership now exceeded a million, with more than 1.1 million men enrolled as Knights. These million-plus men also led the Order to surpass a billion dollars of insurance in force, which now totaled $1.4 billion.

Jacqueline Kennedy walks down the steps of the Capitol
with her children, John Jr. and Caroline. Robert Kennedy
and Patricia Kennedy Lawford follow close behind.

In memory of Kennedy as a Fourth Degree Knight, Cristo Rey Assembly presented a chalice to his widow, Jaqueline, which she directed to Army chaplain Major Lasalle Lenk, who had helped establish the Order in Hawaii. The Order also distributed nationally more than 250,000 of the funeral prayer cards Jacqueline had designed. On May 29, 1964, which would have been JFK's forty-seventh birthday, the Order participated in a requiem Mass at the National Shrine of the Immaculate Conception. Among the nearly 4,000 attendees were Kennedy's sister Eunice Kennedy Shriver and her husband, Sargent Shriver; President Eamon de Valera of Ireland; and numerous diplomats and members of Congress. Representing the Order were Supreme Advocate Judge Harold Lamboley and Deputy Supreme Knight Dr. John H. Griffin, who laid a wreath at Arlington National Cemetery during the graveside ceremony that followed the Mass.

Despite President Kennedy's untimely death, Catholics in the United States felt they had finally come into their own. Some in America had questioned whether Catholics could be devoted to both their faith and their country. It was a question that Father McGivney and the founders of the Order had sought to answer in 1882 when they chose Christopher Columbus as their namesake, and public figures for the Order's leaders. John Kennedy's presidency had answered the question definitively. Even in death, his Catholic funeral reminded the country of the full measure of American life that Catholicism now shared.

Supreme Knight Hart attended Kennedy's funeral as both a representative of the Order and as a friend. He jotted the following notes in his journal on that day:

*Apostolic Delegate asked me to wear my uniform and be seated in Sanctuary.*

*– Tenseness everywhere.*

*– At the Capitol, 500,000 watched transfer of body.*

*– John-John asked for flag for father.*

*– In rotunda–immense throng–line 4 abreast for 5 miles.*

*– Announced Capitol Rotunda would be closed at 10:00, [it was] kept open all night.*

*– Sorrowful scene–family–sorrowing Caroline, Jacqueline, John-John, Rose, Bobby, [Lyndon] Johnson and family.*

*– Millions lined the way to Arlington.*

*– The circumstances of his funeral, the flag draped casket on Lincoln's Catafalque, the funeral mass celebrated by his long time family friend, the funeral procession passing by Lincoln's monument and a vast throng of sorrowing countrymen, then interment with the prayers of the Church in Arlington cemetery, demonstrated not merely the Catholic's loyalty to America, but what is more, the Catholic's love and reverence for America's traditions and heritage.*

## END OF AN ERA

Shortly after Kennedy's assassination, the Order lost its twenty-five-year supreme secretary, Francis Lamb; Supreme Knight Hart passed a month later. Having known every previous supreme knight but Mullen, Hart's death marked a pivotal transition to a new era. Direct and sometimes combative and autocratic, Hart, a widower, had given his life to the Knights, even living in an apartment within the headquarters. Although Order-wide charitable programs—as had occurred during the world wars and the Depression—waned, the growing Order engaged in other new ways to reach out. It embraced "under God" as an expression of faith-filled patriotism, and continued its commitment to evangelization and to religious freedom at home and even behind the Iron Curtain.

An era had ended, but the Order's relevance had not. Catholicism seemed to come of age in America, but new challenges would emerge, and the principled voice of the Knights would be needed anew.

During the 1960s, the Second Vatican Council brought together more than 2,000 bishops to shape the Catholic Church's response to the modern world. It produced guiding documents on topics including the Church in contemporary society, the relationship of Catholics with non-Christians, religious freedom, communications, education, the laity, priestly formation, and more.

# 8.
# Balancing Modernization with Preservation
## 1964 to 1977

The 1960s and 1970s brought change for the Church and for the world. Public support for previous twentieth-century wars gave way to anti-Vietnam War protests. The sexual revolution and drug use—exemplified by Woodstock—coincided with an explosion of divorce and contraceptive use and with the legalization of abortion. Many Americans' fear of communism faded. Secularism and even Marxism gained ground. Simultaneously, the Civil Rights Movement took root, and the country began moving towards equal rights and integration—but Martin Luther King Jr. and others were violently killed. Political upheaval accompanied cultural upheaval; JFK and RFK were assassinated. Watergate brought Nixon's impeachment and resignation. Political violence in Latin America was also common, while the Philippines endured martial law.

For Catholics, there was dramatic change within the Church. The "new Mass" notably moved from Latin to the vernacular. Catholic theological dissent became common, and was voiced by progressives against teaching on contraception and by traditionalists on some of Vatican II's liturgical and theological interpretations.

Although these changes began in the twilight of Luke Hart's tenure, his successor, John W. McDevitt, would have to guide the Knights through these complicated times. The Order was uniquely positioned to respond, combining its nonnegotiable commitment to the Church with its long-standing embrace of Catholic social teaching as foundational to the Order's mission. With councils embodying charity and advocacy in many communities, the Order would tackle specific societal challenges with characteristic faith and action.

The turbulence of the era playing out in the American family was captured on the November 1970 cover of *Columbia* in this humorous illustration by John McDermott.

Sworn in as president after Kennedy's assassination, Lyndon B. Johnson won a second term in 1964. Johnson declared a "War on Poverty" with lasting social agendas that included the Medicare and Medicaid health care coverage programs, and the anti-discrimination Civil Rights Act. He also ramped up American involvement in Vietnam.

The first supreme chaplain who was not a relative of Father McGivney's, Bishop Charles Greco of Alexandria, Louisiana, served as supreme chaplain during the 1960s, 1970s, and most of the 1980s. His episcopal motto, "Vivat Jesus" ("Jesus Lives"), quoting Saint Bernardine of Siena, is now used Order-wide.

# AN EDUCATOR TAKES THE LEAD

Upon Luke Hart's sudden passing, Deputy Supreme Knight John McDevitt succeeded him. A Boston College graduate, Massachusetts native, and educator, McDevitt served as high school teacher, principal, superintendent, and chairman of the Massachusetts Board of Education. In Massachusetts, McDevitt had helped the Knights regain the ability to sell insurance in the state, and had also helped overcome internal disputes. As supreme knight, his resolution skills were immediately put to use with a divisive insurance dispute in Mexico and the enforcement of the Order's nondiscrimination policy.

McDevitt's background as an educator was often evident, and the Order soon partnered with the National Catholic Education Association to produce a booklet, "The Human Purpose of Catholic Education." Approximately 75,000 copies were distributed at the Vatican's World's Fair Pavilion, and another 100,000 were handed out subsequently. The Knights also began providing religious-themed covers for children's schoolbooks. New scholarships and fellowships were offered, and the Order even began presenting student loans.

Initially, McDevitt believed that Catholics had triumphed in America, telling the 1966 convention, "It is high time we abandon the concept of our Order as mainly a fortress to protect us from a hostile world. We are not a besieged minority." After a decade of cultural changes including the sexual revolution challenging previously normative Christian values, McDevitt's view changed. "A principal peril to the freedoms of those who believe in God is the increasing secularization of society," he said, adding that his goal had been to "rally our brother Knights in this great battle with the forces of secularism."

The Knights' response to cultural and Catholic currents animated McDevitt's tenure. Following Vatican II, he guided the Order's efforts of reform and renewal to help serve and shape the modern world. Driving the Order's action was a focus on the dignity of each person—especially racial minorities, the disabled, and the unborn—who faced various forms of marginalization.

**John W. McDevitt**
Eleventh supreme knight.

Vatican II opened under
Pope John XXIII and concluded
under Pope Paul VI.

# IMPLEMENTING THE VISION OF VATICAN II

The Second Vatican Council, often referred to as Vatican II, convened in 1962 under Pope John XXIII and concluded under Pope Paul VI in 1965. Over 2,600 bishops participated in the council, which was designed to bring about a spiritual renewal of the Church and an evangelization of the modern world by renewed Catholic engagement with it. In four annual two-month sessions, the group considered how the Church might respond to the new challenges it faced in the rapidly changing world. Sixteen major documents resulted from

At the 1964 New York World's Fair, whose theme was "Peace Through Understanding," Knights volunteered at the Vatican Pavilion. Guiding 77,000 daily visitors through treasures including Michelangelo's *Pieta*, they fielded questions about the Church and its teachings and distributed reading material to visitors.

On October 4, 1965, Paul VI landed in New York, beginning the Western Hemisphere's first papal visit. His blessing, he said, "renew[ed], as it were, the gesture of your discoverer, Christopher Columbus, when he planted the Cross of Christ on this blessed soil." The pope also addressed the UN and celebrated Mass at Yankee Stadium.

# Call for the Embrace of the Lay Vocation

Vatican II's call for the laity to consider new possibilities with their vocation resonated with the Knights, who were pioneers of the active role of the laity. As a 1900 *Columbiad* article described, "The effect of the Society of the Knights of Columbus has . . . become extraordinary; the Catholic layman has been brought to realize the preciousness of his birthright as a son of the Church." Representing the Order, Supreme Knight McDevitt attended the Third World Congress of the Lay Apostolate in Rome in 1967. He returned energized, with some concerns about those who sought to change Church teaching on contraception, and praise for the Vatican II documents that called the laity "to infuse a Christian spirit into the mentality, customs, laws and structure of the community."

McDevitt was not alone in calling the Knights to help shape the Church and the world with a lay response. Archbishop Fulton Sheen suggested something similar in the wake of Vatican II. At the 1970 convention, Sheen urged Knights to become "a new kind of laity," which would seek to build the Kingdom of God by collaborating with those of good will in doing good work:

Your theology is the theology of action. It is related to the world, to social problems, to economic problems, to the 250,000 who sleep in the streets of Calcutta, to the increasing poverty of Latin America, to our slums. The basis of your theology also must be charity, but not the charity that is private, or personal, or of the neighborhood or the I-thou type. Lay theology of charity is related to the world—not just to the membership— but to the same problems which concern our politicians and economists. But you will do it with a different [Christian] motivation.

In 1972, addressing the Pennsylvania Knights' annual pilgrimage to the shrine of Our Lady of Czestochowa in Doylestown, Pennsylvania, Sheen added a vital responsibility to the laity, saying: "Who is going to save our Church? Not our bishops, not our priests and religious. It is up to you, the people. You have the minds, the eyes, and the ears to save the Church. Your mission is to see that your priests act like priests, your bishops act like bishops, and your religious act like religious."

John McDevitt (second from left) and Count Enrico Galeazzi (far left) attending the Third World Congress of the Lay Apostolate at the Vatican in 1967.

On December 8, 1965, Pope Paul VI concluded the Second Vatican Council. He noted that although "secular humanism, revealing itself in its horrible anti-clerical reality has, in a certain sense, defied the council," there was no clash, battle, or condemnation. Rather, the council's spirituality was that of the Good Samaritan.

Known as the "Rosary Priest," Father Patrick Peyton dedicated his life to advocating the family rosary, proclaiming, "The family that prays together stays together." In the 1950s, Peyton received the first honorary Fourth Degree membership bestowed by the Knights. In 1965, the Knights' friendship continued with $25,000 to help foster Marian devotion worldwide.

these historic meetings, covering a host of issues. Among these works were *Gaudium et Spes,* the Pastoral Constitution on the Church in the Modern World; *Dignitatis Humanae,* the Declaration on Religious Freedom; and *Nostra Aetate,* the Declaration on the Relation of the Church to Non-Christian Religions.

Supreme Knight McDevitt urged "early and complete acceptance of the decisions of the Vatican Council and an earnest effort by all of us to attain the objectives to which they are directed." In particular, he interpreted this as invigorating Christian life, adapting changeable institutions to the needs of the times, fostering unity among Christians, and evangelization, which he described as "strengthen[ing] whatever can help to call the whole of mankind into the household of the Church."

Reflecting this, the Order revised its ceremonials, updating aspects that seemed dated in a more modern setting. Responding to objections, McDevitt explained that "Today's Catholic man . . . tends to be more moved by ideas than by rituals, and to resent being forced into contrived situations of crisis." He believed that "the new ceremonials, properly performed, can talk to this modern man on his terms."

The Order also undertook an educational role in response to rising confusion—and hostility—regarding Church teaching. Supreme Chaplain Bishop Greco noted sadly that the Church was plagued by "dissent, disunity, [and] rebellion on the part of those who seek to change beyond recognition the Church's structure, discipline, worship, [and] dogmas." On controversial subjects like abortion, contraception, and human sexuality, the Order continued to promote the Church's clearly defined doctrine. *Columbia* and the Order's Religious Information Bureau (soon renamed Catholic Information Service) diligently clarified and defended unchanging (but challenged) Church teachings, while also reporting neutrally other elements of the post-Vatican II debates. Not surprisingly, requests for pamphlets and correspondence courses increased, and many people praised their usefulness in clarifying Catholic teaching and aiding conversions and apologetics.

Vatican II's push for considering the concrete needs of humanity found expression, too, both in councils' charitable activities and in *Columbia.* Councils were encouraged to collaborate with community organizations and reach out to ecumenical groups, while pursuing solutions to injustice, poverty, marginalization, and discrimination. Further highlighting the Order's shift towards being a family-oriented organization, *Columbia* often treated the dynamics, struggles, and solutions of family life, providing practical advice that could nurture strong, faith-filled families and inoculate against family breakup. The mosaic of action showed that councils took to heart McDevitt's advice to embrace Vatican II's *Gaudium et Spes* as "a veritable banquet table from which our councils can choose additional programs to fit their interests and capabilities."

The themes and content of the Second Vatican Council, as well as papal documents, were made available and accessible in the Order's Religious Information Bureau booklets. Included were simplified versions of the Council's documents on the Scripture and the Church, and Pope Paul VI's encyclical on human life, *Humanae Vitae.*

In 1967, the 1914 *Catholic Encyclopedia* was updated with the Knights' support utilizing new technologies. Making trustworthy knowledge about the Catholic Church, its teaching, and its history more available, councils like Msgr. Martin C. Murphy Council 6847 of East Columbia, South Carolina, donated copies to local parishes and schools.

# Jeremiah Denton
## Notable Knight

Born in 1924, Jeremiah Denton, a native of Mobile, Alabama, was brought up in the Catholic faith by his mother. He attributed the fortitude he would have to rely on later in life to one of his teachers, a religious sister who, after he led his class to skip school, acknowledged Jeremiah's gift for leadership but challenged his use of that gift. A military career beginning at the Naval Academy in Annapolis allowed him to put his talents to good use. Nothing, however, tested his leadership ability more than being a senior ranking officer among American POWs during the Vietnam War.

Beginning in 1965 and continuing for more than seven years, Denton endured physical and mental torture and severe living conditions as a POW. He spent four years in solitary confinement in the most infamous prisons in the region, including the "Hanoi Hilton," "Las Vegas," and—for more resistant POWs—"Alcatraz." For Denton, lightless rooms, starvation, beatings, leg irons, and other forms of torture became all too familiar.

One of the greatest challenges faced by the American prisoners was the ability to communicate, a key element of POW survival. The guards were on constant watch for any signs of insurrection and inflicted swift punishment on offenders. As one of the highest-ranking prisoners, Denton led his fellow POWs as best he could to keep up morale and to maintain military cohesion. He devised a system of communicating in Morse code by tapping on a wall or, capitalizing on the constant ill health of his comrades, by using coughs and sneezes.

In a moment that gained national attention, Denton used his communication method to "speak" to the entire world. As a propoganda stunt, the North Vietnamese filmed him in a scripted interview that was broadcast in 1966. In it, his captors instructed him to say that American prisoners were receiving fair treatment and adequate care. Although he adhered to the script, he communicated the true situation with his eyes, using Morse code to blink the word "T-O-R-T-U-R-E." And then, in an even more courageous act, he deviated from the script and pledged his allegiance to the United States and its policies.

Upon his release, Denton continued to serve in the military, rising to the rank of rear admiral. In 1981, he took public office as US Senator from Alabama, a position he held until 1987. Concerned about cultural shifts that had been made more obvious by his seven-year absence, he founded the Coalition for Decency for the promotion of morality.

In 1975, Denton wrote an article for *Columbia* on the United States and the importance of morality in culture. Two years later, he addressed the delegates at the 94th Supreme Convention. He praised his fellow knights as "valiant fighters for the preservation and application of values which I, as a Catholic, as a professional Navy officer and former captive of Communism, see as essential, not only to pleasing God, but to the survival of this nation and of the free world."

# FOSTERING RACIAL HARMONY

During the early 1960s, as the Civil Rights Movement gained momentum, the Knights again turned their attention to racial issues—both within and outside the Order. As mentioned in Chapter 2 (see page 27), the Knights of Columbus was considered an organization whose fraternal spirit brought together Catholics of all races and colors. The examples were many. The Order welcomed its first African-American member in the 1890s. The Knights also urged those outside the Order to look past race and color. The Knights ran integrated facilities for troops (huts) during World War I, decades before the US military was integrated. In 1924, it commissioned *The Gift of Black Folk* by NAACP co-founder W.E.B. Du Bois, making a substantial contribution to black history.

Dr. Martin Luther King Jr. calls for an end to racism in his inspirational "I Have a Dream" speech, delivered during the March on Washington for Jobs and Freedom on August 28, 1963.

The 1960s saw the Knights give this issue solid attention once again. As mentioned in Chapter 6, in June 1963, President Kennedy invited Supreme Knight Hart to attend a White House meeting of religious leaders to consider ways to eliminate racial discrimination. Just a few months later, when Martin Luther King Jr. delivered his "I Have a Dream" speech at the pivotal March on Washington for Jobs and Freedom, the Knights donated $25,000 for lodgings so that Catholic clergy—including brother Knight Father Wiliam Ryan—could attend the event.

Supreme Knight Hart and then McDevitt sought to eradicate racism among those who wanted to do business with the Knights, as well as among some members. Unfortunately, some Knights resisted these efforts. Although the Order had African-American members as far back as the 1800s, and candidates were not required to state their race on applications, it became known that some members were manipulating the admissions process to exclude certain applicants based on race. (At that time, a blackball system was used in which five votes against any applicant would block his entry.) Aware of this misuse of the admissions system, Hart spoke out against racism and encouraged integration within the councils.

In 1963, an incident prompted Hart to do more than simply encourage racial tolerance. When the membership application of black Notre Dame alumnus Joe Bertrand was rejected, six council members resigned in protest of the vote. Previously, Bertrand had had a positive experience with the Knights. When he and his fellow athletes were travelling and were refused

Countering racism with love, forgiveness, and a sense of humor, Ernest I. King worked for integration and helped found the interracial North Carolina Catholic Laymen's Association. A member of Council 1074 in Wilmington, he proved a skilled leader and was the Order's first black state deputy south of the Mason-Dixon Line.

In the 1960s, the Knights showed a strong commitment to racial equality on both state and local levels. In Harlem, New York, Dr. Martin Luther King, Jr. Council 6135 was formed. Supreme Knight McDevitt celebrated its inauguration with the grand knight, chaplain, and state deputy (pictured left to right).

# Floyd Patterson
## Notable Knight

Raised in an impoverished Brooklyn family, young Floyd Patterson struggled. Shy, virtually illiterate, and often truant or stealing food, Patterson ended up in reform school. Surrounded by supportive instructors, he was introduced to boxing—and it helped him rebuild his life. His skill swiftly catapulted him to the top. A protégé of Constantine (Cus) D'Amato, the teenage Patterson won the 1952 middleweight Olympic gold medal. At age twenty-one, he become the youngest world heavyweight champion, holding the title for three years, then regaining it in 1960—another first. Along with his hallmark "peek-a-boo" style, his sportsmanship stood out in gestures like helping an opponent up off the mat or refusing to gain an "unfair advantage" by watching a future opponent train.

There were battles outsides the ring too. Patterson strongly promoted civil rights and integration, despite opposition. In 1957, a hostile crowd of white locals impeded his arrival in Fort Smith, Arkansas, where he had a scheduled stop on an exhibition tour. A priest—himself an integration supporter—intervened, bringing Patterson and his entourage to the church and hosting them at the rectory. Soon after, Patterson demanded integrated venues for boxing.

He later traveled to Birmingham, Alabama, standing with Martin Luther King Jr. amid death threats, and he decried his opponent Muhammad Ali's embrace of the Nation of Islam for its divisive outlook on race, stating that it "preach[ed] hate and separation instead of love and integration."

While heavyweight champion, Patterson converted to Catholicism in 1957. He later joined the Knights of Columbus in New Paltz, New York, and became, in biographer W. Stratton's words, "a mainstay" of Knights' events. He also helped the parish by distributing Holy Communion at the local nursing home, calling himself "the Eucharistic minister with the biggest hands." Despite his love of his sport, he once mused that if the Church forbade boxing, he would give it up. When an interviewer later recalled these words for Patterson and asked if his faith was still as strong, he replied that it was even stronger.

accommodations because they were a multiracial team, the local Knights took them in and provided housing at the K of C Hall. After the situation regarding Bertrand's membership was rectified, Hart became adamant that a change in the Order's admissions system was needed. Preventing even isolated incidents of this kind was essential, and he began making plans to have the system revised at the Supreme Convention later that year.

On June 17, 1972, the Watergate scandal began when burglars with ties to the Nixon White House were arrested for breaking into the Democratic National Committee's office at the Watergate complex in Washington, DC. The scandal brought down President Richard Nixon, who resigned as removal from office appeared increasingly likely.

In 1970, when disaster struck Apollo 13, flight director Gene Kranz, a member of Council 6234, successfully managed the astronauts' safe return. That same year, Kranz received an award on NASA's behalf from the Knights, honoring the space agency's accomplishments, particularly the first lunar landing in 1969 by Apollo 11.

In the photo above, professor of history Arthur Wright speaks on the subject of interracial justice at the 1965 Conference on Human Rights at Yale University.

At right, noted activist and chairman of the Congress of Racial Equality, Roy Innis (seated at center) is among the attendees at the 1968 conference on social awareness at the LaFarge Institute.

Luke Hart died unexpectedly before the convention took place, but his successor, John W. McDevitt, was just as determined to ensure that the racial harmony the Knights had always stood for would become a reality. Shortly before the convention, which was to be held at the Roosevelt Hotel in New Orleans, McDevitt discovered that the hotel was segregated and admitted only white guests. When he threatened to relocate the convention to another hotel, the Roosevelt began welcoming black guests that very day.

During the convention, as a sign of his commitment to fighting prejudice, McDevitt seated Father Harold R. Perry—a black priest who would later serve as an auxiliary bishop in New Orleans—at the head table during the States Dinner. It was also at this convention that the admissions system was amended. According to the new rule, a potential member could be refused admission only if one-third of the voting members voted against him. A few years later in 1972, the policy was amended once again. This time, a majority of votes was needed to deny a candidate's admission—a policy that curtailed further abuse of the system.

Supreme Knight McDevitt remained committed to the fight against racial discrimination. Close to home, at Yale University, in the spring of 1965, the Order co-sponsored a conference with the Archdiocese of Hartford. Focused on racial justice, the human rights conference drew 2,000 people. One of the programs to emerge from this conference was the Project of Equality. Under it, all firms doing business with the archdiocese were required to submit their equal employment policies and practices for review.

In 1967, the Order collaborated with the LaFarge Institute to help further increase social justice awareness among members. Named for Father John

Marian devotion drew up to 10,000 Knights and their families yearly for Knights of Columbus Day at the National Shrine of Our Lady of Czestochowa in Doylestown, Pennsylvania. Receiving the Pennsylvania State Council award there in 1972, Archbishop Fulton Sheen urged the laity to take responsibility for saving the Church.

In what would later be considered a "livelihood" program that provided support for workers in the Philippines, in 1971, Knights of Muñoz Council 4268 in Nueva Ecija, Luzon, distributed piglets to the area's farmers, helping to improve their living conditions.

LaFarge, former editor of *America* magazine and a champion of racial equality, the institute focused on the study of racial issues, poverty, and peace. In the past, the Knights had collaborated with LaFarge personally, including a donation of $35,000 for building the Gibbons Institute, a school for African Americans. Taking up his causes, the LaFarge Institute created and disseminated material on subjects such as race relations, economic issues, social problems, and civic responsibilities. It also created outlines for dialogue and sent them to councils to facilitate ecumenical and civil rights discussions. Over 800 councils participated in the ongoing discussion series, which lasted into the early 1970s and led to the establishment of a number of successful programs.

# VATICAN COMMUNICATIONS

One significant concern of the Holy See in the 1960s was its limited ability to reach out and communicate to a widespread audience. As the Second Vatican Council showed, the Catholic Church was very much a global Church, but its ability to communicate worldwide had not kept pace. There was still a need to disseminate news and information from the Vatican more effectively.

Aware of this need, Supreme Knight McDevitt and Cardinal Francis Spellman led a successful campaign to provide the Vatican with shortwave transmitters for its radio station. In 1966, Pope Paul VI formally dedicated three new transmitters—one donated by the Order—for Vatican Radio. With McDevitt in attendance at the dedication as a guest of honor, the Holy Father voiced his gratitude to the Knights "for this valuable contribution." The Holy See was now able to make Vatican Radio a more effective instrument in preaching the message of the Gospel to all nations.

Pope Paul VI at the control panel during the 1966 blessing and dedication of the newly donated radio transmitters for Vatican Radio. Count Enrico Galeazzi and others look on.

While radio broadcasts were certainly an improved means of communication, a decade later, the Order helped take Vatican communications to an even higher level by financing the satellite "uplink" signal the Vatican needed to transmit various telecasts worldwide. Funding these televised broadcasts exemplified the Knights' ongoing commitment to help the Holy See communicate Catholic teachings to every corner of the world.

According to Supreme Knight McDevitt, "Our Holy Father offers the one respected voice of conscience that can guide a world floundering in the sands of shifting morality." With the Knights' help, television stations worldwide were able to air (for free) papal messages and programs from the Vatican such as Midnight Mass and Easter Sunday service.

As the Order improved the Holy See's reach through communications, the Knights in Alaska helped build personal communications as well. In 1971, the Knights donated an amphibious plane to the Juneau diocese, enabling the auxiliary bishop—a pilot—to visit outposts unreachable by other modes of transportation.

In 1973, faith's timelessness found expression in Maine as Knights celebrated Mass and dedicated a plaque on the shores of the St. Croix River. In 1604, the first Mass had been offered in New England by Parisian priest Nicholas Augray, as part of Samuel de Champlain's exploration of the New World.

## BUILDING FOR THE FUTURE

In the mid-1960s, Supreme Knight McDevitt set the wheels in motion for the building of a new headquarters to serve the growing organization. Located in New Haven, Connecticut, the building was to exemplify the modernization of the Order. Auxiliary Bishop John F. Hackett of Hartford, Mayor Richard C. Lee of New Haven, and the supreme officers attended the 1967 groundbreaking ceremony, which was described as "an historic and momentous occasion" by McDevitt.

Built a stone's throw from where the early Knights celebrated their fifth anniversary, the new headquarters for the Knights of Columbus was dedicated in 1969. The cylindrical corner towers represent charity, unity, fraternity, and patriotism—the founding principles of the Order.

Designed by the architectural firm of Kevin Roche, John Dinkeloo, and Associates, the soaring twenty-three story glass, steel, and concrete structure was completed in 1969. Its four 320-foot-tall cylindrical towers—one at each corner of the building—represent the Order's four principles of charity, unity, fraternity, and patriotism. At the dedication ceremony, Mayor Lee stated: "It is not just a structure, it is almost a piece of art . . . a monument to an exciting city by a fine architect and a great organization which is preparing for the twenty-first century." The distinctive high-rise became an immediate focal point of the New Haven skyline, where it continues to stand prominently as one of the city's tallest buildings.

When it opened, the new headquarters was equipped with state-of-the-art computers and other cutting-edge technology. As the headquarters grew, so did the already successful insurance program. In 1960, the insurance in force had reached $1 billion. By 1971, that number had doubled, and four years later, it topped the $3 billion mark.

The Order's spacious new headquarters also allowed the Religious Information Bureau, which published information on the teachings of the Church, to move to New Haven from St. Louis. With the move, the Supreme Council renamed it the Catholic Information Service (CIS), and appointed Father John V. McGuire, CSsR, as program director. The Missouri Knights, who had run the initial program since 1944, continued to fund their own program, which retained the original name of Religious Information Bureau.

In August 1971, Richard M. Nixon became the first US president to address a Supreme Convention. "No one could be more aware than I of your significant role in building a better and more just society," he said. "Your devotion to both God and country sets an inspiring message for all men."

Preserving early Christian historical sites was a personal calling for George B. Quatman, a telecommunications pioneer and supreme director respected for his deep faith. The Order encouraged councils to support the ecumenical work of his American Society of Ephesus, restoring sacred sites including Mary's last abode, revered by Catholics, Christians, and Muslims.

# Vietnam: A Catalyst for Brotherly Concern

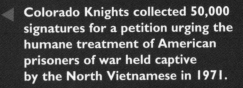

Colorado Knights collected 50,000 signatures for a petition urging the humane treatment of American prisoners of war held captive by the North Vietnamese in 1971.

A collection by employees at Supreme Council headquarters and a matching gift by management procured a half ton of Christmas gifts for American servicemen in Vietnam in 1967.

Care for the spiritual welfare of troops led New York councils to provide 10,000 rosaries and 25,000 Saint Michael Medals blessed by Cardinal Terence Cooke (pictured) for distribution during his annual Christmas visit to Americans serving in Vietnam.

Like many other councils that helped Vietnamese refugees establish homes and lives in a new country, in 1976, Hutchinson Council 612 in Kansas provided a warm welcome and necessities for this family of sixteen from South Vietnam.

Chaplain (Major) Charles Watters, a brother Knight and Medal of Honor recipient, gave his life after repeatedly leaving the defensive perimeter and rescuing wounded under enemy fire. Unarmed, he ministered to soldiers on the front lines with total disregard for his own safety.

# Sargent Shriver
## Notable Knight

A member of Mater Dei Council 9774 in Rockville, Maryland, Robert Sargent Shriver enjoyed a long and prestigious career as a dedicated public servant. He was a great humanitarian and tireless advocate for the poor. A graduate of Yale Law School, Shriver served as a naval officer during World War II. Shortly after, he began working for Joseph P. Kennedy, father of the future president. He married Kennedy's daughter Eunice in 1953.

While campaigning for the presidency in early 1960, then Senator John F. Kennedy first mentioned the concept of a "peace corps" while speaking at the University of Michigan. During that speech, he challenged the students to serve their country for the cause of peace by living and working in developing nations. Shriver loved his brother-in-law's idea.

When Kennedy won the election, a determined Shriver was instrumental in developing the program even further as part of the administration's New Frontier initiative. In 1961, the pilot Peace Corps, with Shriver as its organizer and director, was underway. What began over fifty years ago as an experimental venture, continues to be a program of great significance—one that has welcomed over 200,000 volunteers who have contributed their efforts to the people of nearly 140 countries.

Shriver's contributions did not end with the Peace Corps. During the Johnson Administration, he was appointed head of the Office of Economic Opportunity's War on Poverty. Through his involvement with educational and community development, he oversaw the creation of a number of national projects designed to reduce poverty. Among these programs—which are still in existence today—were Head Start, VISTA, and the Job Corps. Shriver was also responsible for establishing community health centers and law offices that offered services to the poor.

Shriver assisted his wife, Eunice, in founding the Special Olympics in 1968, further highlighting his concern for the dignity of all people. Upon Shriver's death in 2011, Special Olympics President Brady Lum said, "Sargent Shriver was a pioneer for our movement, helping us establish and build programs in the far corners of the world."

Sargent Shriver was a visionary man whose life and role in public service exemplified the principles of charity, unity, fraternity, and patriotism. His generosity, compassion, and tireless outreach touched countless lives and has helped make the world a better place.

On January 22, 1973, the Supreme Court decision *Roe v. Wade* legalized abortion in the United States. More than 40 million abortions followed over the next few decades. Norma McCorvey—the case's "Jane Roe"—would later become a pro-life advocate, calling the case "the biggest mistake of my life."

On January 27, 1973, after years of secret negotiations, the Paris Peace Accords were signed with the intention of ending the Vietnam War. Although the Accords effectively removed the United States from the conflict in Vietnam, the ceasefire collapsed in 1975, and in April 1975, Saigon fell to the North Vietnamese army.

# The New York Knights and Fifty Years of Sports Excellence
## Visionary Council Initiative

From baseball and bowling leagues, to sporting events for youth and military servicemen, the Knights has long embraced athletic pursuits for the self-discipline, camaraderie, and achievement they foster. For decades, one such initiative stood out in terms of both excellence and longevity: the Annual Indoor Track Meet of the New York Knights of Columbus.

Considered one of the most prestigious track competitions in the world, the meet featured Olympic athletes and record-setting performances. Councils in the Bronx and Manhattan began the meet in 1918 through the efforts of track promoter Frank A. Brennan. First held at the 22nd Engineers Armory in the Fort Washington section of Manhattan, the yearly games moved to Madison Square Garden in 1925 and remained a fixture there for many years.

During World War II, although many track competitions—including the 1944 Summer Olympics—were cancelled, the Knights' meet continued. The Olympic Committee later formally thanked the New York Knights for enabling athletes to maintain a high level of athleticism during that time.

The K of C's track meet was renowned for the high caliber of its participants. World-class athletes competed in a variety of events, including running, hurdles, pole vaulting, and the famous Columbian Mile, which was eventually renamed the Frank A. Brennan Columbian Mile in honor of the meet's founder. Among the records set in the 1960s was a new indoor mark in the high jump set by the Soviet Union's Valeriy Brumel in 1961, and Noel Carroll of Ireland's indoor half mile in 1967.

The last meet was held in 1970, concluding over half a century of track meets that enriched the lives of New York Knights and dedicated athletes from around the world. Following in New York's footsteps, Knights launched similar events in other cities, including Boston and Cleveland.

In many parts of the world, reliable sources of water are in short supply, causing great hardship. In the Philippines, Knights helped improve the water supply with more than a few helping hands from Bishop Acebedo Council 5478 in Caubig, which built a reservoir for the whole town in 1975.

Brother Knight Archbishop Fulton Sheen (shown here with John McDevitt) urged the 1975 Supreme Convention not to support "Catholic" schools using "Christless" catechisms that reduced faith to "love your neighbor" without sacrificial love. He also urged the Knights to "teach respect for all life," calling abortion and euthanasia national sins.

# Celebrating the Special Olympics Through the Years

Supreme Knight Virgil Dechant with athletes at the 1987 Special Olympics opening ceremony.

A volunteer from Council 2883 in Danielson, Connecticut, provides on-field support to an athlete at the Connecticut Summer Olympic Games in New Haven, 2010.

Supreme Knight Dechant and Eunice Shriver at a Mass for the 1991 Special Olympics in St. Paul, Minnesota.

At the first International Special Olympics Games at the University of Notre Dame, nearly 5,000 local Knights volunteered, including the school's Council 1477.

Sargent Shriver and Supreme Knight Anderson in 2003.

# PARTNERING WITH THE SPECIAL OLYMPICS

Recognizing the dignity of every person and caring for the marginalized was a founding hallmark of the Order's charitable efforts. Some of these efforts have long involved activities for people with physical and mental disabilities. To support and empower such individuals, in the 1960s and 1970s, councils and assemblies helped in a variety of ways, providing both concrete help for individuals and monetary support for organizations, schools, and camps. Some state councils took up particular causes, such as when the New York state council pioneered large-scale funding for Catholic special needs programs, noting that the Blaine Amendment "discriminate[s] against the mentally handicapped [*sic*] if a parent wishes to send the child to a religious-oriented school." By the 1970s, "Tootsie Roll" drives became an Order-wide fundraising mechanism for the intellectually disabled—with success. The 1972 Illinois drive—attended by the governor—netted $150,000 in two days. The Supreme Council also embraced the well-being and potential of individuals with special needs, launching a fellowship, named for Supreme Chaplain Charles Greco, for those doing graduate work in the teaching of individuals with intellectual disabilities. Bishop Greco had established the first school for the intellectually disabled in the state of Louisiana in 1954.

In the 1960s, the Order began a lasting and rewarding partnership with Special Olympics that was embraced by councils and jurisdictions throughout the Order. The Special Olympics was founded by Eunice Kennedy Shriver, who, besides being a sister of John F. Kennedy and wife of Sargent Shriver (see Notable Knight on page 168), was a pioneer in the struggle to secure rights for people with intellectual disabilities. Of special concern was the lack of recreational opportunities for these children—opportunities that would help them realize their full physical potential.

In July 1968, the first Special Olympics Summer Games were held at Soldier Field in Chicago, Illinois. The Games included 1,000 participants from throughout the United States and Canada. The Knights of Columbus was supportive of the Special Olympics from the start. Members eagerly volunteered their time and service for this inaugural event, while many more attended the games to cheer on and support the participants.

Since that opening game, the Special Olympics has evolved into an international competition involving more than 4 million people in over 170 countries. Through the years, the Knights, at the Supreme Council and local levels, have generously donated both time and funding to the event. As of 2018, the Knights raised and donated more than $600 million for the Special Olympics and programs for people with intellectual disabilities, and since 2014 alone, the Knights have volunteered about 4 million hours.

From hands-on help to financial support, many local councils prioritized the needs and well-being of people with disabilities. Here, a check from Michael O'Connor Council 5026 in Beaufort, South Carolina, is given to Camp Dynamite, a day camp for people with intellectual disabilities.

PROTECT RELIGIOUS FREEDOM

Foreseeing that an increasingly militant secularism would threaten religious freedom, in 1976, the Order established a $500,000 fund for the legal defense of religious liberties of Catholics and other believers. Supreme Knight McDevitt noted that "The Constitution of the United States never was meant to turn believers into second-class citizens."

## CHAMPIONING THE RIGHT TO LIFE

As the decades progressed, new groups of people were overlooked or marginalized by society. In 1882, widows, orphans, and Catholic immigrants had occupied the margins, earning the Knights' attentive protection. By the late 1960s, it became clear that for some newcomers to society's margins, the concern was not how to improve their lives, but whether they would be allowed to live at all.

Even before abortion's widespread legalization, the Knights took action. As acceptance of abortion rose, the Knights petitioned politicians. Councils showed the film *The Right to Life,* narrated by Lorretta Young, which answered common objections. Council programs, *Columbia* articles, and speeches reflected how the Knights saw safeguarding vulnerable unborn human lives as consistent with their founding mission of protecting Catholic families and their children as well as assisting those on the margins of society. At the 1970 convention, noting that "knights" being "protectors" was "a solid reason" why Father McGivney accepted the term for the Order's name, Supreme Knight McDevitt urged, "We, the knights of today, likewise must serve in the role of protectors. In an age suffering from loss of faith in God and lack of confidence in man we must be the knights who will hold up the banner of life. We must be for life. We must protect life."

The first March for Life, held on the anniversary of the *Roe v. Wade* decision, was organized to inspire congressional support for the unborn. According to march founder Nellie Gray, she "received a call from [some] Knights of Columbus," who suggested the idea. Brother Knight William Devlin also designed the logo, depicting the roses given to congressmen.

In 1973, the Supreme Convention held a special session on life issues, and passed a resolution supporting a pro-life constitutional amendment. McDevitt denounced the Supreme Court decision in *Roe v. Wade,* which legalized abortion nationwide, as "shocking and unfortunate." He urged councils to take action to "offset the harmful effects of this lamentable decision."

From this point forward, the Order—consistent with Church teachings—stepped up its resolve to campaign for the sanctity of human life and to oppose abortion as a threat to innocent life. For example, in 1975, the Knights gave a $50,000 grant to the US bishops in support of their pro-life efforts; the grant was renewed the following year. In 1977, the "Save the Baby" campaign was launched, distributing bumper stickers and posters with this message to councils nationwide. The "One Rose, One Life" fundraising campaigns would provide tremendous assistance to pro-life and pregnancy support programs. Over the years, as abortion took the lives of a million unborn children annually, the Order—at every level—would continue its defense of human life at home and abroad in ways large and small.

The first March for Life drew some 30,000 participants, including groups from hundreds of miles away.

---

"We must not be taken in by candidates who state that they personally are opposed to abortion but assert it would be wrong to impose their conviction on others by legislative or constitutional means. Killing innocent human life is so monumental an injustice that the question of whether or not to commit the crime cannot be left to private option. . . . We must disagree with the contention made in the platform of a major American political party that it is "undesirable to attempt to amend the United States Constitution to overturn the Supreme Court decision." The fact that the option to kill the unborn is the law of the land does not make it either right or just. . . . Abortion is a cancerous iniquity in our society which must be excised to save the social structure from total deterioration. Nor must we succumb to defeatism by the enormity of the task. We cannot permit the fiber of our will to yield to the callousness of a secular conscience . . . "

—Supreme Knight McDevitt, 1976 Supreme Knight's Report

From local councils to the Supreme Council, Knights promoted "choosing life." For example, Hawaii councils raised $100,000 for the Mary Jane Home for Unwed Mothers with a 1974 dinner headlined by Archbishop Sheen, while the Supreme Council provided printing services for the March for Life and its founder, Nellie Gray (pictured).

Pro-life essay contests were held by many councils. Urging youth to consider the sanctity of all human life, Spalding Council 417 in Washington, DC, held such an essay contest for fifth and sixth graders. These students, all attendees of St. Francis de Sales Catholic school, wrote the winning essays.

# Vince Lombardi
## Notable Knight

*"The greatest accomplishment is not in never failing, but in rising again after you fall."*

A man with strong Catholic faith and an unparalleled coaching career, Vincent "Vince" T. Lombardi is rightly one of the most revered coaches in NFL history. Within two years of taking over the struggling Green Bay Packers in 1959, he led them to two consecutive NFL championships, soon followed by a third championship, as well as victories in Super Bowls I and II. When he retired, Lombardi's career coaching record stood at 105 wins, 36 losses, and 6 ties.

But beyond his coaching expertise, he earned regard for his values, which he both lived on his own and instilled in his team, urging hard work and discipline for overcoming problems and achieving goals. Believing faith was important in every life, he considered daily Mass and communion the source of his strength, and he often led his Catholic players to Mass. Lombardi joined Monsignor Basche Council 4505 in Green Bay, Wisconsin, and later became a Fourth Degree Knight.

A believer in civil rights, Lombardi famously would not tolerate racial prejudice—and not just among his players. He made it clear to local shops and restaurants that if they refused to serve any of his players because of their skin color, they would be boycotted by the entire team. And players who displayed any act of prejudice would be dropped from the team.

When Lombardi died in 1970 at age fifty-seven, thousands attended his funeral at New York's St. Patrick's Cathedral. Decades later, he remains one of the most notable sports figures of all time. Despite his success and the high regard in which he was held, Lombardi never lost sight of his purpose in life. This was perhaps best expressed by the following words, which he spoke to his players:

> After all the cheers have died down and the stadium is empty, after the headlines have been written, and after you are back in the quiet of your room and the championship ring has been placed on the dresser, and after all the pomp and fanfare have faded, the enduring thing that is left is the dedication to doing with our lives the very best we can to make the world a better place in which to live.

In 1971, the Super Bowl championship trophy was named after Vince Lombardi. And in Middletown, New Jersey, Council 6522 was also named in his honor.

When an earthquake struck Guatemala in February 1976, killing 23,000 and making one million homeless, the Guatemala Knights—although a small, newly created district—established an aid station in Guatemala City. With donations from Mexican and US councils, they distributed 6,000 tons of food, clothing, and medicine.

In the 1970s, the Order began reporting not just membership and insurance, but also man-hours and dollars given in charity. In 1977, membership had grown to 1.3 million Knights, and insurance had tripled to $5 million in force. At the same time, 7 million hours of community service and 20.5 million charitable dollars were given.

# A SUPREME KNIGHT FROM KANSAS

After leading the Knights for thirteen years, during and after Vatican II and through the changing social climate, John McDevitt—whose fraternal spirit was even broadcast on his "1492" license plate—retired in January of 1977. Supreme Secretary Virgil C. Dechant, an astute businessman from Kansas and a member of LaCrosse Council 2970, was elected his successor.

In many ways, Dechant's future—and that of the entire Order—were shaped by the fraternal charity of one council in Kansas. Shortly after Dechant joined the St. Augustine Council 2340 at age eighteen, a car crash sent him to the hospital for two months. Every evening, brother Knights visited him there. When complications later arose along his road to recovery and he was hospitalized again, the Knights resumed their visits.

Dechant was so impressed by the Knights' fraternal spirit that he resolved to get more involved in the Order. During his twenty-nine-year rise to supreme knight, Dechant held many positions, including state treasurer, state membership director, and state deputy of Kansas, all before age thirty. By the 1960s, Dechant's work had drawn the attention of the Order's Board of Directors and Luke Hart, who introduced Dechant to McDevitt and recommended the young man as someone who could help with the insurance program.

**Virgil C. Dechant**
Twelfth supreme knight.

Dechant became assistant supreme secretary, supreme master of the Fourth Degree, and soon, supreme secretary. As recounted in his biography, *The Fraternalist,* Dechant grew concerned about the Order's insurance program, and he asked McDevitt for responsibility of both the insurance and service departments, saying he could make improvements "with my eyes closed." Given the chance, he quarterbacked a professionalization of the insurance program and made a number of improvements to the service department.

Virgil Dechant was assertive yet patient—strong qualities exhibited in his successful twenty-three years as supreme knight. He began his administration with a visit to the National Shrine in Washington, DC. There, he placed his stewardship under the protection of the Blessed Virgin. As a further sign of devotion to "Our Lady of the Rosary," he began the practice of distributing a Knights of Columbus rosary, blessed by the supreme chaplain, to each new member of the Order. A man of deep faith, he wanted a chapel built within the Knight's new headquarters. This came to fruition within a few short years.

As the 1970s came to a close, Dechant would be at the helm to usher in a special decade—one that would mark the Order's hundred-year anniversary.

Designed for use in the Sistine Chapel and
Hall of Blessings, this portable organ was gifted
to the Vatican by the Knights in 1995.

# 9.
# One Christian Family
# 1978 to 1999

The last two decades of the twentieth century were a time of continued change. Communism, which seemed strong in Europe in 1980, collapsed by 1990. A bipolar world had changed into a multi-polar one. Concurrently, other cultural shifts became even more apparent, presenting new challenges to the Church as a whole, and the Church in America specifically. Secularization in American society had been increasing noticeably for decades, while at the same time, Mass attendance among Catholics had fallen from 75 percent in 1955 to 54 percent in 1975. Religious communities also continued to shrink as vocations to consecrated life declined. Most fraternal organizations were losing significant numbers of members, as well.

Adding to the upheaval, in 1978, the Catholic Church was led by three popes in quick succession. When Paul VI died that year, John Paul I succeeded him. Upon his sudden death about a month later, John Paul II was elected. His nearly three-decade pontificate would become a stabilizing force for the Church, as this future saint invigorated the faith of millions. A brilliant theologian and genuine pastor, John Paul lent his name to an entire generation of Catholics who grew up during his tenure.

The Knights would work with this pope from Poland on projects related to the family and religious freedom in Eastern Europe. His contemporary and ally in helping bring down European communism was US President Ronald Reagan, whose father had been a Knight (see page 106), and who also had great respect for the Order. The president and pope also shared priorities on the protection of human life and other values-based

Following the death of Pope Paul VI, in August of 1978, Cardinal Albino Luciani was elected, taking the name John Paul I in honor of his two immediate predecessors. He would die just thirty-three days later, but during his brief pontificate, the first layman he met with was Virgil Dechant.

In 1978's second conclave, Polish Cardinal Karol Wojtyła was elected, taking the name John Paul II. The first non-Italian pope in four centuries, his papacy would last almost thirty years, shaping a remarkable theological and historical legacy. The pope and the Order would work closely together on many projects.

From 1981 to 2018, councils and assemblies raised and donated more than $79 million through the RSVP program, providing approximately 130,000 grants to seminarians as well as to those entering women's and men's religious communities. This 1978 vocations billboard of the Iowa Knights of Columbus captured the spirit of the Order's vocation program.

issues. Both were opponents of communism and ardent supporters of the pro-life movement and international religious freedom. In 1982, the Order's hundred-year anniversary, Ronald Reagan would become the second president to speak at a Supreme Convention, which was held that year in Hartford, Connecticut.

During this time, the Order embraced its history and told its story, which came to light in greater detail through research as it prepared to celebrate its hundredth anniversary and launch Father McGivney's cause for sainthood. The Knights of Columbus also continued to work to balance modernization with the embrace of Catholic values. Even before becoming supreme knight, Virgil Dechant had led efforts to improve the insurance operations and revamp the sales force while he was supreme secretary. As supreme knight, Dechant again put his business and leadership skills to work, directing the exponential increase of the insurance program from $3 billion of insurance in force to nearly $40 billion. Under his leadership, the Order would also expand its charitable work and continue to grow its membership while highlighting and adhering to the vision of its founder and the principles of the Church. New records would be set for charity and membership, as well.

## SUPPORT FOR VOCATIONS

Like the people who had been touched by Father McGivney's work during his lifetime, the Knights of Columbus was profoundly grateful that its founder had embraced his priestly vocation. But Father McGivney himself might never have been ordained if it weren't for the financial support of his family and the financial sacrifices made by its members—and, later, his diocese. In the 1960s and 1970s, vocations to the priesthood and religious life had begun to seriously decline in many parts of the world. In the United States, ordinations fell, as did the overall number of priests and religious. By the 1980s and 1990s, the decline continued at such a rate that in the year 2000, there were only about half the number of religious sisters, religious brothers, and ordinations as there had been in 1965.

From early in his tenure, Supreme Knight Dechant—who as a young man had attended the Pontifical College Josephinum seminary—believed that fostering vocations should be a crucial cause for the Knights. In his first address as supreme knight, he expressed his intention to further promote vocations. Shortly thereafter, Dechant personally discussed his plan with Pope Paul VI in a private audience. The pope wholeheartedly agreed that the cause was important and suggested a more personal solution. Noting that the number of members, their wives, and their children comprised a population double that of vocation-rich Ireland, he was sure that the Order

The Pope John XXIII Medical-Moral Research and Education Center began in 1972. In 1980, with the support of the Knights of Columbus, it launched a bi-annual medical ethics workshop in Dallas, Texas. Now known as the National Catholic Bioethics Center, its workshops continue providing this service for bishops.

Combining family activity, parish involvement, and Marian devotion, the Order launched the Marian Hour of Prayer program in 1979 with a papally blessed image of the Our Lady of Guadalupe provided to state jurisdictions for use in their prayer hours. Later programs included other images, including Our Lady of Częstochowa (pictured).

could foster vocations with similar results. As Dechant recalled in his mem-
oir, *The Fraternalist*, Pope Paul VI stated that "the vocations must come from
your own families."

Over the next two decades, the Knights would make vocations a priority
both in its families and in its funding. To spearhead support for seminarians,
priests, and men and women entering religious life, the Vocations Program
was soon launched, headed by Father John V. McGuire, CSsR. To help assess
the beliefs and practices of Catholic youth, a major poll was commissioned
in 1978 by the Knights using the National Opinion Research Center of
Chicago. The poll surveyed issues related to Church attendance, vocations,
marriage, and Marian devotion. The resulting data led to the 1981 publication of *Young Catholics in the United States and Canada*.

Due to the Vocations Program, in 1981, Supreme Knight Dechant and
Father McGuire were invited to the International Congress for Vocations in
Rome. Most participants were bishops; Dechant was one of the few laymen.
During this trip, Dechant witnessed the attempted assassination of Pope
John Paul II. The pope had planned to announce a significant initiative for
lay vocations that day: the foundation of the Pontifical John Paul II Institute
for Studies on Marriage and Family, a project that the Knights would later
sponsor in the United States.

The financial burdens associated with pursuing a religious vocation
also received keen attention at this time. Supreme and local councils
worked closely on solutions through the new Refund Support Vocations
Program (RSVP) and several scholarship funds. Begun in 1981, RSVP
encouraged the councils' financial support of seminarians and those entering religious life by offering each council a $100 refund for every $500 given
in support of an individual.

The Order also established several scholarship funds for seminarians
and priests. Some of these scholarships funded studies at specific institutions. In 1982, for example, the Count Enrico Galeazzi Fund was formed to
provide scholarships for those attending the North American College in
Rome. A year later, a similar fund—Our Lady of Guadalupe—was set up
for the Mexican Pontifical College in Rome. Over the years, additional
funds were established for priests in Canada, Puerto Rico, and the
Philippines, as well as for those attending the American College in Louvain,
Belgium. General funds were also established based on financial need and
academic merit. In 2000, the funds totaled nearly $16 million, a figure that
has continued to increase.

Over time, numerous priests and religious have been assisted financially through these programs. These scholarships also helped councils con-
cretely support upcoming generations of priests, as well as religious
women and religious men.

From vocation stories featured on its back
cover to its 1987 article on how K of C
experiences emboldened some Knights to
become priests, *Columbia* magazine shed
light on how people decide whether to
pursue a religious vocation and highlighted
the uniquely fulfilling closeness to God
found by seminarians, new priests, and
religious sisters and brothers. *Columbia's*
former editor Tim Hickey (kneeling)
himself was ordained a priest after
twenty-five years at the magazine.

In January 1981, Ronald Reagan was sworn
in as the fortieth president of the United
States. President Reagan worked closely
with Pope John Paul II to confront Soviet
communism, and both men are often
credited with being key to the collapse
of the Iron Curtain in the 1980s.

The Eternal Word Television Network (EWTN)
was launched in 1981. Founded by a Poor Clare
nun named Mother Angelica in Alabama, the network
offers Catholic-themed programming, including talk
shows, documentaries, and news programs. The
Order was an early supporter of EWTN, which
now has a presence around the world.

# FUNDING WORK AT THE VATICAN

For more than half a century, the Order's support for the Vatican across many papacies was already well known. However, in the 1980s, the Order stepped up its assistance even further, taking a unique and leading role in supporting strategic Vatican building projects for Pope John Paul II by sponsoring works of the Fabbrica di San Pietro, the Vatican office responsible for the basilica's upkeep.

In 1981, communism continued to divide Europe. Its atheistic ideology was hostile to Christianity's importance, both in terms of Europe's history and in terms of the religion's significance to the people themselves. Against this backdrop, the Order assisted the Holy See with prominent chapels in the Vatican grottoes celebrating Europe's Christian history. The Three Saints Chapel was created and dedicated to the three saints declared by Pope John Paul as the "co-patrons" of Europe: Saint Benedict, whose founding of monasticism was decisive in Catholicism in Western Europe; and Saints Cyril and Methodius, the evangelists of the Slavic peoples. As reported in *Columbia,* Supreme Knight Dechant noted that it was the Vatican's hope that this chapel would "contribute to a greater solidarity among the European peoples and emphasize their common spiritual and cultural patrimony." This new chapel was constructed adjacent to the existing Polish Chapel, which featured an image of Our Lady of Częstochowa—Poland's patroness. To serve the many Polish pilgrims visiting during John Paul's papacy, that chapel, too, was enlarged with the Knights' financial support.

Both the Three Saints Chapel (left) and the expanded Chapel of Our Lady of Częstochowa (right) celebrated the unified Christian roots of Europe.

During the Knights-funded restoration of the façade of St. Peter's Basilica, columns, statues, and other elements of the famous structure were restored and reinforced to repair and reduce further breakage and crumbling.

On the Feast of Our Lady of Fatima (May 13, 1981), Pope John Paul II was shot and nearly killed by Mehmet Ali Ağca. A year later, he visited Fatima, Portugal to thank Our Lady for her protection. The pope also met with, embraced, and forgave his would-be assassin.

This 1988 meeting of the Order's board of directors took place in one of the rooms created at St. Peter's Basilica through Order funding—the room named for the Knights of Columbus. The meeting was scheduled in Rome to mark the tenth anniversary of Pope John Paul II's election and to deliver the annual proceeds of the Vicarius Christi Fund.

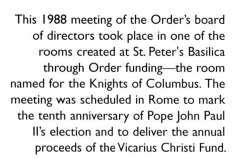

Designed by Italian architect Carlo Maderno, the Maderno Atrium depicts the cardinal and theological virtues as well as key moments and leaders in the history of the Church.

Perhaps the most visible of the Knights' projects in Rome was the restoration of the 65,000-square-foot façade of St. Peter's Basilica. In the three and a half centuries since the basilica opened its doors, the elements had taken their toll. The restoration project would begin in 1984 and take almost two years. During the process, cracks and pitting was repaired, and the gray patina was removed from the surface, revealing the gleaming white of the original stone. Statues atop the façade were also refurbished and retrofitted with steel supports. Later, the towering statues of Saints Peter and Paul flanking the stairs leading to the basilica were also returned to their original glory.

This was just the beginning. In 1993, the Knights stepped forward with funds to save the spiritual heart of the basilica—the Blessed Sacrament Chapel—after a leaking roof damaged it and its sixteenth-century mosaics. The logistical burden of caring for the basilica's items was also eased through funding the creation of six rooms within the basilica for the Fabbrica di San Pietro's collections.

In anticipation of the celebration of the new millennium, the Knights financed the cleaning and restoration of an area central to the coming Holy Year: the Maderno Atrium. The atrium serves as the basilica's front portico or entrance area, and includes the massive bronze Holy Door, which is opened for pilgrims only during designated "Holy Years," such as the Jubilee Year 2000. The atrium project began in 1998 and was completed the next year, in time for the opening of the Holy Door on Christmas Eve. It would be the last of the Knights' twentieth-century Vatican undertakings.

In 1981, the Knights of Columbus established the $10 million Vicarius Christi Fund, and in 1988, the initial amount was doubled to $20 million. The interest is presented annually to the pope to support his personal charities. Popes John Paul II, Benedict XVI, and Francis have all been supported by the fund since its establishment.

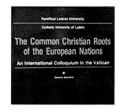

With communism still dominant in half of Europe, in 1981, the Knights sponsored an international colloquium in Rome on "The Common Christian Roots of the European Nations." The pope addressed the conference, and the Knights presented him with 1,500 sets of the proceedings, which were also smuggled into Eastern Europe.

# The Fight for Human Rights Behind the Iron Curtain

When Cardinal Karol Wojtyła became Pope John Paul II in 1978, the Soviet Union and its surrogates were uneasy—and with good reason. An adamant advocate for human rights, the pope presented a challenge to communism throughout Europe, and especially in Poland. Along with British Prime Minister Margaret Thatcher and US President Ronald Reagan, with whom he had a strong relationship, Pope John Paul II would be instrumental in the downfall of European communism.

The pope's successful efforts began in June 1979, when he made his first papal visit to his homeland, Poland. Communist authorities there feared that the charismatic pope would inspire the Polish people, who were experiencing religious oppression under Communist domination. They had tried—unsuccessfully—to prevent his visit. The Knights helped fund a documentary to inspire the people of Poland and prepare them for the event. The film captured the tremendously positive welcome the pope had received in Mexico. The film was then smuggled into Poland, where it was shown discreetly to the people there, enabling them to see how the pope was received in another country where the people—but not the government—embraced the Church.

Pope John Paul II's eight-day pilgrimage to his homeland was transformative. An estimated 13 million people attended at least one of the pope's public events. During the visit, the regime that had once been present everywhere seemed to hide from public view. Certainly, the Polish people's love of freedom, including the freedom to believe and worship as they chose, was strengthened.

Countering the regime's strategy of downplaying crowd size through the use of close-up photography, after the pilgrimage, the Knights were involved with editing the raw filmed footage of the trip. This resulted in a number of films that were shown throughout the country and helped spread the pope's message of faith and unity.

Two years later, in 1981, the Knights helped convey another message to Poland through its funding of the International Colloquium on the Common Christian Roots of the European Nations. Held at the Vatican, the colloquium emphasized Europe's cultural and moral debt to Christianity, and encouraged celebrating that history. Its message challenged the Communist narrative in Eastern and Central Europe, including Poland. The Knights helped finance the printing of the conference proceedings. At the pope's request, copies were then smuggled into Poland to further strengthen the people's resolve to resist communism and fight for the right to worship as they chose.

These efforts in support of freedom and the Church bore fruit in August 1989, with the election of Poland's first non-Communist prime minister, as that country become one of the first Eastern Bloc countries to reject communism. In its wake, the Order assisted the understanding of the faith and Church history by funding the printing of a Polish-language Catholic encyclopedia. In a gesture that reflected the Knights' larger commitment to facilitating vocations, in 1992, the Order also provided funding to educate priests for Eastern Europe at the Pontifical Academy of Theology in Kraków.

# CELEBRATING THE
# CENTENNIAL ANNIVERSARY

In 1982, the Order recalled a hundred years of incredible successes and looked ahead to its second century of service. Throughout the year, the nearly 1.4 million Knights embraced and celebrated the Order's storied past.

In 1981, in celebration of its upcoming centennial year, the Order established the Vicarius Christi Fund, which provided an endowment of $10 million. The annual earnings would be presented to the Holy Father, who would use the money at his discretion for his personal charities or emergency situations. In 1988, the amount was raised to $20 million. To date, the fund has earned over $57 million for papal charities.

Many others joined the Knights in these celebrations. In a warm letter congratulating the Order on this milestone, President Ronald Reagan stated:

> Your creed of charity, unity, fraternity and patriotism has made the Knights and their family members leaders in aiding their fellow citizens. You play an important role in the life of your communities by distributing funds and giving of your time to worthy projects. Throughout the century of your existence, the Knights have stood not only for help to their neighbors, but also for the finest ideals of American fair play and equal treatment for everyone.

That summer, on August 3, over 8,000 Knights and their families gathered with official delegates at the Order's centennial convention, held at the Hartford Civic Center Coliseum in Connecticut. Among the many distinguished guests was His Eminence Cardinal Agostino Casaroli, Pope John Paul's personal envoy and Vatican Secretary of State. Surrounded by more than 400 priests, bishops, and cardinals, Cardinal Casaroli was the principal celebrant at the morning Mass that began the day's events.

President Reagan also attended, addressing what had grown into a crowd of 10,000 people. In his opening remarks, the president spoke of the "crucial values of family, work, neighborhood, religion, and personal freedom" in a speech that received thunderous applause from the packed arena.

Supreme Knight Dechant also delivered his annual report, entitled "A Tradition of Devotion—A Century of Service." The report took the anniversary as its theme, with Dechant noting, "Let no one suppose that, in celebrating the half a millennium of evangelization inaugurated by Columbus's first voyage, the Knights of Columbus look only to the past. From our patron's example we draw inspiration to respond to the challenge of the future, to participate to the full in that 'new evangelization' of the contemporary world, to which our Holy Father Pope John Paul II summons Catholics today."

More than 2,800 people attended the States Dinner, and during that festive evening, Supreme Knight Dechant presented Cardinal Casaroli with a check for $1,225,000 for the Holy Father's charities—the Order's first annual contribution to the Vicarius Christi Fund.

For the centennial of the Order's founding, Father McGivney's remains were reinterred in St. Mary's Church in New Haven on March 29, 1982. Members of the board of directors and the McGivney family served as pallbearers. The new tomb has become a place of pilgrimage for Knights from around the world.

During the 1982 Supreme Convention, Vatican Secretary of State Cardinal Agostino Casaroli and President Ronald Reagan met to discuss formalizing relations between the United States and the Holy See. Less than two years later, diplomatic relations were established, and William Wilson became the first US ambassador to the Vatican.

During the convention, Dechant also arranged a private lunch for President Reagan and Cardinal Casaroli. The men discussed, among other issues, the need for a US ambassador to the Holy See and for formal relations between the two states. It was during this meeting that the foundation for formal diplomatic relations between the United States and the Vatican was laid.

The centennial convention was not an invitation for the Order to rest on its laurels. Even as it celebrated a century of incredible achievements, the Order embraced the needed role it would play—for the Church, for communities, and for its members—in its second century.

President Ronald Reagan addresses the Knights at the 1982 Centennial Convention in Hartford, Connecticut.

Long dedicated to the spiritual as well as financial viability of Catholic families, the Knights' emphasis on sacramental marriage was evident when twenty-five couples had their civil marriages validated in a Catholic ceremony sponsored by Santo Nino de Oro Council 6603 in Cagayan de Oro City, Philippines in 1987.

One of several honors bestowed on Supreme Knight Dechant, in 1983, he was named Knight Grand Cross in the Order of Pius IX—the highest honor bestowed on a Catholic layman who is not a head of state. The cross bears the words *Virtuti et Merito*—Virtue and Merit.

# The Renovation of St. Mary's Church

The renovation of St. Mary's included construction on the existing choir loft in preparation for a historic three-manual, tracker-action organ by E & GG Hook & Hastings.

In conjunction with the centennial, the Knights undertook the renovation of its birthplace—St. Mary's Church. Both time and cold Connecticut winters had taken their toll on the 108-year-old structure, rendering it in dire need of a makeover inside and out. The Knights turned to architect Kevin Roche, who had designed the Order's headquarters. As a parishioner of St. Mary's for fifteen years, Roche's interest in the project was both personal and professional. He and the Knights worked alongside a team of architects, engineers, and other specialists on the undertaking.

The sanctuary was restructured with a revised floor plan that allowed the altar to be moved forward so that it was situated closer to the congregation. A new 400-pound bronze crucifix installed above the altar was a replica of the one commissioned by the Knights for the Three Saints Chapel in the grottoes below St. Peter's.

The church was repainted in its original colors, a new wood floor was laid, and the pews were refurbished with funds supplied by each of the state councils. The Columbian Squires raised money to construct a handicap-accessible entrance/exit, while members of the Fourth Degree contributed to the landscaping and beautification of the grounds around the church.

Along with its restored aesthetic beauty, St. Mary's received a musical gift—a magnificent nineteenth-century organ that had once provided liturgical music for St. Alphonsus Church in New York City. In 1980, after the church was closed and slated for demolition, the organ was given a new home at St. Mary's.

Although the blueprints for the original St. Mary's had included a steeple, a lack of funds had prevented its construction. In 1984, the Order added the final touch to the church in the form of a 179-foot steeple that houses three bells. The structure is now one of the tallest in the city.

The bulk of the renovation, which began in 1981, was completed in early 1982, in time for what was possibly the most significant observance of the centennial year—the reinterment of Father McGivney's body. With the approval of his living relatives and the Holy See, Father's body was disinterred from Old St. Joseph's Cemetery. On March 29, in a solemn ceremony, his remains were returned to St. Mary's, where they were placed in a granite sarcophagus in the back of the church. People from all walks of life and from all over the world come to St. Mary's to visit Father McGivney's tomb.

At a 1982 Mass, dozens of bishops and priests joined Cardinal Agostino Casaroli (center) to mark the Knights of Columbus' centennial year.

# PRESERVING HISTORY

The Order's hundred-year anniversary provided the initiative to research, remember, and communicate its history while planning for the future. One of the first major tasks was the publication of *Faith and Fraternalism* by Christopher J. Kauffman. About six decades had passed since a large-scale history of the Order had been undertaken, and this book documented the organization from its origin to the time of the book's printing in 1982. It was updated in 1992. Kauffman would later expand upon his work with an examination of the Order and its namesake in *Columbianism and the Knights of Columbus*, published for the quincentennial anniversary of the explorer's landing. In *Patriotism and Fraternalism in the Knights of Columbus*, he would highlight the unique mission, spirit, and contributions of the Order's patriotic Fourth Degree. Its 2000 publication date marked the Fourth Degree's hundred-year anniversary.

Church historian Christopher Kauffman waded through a century of manuscripts, records, correspondence, and archival research notes to produce the massive *Faith and Fraternalism: The History of the Knights of Columbus 1882–1982*, and subsequent works.

Telling the story of the Knights through objects rather than words, the Knights of Columbus Museum was also established during the centennial year. First housed in the Order's New Haven headquarters, the museum displayed items of significance to the Order's founding and history. The non-profit institution remained there for nearly two decades, but as the collection and its significance grew, a larger location was needed.

In 1993, the Order purchased property a block away at One State Street that would eventually become the museum's new home. The state-of-the-art facility was blessed and dedicated on September 24, 2000, with its official grand opening on March 9, 2001. Designed to house both permanent and temporary gallery collections, as well as documents and artifacts that reflect the history and activities of the Order, the museum also serves as an education center with its extensive archive of historical material and exhibits representing the "heritage of Catholicism."  (See "The Knights of Columbus Museum" beginning on page 194.)

The Knights of Columbus Museum, now located a block away from the supreme headquarters, opened its doors at this location in 2001.

In addition to funding priests' education, the Order looked to improve the schooling of Catholic children by establishing the $1 million Father Michael J. McGivney Fund for Catholic education research. The Knights were awarded by the National Catholic Educational Association and participated in a presidential meeting on education.

A supporter of human rights and a critic of the Marcos regime's abuses in the Philippines, brother Knight Hilario Davide was named to the country's Constitutional Commission following Marcos' overthrow. He later became the Ambassador of the Philippines to the UN and then Chief Justice of the Filipino Supreme Court.

# CHAMPIONING LIFE AND FAMILY

"With some 1.2 million unborn babies being killed by abortion each year in the United States alone, we are confronted with an outrage against human life paralleled only by the ravages of a bloody war."

–Supreme Knight Virgil Dechant, 1977 Supreme Knight's Report

In 1973, during Supreme Knight John McDevitt's tenure, the US Supreme Court handed down its *Roe v. Wade* decision, ruling that abortion was a constitutional right. Consistent with the Order's long history of supporting those on the margins, as well as Church teaching on human life and sexuality, the Knights turned its attention to protecting the unborn. During Supreme Knight Dechant's tenure, the Knights continued to champion the cause of life at all stages and to support marriage and family at both fraternal and institutional levels.

Pro-life efforts included unifying Knights' messaging and actions through the "Save the Baby" and "Crusade for Life" campaigns. So important was the cause that a pro-life chair was established in each council to spearhead local right-to-life programs. Uniquely, the pro-life chairs were to be held not by a Knight alone, but by a married couple—in a move that reflected a growing emphasis on family-focused fraternalism.

The Order also lent its support and voice to a number of pro-life efforts and legal battles. For example, the Knights provided funding for the US Bishops' efforts, including its "Natural Choice is Life" campaign. The Order also opposed abortion-inducing drugs in the United States. When the US Congress took up the issue of partial-birth abortion in 1996, the Knights printed 2.5 million postcards to allow the public to register support with

Undeterred by blizzard-like conditions at the 1987 March for Life in Washington, DC, Knights of Columbus Council 947 joined thousands of others protesting abortion, showing resolve and a commitment to the cause.

George H.W. Bush was inaugurated as forty-first president of the United States on January 20, 1989. Describing a moment "rich with promise," he pledged to help build "a kinder and gentler nation." Bush also praised the work done by community organizations as a "thousand points of light … doing good."

The notorious Berlin Wall fell on November 9, 1989. East Germany and the rest of Eastern Europe would soon be free of the Communist regimes that had been imposed on them for almost half a century. The fall of the wall would become a symbol for the collapse of communism.

Congress for legislation that would end such procedures. The bill was passed, but was vetoed by President Bill Clinton. A similar bill was ultimately passed and signed into law in 2003 by President George W. Bush.

In 1992, the Knights began a program that would convey the value of every life and the sadness of a life lost. At the Supreme Convention held in New York, Cardinal John O'Connor urged the Order to build a memorial for the unborn in every Catholic cemetery. In a resolution, the Knights took up this initiative to "give eloquent, lasting testimony to the unique sanctity and dignity of each unborn human life." Thousands of memorials, from elaborate monuments to simple gravestones, were built by the councils, including at many parishes. Each served as both a tangible reminder of lost lives and a place of prayerful remembrance.

As abortion ended more than a million unborn lives a year, the Knights saw that issue as qualitatively and quantitatively unique. It was, however, far from the only issue that the Order championed with respect to human dignity and those on society's margins. The Knights took a particular interest in people with intellectual disabilities—often excluded or looked down on by society generally, and later, often the targets of abortion. From the famous Tootsie Roll drives to Order-wide support for the Special Olympics, Knights at every level worked to help others to live—with dignity. This was also accomplished through many charitable programs and a redoubling of efforts at food pantries and soup kitchens at the urging of Mother Teresa.

Life and family were naturally connected, and the Order championed a number of Natural Family Planning (NFP) initiatives, including printing NFP material for participants at the Synod of Bishops in Rome. In this, the Order also continued to support Church teaching as it related to contraception and reproduction. In 1987, the Order established the Knights of Columbus Family Life Bureau in Washington, DC, to promote Catholic teaching on issues related to life and family. Notably, it would launch and administer the Washington session of the Pontifical John Paul II Institute for Studies on Marriage and Family. (See page 190.)

Attendees sign a giant postcard at a K of C site for the 1995 Special Olympics World Games in New Haven, Connecticut. More than 5,000 Knights volunteered in the preparation and organization of innovative programs for the event.

In a 1992 homily at the Supreme Convention, Cardinal John O'Connor urged Knights to erect tombs to the unborn in every state as a memorial to victims of abortion. Just one of many monuments placed around the country, this was sponsored by Marian Council 3768 in Kansas City.

Educated in an Indian mission school, Bud Jetty—a former state deputy of South Dakota—sought to bring about reconciliation and harmony between society at large and Native Americans. His dream was realized in 1992, when South Dakota declared "Reconciliation Day"—a day that brought the two communities closer together.

## THE PONTIFICAL JOHN PAUL II INSTITUTE

Through many initiatives during his papacy, John Paul II displayed his earnest commitment to the family. He encouraged couples to maintain a healthy marriage and home life, to create a "domestic church" in which children would be shaped through faith and love, and to embrace the moral teachings of the Catholic Church as an alternative to the empty promises of the secular world.

One especially significant initiative was the establishment of the Pontifical John Paul II Institute for Studies on Marriage and Family. The pope had actually planned to announce the foundation of the institute on the day he was shot, May

The 2018 class from the Washington, DC session of the international Pontifical John Paul II Institute for Studies on Marriage and Family gathers at graduation.

13, 1981. Founded in 1982 at the Lateran University in Rome, the institute would offer graduate-level theology degrees. In addition, a number of "sessions" of the institute would be founded in other countries, including Mexico, Spain, Australia, and Brazil.

Five years after the institute's launch in Rome, Cardinal James Hickey, Archbishop of Washington, and Supreme Knight Dechant requested permission from the Holy See to open a session of the institute in the United States for English-speaking students. Permission was granted, and in 1988, the Pontifical John Paul II Institute for Studies on Marriage and Family opened in Washington, DC. It is now located at The Catholic University of America. Cardinal Hickey served as the Washington session's vice chancellor and Carl Anderson (then the Order's vice president for public policy) was its founding dean and first vice president. He continued to serve as vice president for many years, even after becoming supreme knight.

The institute would go on to prepare numerous clergy and lay people—many of whom would have roles in parishes, dioceses, or other apostolic work. In addition to its pontifical degrees, the Washington session would receive civil accreditation and offer civil degrees, as well.

## AMERICA'S QUINCENTENNIAL OF EVANGELIZATION

The year 1992 marked five hundred years since Christopher Columbus' 1492 voyage to this hemisphere. The year before the anniversary, the Order produced a sixteen-minute video titled *Christopher Columbus: Faithful Christ Bearer*, which focused on Columbus' role in evangelization. In addition to being seen by an estimated 2 million television viewers, the film was in high demand at parishes and local councils, with the Order loaning out copies more than 5,000 times for local showings. The Knights also supported the planning of celebrations in New Haven and elsewhere.

As 1991 closed, the Knights kicked off the observance of Columbus Day in the largest parade Connecticut had ever seen for that holiday. That same day, a special Mass in honor of Columbus was celebrated at the Basilica of the National Shrine of the Immaculate Conception in Washington, DC.

In a series of events that took place between 1989 and 1991—from the rise of the Solidarity movement in Poland to the destruction of the Berlin Wall—Communist-led regimes collapsed throughout Eastern Europe and the Soviet Union. Pope John Paul II is often credited as one of the individuals who helped precipitate the fall of these oppressive social systems.

Virgil Dechant oversaw explosive growth in insurance and membership. In addition to modernizing the insurance operation, he made it a priority as supreme knight to stay in regular contact with local councils, visiting councils in many jurisdictions and even placing Christmas morning phone calls to state deputies.

The Knights began 1992 with a float sponsored by the California State Council honoring Columbus in the New Year's Day Tournament of Roses Parade in Pasadena, California, which also had a global television audience. Orderwide, the year was filled with commemorations of this important anniversary. *Columbia* ran a series that year on Columbus, bringing out key aspects of the explorer's faith. The Order also ran an essay contest and museum exhibit centered on the quincentennial of Columbus' voyage. That exhibit laid the groundwork for the current Columbus Gallery that is now part of the Knights of Columbus Museum.

In August of 1992, the 110th annual Supreme Convention in New York City again focused on the celebration of the Order's namesake. Supreme Knight Dechant's remarks echoed those of Pope John Paul II in his greeting to the convention, which linked the evangelization of 1492 with the "new evangelization" of the current moment. Dechant noted, "We honor Columbus . . . in the work of preaching the Gospel to all nations in response to Christ's command."

Columbus wasn't the only famous person honored at the convention. It was also there that the Order presented its first Gaudium et Spes Award to Mother Teresa, who was a potent example of evangelization through the witness of Christian charity.

The Knights were in good company celebrating the quincentennial of Columbus' voyage. In October, Pope John Paul II made his third trip to the Dominican Republic, this time planning his journey around the celebration of the of the five hundredth anniversary of Columbus' arrival in the Americas. He celebrated an outdoor Mass in Santo Domingo, one of the islands Columbus had explored on his first journey to what would soon be called the "New World." There, the Holy Father spoke of the quincentennial of evangelization as "a great day for the Church."

Earlier that month, in Santo Domingo, a new lighthouse was dedicated that projected an image of a cross into the night sky that could be seen for 150 miles. There, the bones believed to be those of Christopher Columbus were reinterred, having been escorted to their final resting place by an honor guard of ten Fourth Degree Knights. Supreme Knight Dechant and his wife were among those in attendance at the ceremony.

The quincentennial celebration of Columbus was another important element connecting the Order to its early roots. The year-long emphasis helped remind Knights of the importance of the explorer—to the history of the Order and of the hemisphere. Cerainly, Father McGivney had selected Columbus as the Order's namesake because at that time, the explorer was the only Catholic widely regarded as an American hero. However, the celebrations in 1992 also reminded Knights that Columbus had played an important role in evangelization—an evangelization that Pope John Paul II had called the Knights—and other Catholics—to continue in a "new" way.

"You are united with the whole Church in giving thanks to God for five hundred years of the Church's presence in the Americas. . . . 1492 represented a *kairos*, a "salvific occasion" of the first magnitude, to which the Church responded promptly and decisively, in a great saga of evangelization. . . . The depth and the fruitfulness of the acceptance of the Gospel clearly indicate that the first evangelization of the Americas was truly a work of love. . . . Today, a new proclamation of the salvific message of the Gospel is needed. May the Cross of Evangelization which symbolizes your commitment to advancing the Kingdom of our Lord Jesus Christ inspire you with renewed vigor in Christian living, so that the Successor of Peter and the Church at large may continue to rely on the Knights of Columbus in the new evangelization."

–Pope John Paul II, letter to the Knights of Columbus for the 1992 Supreme Convention

President George H.W. Bush addressed the Supreme Convention in 1992 in New York during the quincentennial celebration of Columbus' first voyage west. Bush had previously mentioned the Knights as a force for good in his 1988 nomination acceptance speech and had also addressed the 1984 Supreme Convention as vice president.

The Knights of Columbus website was launched in July 1991. The site features information on membership, activities, and insurance products, along with news releases and an abridged version of *Columbia* magazine. A section devoted to the Catholic faith has included discussions of religious vocations and a searchable copy of the *Catechism of the Catholic Church*.

# Joy and Hope
## Mother Teresa and the Knights

During the late 1980s, the relationship between the Knights of Columbus and the Missionaries of Charity grew significantly. Founded in 1950 by Mother Teresa (now Saint Teresa of Kolkata) in India, what began as a small community of 12 sisters—dedicated to servicing the poor, the infirm, the homeless, and the unloved—grew to nearly 5,000 sisters and more than 500 missions in more than 130 countries. Along with caring for the poor and the disabled, the missionaries run orphanages and hospices, as well as charity centers, clinics, and soup kitchens. They also visit families in need and hold catechism classes for children in impoverished parishes. In 1976, New York's South Bronx became the first home of the Missionaries of Charity in the United States.

The Knights considered it a great privilege to support Mother Teresa in her charitable work. In 1987, in response to her plea to "help us with the soup kitchens . . . with the poorest of the poor," the Order launched "Operation Share." This program encouraged members to serve the poor by volunteering at local food pantries and soup kitchens. That year, while attending the Synod of Bishops in Rome, Supreme Knight Dechant and his wife worked in one of the mission's soup kitchens there.

The Order also put its printing operation to work for the Missionaries of Charity. In 1988, when it agreed to publish the Constitutions of the Missionaries of Charity, it was Mother Teresa herself who delivered the manuscript in a surprise visit to the New Haven headquarters. She spoke to the hundreds of employees who had gathered around her, telling them about her work and encouraging them to join her mission. "We invite you to come and share the joy of loving," she said. "Come and see, and do not be afraid to share that joy of loving," she said. She also challenged the employees to the universal call to holiness, saying, "Holiness is not the luxury of the few—it is the simple duty for you and for me."

Inspired by her words and example, councils everywhere stepped up their involvement with charitable programs and outreach to the poor. Mother Teresa's visit was described in *Knightline,* the Order's newsletter:

Mother Teresa addressed hundreds of employees at the Knights of Columbus' New Haven headquarters during her unexpected 1988 visit. She encouraged their involvement in charitable acts of giving.

The official canonization portrait by noted American artist Chas Fagan.

Supreme Knight Dechant presents Mother Teresa with the first Gaudium et Spes Award in 1992.

The surprise visit of the Nobel Peace Prize recipient and founder of the order of the Missionaries of Charity to the New Haven office left some in tears, others in delightful amazement and most with the feeling that they had indeed been in the presence of one who has been called by many a modern day saint.

Along with publishing the Constitutions, the Order began printing many other items for Mother Teresa's community, including prayer books, prayer cards, leaflets, and missionary directories. This tradition continued for decades and notably included the production of hundreds and thousands of prayer cards and other material for her canonization.

In 1990, the Order sponsored a PBS documentary on Mother Teresa in conjunction with her eightieth birthday. Then in 1992, the Knights bestowed upon her the Gaudium et Spes Award—the Order's highest honor—

for her unconditional service to mankind in the name of Jesus Christ. The first recipient of this award, she made the journey from India to the United States to receive it.

In 2010, in observance of what would have been Mother Teresa's hundredth birthday, a year-long exhibit on her life and works was presented at the Knights of Columbus Museum. Entitled "Mother Teresa: Life, Spirituality and Message," the historical presentation chronicled her life from childhood to beatification and detailed her close relationship with the Order.

More recently, the Knights commissioned the official canonization portrait of Mother Teresa. Painted by renowned American artist Chas Fagan, the original portrait was unveiled in 2016 at the Saint John Paul II National Shrine in Washington, DC. An enlarged copy of the portrait was hung from St. Peter's Basilica for Mother Teresa's September 4, 2016 canonization.

# The Knights of Columbus Museum

High above the main staircase in the entrance hall of the Knights of Columbus Museum hangs a priceless relic: the seventeenth-century bronze cross that had once been part of the statue of Christ the Redeemer, which stands atop St. Peter's Basilica. Pope John Paul II had given it to the Order in appreciation for its role in restoring the basilica's façade in 1984. (See page 182.) The cross, which once greeted millions who made their way to the heart of the Church, now greets those who visit the museum to discover the heart of the Order's history and its present-day missions.

Along with the Wall of History, the museum houses a number of permanent exhibits. Included among them are the Father McGivney Gallery and the Papal Gallery. Each contains artwork, artifacts, and historical material that tell the story of these men and their relationship with the Knights of Columbus.

Visitors are also drawn to the many temporary exhibits featured at the museum. Past exhibits have included sacred art collections, tributes to notable figures like Pope John Paul II and Mother Teresa, and an annual Christmas exhibition that highlights crèches from around the world, as well as festive Christmas trees that are decorated by area children. Two unique past exhibits were created in participation with the Vatican: an exposition of the Swiss Guards and a presentation on the building and design of St. Peter's Basilica, which featured a sixteenth-century wooden model of the famous dome commissioned and designed by Michelangelo.

The museum also contains the Supreme Council Archives and the Multimedia Archives. The former includes publications, correspondence, pamphlets, programs, newspaper articles, and books related to the history of the Order. It also houses the proceedings of the Supreme Council and important papers of the supreme officers, which contribute significantly to the history of the organization.

The Multimedia Archives preserves the many decades of images depicting and related to the Knights, as well as video footage dating back to the early 1920s.

Open year-round, the Knights of Columbus Museum welcomes thousands of visitors annually. It has become a premier destination not only for learning about the Knights but also for experiencing Christian art and Church history.

The permanent Wall of History exhibit takes visitors from the Knights' founding and early years to the present day, highlighting the key work and individuals who have shaped the Order.

Through images, memorabilia, interactive elements, and artifacts, major historical moments are brought to life, such as the World War I hut program, including personal items from K of C secretaries ("Caseys") as well as items provided to troops.

Along with the Papal Gallery and the large cross formerly found atop the façade of St. Peter's Basilica, the Knights' century-long relationship with the papacy punctuates the Wall of History. Here, the beginning of the Knights' work with the Holy See is presented.

In addition to the Wall of History are other unique permanent and temporary exhibits. The McGivney Gallery includes relics and artifacts from the founder's life and death.

Using documents, correspondence, prints, and more, the Supreme Council Archives' changing exhibits tell the stories of important moments in the Order's history, as well as the voices and discussions that brought them about.

Special exhibits often cover themes of broader interest to Catholics and the general public, including a yearly display of crèches that highlight how the birth of Christ is celebrated and represented in art around the world.

# Defending Faith in the Public Square
## Visionary Council Initiative

As the celebration of Christmas became more of a consumer holiday than a religious one, many councils encouraged the public to "Keep Christ in Christmas" by highlighting the spiritual nature of the holiday. Setting up nativity scenes in public places was a time-honored way to observe the religious roots of a holiday celebrated by most Americans. Despite America's long history of such religious displays, efforts were made in some quarters to sideline or even ban nativity scenes from the public square.

In 1994, a town-sponsored Christmas tree and privately sponsored menorah decorated the public green adjacent to the Town Hall of Trumbull, Connecticut, as they had each December for years. Spearheaded by Donald Creatore, one of St. Theresa Council 2961's leading members, that council requested permission to set up a nativity scene on the green the following year. The permission was granted, and then was rescinded at the last minute specifically because of the display's religious nature.

The council did not give up. It sued for the right to have its display on the green with the others. The Becket Fund—a public interest law firm specializing in defending religious freedom cases—took up the case together with attorney Pat Cipollone, who was then of the law firm Kirkland & Ellis of Washington, DC, and later became supreme advocate, the general counsel of the Order. Support from the Supreme Council's McDevitt Fund for Religious Liberties helped finance the case.

It was not an easy road. First the district court and then the Second Circuit Court of Appeals rejected the Knights' case, claiming that proximity to the Town Hall might give the impression that the government endorsed a specific religion. The council then appealed to the US Supreme Court. The high court vacated the district court's ruling and remanded the case back to the lower court for reconsideration, with the result that the Knights were permitted to display their crèche. Becket Fund founder Kevin "Seamus" Hasson later told the *National Catholic Register* that the Supreme Court's order for the lower court to revisit and rethink the case "made clear [that] Nativity scenes, like other cultural symbols, should be welcome in the town square, literally."

The legal victory had national implications for allowing nativity scenes on public property in towns and cities throughout America. In the public square, the Knights had literally helped keep Christ in Christmas. The crèche was displayed that year and has been in years since.

Known as "the Vatican spy catcher," Jesuit Father Robert Graham spent his life both researching Church history and making it.

Born in 1912 and ordained in 1941, the California native's priestly service would incorporate both very public and very private work. He spent two decades at the Jesuit magazine *America,* including as an editor, and published his first book, *Vatican Diplomacy,* after earning a doctorate in political science and international law from the University of Geneva.

With Soviet-backed disinformation slandering Pope Pius XII as pro-Nazi, Graham was brought to the Vatican to research and report the truth. While working on an eleven-volume series of Vatican documents, he had access to Vatican archives and European public figures and became a leading expert on the Vatican's diplomatic and public engagement efforts. Although best known for making public Pope Pius XII's efforts to save the Jews during the Holocaust, Graham's research also uncovered anti-Vatican espionage by Nazi, Fascist, and Soviet entities. His second book, *The Pope and Poland During World War II,* was fortuitous—published a decade before the election of Polish Cardinal Karol Wojtyła as Pope John Paul II.

Father Graham also wrote a monthly "Vatican" column for the Knights of Columbus' *Columbia* magazine from the 1960s to the early 1990s. Combining his knowledge of the Church with diplomatic acumen and journalistic skill, his column analyzed Church affairs in a global light.

Working in Rome during the Cold War, Graham's knowledge of tactics against the Catholic Church proved particularly relevant. As Soviet-era documents continue to reveal, the KGB—and its affiliates, including the Polish SB, East German Stasi, and others—attempted to destabilize the Church with "active measures."

These tactics sought to undermine the Vatican and promote Soviet-friendly orientations and ideologies within the Church itself, with attempts to manipulate both local churches and the Vatican.

With the global superpowers waging a high-profile Cold War, espionage against the Vatican rarely made headlines. Father Graham, however, had more than an academic interest in Vatican counterintelligence operations: he helped lead them. Occasionally he even discussed such issues in *Columbia.* One 1969 column was entitled "The Story of Bugging at the Vatican." Graham wrote: "The Vatican telephones have been tapped, confidential messages by radio or telegraph intercepted and decoded, files rifled, and the Holy See's representatives abroad surrounded by informers. It has had to cope with hidden radio transmitters, fake students planted in Roman seminaries, traitorous workers in its offices and agents sent from the world's capitals to gather classified information."

Disinformation and attempted manipulation of the Church were among the Soviet tactics, as was the use of moles, blackmail, surveillance, bugs, and infiltration of the Vatican using priests and seminarians groomed for the Soviet cause. Graham confirmed that "espionage by governments hostile to the Catholic Church" was a "security question . . . of abiding concern to papal aides."

Graham's ability to detect and expose those spying for the Soviets became legendary. Although details were often kept secret, he became the Vatican's unofficial "spy catcher" and its de facto head of counterintelligence. His efforts were highlighted in the book *Spies in the Vatican* by John Koehler, a former AP journalist and American OSS intelligence officer. One example described by Koehler involved a group of KGB-trained "sleeper agents" from Ukraine—then part of the Soviet Union—who were sent to Rome to enroll in the seminary. The plot was thwarted when Graham discovered the scheme, causing their expulsion.

A member of Monsignor John T. Dwyer Council 9851 in Saratoga, California, Father Graham witnessed the rise and fall of both fascism and communism in Europe during his lifetime. He moved back to the Golden State, publishing two more books related to World War II—one with David Alvarez on Nazi espionage against the Vatican, another on the Vatican's experience with communism—before his death in 1997.

# THE PAPAL MASS AT AQUEDUCT RACETRACK

One of the chalices used during Pope John Paul II's 1995 Papal Mass at Aqueduct Racetrack had been commissioned by the Order five years earlier for the hundred-year anniversary of Father McGivney's death. Bearing an orb representing Columbus' journey and a medallion image of Father McGivney, the chalice is displayed at the Knights of Columbus Museum when it is not being used for special Masses.

During his five-day apostolic visit to the United States in 1995, Pope John Paul II celebrated Mass in four locations—at Camden Yards in Baltimore, Maryland; at Giants Stadium in Newark, New Jersey; in Manhattan's Central Park; and at Aqueduct Racetrack in Queens, New York.

In conjunction with the Diocese of Brooklyn, the Knights co-sponsored the Aqueduct Mass. It was believed to be the first time a lay organization had sponsored such a papal event. Since Aqueduct was located in the diocese of Supreme Chaplain Bishop Thomas Daily of Brooklyn, the collaboration came very naturally, and Knights volunteered in many ways. Knights were also encouraged to attend, with each jurisdiction allotted tickets for members and their families.

The Knights commissioned a papal chair for the event to be built by local artisans. Although not obvious, it had a number of special features, including a bulletproof back plate and a height designed specifically to enable its ease of use by the pope, who had recently undergone hip surgery. The chair would be used again when Pope Benedict XVI visited the United States in 2008, and is now a permanent part of the Papal Gallery at the Knights of Columbus Museum.

Prior to the Mass, hundreds of Knights helped to get everything ready for the pope. On October 6, under clear blue skies, the capacity crowd of 75,000 gathered for Mass with the Holy Father.

Interest in the event was further heightened by the fact that earlier that year, Pope John Paul II had published his landmark encyclical, *Evangelium Vitae* ("The Gospel of Life"). His homily included similar themes, all of which were of substantial interest to the Knights. Grounding the "progress of peoples" in the cross and resurrection, the pope proposed practical markers for a society that both treated the human person with dignity and love, and facilitated man's ultimate spiritual needs:

> People everywhere thirst for a full and free life worthy of the human person. There is a great desire for political, social and economic institutions which will help individuals and nations to affirm and develop their dignity. . . .
>
> In practical terms, this truth tells us that there can be no life worthy of the human person without a culture—and a legal system—that honors and defends marriage and the family. The well-being of individuals and communities depends on the healthy state of the family. . . .

In January 1993, former Arkansas governor Bill Clinton became the forty-second President of the United States. A Democrat, he would sign into law the International Religious Freedom Act, the Religious Freedom Restoration Act, and the Defense of Marriage Act. Impeached by the House, he was not convicted by the Senate.

On February 26, 1993, terrorists struck the World Trade Center, detonating the largest bomb of its type up to that point in the underground parking garage of the center's north tower. Six died and a thousand more were injured. Eight years later, the 9/11 attacks there would take nearly three thousand lives.

Catholic parents must learn to form their family as a 'domestic church,' a church in the home as it were, where God is honored, his law is respected, prayer is a normal event, virtue is transmitted by work and example, and everyone shares the hopes, the problems and sufferings of everyone else.

Pope John Paul II's historic Mass at Aqueduct Racetrack touched the hearts and souls of millions—whether they attended the actual event or watched it on television. The Order was justifiably proud of its role. Supreme Knight Dechant told the media: "In 113 years, we've never had this type of privilege."

## EXPANDING FRATERNALISM

Supreme Knight Dechant's personal goal for leading the Knights was famously simple: to leave it better than he found it. During his tenure, he proved to be a leader with both a keen, appreciative grasp of the experience of everyday Knights and a dedication to improving the Order in terms of

During his 1995 US visit, Pope John Paul II celebrates Mass at Aqueduct Racetrack in Queens, New York, for a crowd of over 75,000.

charity, insurance, and function. While the Order's external collaborations and services to the Church—like projects for the Vatican and the Missionaries of Charity—received public notice, Dechant's attention to improving and strengthening the Order at home made a tremendous impact on the fraternal experience of the Knights, their families, and their parishes.

Understanding that recruiting was key to the Order's good work, membership growth was also a priority. During the 1970s, the Order had experienced a brief period of stagnation and even decline in membership growth, as well as a reluctance to form new councils. In response, the idea of creating councils within individual parishes took center stage. Parishioners showed interest in these parish-based councils and began joining at a steady pace. Priests who joined were granted honorary lifetime memberships.

Although the Order aimed to provide a council in every parish, some parishes did not have enough members to support a full council. To help Knights in those parishes maintain a sense of unity and visibility and better serve their community, the Parish Round Table Program was formed. With the assistance of local priests, members of a "round table" represent the Order in serving their parish and community. Once membership reaches thirty and demonstrates the potential to grow further, round tables are eligible to become new councils. The model is also employed with success in other situations where meeting an initial threshold of thirty members could be difficult—for example, on foreign military bases and in new countries.

The shift toward an emphasis on parish-based councils succeeded. When Dechant became supreme knight, there were 6,066 active councils in existence; when he left, that number had nearly doubled to 11,644. Membership had also increased by 31 percent.

Better integrating families into the Order's activities was a personal goal for Dechant. He encouraged Knights' activities to include wives and children, accentuating the Order as a service organization that brought families together. Decisions such as seating wives along with their husbands and distinguished Church hierarchy at the main dais of the Supreme Convention's States Dinner telegraphed the importance of this holistic view.

The Order's mission of caring for the families of deceased members—especially their widows—continued to develop, as well. The experience of widows was on Dechant's mind from his first year as supreme knight on, when he urged Knights to continue to involve the families of deceased members in the Order's programs and activities and to enable them to receive its publication. Committees were established to maintain contact with the widows and dependent children, who remained eligible for student loans, fellowships, and other educational benefits sponsored by the Knights. Upon a member's death, a condolence letter was sent to the next of kin by the supreme knight. The family was informed of the loved one's enrollment in a Mass at St. Mary's Church in New Haven every day for a year.

When Virgil Dechant (center) took the reins of the Order, its insurance in force had recently surpassed $3 billion. In less than a quarter century under his leadership, that total would grow to $40 billion.

Entering into force on January 1, 1994, the North American Free Trade Agreement (NAFTA) gradually eliminated most tariffs and other trade barriers on services and products passing between the United States, Canada, and Mexico. In 2004, NAFTA was expanded to include five Central American countries.

In 1994, Cardinal John O'Connor, Archbishop of New York from 1984 to 2000, and founder of the Sisters of Life, received the Gaudium et Spes Award for his pastoral leadership and service to the Church, his ministry as a military chaplain, and his pro-life work in promoting the Culture of Life. He was a member of Our Lady, Star of the Sea Council 6701 in New York City.

# FATHER MICHAEL JOSEPH McGIVNEY'S CAUSE FOR CANONIZATION

During his lifetime, Father Michael J. McGivney's holiness made an impression on all who knew him. It was noted that those to whom he ministered called him a "positive saint and meant it"—a sentiment echoed by Chip Smith, the man under sentence of death to whom Father McGivney tended. (See page 17.) Smith extolled Father McGivney for "saintly" ministry in prison. In the decades that followed, the Knights and many others turned to the founder as a model of holiness and heavenly intercessor.

While many people have recognized the founder's virtues, it takes a more formal investigation for the Catholic Church to officially declare him a saint. Such an investigation, or *cause for canonization,* is usually long and fairly arduous—often taking decades or even centuries of research and review. While canonization is never assured until a proclamation is issued by the Vatican, the holy life led by Father McGivney and the continued devotion to him by many have helped his cause move ahead.

Before the cause could be officially opened, preparatory steps were needed. Preliminary research was conducted, including a 1981 survey of the Knights that showed remarkable and fruitful devotion to the founder. A little more than a decade later, the US Conference of Catholic Bishops gave unanimous support for pursuing the cause.

In 1997, the Father McGivney Guild was established to promote this cause for sainthood, which was opened by Archbishop Daniel A. Cronin of Hartford, Connecticut. Dominican Father Gabriel B. O'Donnell was named

Archbishop Daniel A. Cronin of Hartford, Connecticut, officially opens Father McGivney's cause for sainthood in 1997.

Albert Zagrodnik is one of eleven members of Manitowoc, Wisconsin Council 710 who have volunteered to man video cameras for a televised daily Mass at Holy Family Medical Center in Manitowoc. Patients at the center unable to make it to the chapel can participate in the Mass each day through closed-circuit television.

In addition to assisting with the satellite uplink for papal events, the Knights of Columbus has funded other Vatican communications initiatives. The Order has provided support for several mobile production trucks for Vatican television, including this one being presented to Pope John Paul II by Virgil Dechant in 1995.

*postulator*—the person in charge of promoting the process through the investigation and compilation of evidence. For three years, Father O'Donnell worked with the archdiocese and members of the Order, gathering historical records of Father McGivney's life, works, and other accomplishments. In the year 2000, nearly 700 pages of documents were presented to Archbishop Cronin, who verified their authenticity.

The documents were then submitted to the Congregation for the Causes of Saints at the Vatican. After examining the material, the congregation decided that the criteria had been met for the process to move on to the next phase—the writing of a detailed argument for canonization called a *positio*. For this, the congregation assigned an advocate or *relator* to work with Father O'Donnell in preparing the dissertation-like work. Dominican Father Ambrose Eszer, who had shown special interest in Father McGivney's cause, was assigned the position. He was instrumental in helping prepare the nearly 1,000-page positio, which was presented in two volumes. One volume contained Father McGivney's biography, based on the writing of Christopher Kauffman, historian of the Order. The second volume explored Father McGivney's spirituality and life of virtue.

In January 2002, the positio was submitted to the Congregation for the Causes of Saints. Approved by the congregation in 2008, it was then submitted to Pope Benedict XVI, who also gave his approval. With his cause reaching this phase of the process, Father McGivney was declared "Venerable" in 2009.

*Beatification* would be the next step on Father McGivney's road to sainthood. This involves the confirmation of a miracle attributed to the candidate after his or her death. This step can vary significantly in length, since possible miracles must be reported and investigated. Once a miracle has been verified, the candidate can be beatified and declared "Blessed." The next and final step to sainthood, *canonization*, requires one more confirmed miracle.

With beatification as the next phase in Father's cause, the Father McGivney Guild continues its efforts. Along with encouraging continued

*God, our Father, protector of the poor and defender of the widow and orphan, you called your priest, Father Michael J. McGivney, to be an apostle of Christian family life and to lead the young to the generous service of their neighbor. Through the example of his life and virtue may we follow your Son, Jesus Christ, more closely, fulfilling his commandment of charity and building up his Body, which is the Church. Let the inspiration of your servant prompt us to greater confidence in your love so that we may continue his work of caring for the needy and the outcast.*

*We humbly ask that you glorify your venerable servant Father Michael J. McGivney on earth according to the design of your holy will. Through his intercession, grant the favor I now present (here make your request). Through Christ our Lord. Amen. (Our Father, Hail Mary, Glory Be.)*

Rectifying issues of family discord, livelihood, or renewed faith are among the favors commonly reported as occurring through prayer to Father McGivney. This is a frequent prayer at K of C events and at St. Mary's Church in New Haven.

To assist the Holy See in its work at the United Nations by providing it with a permanent embassy there in the 1990s, the Knights of Columbus paid the mortgage on the headquarters of the Permanent Observer of the Holy See to the United Nations in New York City.

Between 1975 and 2000, the Order's business growth was unprecedented, with insurance in force rising about 1,200 percent, from $3.2 billion to $39.3 billion. Charitable giving grew from $14 million and 6.7 million hours to $109 million and 55.3 million hours. Membership grew from 1.2 million to 1.6 million members.

devotion to Father McGivney, the guild collects reports of favors received through his intercession. In the words of Father O'Donnell, the purpose of the guild is to "spread the good word about Father McGivney's holiness of life, to encourage devotion to his memory, and to seek his intercession before the throne of God."

The Order also actively encourages devotion to the founder, including a prayer for his canonization. (See page at left.) This prayer is recited during Mass at the Supreme Office, at Supreme Conventions, and at St. Mary's Parish. Local councils are encouraged to say the prayer during meetings, as are all who have a devotion to Father McGivney.

## THE CENTURY COMES TO A CLOSE

As the end of 1999 approached, all eyes turned to the upcoming century and millennium. But even while planning for the new millennium, the Order was able to draw upon more than a hundred years of experience in meeting the needs of its members, its Church, and its communities.

The Knights of Columbus also faced a transition of eras. Virgil Dechant would be the last supreme knight to have a direct tie to Luke Hart, the supreme knight who himself had served on the board with every supreme knight since Flaherty and had attended conventions with some of the first leaders of the Order—past Supreme Knights Phelan and Cone.

During his twenty-three years at the helm, Dechant had skillfully guided the organization's expansion and outreach. The insurance operation had flourished—insurance in force alone grew from $3.2 billion to $39.3 billion—supporting greater charitable outreach. The focus was not just inward. The Knights' charitable activities responded to the needs of the Church at every level, and to communities, countries, and members around the world. Dechant's contributions did not go unnoticed, and he became the recipient of numerous external awards, honors, and degrees.

The Knights, too, recognized Dechant's contribution, honoring him in 2012 with the Gaudium et Spes Award. At the ceremony, Supreme Knight Anderson called his predecessor "the model of Catholic fraternalism for an entire generation."

Ready to respond to the challenges of the time, the Knights of Columbus was poised for the future. In 2000, the Order's supreme secretary, Carl Anderson, would be elected to succeed Virgil Dechant and lead the Order into the new era.

After their homeland was liberated from Isis control, Iraqi Christians are seen here raising a wooden cross on April 24, 2017 near St. George's Monastery in Mosul.

# 10.

# Into the New Millennium

## 2000 to Present

Together with the Church, the Knights welcomed the twenty-first century with great anticipation. The year 2000 marked the start of the third millennium of Christianity and began with the celebration of the Great Jubilee Year proclaimed by Pope John Paul II.

On Christmas Eve of 1999, in the newly refurbished Maderno Atrium of St. Peter's Basilica, the pope opened the great Holy Door. During that Jubilee Year, millions of faithful pilgrims would walk through the door to receive a special holy year indulgence. Other churches around the world, including St. Mary's in New Haven, were also designated as pilgrimage sites.

The Knights had another reason to celebrate in May of that year, when Pope John Paul II canonized six of its members. The new saints were priests who had been among twenty-five martyrs who gave their lives during the persecution of the Catholic Church in Mexico during the late 1920s. (See page 86.) They were the first Knights of Columbus to be recognized by the Church as saints.

The Jubilee also marked the beginning of new leadership for the Order with the election of Carl Anderson as the thirteenth supreme knight. In some areas, the world during his tenure struggled in ways reminiscent of the Order's first five decades. Similar destabilizing forces were shaping the cultures and countries that the Knights call home, including contentious political environments, economic recession, foreign wars, and international religious persecution. The retreat of men from actively engaging in parish life again accentuated the need for spiritually focused initiatives. Other con-

"In fidelity to the vision of Father Michael McGivney, may you continue to seek new ways of being a leaven of the Gospel in the world and a spiritual force for the renewal of the Church in holiness, unity, and truth."

–Pope John Paul II to the Knights of Columbus Board of Directors, 2003

While Supreme Secretary Charlie Foos looks on, Carl Anderson signs his first charter as supreme knight for the newly instituted Padre Miguel Agustin Pro Juarez Council 12789 in McAllen, Texas. Pro was a Jesuit priest killed during the persecution of the Church by the Mexican government in 1927.

On January 21, 2001, George W. Bush was sworn in as the forty-third US president. At the 2004 Supreme Convention, he praised the Knights' work to promote human dignity for all "born and unborn," adding that in this arena "few organizations have worked harder and done more . . . than the Knights of Columbus."

"Concerning the theological virtues of Faith, Hope and Love both toward God and neighbor, as well as the cardinal virtues of Prudence, Justice, Temperance and Fortitude, and those others joined to them, they existed to a heroic degree in the Servant of God Michael McGivney, Diocesan Priest and founder of the Fraternal Order the Knights of Columbus."

–Pope Benedict XVI's statement declaring Father McGivney "Venerable," March 15, 2008

cerns, such as the impact of technological advancements on how people engage socially, presented entirely new challenges.

Acceptance of Catholics in society had become more complicated. Fifty years after John F. Kennedy's election, animosity toward certain Church teachings sometimes marginalized Catholics committed to those beliefs. One notable difference, however, was that the fault lines of contention were increasing between secular and religious ideals, rather than mirroring the Protestant versus Catholic tensions characteristic of earlier American anti-Catholicism. Secular suspicion or hostility was now directed not only at Catholics, but at many Protestant and even non-Christian groups as well. As this secular outlook gained strength, greater attempts would be made to bring Catholics into conformity with politically progressive norms. This created an environment with challenges that had to be carefully addressed and managed, especially when combined with the other challenges of the period.

Drawing on the Order's mission and history as a champion for Catholics and the marginalized, Anderson would take an involved role in catalyzing important action in new ways. The Order would again strongly embrace the defense of civil and religious rights, particularly of Catholics, something that had been important to the Knights from the time of its founding.

Even as the Order grew globally, its uniquely Catholic nature would be brought to the fore, with programs designed to strengthen the faith of families while putting parishes at the center of the Knights' work, which could revitalize parishes and councils alike. Charitable programs meeting the concrete needs of families and communities would also be introduced, with the Knights' commitment to charity and faith formally united under the heading of "Faith in Action."

The Order's growth from a small group of men in Connecticut, to the international brotherhood of millions it is, gave weight to its perspective on issues of importance, including faith, humanitarian concerns, and religious freedom. The supreme knight ensured that the Order's Catholic voice on these matters was heard not only through words but also in action. The Knights' pro-life work would expand with life-saving initiatives. The Supreme Council would take a direct hand in engaging and evangelizing an increasingly secular culture, and offering resources for local Knights and councils to do the same—through a robust publishing program, documentary film production, public opinion polling, museum exhibits, and the construction of the Saint John Paul II National Shrine in Washington, DC.

In response to religious freedom threats that had seemed unthinkable for five decades, the Order and Anderson personally would strongly defend the rights of Catholics to exercise their faith free from legal compulsion or encroachment, both domestic and foreign. The issue of religious freedom would become prominent internationally, as well, and the Order

On Tuesday, September 11, 2001, Al-Qaeda launched attacks on American soil. Two hijacked planes were flown into the Twin Towers of New York's World Trade Center, another hit the Pentagon. The last plane crashed into a Pennsylvania field. American military response focused on terrorist-haven Afghanistan and—more controversially—on Iraq.

The Order established the $2 million Pacem in Terris (Peace on Earth) Fund in April of 2002 to promote the Church's efforts for peace in the Middle East, and to provide support for the Christian community there.

would also successfully advocate on behalf of Christians and others persecuted in the Middle East.

The fraternal health of the Order would also receive dedicated attention, resulting in impressive growth in terms of both membership (reaching nearly 2 million members) and insurance (more than a doubling of insurance in force, surpassing $100 billion). Seeing a global need for the Knights of Columbus, Anderson would directly spearhead the Order's first expansion outside North America in more than a century, adding new countries and new continents. The Order's ceremonials would be updated. Embracing technological innovation would set the Order on solid, competitive, and relevant business footing for the future, with a strong emphasis on ethics.

# O Holy Knights

In May 2000, the Knights had a very special reason to celebrate with the canonization of six members of the Order. Canonized by Pope John Paul II, the men were priest-martyrs who had given their lives during Mexico's Cristero War—the fight for religious persecution that began in the late 1920s. (See page 84.) They were the first Knights to be declared saints. The seventh, Rafael Guizar Valencia, also active in Mexico during the war, was the first bishop/Knight to be canonized.

In addition to these men, a number of Knights, including the founder of the Order, have been recognized for their holiness and placed on the road to sainthood.

## Saints

| | |
|---|---|
| Luis Batiz Sainz | José Maria Robles Hurtado |
| Mateo Correa Magallanes | Pedro de Jesus Maldonado Lucero |
| Miguel de la Mora de la Mora | Rodrigo Aguilar Alemán |
| | Rafael Guízar Valencia |

## Blesseds

| | |
|---|---|
| Carlos Manuel Rodríguez | Andrés Sola Molist |
| José Rangel Montaño | Leonardo Pérez Larios |

## Venerables

| | |
|---|---|
| Michael J. McGivney | Aloysius Schwartz |
| Patrick Peyton | Alphonse Gallegos |
| Fulton J. Sheen | |

Reliquary holding the relics of the six canonized Mexican priest-martyrs—the first Knights to be declared saints.

Building on the Order's devotion to the Eucharist and its long history of taking part in Eucharistic Congresses, the Order launched its first Knights of Columbus Eucharistic Congress in 2002. The two-day event received a papal letter of greeting and its program featured Masses, perpetual adoration, and talks on the Eucharist.

In 2002, Juan Diego—a Native Mexican—was declared a saint. After appearing to him in 1531, Our Lady of Guadalupe left her image on his tilma. Msgr. Eduardo Chavez (postulator of Saint Juan Diego's cause for canonization) and Supreme Knight Anderson co-authored a best-selling book on the apparitions in 2009.

These efforts and many more would continue well into the twenty-first century, and are written so freshly in the pages of history that the ink is scarcely dry. But it is an important history, not only because of the deeds' importance, but also because such recent labors inform so deeply who the Knights of Columbus currently are and, from that, who they might become. So this chapter, more than any other, is the story of the Catholic men of the Knights of Columbus today—family men, parish men, spiritual men, and men who "get things done." They are the men who give life to Venerable Father McGivney's dream. It is the story of their present and a hint of their future.

## CARL ANDERSON AT THE HELM

In October of 2000, at the age of forty-nine, Carl A. Anderson succeeded Virgil Dechant in becoming the Order's thirteenth supreme knight. From the very beginning of his tenure, Anderson highlighted the Order's unique ability to unify Catholics, as well as to develop its unique capacity as a force for good for Catholic families, for the Church, and for the Americas. Reflecting this, Anderson chose to be installed as supreme knight at the Basilica of Our Lady of Guadalupe in Mexico City. There, in the "spirit of unity that transcends all national boundaries," he dedicated his tenure and the Order itself to Our Lady of Guadalupe. She, more than any European missionaries, played a tremendous part in evangelizing the hemisphere and thereby unifying disparate peoples through a common faith in Jesus Christ.

A long-time member of Potomac Council 433, Anderson served the Order in a number of positions, including grand knight of Potomac Council 433 and state deputy of the District of Columbia. His experience of the "boots on the ground" brotherhood, and of how Knights engaged for transcendent reasons of love of God and neighbor rather than partisan ones, would stay with him. Later, he would bring that experience with him as, for thirteen years, he served the Order full time as its vice president for public policy, as assistant supreme secretary, and finally as supreme secretary.

Complementing his fraternal experience, at the time of his election as supreme knight, Anderson was already well known both inside and outside the Order as an effective visionary who had made substantial contributions in Church and government realms.

Like the majority of supreme knights before him, he had a background in both law and in public service. A graduate of Seattle University, Anderson earned his law degree at the University of Denver, putting his degree to use as a member of the bar in Washington, DC, and helping to defend key pro-life legislation before the US Supreme Court. At the Department of Health and Human Services, he worked to end discrimination against handicapped

**Carl A. Anderson**
Thirteenth supreme knight.

With the purchase of 2,000 wheelchairs in 2003, the Knights began an initiative called the Global Wheelchair Mission. Since its inception, the mission has distributed more than 60,000 wheelchairs throughout the United States, Canada, Mexico, the Philippines, Haiti, Chile, Israel, Vietnam, and Kenya.

Against a post-9/11 backdrop rife with reports of terrorism, religious conflict, and distrust, the Knights sponsored a "Concert of Reconciliation" at the Vatican, bringing together leaders of Catholic, Jewish, and Muslim faiths. The concert was performed by the Pittsburgh Symphony Orchestra—the first US orchestra to perform at the Vatican.

newborns. He also served nearly a decade on the US Commission on Civil Rights. During the administration of Ronald Reagan, he had held various positions, including special assistant to the president and acting director of the White House Office of Public Liaison. Of his decision to leave the White House staff in order to work at the Knights of Columbus, Anderson has said: "As I told President Reagan then, I left politics to serve a higher calling."

Trusted by the Holy See as an expert and advisor in several capacities, Anderson brought with him a close relationship with the Vatican unique among his predecessors, which would further grow. At the John Paul II Institute for Studies on Marriage and Family, he helped foster two generations of Catholics, first as a visiting professor teaching family law (1983–1998) at its Rome session, and then as the founding vice president and first dean of the institute's Washington, DC session. He attended the 1994 meeting of the International Catholic-Jewish Liaison Committee, which produced the Common Declaration on the Family, and in 1998, Pope John Paul II appointed him to the Pontifical Academy for Life, to which he would be reappointed by Pope Francis. Reflecting both Anderson's personal experience and the importance of the Order's perspective in the Church, over the years, popes would call on him to serve through additional Vatican positions including on the Pontifical Council for Justice and Peace, the Pontifical Council for the Laity, the Pontifical Council for Social Communications, and the Pontifical Council for the Family.

This range of experience proved uniquely relevant at the dawn of the new millennium. Bringing to bear the Order's founding principles and its long history of defending the beliefs and free exercise of the Catholic faith, he would take an involved role in steering an engaged Order through various challenges and into rewarding endeavors.

Carl Anderson (left) became the first supreme knight installed outside the United States. He underscored his prioritization of Catholic unity by dedicating his administration to Our Lady of Guadalupe and holding his installation at her Basilica in Mexico City. Our Lady of Guadalupe is the patroness of the American hemisphere and the Philippines.

# FOR THE GOOD OF THE ORDER

Following Father McGivney's founding vision, Carl Anderson made clear that the Knights played a key role in preserving the well-being of families in terms of both their faith and their financial stability. Regarding the latter, Father McGivney had described the goal of offering "the same, if not better, advantages" as other societies, and in the twenty-first century, "better" was the accurate description.

But maintaining its "better" status required significant updating. One of the earliest organizational challenges Anderson faced as supreme knight involved the rapid advancements in the field of technology—an area in which the organization had lagged. Computers were in short supply at the New Haven headquarters in 2000, and the software was so dated that it couldn't be used outside the building. Typewriters and carbon paper were often still the norm, and manual systems predominated.

To build for the future and remain competitive, Anderson understood that improving the Order's technological footing had to be a priority. Information technology and business process upgrades moved the daily operations of the Knights firmly into the twenty-first century. These upgrades continued periodically to keep the Order up to speed with technological developments and to reorganize its departments and processes in a way that would ensure the Order's long-term competitiveness. A major restructuring of the insurance business of the Order was also undertaken, and the agency force was reorganized for the first time in decades.

Throughout these changes, the Catholic faith continued to shape the Order's financial services to Catholics. New products were rolled out to meet the changing needs of families, as were new lines of business, with K of C Asset Advisors, which put the investment team that had engineered the Order's strong track record at the service of others. These advisors provided Catholic-compliant investments to both individual and institutional investors. In this area, and throughout the company, a strong Catholic ethical foundation was embraced and further strengthened. Beginning in 2014, the Knights of Columbus also became one of the companies named several times as a "World's Most Ethical Company" by the Ethisphere® Institute.

The embrace of technological advancements improved aspects of the fraternal experience, as well. A strong and regularly updated online and social media presence allowed the Knights, its activities, and its messages to reach digital audiences and stay current in a swiftly developing technological landscape. Joining the Order also became easier. Potential members were allowed to obtain their First Degree via video, rather than having to wait for a scheduled, in-person degree team. Joining became easier still in 2017, when online membership was introduced. Through this online connection,

Melding Eastern and Western Christian artistic styles, the 2005 renovation of the Supreme Office's Holy Family Chapel featured mosaics by renowned artist Jesuit Father Marko Rupnik. In addition to hosting daily Mass for employees, the chapel provides a place for visiting priests and bishops to celebrate Mass as well.

Bringing founder and founding to life, *He Was Our Father*, a play by Fr. Peter John Cameron, debuted in 2005. The next year, Douglas Brinkley and Julie Fenster published a best-selling biography of Father McGivney, *Parish Priest*. Its publication in Italian by the Vatican publisher was one of many foreign language editions.

In 2005, after a papacy of almost three decades, Pope John Paul II died on the vigil of Divine Mercy Sunday at age eighty-four. Cardinal Joseph Ratzinger presided over his funeral, which was attended by Supreme Knight Anderson. Ratzinger would soon be elected pope, taking the name Benedict XVI.

Catholic men could join the Order quickly, even before contacting a council. In addition, ceremonials were updated to better embrace the needs of twenty-first century men.

Such changes reflected important strategic choices, as did avoiding risky monetary investments. With the financial crisis of 2008, driven by speculative investments of dubious quality, the world suddenly faced the worst economic crisis since the Great Depression. Committed to ethical and sustainable investing based on Catholic principles, the Knights had largely avoided the sort of investments that helped trigger the crash, and thus the Order weathered the storm better than many.

The Order would prove that it was capable of embracing its Catholic roots and key elements of its past even as it positioned itself for future growth and expanded into new territories, new digital frontiers, and new programs.

# Captain Alfredo "Al" Fuentes
## Notable Knight

On the morning of September 11, 2001, when two hijacked planes flew into the Twin Towers of the World Trade Center, Captain Alfredo Fuentes of the New York City Fire Department was among the first responders. In the midst of the chaos and destruction, he led fireboat rescue teams from the Brooklyn Naval Yard to lower Manhattan to ferry survivors to hospitals across the Hudson River.

Before the south tower fell, Captain Fuentes had helped move a number of the wounded from the wreckage to the fireboats. When he went to the north tower in search of more survivors, the building suddenly began to collapse around him. A steel girder pinned him to the ground. His skull was fractured, ribs were broken, his left hand was smashed, and he had a collapsed lung. While in excruciating pain, he drifted in and out of consciousness for nearly an hour. During lucid moments, he maintained radio contact with other rescuers and guided them to where he lay.

Captain Fuentes' injuries kept him hospitalized for many months. While he was recuperating, fellow Knights from the George W. Hudson Council 3701, of which he had been a member for over two decades, visited regularly. During that time, Fuentes often spoke of his near-death experience, claiming that prayer—the Hail Mary in particular—was his constant companion and gave him the strength to survive.

When he recovered, Fuentes published his autobiography, *American by Choice*. In it, he shares a detailed account of that fateful day and professes his great love of country, the Catholic Church, and his fellow man.

On the first anniversary of the September 11th attacks, the Knights sponsored a memorial Mass, followed by a patriotic program at the National Shrine in Washington, DC. Although he was in constant pain, Al Fuentes attended the event, during which he led those assembled in the Pledge of Allegiance. He viewed being there that day and leading the pledge as a true honor.

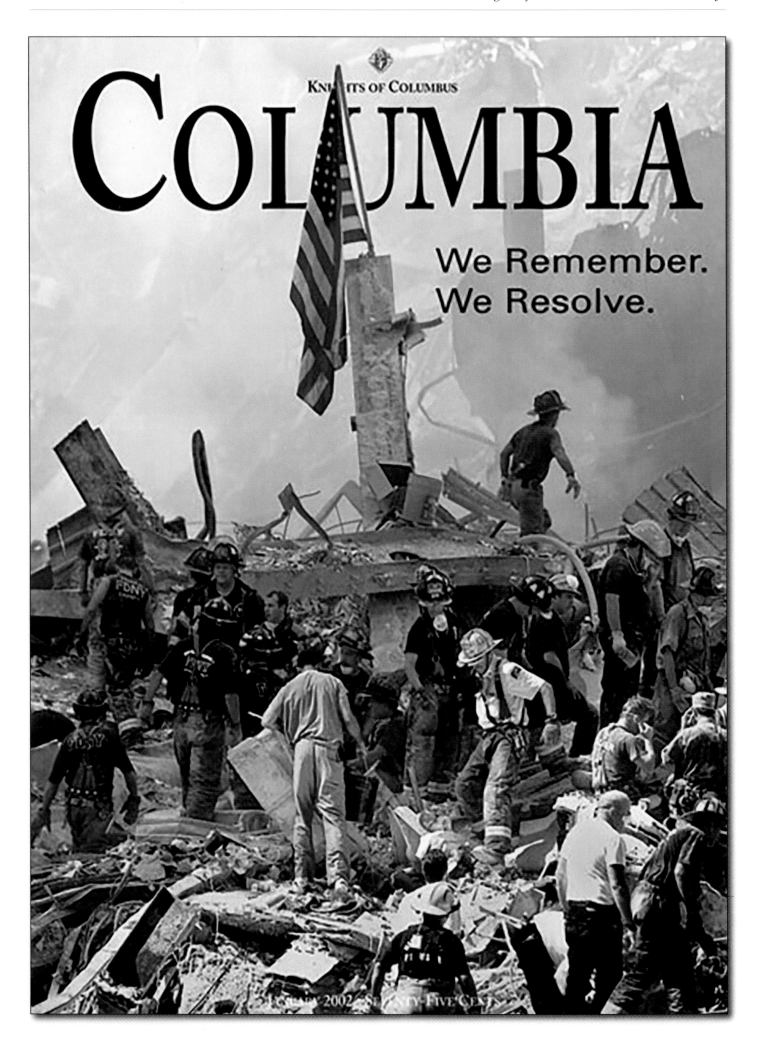

# DISASTER RESPONSE AND RELIEF

Every year, hundreds of disasters—natural and manmade—strike throughout the world. Although the Knights of Columbus had provided relief assistance for such disasters as far back as the Great San Francisco Earthquake of 1906, its outreach continued to develop during the first years of the new millennium. What follows are just a few of the many instances illustrating the Knights' charitable outreach during times of crisis. They also highlight the innovative ways in which the Order's response to disasters became increasingly effective.

## 9/11 Terrorist Attacks

When the United States was targeted with previously unimaginable acts of terrorism on September 11, 2001, the entire world watched in shock. Along with witnessing the horrors of that day, the world also saw an impressive outpouring of heroism as first responders—firefighters, law enforcement officers, and emergency medical personnel—risked their lives in an effort to save others. The risk was not without cost, and many of these brave first responders showed the greatest love of all by giving their lives for their neighbors.

The families of the fallen first responders had no time to prepare for such a tragedy. In addition to the emotional toll of losing their loved ones, many of these families would be facing immediate financial needs.

Their plight resonated with the Knights. The very next day, Anderson led the Order to swiftly establish the $1 million Heroes Fund, which gave immediate support to families of fallen first responders regardless of their religion or affiliation with the Knights. Days later, local K of C insurance agents delivered the first of 419 checks in the amount of $3,000 to families of first responders. A second check for about $500 followed shortly after. Donations began pouring in from around the world, adding almost $500,000 more to the fund. Anderson said that because of the fraternal infrastructure of councils, "we knew we could be there, because we were there."

Building on the success of the Heroes Fund, the Knights would continue to increase its efforts when responding to disasters.

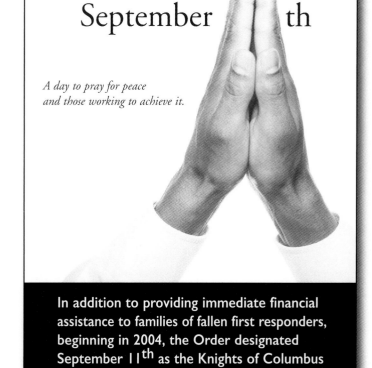

September 11th

*A day to pray for peace
and those working to achieve it.*

In addition to providing immediate financial assistance to families of fallen first responders, beginning in 2004, the Order designated September 11th as the Knights of Columbus World Day of Prayer for Peace, and invited people of all faiths to join in. This action added a spiritual element to the Order's response, with councils organizing events like "Blue Masses" for public safety personnel and ecumenical prayer services.

◀ *Columbia* magazine captures first responders making their way through the rubble that was once New York's World Trade Center.

At the K of C Museum, twisted girders from the World Trade Center stand before a metal woven plaque with the names of more than forty Knights who were killed on 9/11. Among the fallen was Lieutenant Daniel O'Callaghan, whose body was found with his K of C rosary in hand.

## Hurricane Katrina

When Hurricane Katrina made landfall in August 2005, it was the largest and one of the strongest hurricanes ever recorded in the United States. The category 5 storm devastated the Gulf Coast from Florida to Texas. In New Orleans, the twenty-foot-high storm surge broke through the levees, flooding nearly 80 percent of the city. The death and destruction left in the storm's wake were unprecedented. Nearly 2,000 people lost their lives, while hundreds of thousands were left homeless. (Adding to this devastation, a second hurricane—Hurricane Rita—made landfall along the Gulf Coast less than a month after Katrina.) With upwards of $81 billion in property damage, Katrina became the costliest hurricane in the country's history.

The Knights stepped up in ways large and small, executing a two-part approach that included giving a hand locally while raising funds nationally. This approach would become the Order's signature model for responding to major disasters.

Before even receiving a call for help, the Knights had already sprung into action. Volunteers from local councils in and around the region got to work setting up staging areas for first responders. A number of council homes in the region served as temporary police headquarters, while others became aid

Churches along the path of Hurricane Katrina sustained tremendous damage. This statue was the only thing left standing at St. Michael's Catholic Church in Biloxi, Mississippi.

In the new millennium's first decade, the Order celebrated several important anniversaries. In addition to centennials in Mexico (2005), the Philippines (2005), Panama (2009), and Cuba (2009), in 2007, the Order celebrated the 125th anniversary of its founding.

When the 2008 financial collapse caused a severe recession, the Order responded with food and clothing programs. Several Missouri councils launched the "Journey for Charity," a food collection parade of 80+ tractors over thirty miles. The annual event has raised tens of thousands of dollars and tons of food.

distribution centers. Members operated soup kitchens and organized temporary shelters for the displaced. In the months following the storm, countless Knights volunteered hundreds of thousands of hours, making 2005 a record year of charitable giving.

Supplementing immediate responses by local councils in the region, the Supreme Council established the Gulf States Hurricane Relief Fund. Of the $10 million that was raised, $5.4 million came from councils, individual donors, and other organizations, with the Supreme Council matching all donations that came in during September and October. The direct raising of money at this level through the Knights of Columbus Charities paved the way for the Order's response to future large-scale crises. Similar efforts were later mounted after other disasters, including the 2013 chemical plant explosion in West, Texas, the 2016 flooding in Louisiana, Hurricane Sandy in 2012, and Hurricanes Harvey and Maria in 2017.

The devastation following Hurricane Katrina in 2005 was unprecedented. It left hundreds of thousands homeless.

In 2008, Pope Benedict XVI named Father McGivney a "Venerable Servant of God"—a key step toward sainthood. Visiting America a month later, the pope met with the supreme knight. Knights volunteered at papal events and served as honor guards. At St. Patrick's Cathedral, the pope again praised Father McGivney.

Beginning in 2008, the Knights partnered with The Marist Poll for surveys on key social issues. The polling on abortion was particularly notable, diving deep to help shape the national conversation on life issues by consistently finding widespread consensus among Americans of both parties in favor of abortion restrictions.

## Super Typhoon Haiyan

In 2013, the Knights' work after Super Typhoon Haiyan in the Philippines also capitalized on the effective network of hard-working councils and pursued strategic longer-term relief initiatives. The typhoon's 200-mile-an-hour winds and massive wave surge devasted the country, killing thousands and destroying the homes of millions. In a country with more than 100 languages, it was reported that government and other aid organizations had difficulty discovering the needs of those in remote areas and distributing aid to them.

Knights in the Philippines responded quickly to the devastation from Super Typhoon Haiyan. In the short term, Knights developed a system for providing food to those affected in remote hard-to-reach areas (above). For the longer term, the Knights helped families rebuild their lives by replacing lost fishing boats (below) and providing seeds to help farmers get back on their feet.

The network of councils and local members proved an essential communications stream for finding out where and what aid was needed. The Supreme Council committed an initial $250,000, with an additional $500,000 of donations pouring in soon after from K of C and others. This helped the Order purchase the most critically needed items for distribution through both stationary food-bank-style sites and distribution-style sites like the one run by the Visayas State Council. This council packaged essentials (rice, canned food, water, etc.) and delivered them to out-of-the-way areas, which otherwise would have had difficulty receiving aid.

The Knights also set its sights on the country's longer-term needs through key livelihood programs. Haiyan had destroyed thousands of boats, leaving many of the area's fishermen without a way to earn a living. Teams of Knights visited affected areas and launched a boat-building program for fishermen whose vessels had been lost in the storm. More than one hundred boats were provided along with other equipment essential to the fishermen's work.

The typhoon had also struck just a month before the end of the planting season, and the felled coconut trees not only wiped out years of cultivation but also made the land inaccessible for replanting. The Knights provided equipment to clear the land as well as thousands of seeds and seedlings to help the farmers begin anew.

# Earthquake in Haiti

The Order has also provided assistance beyond its own territories, notably in Haiti, where it committed to solving a specific longer-term need. On January 13, 2010, an earthquake struck the heart of Haiti, resulting in one of the Western Hemisphere's worst natural disasters in recent memory. The epicenter of the 7.0-magnitude quake devastated Port-au-Prince—the country's most populated area. Over 200,000 people were killed, tens of thousands were critically injured, and an estimated 1.5 million were left homeless.

Within days of the catastrophe, the Order sent an initial $50,000 donation to the Catholic Relief Services for its efforts there. Soon, the Knights had committed $500,000, of which half came from state and local councils. The Order's commitment would soon exceed $1 million.

After initially providing wheelchairs for the injured, the Knights discovered that among the thousands of Haitians injured during the quake were hundreds of children who had lost limbs. Amputation had put these children at a huge disadvantage and also left them culturally stigmatized.

In response, the Knights launched the Healing Haiti's Children project, a joint effort with Project Medishare for Haiti. This group was affiliated with the University of Miami and housed in Hospital Bernard Mevs in Port-au-Prince. Funded by the Knights, Project Medishare fitted the injured children with prosthetic limbs and provided two years of physical therapy and rehabilitation. Initially, then-Supreme Secretary Emilio Moure led the initiative, dedicating inexhaustible heart and effort to its success.

With the Knights' help, Project Medishare was even able to open a prosthesis-production facility on site in Port-au-Prince. This local facility provided access to quality prosthetic devices while also creating sustainable jobs for Haitians, including some who had lost limbs themselves.

A young girl is fitted for a prosthetic limb as part of the Healing Haiti's Children project. She was one of more than one hundred children fitted with prosthetics in 2011.

In 2014, the Knights released an award-winning documentary on the rehabilitation efforts in Haiti. *Unbreakable: A Story of Hope and Healing in Haiti* was aired on PBS stations and shown at film festivals throughout the country.

The earthquake in Haiti was a tragedy marked by the unfortunate failure of many members of the international community to make good on their promised aid. Conversely, the Knights' involvement was both immediate and long lasting, particularly through its involvement with the Healing Haiti's Children project. Over the course of five years, the Knights donated approximately $1.7 million, which provided prosthetic limbs for 1,000 amputees, as well as rehabilitation services for more than 25,000 others who had been injured in the quake.

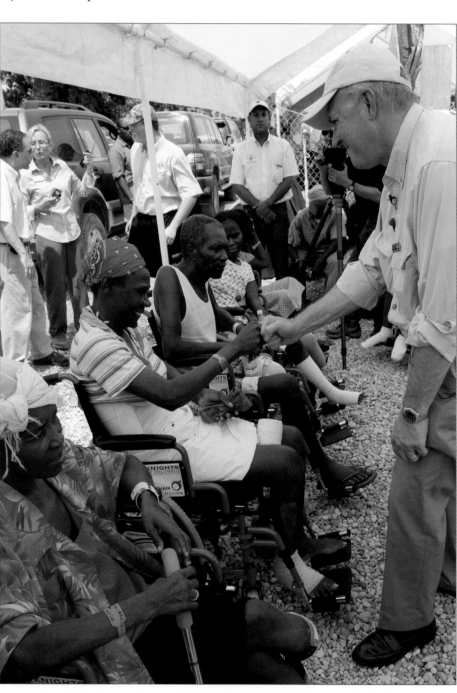

Supreme Knight Carl Anderson distributes wheelchairs and meets with Haitian amputees at the Project Medishare hospital in Port-au-Prince following the 2010 earthquake.

Highlighting the vital work of council chaplains, in 2009, the Order established a position to support chaplains' efforts. The following year, the Order hosted an enriching pilgrimage for dozens of state chaplains—including several bishops— to Rome and Assisi for prayer, discussion, and the concluding Mass of the Year for Priests with Pope Benedict.

Team Zaryen competes in a game against the ▶ US National Amputee Soccer Team during a five-day Knights'-sponsored tour through the northeastern United States in 2011.

# Overcoming Adversity

One of the many worthy outcomes of the Healing Haiti's Children initiative was Team Zaryen—a soccer team of amputee players, most of whom had been injured in the country's 2010 earthquake. Co-sponsored by the Knights and Project Medishare, the team was conceived by Wilfrid Macena, who lost his right leg in the earthquake. He formed the team after receiving a prosthetic limb and regaining his mobility.

Team Zaryen served as a symbol of overcoming adversity. Its members are proud ambassadors of hope, whose mission is to inspire others to triumph over the challenges resulting from limb loss. The name *Zaryen* is Creole for "tarantula," a fearless spider that can function undaunted by the loss of a leg. A tarantula with seven legs serves as the graphic for the team logo.

The players became involved with Project Medishare's programs to help their country's young amputees return to school and its adults return to work. Along with funding its regular operations, the Order has helped the team bring its inspirational mission to others. In 2011, it arranged for Team Zaryen to travel to the United States,

where the players conducted soccer clinics for wounded veterans at the Walter Reed Army Medical Center. They also performed in an exhibition game against the US National Amputee Soccer Team. Witnessing Team Zaryen's spirit, enthusiasm, and skill provided much needed encouragement to new amputees, whose eyes were opened to the real possibility of thriving in spite of their injuries.

In 2015, five years after the Haitian earthquake, the Knights sponsored a trip to Rome for the team. The players attended a Vatican conference on Haitian relief efforts, and met with Pope Francis. They also scrimmaged with local soccer players at the Knights' sports center that overlooked the Vatican.

Like prosthetics, sports have proven to be an important tool in helping the young amputees of Haiti stand tall. Team Zaryen's ability to travel the world and play soccer against teams throughout Europe and the United States has helped underscore an important message of hope—that those living with a disability are entitled to dignity and respect, and that they can overcome the biases of their neighbors while winning international acclaim as well.

## RELIGIOUS FREEDOM AT HOME

While engaging on religious freedom abroad at a level not seen since the 1920s, the Knights were also forced to defend religious freedom at home for the first time in five decades. The threats were varied, with some targeting the Church itself and others affecting Catholic individuals and employers.

In Connecticut, a bill was introduced in 2009 that would have stripped parishes and dioceses of financial control of their own assets. The concept known as "lay trusteeism" was a blatant violation of the First Amendment's establishment and free-exercise clauses. The Knights of Columbus joined with the bishops of Connecticut in opposing the bill. Supreme Knight Carl Anderson spoke out against this bill and published an op-ed in the *Stamford Advocate* entitled "Shredding the First Amendment in the Constitution State." The bill was ultimately defeated.

In March 2009, more than 5,000 Catholics rallied at the Connecticut Capitol against a bill designed to take financial control of parishes away from the Church. Supreme Chaplain Bishop William Lori—then Bishop of Bridgeport—along with the supreme knight and other Church leaders, addressed the crowd and led a successful movement to defeat the bill.

In 2007, the Knights became defendant-interveners in a case challenging the words "under God" in the Pledge of Allegiance. Court decisions subsequently upheld the words' constitutionality. In 2008, the Becket Fund, which was representing the Knights in this case, awarded the Canterbury Medal—its highest award—to Supreme Knight Anderson.

Following his 2008 presidential election, US Senator from Illinois and former community organizer Barack Obama became the first African American to take the oath of office as President of the United States of America. On November 6, 2012, he would be elected to a second term.

The next year, a national issue emerged with the passage of the Affordable Care Act. In its implementation of that law, in 2012, the Department of Health and Human Services (HHS) issued regulations requiring employers to provide health insurance plans that covered various contraception, sterilization, and abortion services for their employees. While a narrow exception seemed to exempt dioceses and parishes, many other Catholic charitable groups and other Catholic employers were left unprotected. Those who wanted to opt out of providing the coverage faced confiscatory fines. In speeches and op-eds, Anderson spoke out forcefully against the mandate's undermining of religious freedom. The Order also filed formal comments calling for the repeal of the mandate with the HHS. While court rulings in 2018 protected Catholic employers, including the Knights, from having to violate their religious freedom, it was clear that after a decades-long hiatus, the issue had resurfaced at a national level for the Catholic Church and its Knights.

As if to underscore the point, in both 2017 and 2018, Catholic judicial nominees were subjected to scrutiny by certain US senators because of their faith. Brian Buescher, a member of the Knights of Columbus, was questioned by two senators specifically about his membership in the Order because of its adherence to Church teaching. A firestorm of controversy ensued.

In light of the Buescher incident, Catholic, Protestant, Jewish, Muslim, and Sikh leaders wrote to the Senate expressing their concern about a religious test being applied and asked all senators to pledge to avoid such religious tests. *America* magazine editorialized in support of the Knights and against religious tests, while the Catholic commentator and journalist John Allen called the senators' line of questioning a "stalking horse" for going after Buescher's Catholicism. The US Conference of Catholic Bishops also issued an alert, asking Catholics to "tell the Senate to reject religious tests for judicial nominees."

In a letter to his brother Knights, Anderson noted that Pope Francis himself had urged the Knights to speak out on the Church's teachings regarding life and human sexuality. He added:

> We must remember that Article VI of the U.S. Constitution forbids a religious test for public office, and the First Amendment guarantees our free exercise of religion, freedom of association and freedom of speech. Any suggestion that the Order's adherence to the beliefs of the Catholic Church makes a Brother Knight unfit for public office blatantly violates those constitutional guarantees.
>
> Let us continue to express our love of God and neighbor by helping those in need and by standing with our Church, regardless of the popularity of doing so. Let us remember that our "Christian witness is to be considered a fundamental obligation."

"First Amendment religious freedom is not something we chose to care about last week, or last year. It is something that has been part of the Catholic experience and the Knights of Columbus experience in America from the very beginning. And where our First Amendment freedom is threatened, we will defend it vigorously. . . . What is at stake is the future of religious liberty in the United States and the right of every individual to practice his faith freely."

–Supreme Knight's Report
Supreme Convention
Anaheim, California, 2012

Shortly after its centennial anniversary in Cuba, the Knights supported San Carlos y San Ambrosio Seminary, the first new seminary in that Communist country in five decades. Supreme Knight Anderson and Cuban-born Supreme Secretary Emilio Moure attended the dedication by Cardinal Ortega, who also received the Order's Gaudium et Spes Award.

In 2011, the Knights defended "Big Mountain Jesus"—a statue erected by Kalispell Council 1328 in 1954, commemorating the 10th Mountain Division's WWII service. An atheist group pushed the US Forest Service to remove it, but in 2015, the Ninth Circuit Court of Appeals ruled the statue could remain.

# PRO-LIFE WORK

The Knights' long-standing promotion of Catholic teaching related to the right to life, marriage, the family, and human sexuality drew specific praise from Pope Francis in his first greeting to a Knights of Columbus convention. He said:

"Conscious of the specific responsibility which the lay faithful have for the Church's mission, [Pope Francis] invites each Knight, and every Council, to bear witness to the authentic nature of marriage and the family, the sanctity and inviolable dignity of human life, and the beauty and truth of human sexuality."

–Papal Greeting from Pope Francis to the Knights of Columbus, 2013

Begun under Supreme Knight McDevitt, and continued by Supreme Knight Dechant, the defense of human life continued to be an important cause for the Knights under the leadership of Supreme Knight Anderson. Involvement in initiatives that proved to save lives and move hearts further cemented the Order's commitment to the unborn—whom the Knights see as one of the most at-risk groups in modern society.

In 2004, the Supreme Council began a concrete partnership with the Sisters of Life, a contemporary religious order dedicated to "the protection and enhancement of the sacredness of every human life." These sisters take part in a variety of outreach initiatives that include taking in pregnant women in difficult situations and providing related assistance. While the sisters had a number of houses for this type of work, it was their decades-old dream to have a retreat house, where people could come closer to God through traditional spiritual retreats. It would also be for retreats focused on post-abortion healing.

The Knights helped make this dream come true by purchasing a property in Stamford, Connecticut, that would become Villa Maria Guadalupe. The old, but very beautiful facility—formerly a convent—needed much work, but the willing hands of Knights in local councils eagerly pitched in. Recognizing the importance and effectiveness of their mission (and their infectious joy), the Order has continued its support of the sisters over the years.

In 2008, the Knights initiated annual surveys on abortion, helping to shape the national discussion of the issue on abortion and other moral issues.

Founded by Cardinal John O'Connor of New York, the Sisters of Life is a community of sisters dedicated to protecting life by aiding women in crisis pregnancies. Here they assemble before their new retreat center in Stamford, Connecticut, purchased by the Knights of Columbus.

Continuing its history of facilitating public discussion on timely issues, the Order sponsored numerous conferences worldwide (several with Vatican entities) addressing pressing religious and humanitarian themes, as well as nuanced family challenges such as abortion's effects on men and paths to healing in the aftermath of divorce and abortion.

When floods devastated Pakistan in 2010, affecting 20 million people, the Order supported the relief efforts—for Christians and Muslims alike—organized by Bishop Andrew Francis of the Diocese of Multan. Women, children, and people with special needs were among those helped with food, medicine, supplies, and transportation.

# The Ultrasound Initiative

The Knights of Columbus has long stood with those on the margins of society. In the twentieth and twenty-first centuries, this included the unborn. In the United States, there are almost twice as many abortions performed as there are deaths from heart disease, which is generally listed as the country's leading cause of death.

Perhaps the greatest debate on the abortion issue is on the question of life itself. There are those who do not consider the unborn child a living being, while others believe the scientific evidence and teaching of the Church that life begins at conception. Regardless of her position, an ultrasound offers a pregnant woman the first encounter with her unborn child. It allows her to see that the child she is carrying is truly a living, moving being. Many women who have considered terminating a pregnancy have changed their minds after having an ultrasound.

But the high cost of ultrasound equipment meant that pregnancy care centers, which are dedicated to helping women with unplanned pregnancies, often were unable to purchase this most important piece of equipment. In response, in 2009, the Order launched the Ultrasound Initiative, encouraging councils to raise half the cost of ultrasound machines, while the Supreme Council provided the other half. Later, mobile units were added to the initiative, enabling this life-saving "window into the womb" to reach women in a greater number of areas.

By 2019, the initiative had raised enough money to place 1,000 ultrasound machines—with the goal of saving a million unborn lives.

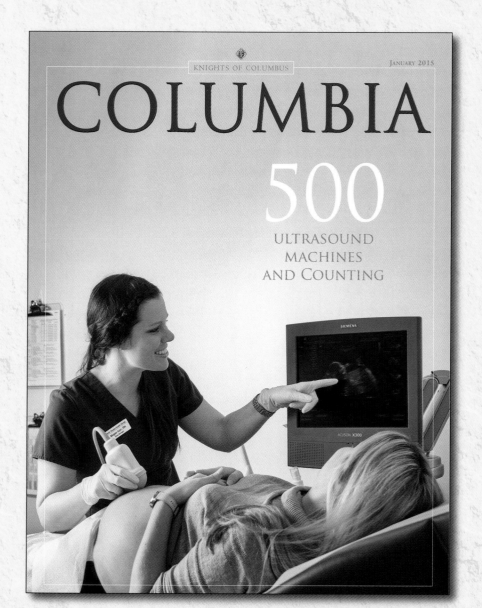

The January 2015 *Columbia* cover celebrated the success of the Ultrasound Initiative. The milestone of 500 ultrasounds would be surpassed and doubled a few years later, when the partnership between local councils and the Supreme Council funded and donated the thousandth ultrasound machine.

In partnership with the Marist Poll—a premier pollster often used by major media outlets—the annual surveys found broad (generally three-quarters or greater) support for substantial restrictions on abortion. This held true even in years when most Americans identified themselves as pro-choice.

The launching of the K of C Ultrasound Initiative (see page 225) took place in 2009. This program brought Supreme Council support to state and local councils that sought to provide ultrasound machines so that pregnant women considering abortion could make a more informed choice based on the clear view of the life growing within them. In a decade, more than 1,000 machines were installed, and center after center reported that mothers chose to keep their child after seeing the ultrasound image. Understanding how pregnant and new mothers needed support and care, councils throughout the Order have continued to aid pregnancy resource centers and provide diapers, formula, and other essentials for expectant and new mothers.

Public advocacy for the rights of the unborn also continued, with the Knights participating in pro-life marches around the world from Mexico to Poland to the Philippines, as well as throughout North America. The Knights brought substantial expertise to such work from the Order's decades-long experience, especially with the March for Life in Washington, DC, whose chairman of the board is current Deputy Supreme Knight Patrick Kelly.

All three popes of the new millennium encouraged the Order's defense of human life, and for the Knights, the issue of abortion transcended politics. Driving the matter home as a humanitarian issue, Supreme Knight Anderson often noted that abortion was the leading cause of death in America. It takes more lives than heart disease, which usually is given that dubious distinction. The sheer number of lives lost, he argued, made it the preeminent human rights issue of the day, and he urged Americans to withhold their vote from candidates of either party who did not support pro-life legislation.

In addition to marching, the Knights provide iconic signs declaring "Defend Life" or "Love Life, Choose Life," which have been used by hundreds of thousands of marchers onsite—in the United States as well as in Manila, Philippines (pictured here).

In 2011, threats to religious freedom—including HHS regulations mandating insurance coverage of sterilization, contraception, and abortion-inducing drugs—prompted the US Conference of Catholic Bishops to create an Ad Hoc Committee for Religious Liberty. It was led by then-Bishop of Bridgeport William Lori, supreme chaplain.

Long a supporter of Vatican communications, in November, 2010, the Knights of Columbus helped sponsor a high-definition television truck created by Sony for use by the Vatican. Pope Benedict XVI blessed the truck, which was designed for use in broadcasting Vatican events to millions around the world.

# EXPANDING INTO EUROPE AND BEYOND

One of the key factors in the Order's massive expansion into new territories and countries a century ago was the enthusiasm of its members. The men were eager to share both the experience of being a Knight and the distinctly Catholic charitable values they grew to call "Columbianism." Similarly, the early twenty-first century would see new international expansion, spurred by an awareness of the Order's benefits for Catholic men, families, the Church, and communities.

In 2005, at the encouragement of Pope John Paul II, the Knights established its presence in Poland—its first in Europe. The councils were set up through collaboration with Cardinal Józef Glemp of Warsaw, Cardinal Stanisław Dziwisz of Kraków, and Cardinal Franciszek Macharski, the emeritus archbishop of Kraków, who served as the first national chaplain for the Order in Poland.

Initial membership in these councils—the first of which was John Paul II Council 14000 in Kraków—totaled more than 300. Polish membership grew quickly, and in 2011, Poland was granted state council status. By 2019, membership numbered well over 5,000.

In 2012 and 2013, the Knights expanded into two more Eastern European countries: Ukraine and Lithuania. The invitation to Ukraine had been raised nearly a decade earlier by Cardinal Lubomyr Husar, the Major Archbishop of Kyiv-Halyč in Ukraine. Speaking at the Supreme Convention in Chicago in 2005, he hailed the Order's expansion into Poland and expressed hope that the Knights would be established soon in Ukraine, as well. He highlighted how important charitable involvement could be in healing the "deep wounds" the country sustained in the wake of Communist oppression.

Less than a decade later, the cardinal's wish came true with the establishment of two councils in Ukraine. The Knights immediately became a unifying force for the country's Catholics. Among the first men initiated—Major Archbishop Sviatoslav Shevchuk and Archbishop Mieczysław Mokrzycki—were leaders of the country's Ukrainian Greek Catholic and Roman Catholic Churches, respectively. This made their membership in the Order—and the Order itself—unique as the Knights became a greater source of unity for Catholics.

In recognition of its substantial growth, in 2018, Ukraine was granted state council status. By 2019, it had more than twenty-five councils and almost 1,300 members.

While the Order was growing in Ukraine, the Knights were also establishing a foothold in Lithuania with the formation of a round table in Vilnius in 2013. Archbishop Gintaras Grušas of Vilnius, who was familiar with the Knights' work for the military, was instrumental in its formation. That round table took root and became that country's first council.

Cardinal Lubomyr Husar, Archbishop of Kyiv (Kiev), Ukraine, at the 2005 Supreme Convention expressed hope that the Knights would come to Ukraine.

Music helps the healing at a recreational and spiritual summer camp organized by St. Peter Council 16252 in Melitopol, Ukraine. Hundreds of children affected by the conflicts in that country have benefited from the camp.

In 2010, Rome's Capitoline Museum—the oldest public museum in the world—hosted an exhibit on the Knights' ninety years in Rome. The Order would later partner with the museum on "The Dream of Rome," a project through which some of the city's most important pieces of art were lent to top US museums.

In 2011, the City of Rome named the area adjacent to the Baths of Caracalla in honor of the Knights of Columbus. Set in a scenic area near well-known landmarks including the Coliseum, "Largo Cavalieri di Colombo" honors the Knights' nine decades of service in the Eternal City.

**Poland.** Prior to establishing in Poland, invited by Cardinal Józef Glemp of Warsaw, a delegation of six Fourth Degree Knights led by Supreme Knight Anderson took part in the third National Eucharistic Congress in Warsaw, June 2005.

**Ukraine.** His Beatitude Sviatoslav Shevchuk, head of the Ukrainian Greek Church, with Knights after celebrating Mass in honor of Ukraine's first council, St. Vladimir Council 15800, in Kyiv, Ukraine, November 2013.

**Lithuania.** First Degree class formed at the Cathedral of St. Ignatius of Loyola, Vilnius, Lithuania, March 9, 2017.

**France.** The 2016 Supreme Convention brought the announcement of five new councils established in France.

**Korea.** Korean members of the Fourth Degree are pictured with Supreme Knight Anderson following the Fourth Degree exemplification, which took place in the base chapel of US Army Garrison Yongsan, South Korea.

For Catholics living in countries that had spent decades under communism, the Knights provided a way to grow in and live out the faith that had been so brutally suppressed. It also gave these men yet another tangible connection to the universal nature of the Catholic Church.

Half a world away, the foundation was being laid for bringing the Knights to South Korea, a country with a rapidly growing Catholic population of at least 5.5 million faithful. Since 2007, a solitary military council, Bishop John J. Kaising Council 14223, had existed there at US Army Garrison Humphreys. The council's charity focused not only on soldiers and their families, but also on impoverished migrant workers. This outreach spoke well of Catholic knighthood.

The idea of a non-military council was planted during Supreme Knight Anderson's visits to Asia in 2010 and 2013. The reception of Bishop Francis Xavier Yu Soo-il into the Order in 2012 meant that the Knights had a strong advocate within the Korean Catholic hierarchy. The first Korean council—St. Andrew Kim Taegon Council 16000 in Seoul—was announced at the 2014 Supreme Convention.

In 2015, the Knights' presence in France began with the creation of three councils—in Lyon, Toulon, and Paris. By 2018, the membership had grown to more than 200 men and fifteen councils in eight dioceses and archdioceses. This expansion came just as the country celebrated the hundredth anniversary of the end of World War I—a war in which the Knights of Columbus had played a strong role.

While Catholicism might seem on the wane in France and on the upswing in Korea, Catholics in both countries embraced the Knights as a way to grow in faith and take meaningful action through service.

Notably, in both Korea and France, the Knights had at least one previous—and famous—member. In France, it was Field Marshall Ferdinand Foch, a hero of World War I. Foch had been given honorary membership in the Order following the war, almost a century before the Order was officially established in France. In Korea, statesman John Chang Myon had become a Knight more than half a century before the Order was established in his homeland. In both cases, these national figures became the "proto-Knights" of their respective countries.

New jurisdictions were just one part of the Knights' story in the early twenty-first century in terms of encouraging Catholic men to join as a way of deepening their faith and committing to charity. In addition to fostering devotion to Our Lady of Guadalupe throughout the Americas, Anderson brought a sharp focus to the Order's work in Mexico and with Hispanics in the United States. As in the Philippines, the number of state jurisdictions in Mexico was increased, as was membership there, and outreach to Hispanic Catholics in the United States was made a priority.

In March 2011, 400 Knights and their families joined Supreme Knight Carl Anderson on a pilgrimage to the Shrine of Christ the King at Cubilete Hill, Mexico. Under Anderson, the Order would expand the number of its state jurisdictions in Mexico from one to five.

In December 2012, the Knights of Columbus and the Pontifical Commission for Latin America co-sponsored the "Ecclesia in America" conference at the Vatican. The conference drew participants from throughout North and South America, and included Mass and remarks by Pope Benedict XVI in St. Peter's Basilica.

On November 21, 2013 in Kyiv, Ukraine, Euromaidan protests erupted against the Ukrainian government's moves favoring Russia over Europe. Newly established Council 15800 in Ukraine was located adjacent to the months-long bloody protests. In addition to the council's other charitable work, it helped care for the injured and their families.

To honor John Paul II's twenty-fifth anniversary as pope in 2003, the supreme knight launched the Divine Mercy Hour of Prayer, which drew 2.2 million people to more than 28,497 prayer services. Meeting with Mr. and Mrs. Anderson, the pope blessed a reproduction of the image for use in the program. The Divine Mercy devotion—begun by Saint Faustina Kowalska in Poland—remains integral to the Order's spirituality and its work at the Saint John Paul II National Shrine, where Saint Faustina's Congregation of Sisters of Our Lady of Mercy now works.

# COLLABORATION WITH THE VATICAN

Projects taken up by the Knights in the twenty-first century focused on nurturing people spiritually and living the Catholic faith personally. At the local level, this meant an increased focus on the role of the Knights in their parishes. On a global level, the Order's focus on faith meant strong relationships with patriarchs and national bishops' conferences, with dioceses around the world, and with the Vatican.

Since the year 2000, three popes have led the Catholic Church—John Paul II, then Benedict XVI, and then Francis. The Order has worked with each of these popes by co-sponsoring Vatican conferences, supporting papal events, and organizing or assisting with projects that introduced people around the world to each of these leaders of the Catholic Church.

Known as the pope of the family, John Paul II and his writings shaped the Knights in the twenty-first century, and the Order supported and collaborated on a number of Vatican initiatives. Shortly after his election, Supreme Knight Anderson was invited to address more than 300,000 people in St. Peter's Square for the Vatican-organized World Meeting of Families in 2000. At the Knights of Columbus Museum, an exhibit highlighting the Holy Father's life entitled "John Paul II: A Passion for Peace" opened in 2003. In 2004, the Order sponsored a concert of reconciliation at the Vatican, bringing together Pope John Paul II, Muslim leaders, and Jewish leaders. The Knights also provided volunteers at key events, and sponsored numerous communications initiatives, including satellite uplinks of papal events around the world.

When Cardinal Joseph Ratzinger became Pope Benedict XVI in 2005, the Knights continued to work closely with the Vatican and drew inspiration from him. Two of his encyclicals focused largely on charity and were seen by the Knights as further affirmation of the need for action based on the Order's first principle.

New evangelization in the American hemisphere and Our Lady of Guadalupe were the focus of the 2012 Ecclesia in America (Church in America) conference. This was the first of several such gatherings the Order co-sponsored with the Vatican during the pontificates of Pope Benedict and Pope Francis that concerned the Americas.

From frescos of Madonnas to larger structural needs, a number of restoration projects undertaken at the Vatican in the new millennium through the Order's assistance have helped keep the Basilica and related architecture structurally sound, beautiful, and inspiring for the millions of pilgrims who visit each year.

After Pope Benedict's resignation in 2013, Argentine Cardinal Jorge Mario Bergoglio was elected, taking the name Francis. He was the first Jesuit and first South American pope. Through *Columbia* and a documentary on his life, the Knights helped introduce the new pope to those outside Argentina, who knew little about him.

That year, the supreme knight would be the only American layman in attendance at the Synod on the Eucharist. The Order was a visible presence during Pope Benedict's visit to the United States in 2008 and commissioned polling on American's attitudes toward him. A month after the Vatican declared Father McGivney "Venerable," Pope Benedict praised the "exemplary American priest" during his visit to New York. In 2012, the Knights co-sponsored a conference with the Vatican on the "Church in America," encouraging a continental understanding of the faith.

When Pope Benedict resigned, and Cardinal Jorge Mario Bergoglio became Pope Francis in 2013, the Knights were excited to have a pope from the "Church in America" and one whose life was so deeply committed to charity. Within weeks, the Knights began producing a documentary on his life, introducing the new, largely unknown pope to viewers internationally. The Knights also began working with the new pope almost immediately, and in 2013, co-sponsored a second conference on the "Church in America" with the Vatican, this time at the Shrine of Our Lady of Guadalupe in Mexico City. Pope Francis addressed the conference by video, and Anderson would also speak at the meeting, calling for "more profound unity and cooperation among the churches of our continent" through Our Lady of Guadalupe.

The Knights would go on to assist the Vatican with two conferences in Rome—one on the Church's post-earthquake reconstruction efforts in Haiti (2015), and one on Saint Junipero Serra (2015)—as well as a conference for the Jubilee of Mercy in Bogota, Colombia (2016). Pope Francis participated in the first two events in person, and in the last event via video. In addition, the Knights would do a great deal in support of Pope Francis' trip to the United States in 2015. Under the auspices of *Columbia* magazine, a seminar for American journalists was held prior to the pope's visit, featuring key figures from the Vatican and the Church in the United States. The Knights also sponsored elements of Saint Junipero Serra's canonization events, presided over by Pope Francis in Washington, DC, and the World Meeting of Families, which the pope addressed in Philadelphia.

In November 2004, less than six months before he died, Pope John Paul II received Supreme Knight Anderson, together with his wife Dorian and daughters Katherine and Clare, in a private audience.

Supreme Knight Anderson and Supreme Chaplain William Lori met with Pope Benedict in a private audience in 2009.

Supreme Knight Anderson presented Pope Francis with an icon related to the Order's Saint John Vianney relic pilgrimage.

At the October 2013 Marian Day for the Year of Faith, an honor guard, including Supreme Master Dennis Stoddard and three supreme directors, carried the original statue of Our Lady of Fatima in a procession prior to the papal Mass in St. Peter's Square—a first for the Order's honor guard.

In summer 2014, Islamic State (ISIS) terrorists swept through Northern Iraq, devastating the region's religious minorities including Christians, who had lived there for almost 2,000 years. In the face of killings, kidnappings, sexual enslavement, theft, torture and demands for conversion, hundreds of thousands fled to safety in Iraq's Kurdish region.

# The Saint John Paul II National Shrine

Even before Pope Francis declared him a saint in 2014, Pope John Paul II was widely respected for his holiness, as well as the impact he had on the history of the Church and the world. John Paul II's geopolitical and theological contributions were unparalleled, having a role in the fall of communism and creating a matrix for the way we understand human sexuality.

In August 2011, after the Knights purchased what had once been the John Paul II Cultural Center in Washington, DC, Supreme Knight Anderson announced that the Order would be transforming the site into a shrine-museum to celebrate the beloved saint. The twelve-acre plot, located in the heart of the city's northeast section, is situated across from two major Catholic sites—the Basilica of the National Shrine of the Immaculate Conception and The Catholic University of America.

To implement his vision of the shrine, Anderson appointed Patrick Kelly executive director and brought in a team of experts to help create what would become a world-class permanent exhibit on the life of John Paul II. The exhibit would blend biography, theology, and prayer in a multi-media spiritual experience. Biographical research experts uncovered details of his life, as did interviews with his friends and close acquaintants. Theologians molded the content in a manner consistent with his thinking and highlighted his ideas that helped shape the world. The esteemed museum-design firm of Gallagher & Associates helped bring the world of John Paul II to life.

Opened in 2014, the exhibit—A Gift of Love: The Life of Saint John Paul II—began welcoming visitors from all over the world, taking them on a journey through the life of Karol Wojtyła. Impressive displays, filled with his personal artifacts, photos, and scholarly writings, begin with his birth and young adulthood in Nazi-occupied Poland, and continue with his ministry first as a priest and then as a bishop during the Communist period. Special galleries highlight his election to the papacy and focus on the major themes and events of his twenty-six years as pope, including his final days and eventual canonization on Divine Mercy Sunday in 2014.

"A Gift of Love" is an ideal name for this exhibit since it perfectly describes the life of the pilgrim pope. Saint John Paul II lived a life filled with Christ—a life focused on sharing God's love with the world.

Along with the exhibit, the museum houses two places of worship: the Redemptor Hominis (Redeemer of Man) Church, which is named for Pope John Paul's first encyclical, and the Luminous Mysteries Chapel. Both are designed to bring visitors to God—John Paul II's first and greatest love—through prayer and the sacraments. The Luminous Mysteries Chapel also houses a precious relic, a vial of Saint John Paul's blood, displayed as part of the chapel's altar.

On March 14, 2014, the US Conference of Catholic Bishops designated the museum as a national shrine. It has since become a focal point for Catholic events throughout the year, including retreats, spiritual evenings, and World Youth reunions for young Catholics.

Defining the shrine first and foremost as a place for encountering God, several spaces provide opportunities for liturgies and the sacraments, as well as for personal prayer and veneration.

Redemptor Hominis Church provides the main liturgical space; its altar was dedicated on October 2, 2015 by John Paul's former secretary Cardinal Stanisław Dziwisz, archbishop of Kraków. Its name is taken from the title of Saint John Paul II's first encyclical on "The Redeemer of Man"—a theme taken up in the artwork, which surrounds pilgrims with images of Old Testament and New Testament events related to the redemption of man.

A second space, the Luminous Mysteries Chapel, houses a blood relic of Saint John Paul II and provides a more intimate space for Mass, prayer, and veneration. The relic housed in the chapel was entrusted to the Knights of Columbus in October 2011, and was later brought on pilgrimage throughout the United States before the chapel's completion.

The chapel's name and artwork are inspired by the Luminous Mysteries of the Rosary, which Saint John Paul II added to the traditional fifteen mysteries of the rosary in 2002. These five "new" mysteries present five events from Christ's public life, which John Paul described as a time when *"the mystery of Christ is most evidently a mystery of light:* 'While I am in the world, I am the light of the world.'" The artwork visually presents those five

**Grand and welcoming, this entrance to Redemptor Hominis Church evokes the famous words of Saint John Paul II: "Open wide the doors to Christ."**

Artist and Jesuit Father Marko Rupnik discusses the installation of the mosaics at Saint John Paul II National Shrine with Supreme Knight Anderson and wife Dorian, in September 2015.

events: the Baptism of Christ, the Wedding Feast at Cana, the Proclamation of the Kingdom, the Transfiguration, and the Institution of the Eucharist.

In both the Shrine's church and chapel, particular care was given not simply to the functionality, but to the art. This too evoked a priority for Saint John Paul, who, in his 1999 *Letter to Artists* wrote: "In order to communicate the message entrusted to her by Christ, the Church needs art. Art must make perceptible, and as far as possible attractive, the world of the spirit, of the invisible, of God."

To accomplish this vision, artist and Jesuit Father Marko Rupnik, leading the Centro Aletti studio, was chosen to create massive mosaics to adorn both spaces. Rupnik had previously been commissioned by Saint John Paul II himself to create mosaics for the Redemptoris Mater Chapel at the Vatican. Father Rupnik has also created mosaics for the façade of the church at Lourdes, for the crypt chapel in San Giovanni Rotondo (where Saint Padre Pio of Pietrelcina lived), and for the Supreme Office's Holy Family Chapel. Reflecting on liturgical art, Father Rupnik has said: "The great difference is this: an art work can rouse wonder and admiration, but the art that enters the liturgical space must stir veneration."

Through Mass, confession, and devotions to Divine Mercy, as well as special events, retreats, and lectures throughout the year, the Shrine not only presents the life and thought of Saint John Paul, but also helps people grow in their own spiritual life by helping pilgrims to "enter into our patron's deep love for God and for man."

The Shrine's Luminous Mysteries Chapel includes a blood relic of Saint John Paul II, which is permanently enshrined in the altar.

# A Gift of Love: The Museum Galleries on Saint John Paul's Life and Thought

### Beginning

**1** *Beginning* is a powerful introductory film, offered in a large circular theater that evokes St. Peter's Square.

### Light in Darkness

**2** Discover Karol Wojtyła's life from his childhood and youth to his ministry as a priest and cardinal during the Communist period.

### Election to the Papacy

**3** Learn about the conclave that elected Cardinal Karol Wojtyła and the opening message of his pontificate, "Be not afraid!"

### Man, the Way of the Church

**4** Walk in the footsteps of the pilgrim pope on his apostolic visits around the globe, including his historic 1979 return to Poland.

### *Totus Tuus*: Mary, Mother of Mercy

**5** Explore John Paul II's lifelong devotion to Mary, the inspiration behind his papal motto, *Totus Tuus*—"I am completely yours."

### The Dignity of the Human Person

**6** The pope's defense of the sacredness of human life is presented here. Also included is his involvement in World Youth Days.

### The Mysteries of Light

**7** In 2002, Pope John Paul II added five "mysteries" to the rosary highlighting key moments in Christ's public ministry.

### A Great Gift

**8** As the end of Pope John Paul II's life draws near, pilgrims reflect on two themes—the Eucharist and the priesthood.

### The Communion of Saints

**9** This is a memorable display of all the blesseds and saints raised to the altar by Pope John Paul II.

### The Life of Saint John Paul II

**10** A timeline wall of poignant, large-scale images leads visitors through significant moments in the life and papacy of Saint John Paul II.

**Gallery 1  Beginning**

**Gallery 2  Light in Darkness**

**Gallery 3** Election to the Papacy

**Gallery 4** Man, the Way of the Church

**A full-scale replica of the Holy Door
at St. Peter's Basilica in Rome.**

**Gallery 5** *Totus Tuus*: Mary, Mother of Mercy

**Gallery 6** The Dignity of the Human Person

**Gallery 7** The Mysteries of Light

**Gallery 8** A Great Gift

**Gallery 9** The Communion of Saints

**Gallery 10** The Life of Saint John Paul II

# Shaping the Conversation Through Books and Film

During the 1920s, the Knights launched an influential publishing initiative to counter the Ku Klux Klan and other anti-Catholic forces. Many of the publications were designed to fight such groups through heightened public awareness. Under Carl Anderson's leadership, the Order once again became a thought-inspiring leader through the publication of several books and the production of a number of films.

On topics ranging from spiritual reflections and cultural analyses to calls-to-action for Knights, Catholics, and society at large, the books reflect the Order's charitable and spiritual priorities. Three of the publications made their way to the *New York Times* Best Sellers list, including *Parish Priest: Father Michael McGivney and American Catholicism* (2006), co-authored by Douglas Brinkley and Julie Fenster. Supreme Knight Anderson's books were the other two. He wrote *A Civilization of Love: What Every Catholic Can Do to Transform the World* (2008), and he co-authored *Our Lady of Guadalupe: Mother of the Civilization of Love* (2009) with Monsignor Eduardo Chavez.

Along with these titles, Anderson also wrote *Beyond a House Divided: The Moral Consensus Ignored by Washington, Wall Street, and the Media* (2010), and *Proclaim Liberty: Notes on the Next Great Awakening in America* (2012). He also teamed with Father Jose Granados for the publication of *Called to Love: Approaching John Paul II's Theology of the Body* (2009). In each case, Anderson donated his royalties from these publications to Knights of Columbus Charities.

The Knights were also involved with the republication of other important books, including the W.E.B. Du Bois classic *The Gift of Black Folk* and Jean Meyer's *La Cristiada: The Mexican People's War for Religious Liberty*. From the Vatican, the Order also secured the English-language rights for all of the works written by Saint John Paul II.

In addition to books, the Knights were involved in the production of several documentaries, many of which won awards, including Emmys. Some were specific to the Order, while others were publicly released full-length films. Among these works, *Unbreakable: A Story of Hope and Healing in Haiti* (2014) tells of the Knights' work after the 2010 earthquake; *Guadalupe: The Miracle and the Message* (2015) traces the story of Our Lady's apparition to Mexican peasant Juan Diego; and *The Face of Mercy* (2016) highlights the inspiring personal stories of individuals who have experienced mercy and forgiveness in their own lives. *Francis: The Pope from the New World* (2013) presents the life of the Holy Father; while *John Paul II in America: Uniting a Continent* (2014) and *Liberating a Continent: John Paul II and the Fall of Communism* (2016) outline Pope John Paul II's key contributions in the history of America and Europe.

All of these works helped bring key themes of both the Church and the Knights to new audiences, while telling—and preserving—timeless stories of notable figures and moments in history.

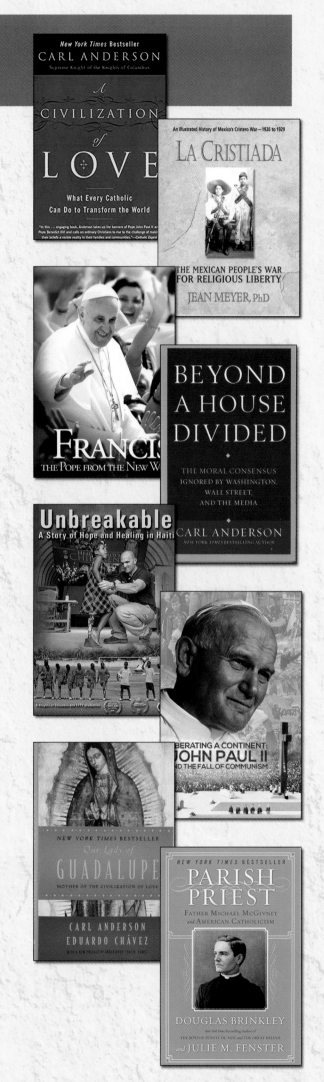

## SERVING PILGRIMS AT WORLD YOUTH DAYS

Knowing the importance of forming future generations of Catholics, the Knights have been strong supporters of World Youth Day (WYD)—an initiative of Pope John Paul II that has been continued by his successors. During these joyful events, young pilgrims come together to learn about and celebrate their faith. The personal presence of the pope is always the highlight of World Youth Day, whose events conclude with the Holy Father's celebration of Mass.

The Knights of Columbus supported and participated in previous World Youth Days, both financially and through voluntary services. For example, at the 1993 WYD in Denver, Colorado, the Order distributed prayer cards, rosaries, and other religious items. In Manila in 1995, it funded the satellite telecasts of the papal Mass.

In the twenty-first century, the Order became even more actively involved. At the 2002 celebration in Toronto, Canada, the Order provided a $1 million grant to fund a reconciliation site in the city's Coronation Park. A delegation of Knights also assisted in carrying the iconic World Youth Cross through hundreds of cities on its pilgrimage to the celebration.

In 2008, the Order's involvement focused on creating programming and events for pilgrims. Working closely with the Sisters of Life, the Knights helped contribute to the experience of those in attendance by sponsoring sites that were places of prayer, sacramental life, religious education, and social centers for the young people. During 2008's World Youth Day in Australia, the Order sponsored the Love and Life Site, located on the campus of Notre Dame University in downtown Sydney.

At the 2011 World Youth Day in Madrid, Spain, the Knights stepped up its involvement even further. Again working with the Sisters of Life and with help from Holy Cross Family Ministries and other Catholic organizations, the Order took charge of the official English-language center there. Located in a 15,000-seat sports arena, the center offered daily catechesis and devotions, Mass, educational programming, panel discussions, and inspiring speakers. Internationally acclaimed musicians also performed in the center, and its confession hall and two Eucharistic adoration chapels saw continuous pilgrim use. During the celebration, the center drew more than 100,000 people.

The 2016 celebration in Kraków, Poland, was especially significant. Kraków was the home of the recently canonized John Paul II, the founder of World Youth Day, and Poland was a Knights of Columbus jurisdiction. Also significant was that this WYD occurred during the "Year of Mercy," proclaimed by Pope Francis.

*Pilgrims show their love of country and of the Order at World Youth Day in Sydney, Australia. The Order's WYD efforts would take on even more significance in Madrid and Kraków, with major centers serving both pilgrims from English-speaking nations and those from Europe, Asia, and Africa who were more at home with English than with the host-country's language.*

In 2013, the Knights of Columbus, the Pontifical Commission for Latin America, and the Guadalupe Basilica and Institute of Higher Studies co-sponsored a conference on Our Lady of Guadalupe: Star of the New Evangelization. Supreme Knight Anderson was among the speakers and Pope Francis addressed the gathering in video remarks.

Environmental stewardship was underscored in Pope Francis' encyclical *Laudato Si'* in 2015 and in Knights' projects during the decade, from Council 10775 planting mangroves to safeguard a Philippine coral ecosystem, to the Supreme Council partnering with Charity: Water to provide clean water to tens of thousands in Sub-Saharan Africa.

Devotion to Divine Mercy had begun in Kraków in the early twentieth century, and had been embraced and advanced by John Paul II when he was pope.

As in Madrid, the Knights ran an official English-language site at WYD Kraków. Among its co-sponsors were the Sisters of Life; the Sisters of Our Lady of Mercy; and the Saint John Paul II National Shrine in Washington, DC. The site was located at the Tauron Arena, one of the most modern sports facilities in Europe, with seating for more than 20,000. An estimated 100,000 young people attended the Order's WYD programs that year, and Pope Francis himself visited the arena for one of World Youth Day's events.

Knights helped in important ways at other World Youth Days, as well. Following the celebration in Kraków, the Order began holding reunions for WYD participants at the Saint John Paul II National Shrine in Washington, DC. In this way, the Knights continue the World Youth Day vision of community and growth in faith that was imagined by Pope John Paul II and continued by Popes Benedict XVI and Francis.

Pope Francis met with World Youth Day volunteers at Tauron Arena in Kraków in 2016. The site served as the WYD Mercy Centre run by the Knights of Columbus and the Sisters of Life.

For 2019 World Youth Day in Panama City, the Knights co-sponsored a "Fiat Festival" along with the Fellowship of Catholic University Students and the US Conference of Catholic Bishops. Supreme Council staff and three Panamanian councils helped organizers before and during the one-day program of liturgies, talks, and music.

On April 27, 2014, Pope Francis celebrated the canonization Mass for Popes John Paul II and John XXIII. Supreme Knight Anderson was among the millions in attendance. Polish pilgrims at the event camped at the Order's sports facilities in Rome. The ceremony was broadcast live at the John Paul II National Shrine in Washington, DC.

# SPIRITUAL INITIATIVES

The Knights' twenty-first century involvement in World Youth Days grew out of the Order's history of providing spiritual and moral enrichment. True to its Catholic identity, the Order was involved in a number of spiritual events during the early years of the new millennium—not only in partnership with the Vatican, but also at local and regional levels.

In 2009, the Knights co-sponsored the First International Marian Congress dedicated to Our Lady of Guadalupe. The three-day congress, held in Phoenix, Arizona, brought together an international group of experts on the 1531 apparition of the Blessed Mother to Juan Diego, a native of Mexico living in Mexico City. This apparition was the catalyst for the conversion of 6 million Native Americans in Mexico to Catholicism. The congress concluded with a jubilant festival. Nearly 20,000 attendees filled Jobing.com Arena (now Gila River Arena)—Glendale's sports and entertainment center—to celebrate with prayer, music, and inspirational speakers. Highlighting the festival was a procession with a precious relic: a small piece of the tilma (cloak) of Juan Diego on which the image of the Blessed Mother had miraculously appeared.

The success of the program in Arizona inspired a second and much larger Guadalupe Festival, held three years later at the Los Angeles Memorial Coliseum. The bilingual event, co-sponsored by the Knights with the Archdiocese of Los Angeles and the Instituto Superior de Estudios Guadalupanos, attracted an estimated 75,000 people, making it one of the largest Catholic events in Los Angeles history.

In addition to sponsoring spiritually enriching events, the Knights launched initiatives geared toward the faith formation of Catholics. One of these projects included the creation of a Catholic Information Service (CIS) series on the new evangelization—a term adopted by Pope John Paul II to describe the preaching of the Gospel in new ways to those familiar with Christianity, but heavily influenced by secularization. The series covered topics such as "Technology and the New Evangelization: Criteria for Discernment" and "In the Image of Love: Marriage, Family and the New Evangelization."

The Order also extended that support to focus specifically on fatherhood. The Fathers for Good website (fathersforgood.org) was designed to promote the positive (and permanent) role that fathers should play in their children's

The 2009 Guadalupe Festival in Phoenix, Arizona, drew more than 20,000 for an afternoon of music, addresses, veneration of the tilma relic, and an international rosary prayed in fifty languages.

Among its Guadalupe-themed efforts, the Order sponsored a nationwide tour of a relic of Saint Juan Diego's tilma in 2003. Pilgrims to the Cathedral of Our Lady of Angels in Los Angeles can now pray before the relic in a chapel the Knights helped fund a decade later.

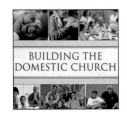

Nurturing Knights as family men and parishioners, the Order launched the "Building the Domestic Church Initiative" in 2014. The program encouraged councils to help revitalize parishes through Faith in Action programs including spiritual, charitable, and communal activities, and through family revitalization using resources like the "Family Fully Alive" program.

lives. It offers articles and information designed to help Catholic fathers grow in their role of forming the minds and hearts of their children and making their families places of faith and stability.

Building on the success of family-oriented projects like the Fathers for Good website and other faith-inspired programs, Supreme Knight Anderson launched the Building the Domestic Church initiative in 2014. This program focused on revitalizing the faith of both the family and the parish. The first aspect of this program, "Building the Domestic Church: The Family Fully Alive," was designed to help families grow in faith through prayers and activities shared together on a regular basis. The second aspect, "Building the Domestic Church While Strengthening Our Parish," presented practical ways in which councils can help invigorate parish life. The Order further supplemented the Domestic Church program with a new CIS series. Titles included "Becoming a Real Man of God"; "The Family in the Modern World"; and "The Good Life, God's Way."

The founding mission of helping Catholic men and their families stay strong spiritually, despite cultural pressures to the contrary, certainly has been and continues to remain relevant. The spiritual programs undertaken by the Order in the new millennium helped further that vision, providing opportunities for members and their families to give back to the community, while growing in their own faith and providing a solid basis for the "action" for which the Knights were so well known.

Archbishop William Lori of Baltimore processes with the relic of the tilma of Saint Juan Diego during the Guadalupe Celebration at the Los Angeles Memorial Coliseum on August 5, 2012. The event drew an estimated 75,000 people.

# FAITH IN ACTION

With charity—based on love of God and love of neighbor—as its first principle, the Knights of Columbus has responded to the spiritual and practical needs of others for more than a century. This response has ranged from local council-level programs to international partnerships with various charitable organizations. One of Carl Anderson's priorities as supreme knight was encouraging the members' "hands-on" involvement. While monetary support is obviously important, true charitable efforts needed to go beyond check writing. During his tenure, the supreme knight introduced "Faith in Action" as an umbrella term that fittingly captured the inseparable religious and practical nature of the Knights' work.

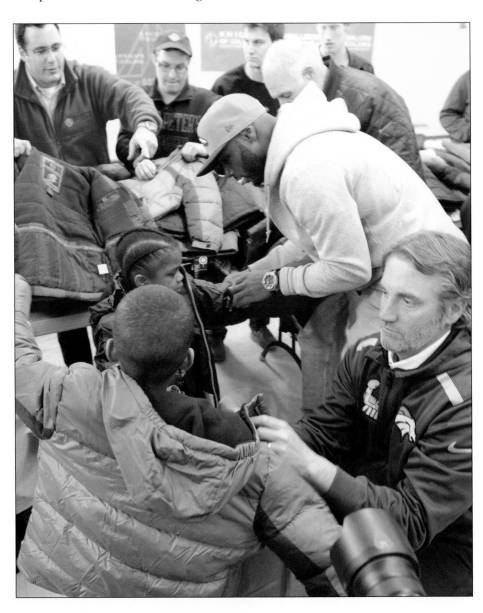

Before the 2014 Super Bowl, team and staff members of the Denver Broncos joined the Knights at a K of C "Coats for Kids" distribution, held at a Catholic school in New Jersey. Bronco players included defensive end Robert Ayers, who returned to his alma mater to participate. Since 2009, councils have provided more than 500,000 new coats to kids in need.

During Pope Francis' 2015 visit to the United States, the Order organized a media briefing and directly supported papal events, including the World Meeting of Families and the canonization of Saint Junipero Serra. The supreme knight and board attended many of the papal events while local Knights provided honor guards and volunteers.

Among their prolific initiatives, councils assist families facing hardship. Members gather resources for family support centers, shelters, and individual families. Easing the average $1,000 annual cost of diapers for a newborn, Knights of Michigan's Ithaca Council 8785 are seen here during its 2018 two-week diaper drive.

# African Orphans and the Apostles of Jesus

One of the benefits of the Knights' record of service is that it inspires others to bring worthy causes to the Order's attention. When former Pennsylvania State Chaplain Father Paul Gaggawala of the Apostles of Jesus returned to Africa, he discovered a problem he thought the Knights would be well suited to help solve. According to the US Agency for International Development, 17 million children have lost one or both parents to AIDS—with 9 of 10 living in Sub-Saharan Africa. Father Gaggawala brought this situation to the Order's attention.

At the Supreme Convention in 2011, plans were announced for the construction of a school in Uganda to serve AIDS orphans, many of whom were HIV-positive themselves. The initiative helped orphans in both Uganda and Kenya and was operated in partnership with the Apostles of Jesus, the first religious missionary order of priests and brothers from Africa.

The Knights' involvement in building that school and supporting other efforts of the Apostles of Jesus helped enrich the lives of those children, who were entirely dependent on the generosity of others. The caring environment offered by the Apostles was a perfect match for the Knights, whose support for widows and orphans had been one of its founding purposes.

The need for hands-on assistance reached a new urgency with the financial crisis of 2008. The subprime mortgage crisis triggered a meltdown that devastated the lives and livelihoods of millions of families. People saw their life savings evaporate; many suddenly found themselves out of work. Home foreclosures reached record levels, and even basics like food and clothing were increasingly out of reach for many families. Even worse, ethical lapses and greed at many levels of the financial sector had helped catalyze the crisis.

Assessing the situation, Anderson focused on a course of action that would be feasible and effective even during times of joblessness and reduced cash flow. The solution was volunteerism—something the Knights knew a great deal about. A summit to formulate possible strategies was held in New York in February 2009. The summit, called Neighbors Helping Neighbors, brought together government and charitable groups, including leaders of more than one hundred organizations.

The summit served as a catalyst for a number of new initiatives to address the immediate and concrete needs of families. One of these programs—K of C Coats for Kids—was created to provide warm weather cloth-

Learning that 60 percent of children live to only age five in the village of Kitakyusa, Uganda, Council 11475 in Virginia took action. With donations of medical equipment and less than $100,000, it established a medical clinic, housing for nurses, and a well to provide clean water for the people there.

In 2015, the Supreme Council and New York State Council gave a combined $600,000 to help the Shrine of the North American Martyrs and birthplace of Saint Kateri Tekakwitha to remain open. Several councils bear Saint Tekakwitha's name, who was the second Native American declared a saint, after Saint Juan Diego.

ing for children in need. Local councils purchase new coats in bulk at a discount. As the weather gets colder, especially on Black Friday, the day after Thanksgiving, councils around the country distribute the coats at parishes, schools, and community centers. Coat distribution on Black Friday has particular symbolism, as the Knights' donation stands in contrast to the secular start of the Christmas season, usually a key shopping day. In addition to distributing the coats themselves, some councils partner with local police and fire departments, placing coats in the vehicles of first responders for distribution as needed. Since the ongoing program's inception in 2009, the Knights have donated more than 400,000 new winter coats.

For decades, individual councils have provided immeasurable support to community food efforts like soup kitchens and food banks. Beginning in 2009, such efforts became an Order-wide cause. Councils were encouraged to step up their involvement in combating hunger in their communities. To spur their efforts, the Supreme Council began offering refunds for their contributions. For every 1,000 pounds of food or $500 donated to a local food-related charity, the council or assembly would receive $100 (up to $500) per year.

Councils personalized their programs to fit local needs and council strengths. They proved both diligent and creative in their efforts, which ranged from planting gardens that produced tons of fresh produce to sponsoring food collection drives. Often the liturgical calendar inspired these efforts, resulting in campaigns like the "40 Cans for Lent" food drive. Since its inception, Food for Families has grown significantly, with the Order collecting more than 21.5 million pounds of food and $10.7 million in donations since 2012.

Along with sponsoring its own programs, the Knights have also partnered with or supported the efforts of many other groups on worthy causes. Habitat for Humanity, which provides low-cost housing to families in need, is one. Members have donated hundreds of thousands of dollars and more than a million hours of service annually to this cause. The Order and its members have also continued their longstanding work with the Special Olympics both domestic and internationally.

Working under the hot sun, Knights of Council 2171 in Tillamook, Oregon, harvest cabbages from its 4,000-square-foot charitable vegetable garden. The garden provides as much as 15,000 pounds of fresh produce annually for the parish food bank—a difficult food to find in food pantries.

From the beginning, the Knights of Columbus has supported Special Olympics at every level—throughout the United States and around the world. In 2015, the Order provided a $1.4 million grant to sponsor the Special Olympics World Games in Los Angeles.

Reminiscent of its support for Native Americans dating back to the early 1900s, the Order renewed its focus on the challenges of US reservations in 2018. It created programs to assist tribes with key needs and urged Americans to learn about the specific Native American history of each state.

# Global Wheelchair Mission

The Healing Haiti's Children initiative was not the only project the Knights undertook to assist the physically disabled with mobility. In 2003, with the purchase of 2,000 wheelchairs that were sent to war-torn Afghanistan, the Knights began what would become a long and fruitful connection with the Global Wheelchair Mission. Headed by Chris Lewis, this nonprofit organization purchases wheelchairs in bulk (at a greatly reduced price) and delivers them around the world where needed.

Councils raise money, and then often assist with the actual distribution of the wheelchairs, sometimes to recipients nearby and sometimes to those halfway around the world. To date, more than 60,000 wheelchairs have been distributed through the Knights sponsorship, transforming lives throughout the United States and Canada, as well as in Mexico, the Philippines, Haiti, Chile, Israel, Vietnam, and Kenya.

In addition to the obvious benefits of the gift of mobility, this program helps build the confidence and dignity of those living with a physical challenge. It also shows how even a relatively small donation can help transform a person's life.

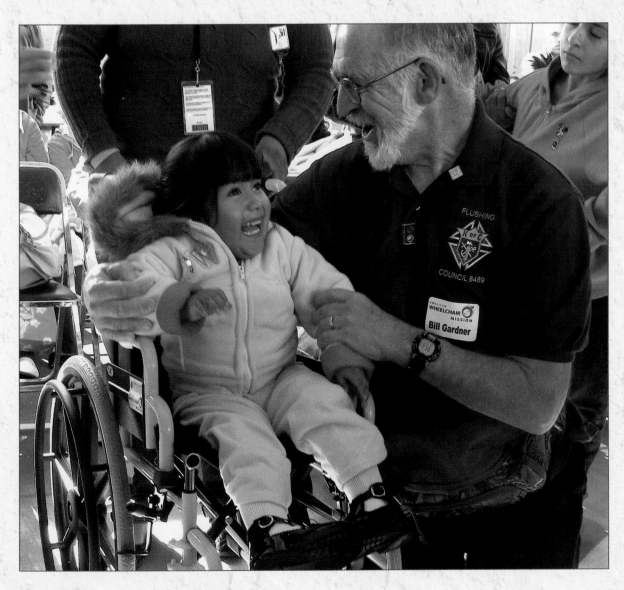

As white supremacists and groups like ANTIFA grew increasingly violent, the Knights spoke out, calling for racial harmony and nonviolent solutions. Anderson co-authored a piece for *Time* magazine, and the Order sponsored a clergy letter and news conference at the MLK memorial urging an end to the hatred and violence.

At the 2019 Supreme Convention, eighteen-year-old Kendrick Castillo, who had been killed protecting classmates during a school shooting, was honored with a posthumous membership and the Caritas Award. Kendrick was planning to join the Knights after graduation. He and his father John (a Knight) had already volunteered a combined 2,600 hours.

## CELEBRATING A CENTURY OF COLLEGE COUNCILS

The year 2010 marked another landmark celebration for the Order—the 100-year anniversary of the first college council. A century earlier, when a group of students first proposed the idea of forming its own council on the University of Notre Dame campus, the idea was met with skepticism. Many members believed that a council of primarily young, inexperienced college students would never survive. But Notre Dame Council 1477 not only survived but became a model that was replicated successfully on college campuses throughout the United States and beyond.

As an important service to Catholic college men, these councils are considered "spiritual homes" by their young members, who place great value on the fraternal relationships they form with their fellow Knights. They also find great comfort and satisfaction in their common spiritual beliefs and similarities of purpose.

Prior to volunteering at the Knights' Mercy Centre at the 2016 World Youth Day in Kraków, these college Knights enjoyed faith and camaraderie on a pilgrimage in Poland.

Not surprisingly, the primary mission of most college councils is service. Members run social gatherings on campus, sponsor fundraisers, volunteer at homeless shelters and soup kitchens, visit the sick, pitch in during disasters, work with troubled youth, and participate in the local Habitat for Humanity projects. Many attend World Youth Days and are active in pro-life activities, including the annual March for Life in Washington, DC.

Every year, council leaders have the opportunity to meet other college Knights at the College Council Conference in New Haven, Connecticut. The young members attend workshops and meetings to develop leadership skills, partake in liturgies, recognize council achievements, and connect with fellow Knights.

What began as a questionable effort among a small group of determined young college men blossomed into an integral part of the Order. A century after the first council was formed, the number of college councils reached 244 with nearly 19,000 members among the college Knights. When these young Knights graduate and join local councils, they bring with them the valuable experiences they had in the college program. They offer a unique combination of youth, experience, and ideas.

While parish councils form the backbone of the Order, college councils represent the next generation of leadership. In 2010, the Order celebrated the hundredth anniversary of the first college council (Council 1477 at Notre Dame University). In 2015, it celebrated fifty years of the college council conference.

Taking to heart the Order's mission of caring for families of deceased members, members of Cargill Council 64 in Putnam, Connecticut, visit the widows of deceased council members at Christmas time. Begun in 1995, the council's program for its widows also includes a fund for helping those in need.

# SERVING THOSE WHO SERVE

With veterans of the Civil War becoming some of the founding members of the Order, it's easy to understand why the Knights' commitment to those who served has always been strong. The influence of veterans on the Order is reflected in part in the Knights' band-of-brothers fraternalism, as well as its willingness to take decisive action in the defense and promotion of Catholic values, including charity. The Knights provided great support to American troops during World War I and World War II. More recently, the Order's principle of patriotism has led its members, especially those of the Fourth Degree, to focus on supporting those who have dedicated their lives in service to their country.

With troops deploying to Afghanistan and Iraq in the early part of the new century, the Knights helped support them spiritually by "arming them with faith." Working with the Archdiocese for Military Services, USA, the Order created and printed prayer books titled *Armed with Faith*. Within a decade, more than 600,000 copies, which were sturdy enough to survive the rough and rugged combat environment of the Middle East, had been distributed to American and Canadian troops.

In 2011, when Supreme Knight Anderson paid a visit to Knights stationed on the USS *Dwight Eisenhower* aircraft carrier, he got a first-hand look at the spiritual desert of military deployment. He also learned how dire the military chaplain situation had become. While roughly 800 priests were needed

To help Catholic institutions—dioceses, hospitals, universities, religious groups, etc.—maintain high ethical investment standards, while availing themselves of the Knights' expertise in asset management, the Order began offering a new kind of financial service: the K of C Asset Advisors. Launched in 2015, this team is designed to help such institutions manage their finances, ensuring that their money is invested according to Christian morals and principles as reflected in Catholic doctrine. This means that, among other things, the advisors avoid industries or companies that provide, promote, or fund such activities as abortion, human cloning, and pornography.

Army Major Michael Ricky (center) holds a copy of *Armed with Faith* while standing with a group of soldiers in Baghdad.

Commemorating World War I's 100th anniversary, the Knights of Columbus in France cosponsored with the Archdiocese of Paris a light show projected onto Notre Dame Cathedral. Entitled "the Lady of Hearts," the show told the story of how the cathedral—and the faith—persisted despite history's many horrors.

In 2016, the Order led efforts to have ISIS' crimes against Christians and other minorities in Syria and Iraq declared "genocide" by Secretary of State John Kerry. Compiling a nearly 300-page report on ISIS' atrocities, the Order also raised awareness with a media campaign. Both Kerry and a unanimous Congress declared ISIS' actions genocide.

Since 2010, Knights in New Jersey have held a "Knights of Columbus Annual Tank Pull" to raise money for veterans. The event has been an enormous success, bringing together Knights and the community to help raise more than $1.5 million in just ten years to serve those who served.

to adequately answer the needs of troops who were stationed throughout the world, only 280 were available. At times, soldiers went weeks without Mass or confession.

One of the main reasons for the chaplain shortage was the cost involved. Chaplains in training depended almost exclusively on donations to cover the expense of their education. Once aware of the problem, the Knights became actively involved. Working again with the Archdiocese of the Military Services, the Order became a major sponsor for military chaplains through the creation of the Father McGivney Military Chaplain Scholarship in 2011. The Fourth Degree Knights stepped up, raising the promised $1 million in scholarships for educating future chaplains.

The Order took up another spiritual initiative with the Archdiocese of the Military Services in 2013, sponsoring its annual pilgrimage to the Marian shrine of Lourdes in France. Bringing active and veteran soldiers, including those with various injuries, often accompanied by their families or caregivers, this pilgrimage is timed to coincide with the annual International Military Pilgrimage, which began in 1946 following World War II. K of C sponsorship has enabled American troops to be part of a larger international gathering, as well as participate in events specific to their group.

Again, the program had deep historical antecedents. During World War I, the Knights' secretaries (the Caseys) ran a hospitality center—a "hut"—in Lourdes and assisted in bringing soldiers to the shrine. In the years that followed, especially after World War II, visits to Lourdes by soldiers and

In 2016, real estate mogul and television personality Donald Trump defied the odds and the predictions of most analysts and was elected the forty-seventh president of the United States. A political outsider, Trump was part of a wave of populist leaders elected around the world.

During the centennial celebration of the end of WWI, in recognition of the Order's century of support for the US Armed Forces, Supreme Knight Anderson received the St. Martin of Tours Medal on behalf of the Knights of Columbus. The medal was presented by US Army Chief of Chaplains, Major General Paul Hurley.

veterans remained a long-standing tradition. Each year since 1946, military personnel from countries around the world have attended the international pilgrimage to spend a few days in prayer and spiritual devotion.

At home, the Order has always supported veterans, with the Fourth Degree leading the way. Knights have provided wheelchairs to VA hospitals and sponsored training clinics for amputee soldiers. Members actively volunteer their services to VA hospitals from coast to coast. Because of its dedication, the Knights of Columbus has become the "single largest volunteer service partner of the Veterans Administration."

Building on this commitment, at the 2014 Supreme Convention, Supreme Knight Anderson announced a new partnership with the Gary Sinise Foundation, whose mission is to support the needs of returning servicemen and women, veterans, first responders, and those in need. Through this partnership, the Knights would help in the building of computer-assisted "smart homes" for wounded veterans whose needs require advanced technological solutions. Each home would be tailored to meet these individual needs. Actor Gary Sinise made an appearance at the convention. Addressing members at the States Dinner, he spoke of his faith and his dedication to veterans. Working with his foundation, the Order has helped build several of these "smart homes."

As has long been the case, whether on active duty or retired, current and former troops have found a reliable "band of brothers" in the Knights of Columbus.

The Knights' co-sponsorship since 2013 has made it possible for American military—many still bearing the effects of war-time injury—to attend the annual International Military Pilgrimage at Lourdes, which includes Masses, a candlelight procession, and the opportunity to visit the miraculous spring. Below, an English-language Mass is celebrated at the Grotto for active and veteran military and their families from the United States, England, and Ireland.

## SUPPORTING CHRISTIANS IN THE MIDDLE EAST

In 2014, a man-made disaster struck halfway around the world. ISIS, the Islamic State of Iraq and Syria, began conquering vast areas in Iraq and Syria with the goal of establishing a caliphate. That summer, ISIS took control of the city of Mosul and the surrounding Nineveh region of Iraq—areas that had been home to a sizeable Christian population since the days of the apostles. Christians living there faced three options: convert, flee, or die. Unthinkable atrocities ensued as ISIS and its sympathizers targeted Christians, Yazidis (a religious group in northern Iraq), Shi'a Muslims, and other religious groups in the area. The small numbers of the Christians and Yazidis placed them at particular risk. Murder, kidnapping, torture, rape, and theft by ISIS were common. Along with the destruction of homes, ISIS desecrated churches and other places of worship, and demolished historical and cultural monuments—all with the intention of eradicating any trace of these people.

As ISIS took control of territory, it targeted Christians and other religious minorities as well as their places of worship. Mar Addai Church in Karamles, Iraq, was desecrated by ISIS during the terrorist group's occupation of the town. It was later rebuilt by the Knights.

Many of the areas' predominately middle-class Christians fled across the desert, seeking safety in Kurdistan, the region adjacent to Nineveh in northern Iraq. Church communities in this region were suddenly entrusted with more than 100,000 refugees who had nothing left but the clothing they wore and their faith.

The shocking images stirred the Order's memory of its actions on behalf of persecuted Catholics in Mexico in the 1920s, and the Knights swiftly set humanitarian relief and advocacy efforts in motion. The K of C's Christian Refugee Relief Fund was launched and began to assist the affected communities through the support of medical clinics, food programs, housing, education, and catechesis. The fund also helped resettle the refugees and, once ISIS was defeated, assisted with their return to and reconstruction of liberated areas. Within five years, more than $25 million would be committed by the Order, much of it raised from its members and the public.

The Knights also worked hard to raise both public and government awareness of this issue at home, asking the US government to take specific steps to address the needs of persecuted minority groups, including Christians. The supreme knight provided congressional testimony several times and, among other efforts, called for assistance that did not overlook Christians and other persecuted religious communities.

In late 2015, to highlight the scale of atrocities, the Knights urged the US government to declare that ISIS was committing genocide. There had been

Mother Teresa—with whom the Order had worked closely—was declared "Blessed" by Pope John Paul II in 2003. She was then declared a saint by Pope Francis in 2016. The official portrait used at her canonization was commissioned by the Knights and painted by artist Chas Fagan.

In 2017, the Knights of Columbus announced that it would rebuild Karamles—a Christian town on the Nineveh Plain devastated by ISIS. Working with the Catholic Church in Iraq, the Knights invested $2 million rebuilding houses, helping hundreds of families move back to their homes, and preserving the town's long-standing Christian identity.

substantial documentation of ISIS' crimes against certain groups, but not against Christians. A senior State Department official told the Knights that the claim that Christians were facing genocide needed to be proven, and suggested that the Knights make the case. Taking up the challenge, the Order spearheaded an in-depth investigation into ISIS crimes against Christians in Iraq. The Knights sent a member of its staff to Iraq to collect evidence with the help of Church leaders. Once collected, the material was sent back home, where it was compiled and edited. Iraqi Knights in California helped with the evidence and with securing the translation of documents in Arabic and Aramaic.

Working with a number of groups, including In Defense of Christians, the investigation broke substantial ground in proving ISIS crimes. The result was a nearly 300-page report that included, among other atrocities, itemized lists of individuals who had been murdered and churches that had been destroyed. It also had an ISIS price list for slave women, including teens and young girls.

The report made a clear case that ISIS atrocities were more than mere acts of violence—they were acts of genocide, committed with the intention of eradicating the region's Christians.

The Knights also launched a far-reaching media campaign—including commercials, op-eds, and articles—urging the United States government to recognize that the deliberate targeting of Christians and other religious groups by ISIS was genocide. A petition drive was initiated as well, and more than 140,000 signatures were collected.

More than 100,000 Christians fled to the Kurdish region of Iraq in 2014, as ISIS invaded Mosul and Nineveh.

The crucial pieces of evidence in the Knights' report influenced the unanimous determination by Congress and the subsequent finding by Secretary of State John Kerry that ISIS had indeed committed genocide. It was only the second time an ongoing situation had been declared genocide by the US government. The declaration was certainly a good first step, but as time went on, it became increasingly clear that the victims of ISIS persecution were often being left out of official government aid channels. What aid did reach them generally came from independent groups, not from the US government. The Knights urged the Obama Administration to follow up its genocide declaration with action. But with that administration winding down, no such action was taken.

The Knights continued urging action on behalf of these shattered communities with the Trump Administration. In October 2017, Vice President Mike Pence announced that the US government would begin to fund these communities directly. American assistance ramped up, through both the United Nations and non-government organizations.

A new Fourth Degree uniform—blue blazer, grey pants, and military guard beret—was unveiled at the 2017 Supreme Convention. Such updates have occurred several times since the Patriotic Degree was established in 1900. In previous eras, members have worn top hats, chapeaux, capes, tuxedos, and military style coats.

When hurricanes devastated Puerto Rico and Texas in 2017, the Knights provided $1.4 million in relief. The supreme knight visited both regions. In Puerto Rico, where recovery was most difficult, K of C insurance agents (shown) led aid distribution, which included up to 200 cooked meals each Sunday for three months.

# Providing Needed Help for the Displaced

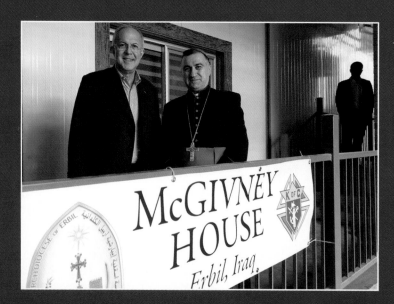

To accommodate Christian families displaced by ISIS, the Knights funded the Archdiocese of Erbil's "McGivney House" in Iraq's Kurdish region. The facility provides a permanent home for those unable to return to their cities or towns of origin. Supreme Knight Anderson, pictured here with Archbishop Bashar Warda, visited the housing on his trip to Iraq.

A warehouse of food purchased with funds from the K of C were distributed to thousands of families displaced by ISIS.

Food packages, sponsored by the K of C, being delivered to displaced families.

Step-In's mobile clinic arrives to provide care for the displaced. The Knights of Columbus is a major sponsor of the Step-In clinics, which serve displaced families in Kurdistan.

# Setting the Political Course for Aiding Christians in the Middle East

Coptic Orthodox Archbishop Anba Angaelos makes the case to the media that ISIS' crimes constituted genocide.

Supreme Knight Carl Anderson addresses the Congressional Subcommittee on Africa, Global Health, Global Human Rights, and International Organizations on May 26, 2016. His testimony served as a basis for H.R. 390: The Iraq and Syria Genocide Relief and Accountability Act.

H.R. 390 received bipartisan support and was passed unanimously by both the House and the Senate. Here, President Trump signs it into law by December of 2018. The act provides for direct funding by the US government of groups targeted for genocide by ISIS.

Syriac Catholic Patriarch Ignatius Joseph III Younan—a long time Knight—addressed the 2016 Supreme Convention in Toronto, bringing further attention to the plight of Christians in the Middle East.

Melkite Greek Catholic Archbishop Jean Clement Jeanbart of Aleppo, Syria, blessed the icon of Our Lady Help of Persecuted Christians at the 2018 Supreme Convention in Baltimore. Archbishop Jeanbart had been made a Knight by acclamation at the 2016 Supreme Convention in Toronto.

As part of the government's effort, the US Agency for International Development also signed a Memorandum of Understanding with the Knights that provided for the sharing of information and the co-creation of programs to help communities affected and targeted by ISIS genocide. Based on testimony given by the supreme knight, and on a Congressional Delegation to Iraq that the Knights helped organize, Congressman Chris Smith introduced the Iraq and Syria Genocide Relief and Accountability Act. It passed both Houses of Congress unanimously and was signed into law by President Trump in an Oval Office ceremony attended by Congressman Smith and the supreme knight.

Even as the US government stepped up to the plate, the Knights continued its support. In August 2017, it committed $2 million toward rebuilding the predominantly Christian town of Karamles, which had been liberated from ISIS. By the end of 2019, the Knights' commitment on behalf of those persecuted by ISIS was nearly $25 million.

Some of the Order's impact had an effect far beyond financial needs. In October of 2012, the Order worked closely with the Catholic Church in Iraq, the US State Department, and the National Security Council to help deescalate the armed conflict that had broken out between the Kurdish Regional Government and the Government of Iraq following a referendum on Kurdish independence in the fall of 2017. With the fate of Christianity in Iraq hanging in the balance, it was timely action by the Knights that proved decisive in not only saving a Christian town from bombardment, but also helping to stop the armed conflict that threatened to tear Iraq apart again.

In early 2019, Supreme Knight Anderson visited Iraq to review Knights of Columbus' relief work there and to meet with those who had suffered so much. During his trip, Anderson announced several projects that the Knights would be funding and met with Church leaders and government officials on the problems still confronting Christians and other targeted communities there.

Archbishop Bashar Warda of Erbil, Iraq, one of the main leaders and de facto relief organizers of one of the largest groups of persecuted Christians, expressed his gratitude to the Knights for its work as philanthropist and peacemaker. In his words:

> After the Daesh (ISIS) invasion, more than 125,000 Christians and others fled Mosul and the Nineveh Plain [to Iraqi Kurdistan]—crying with no one to help, except for the Church. Neither the UN nor the Iraqi government was taking care of these displaced people. Then, the Knights came and worked closely with us to help ease the suffering of those displaced families—and not just

In 2018 and 2019, the Order sponsored and organized a US tour of a relic: the heart of Saint Jean Marie Vianney—the patron saint of parish priests. Against the backdrop of sexual abuse scandals, the tour prayerfully inspired clergy and laity with an example of true priestly holiness.

The Order grew substantially during the millennium's first two decades with membership reaching nearly 2 million in 2018. Volunteer hours rose to 1.3 billion hours, while charitable donations hit $2.9 billion. Insurance in force reached more than $109 billion.

Christians but Yazidis, everyone—by providing them with food, medicine, shelter.

The Knights said, *'We are with you. We will stand with you. We'll support you. We will be in this together.'* 'That gave great hope to the Christian community. And that's why today we have so many families returning to their liberated villages.

Archbishop Warda also noted: "The work of the Knights helping the displaced Christians from Mosul and the Nineveh Plain is a historic work. Without this support, Christianity would disappear in our region." The Order's humanitarian outreach in the region is an ongoing effort.

# Rebuilding the Cradle of Christianity
## Visionary Council Initiative

The Supreme Convention of August 2017 was the first time most Knights heard the name "Karamles." The ancient Iraqi town destroyed by ISIS became immediately personal when the Knights realized that they could have a hand in turning around the town's tragic history and resettling hundreds of Christian families there. Supreme Knight Carl Anderson pledged that the Order would raise and donate the funds needed to rebuild Karamles, house by house, at a cost of about $2,000 per home.

In Fort Calhoun, Nebraska, the Knights of St. John the Baptist Council 10305 took the mission to heart with unmatched enthusiasm, organization, and effectiveness. Inspired by the testimony of Iraqi-born Bishop Yousif Habash and spurred on by fellow council member and Supreme Director Michael Conrad, the council set—and immediately met—an initial goal of funding the rebuilding

Bishop Barnaba Yousif Benham Habash

of five houses at a cost of $10,000. Then, the council decided to "go big" by launching the largest project it had ever sponsored.

In 2018, a three-day event entitled "Rebuilding the Cradle of Christianity" was conceived to raise awareness and donations for Karamles. For attendees, the testimonies of Bishop Habash and of Gabriel Jabbour—a Syrian refugee who had escaped execution and emigrated to Nebraska—vividly conveyed the conditions facing Christians in the Middle East. Together, all celebrated a common experience as God's family in a Syrian Rite Mass at St. Cecilia Cathedral in Omaha.

A crucial part of the Knights' initiative in the Middle East, the members of St. John the Baptist Council exceeded their original goals. For Karamles, a town with several hundred homes, the $163,000 raised by the council provided enough funds to rebuild eighty houses—a great first step in literally bringing Christian refugees back home.

## A LOOK TOWARD THE FUTURE

Sharing the vision of Father McGivney has always been at the heart of the Knights of Columbus. When Carl Anderson led the Order in the new millennium, that drive continued with impressive resolve. Membership grew and insurance set new records, with insurance in force more than doubling. Expansion into Europe and Korea further increased the Order's worldwide presence, and in New Haven, the introduction and periodic updating of technology helped the Order retain its competitive edge and position for the future.

At the same time, Knights at the local level were incredibly active, putting faith into action in ways large and small for a significant cumulative effect. The level of charitable giving set new records for donations and volunteer hours each year. From 2000 to 2018, the Knights donated approximately $2.9 billion toward charitable efforts, and provided nearly 1.3 billion hours of voluntary service in support of outreach initiatives.

Anderson's leadership during the first two decades of the twenty-first century highlighted the enduring nature and mission of the Knights of Columbus. The Order was able to evangelize and engage the culture in the Knights' best tradition. Moreover, when, after fifty years, the Order once again confronted a landscape that included attacks on religious freedom at home and abroad, it quickly and effectively rose to the defense of those principles.

As the vision of Father McGivney continues, the principles at the heart of the organization he founded—charity, unity, fraternity, and patriotism—remain its driving force. Now as then, the Knights stand ready, armed with over a century of faithful experience, to aid the marginalized and forgotten—wherever the margins may be. Now as then, widows, orphans, the poor, the intellectually and physically disabled, and the unborn all have a friend in the Knights. Now as then, the Knights of Columbus helps protect the faith and financial stability of Catholic families, and as it has from the beginning, continues to stand for religious freedom: working to end religious discrimination and persecution, and continuing to promote the principle that faithful Catholics can also be model citizens.

# The Path Ahead

While proud of its past, the Knights of Columbus has long been an organization focused on its future.

Typical of this are the words of Supreme Knight Edward Hearn in 1905: "While regarding the progress of the Order in the past, let us regard even more carefully the future, and let it be the aim and object of every member and officer of the Order that the record of [this year] will surpass and excel the success of [last year]."

In a way, everything about the Knights of Columbus is geared to the future, beginning with the foundational concern for the future of the faith and finances of Catholic men and their families. Being forward-looking has helped lead to accomplishments at every level of society and the Church. At the same time, the forward-looking impulse of the organization has been grounded in its unwavering commitment to its core values and identity.

The vision that Father McGivney presented to the men of his parish in 1882 was something that withstood the test of time, embraced not only by men in 1880s New England but also by every subsequent generation of Knights. While one might discern several factors that have been foundational to the Knights of Columbus' success, the following stand out particularly.

First, there was—and continues to be—a commitment to the principles of charity, unity, fraternity, and patriotism. These ideals were immensely important following the most polarizing moment in American history, the Civil War. Ideals that could help heal a nation, they remain important today, especially in an era of deep political polarization.

Second, there has been a unique ability to respond to the needs of the moment—local, national, or global. Knights historically act within the communities they serve in the wake of a local tragedy. In these cases, no task is too small. Likewise, no task is too large as Knights also act in unison—from many councils—when necessary. Time and again, responses to major events show an awareness of what men can do together to help others: from the survivors of the San Francisco Earthquake and Fire in 1906, to the troops in World War I and World War II, to the families of first responders after the 9/11 terrorist attacks, to persecuted Middle Eastern Christians and other religious minority communities. In each case—and many more—the Order has been witness to the power of fraternal unity focused on charity.

Third, the Order has shown a unique ability to transplant itself into the fertile Catholic soil of diverse communities and countries—from New Haven to Havana, from Paris to Portland, and from Manila to Mexico City. Few organizations have integrated themselves as well and as successfully into the fabric of communities so different from one another. Yet in each of these places, the Knights is as much a local group as a global one. It is that local credibility, built on the commonality of a shared Catholic faith, that gives the Knights an ability to do so much in so many places.

All of this is possible because "faith in action" characterizes this Order, and it always has. Founded by a parish priest, from the beginning, it had a sense of evangelization. This has been expressed in its Catholic spirituality and sense of mission—to help its own members and fellow parishioners, whether with matters of faith or with financial stability. It has also meant reaching out far beyond the parish to respond to and meet the needs of the community—regardless of race or creed, age or disability. In fact, the Order has often given priority to assisting those marginalized for such reasons. Understanding the importance of faith in action has also led the Order to become—and remain—a globally respected advocate for the free exercise of religion. It has also led the Knights to take its patriotic duty seriously, not simply showing that Catholics make excellent citizens, but also working to ensure that fundamental rights are applied to Catholics and to all— regardless of race or creed.

With the Knights of Columbus, Catholic men continue to find a place where their faith is supported, where they are united in a brotherhood of faith, and where they can act on their faith in concrete ways as they seek to live out the love of God and neighbor that is so central to Catholicism.

While the breadth of future actions in all these areas could not have been foreseen in 1882, neither Father McGivney nor the men he gathered in St. Mary's basement would be surprised by what the Knights of Columbus prioritized in the subsequent years. Indeed, they would see the fruits of what they sowed.

In the twenty-first century, as old issues resurface and new ones arise, the Knights of today, and of tomorrow, are well positioned to respond. In late nineteenth-century New England, the most marginalized would have included Catholics, immigrants, and especially their widows and orphans. The margins have not always been static, but in whatever ways they have shifted over the years, the men witnessing to the faith and doing service for those whom society has overlooked still call themselves Knights of Columbus.

In 1894, in the Order's magazine, *Columbiad,* the editors ran a note under the title, "The Ideal Future." It stated: "The ideal future of the Knights of Columbus could be no more truthfully or forcibly emphasized than in these few words: 'It is what we shall do next that will be our best work.'"

In 1894, that spirit was certainly ambitious. The bar is higher now, but the same spirit is still very much alive in the Knights of Columbus. Great things have been done, but the next chapters, yet unwritten, could be the Order's greatest work.

# About the Authors

**Andrew Walther** earned his bachelor's and master's degrees in Classics from the University of Southern California. Since then, he has had a career as an educator, journalist, speechwriter, international religious freedom advocate, and corporate executive. While working as a freelance journalist, he earned the Excellence in Teaching Award for his popular writing courses at his alma mater.

For a decade and a half, Andrew has worked at the Knights of Columbus in a number of senior communications and government affairs roles. His work has included overseeing the Order's multimedia archive, editing several books, and guiding a book publishing operation that included a number of *New York Times* bestsellers. He has also helped draft speeches for leading figures around the world.

Beginning in 2005, Andrew helped to found and build the Knights' modern communications operation. This included planning major conferences and events cosponsored with the Vatican in the United States, Latin America, and Europe, as well as organizing major international exhibits at major museums in Italy and the United States. In the aftermath of the ISIS campaign of terror in the Middle East, Andrew has led international religious freedom advocacy and humanitarian outreach on behalf of persecuted minorities in the region, working with religious leaders, nonprofit organizations, the United States, and other governments in Europe and the Middle East.

**Maureen Hough Walther** graduated from Princeton University with a bachelor's degree, specializing in Medieval Latin and Old English texts, with certificates in Medieval Studies and Creative Writing. Born blocks away from the Order's birthplace in New Haven, Connecticut and a lifelong parishioner at St. Mary's parish, where Father McGivney served, Maureen is a researcher, writer, and editor with more than a decade of experience at the Knights of Columbus. She has worked on a wide range of historical projects while also serving as Special Assistant to the Supreme Knight, and has edited a number of books, including *La Cristiada: The Mexican People's War for Religious Liberty* (2013).

# Index

Abortion, anti-. *See* Pro-life initiatives.
Act of Toleration, 1649, Maryland, 6
Agency for International
    Development. *See* US Agency
    for International Development.
Albert, Enrique, 124, 125, 126, 129
Albrecht, Antonio, 126
Alemán, Rodrigo Aguilar, 86
Alfred E. Smith Memorial Foundation
    Dinner, 80
Ali, Muhammad, 163
Allen, John, 223
Alvarez, David, 199
*America* magazine, 107, 165, 223
*American by Choice* (Fuentes), 213
American City Bureau, 102
*American Negro in the Great War, The*
    (Scott), 63
*American Standard, The*, 49
*American States 1775–1789, The*
    (Nevins), 82
"America's Church." *See* Basilica of
    the National Shrine of the
    Immaculate Conception.
Anderson, Carl A., 150, 190, 205, 207,
    208, 220, 222, 223, 224, 226, 228,
    229, 231, 232, 239, 244, 249, 251,
    254, 255, 256, 257, 258
    background of, 210–211
    and early improvements to the
        Order, 212–213
Angaelos, Anba, 255
Anglicanism, 6
Annual Indoor Track Meet of the NY
    Chapter, 169
Annual Tank Pull, Knights of
    Columbus, 250
Anti-abortion initiatives. *See* Pro-life
    initiatives.
Anti-Catholicism, 52–54, 130–131
    in early days, 5–6, 7, 8–9
    in Mexico, 45
Apostles of Jesus, 245
Aqueduct Racetrack, papal Mass of
    John Paul II, 200–201
Arlington National Cemetery, 155
*Armed with Faith,* 249
Army hut program, 55, 57, 58, 61, 162

and Canadian Knights, 114, 115, 133
    in Lourdes, 250–251
Asset Advisors, 249
*At That Time* (Rodriguez), 141

Babe Ruth Foundation, 73
Baker, Newton D., 62, 63
Ballila, 97
Basilica of Our Lady of Guadalupe,
    210, 211
Basilica of the National Shrine of the
    Immaculate Conception, 149,
    150, 175, 190, 232
Bataan
    Death March, 125, 126
    fall of, 124
Bauernschub, John, 76
Beatification, 204
Becket Fund, 198
Beckman, Francis, 113
Bell tower, Knights. *See* Knights' Tower.
Bellamy, Francis, 139
Bemis, Samuel Flagg, 82
Benedict XV, Pope, 67–68
Benedict XV playground, 69
Benedict XVI, Pope, 35, 86, 88, 204,
    208, 230, 231, 241
Bergoglio, Jorge Mario, 230, 231. *See
    also* Francis, Pope.
Bernard of Clairvaux, Saint, 25
Bertrand, Joe, 162–163
*Beyond a House Divided: The Moral
    Consensus Ignored by
    Washington, Wall Street, and the
    Media* (Anderson), 239
Bigotry, anti-Catholic. *See* Anti-
    Catholicism.
Birmingham Council 635, 78
*Birth of a Nation, The*, 74, 106
Bishop John J. Kaising Council 14223, 229
Bishops Relief Fund, US, 126
Black, Hugo, 78
Black Legend, the, 44
Blanshard, Paul, 131
Blessed Knights, 209
Blood donor program, 117, 119
*Boston Pilot*, 120

Bowman, Louis, 139
Boy Guidance program, 72
Brennan, Frank A., 169
Brinkley, Douglas, 239
Brooklyn Council 60, 36
Brown, Clause, 114, 115
Brumel, Valeriy, 169
Bryan, William Jennings, 53
Buescher, Brian, 223
Building the Domestic Church, 243
Bunker Hill Council 62, 39, 151
Bureau of Employment, New Haven, 93
Burke, Margaret Gibbons, 100
Bush, George W., 188

*Called to Love: Approaching John Paul
    II's Theology of the Body*
    (Anderson, Granados), 239
Calles, Plutarco Elías, 84
Calles Law, 84, 86, 88
Calvert, Cecil, 6
Camp Casisang, 128
Camp O'Donnell, 124, 125, 126, 129
Camp Shriver, 171
*Campi sportivi*, 69
Canada, establishment in, 44
Canadian Legion, 114
Canonization, 204
Canonization, Michael McGivney's
    cause for. *See* Cause for
    Canonization, Michael
    McGivney's.
Canonization, Prayer for Father
    McGivney's, 204, 205
Canonized Knights, 86, 88, 209
Cárdenas, Lázaro, 88
Carillon at the Knights' Tower, 150
Carmody, Martin H., 71, 89, 92, 93, 95,
    101, 102, 103, 107, 109, 111, 113, 114
Carranza, Venustiano, 84
Carroll, Charles of Carrollton, 6, 7
Carroll, Daniel, 7
Carroll, John, 7
Carroll, Noel, 169
Casaroli, Agostino, 184, 185
Casas, Bartolomé de las, 20
Caseys, 56, 57, 59
Castañeda, Carlos, 83

Castro, Fidel, 147
Cathedral of St. Paul, 78
Catholic Action. *See* Mobilization for
    Catholic Action.
Catholic Advertising Program, 142
Catholic Association of Mexican Youth, 84
Catholic Benevolent Legion, 15
Catholic Home Finding Association, 47
Catholic Information Service (CIS), 142,
    166, 242
Catholic Order of Foresters, 15
Catholic Relief Services, 219
Catholic University Endowment Fund,
    47–48
Catholic University of America, 46–47,
    98, 100
*Catholic World,* 120
Cause for Canonization, Michael
    McGivney's, 35, 203–205
Centennial anniversary, 184–185
Ceremonials, 24, 45, 160, 209
Chapel of Our Lady of Częstochowa, 181
Charles Carroll Assembly, 40
Charter of Knights of Columbus, 18, 19
Chavez, Eduardo, 239
Chemical plant explosion, West Texas, 217
Chinese Civil War, 135
*Chivalry in Medieval England* (Saul), 25
Christ Church, 8
Christian Refugee Relief Fund, 252
Christians in Middle East, aiding. *See*
    Middle East, aiding Christians in.
Christie, Alexander, 79
*Christopher Columbus: Faithful Christ
    Bearer,* 190
Church in America conference. 230, 231
Cipollone, Pat, 198
CIS. *See* Catholic Information Service.
Civil Rights Movement, 157, 162
*Civilization of Love: What Every Catholic
    Can Do to Transform the World*
    (Anderson), 239
Clarke, Edward Young, 75
Clinton, Bill, 188
Coalition for Decency, 161
Coats for Kids, 244, 245–246
Coeur de Leon Council 87, 40
Cohen, George, 81
Colayco, Manuel, 126
Cold War, 130, 132, 133, 135, 137, 199
Coletti, Joseph A., 145
College Council Conference, 248
College councils, 46, 248
College of St. Hyacinthe, 16
Collins, Peter W., 54, 64, 93
Colombian Mile, 169

Color Corps, 41
Colorado Knights, 94
*Columbia* magazine, 29, 87, 103, 107,
    108, 109
*Columbiad, The,* 12, 28–29
Columbian Squires, 71–72, 186
Columbianism, 36, 37, 45, 227
*Columbianism and the Knights of
    Columbus* (Kauffman), 24, 37, 187
Columbus, Christopher, 18, 20, 21
*Columbus and the Quest for Jerusalem*
    (Delaney), 20
Columbus Day, 49
Columbus Day 1992, 190–191
Columbus Gallery at K of C Museum, 191
Columbus Memorial, 50–51
Colwell, Daniel, 27, 31, 162
Commission on Religious Prejudices, 54
Common Christian Roots of the
    European Nations, Colloquium
    on the, 183
Communism, 113, 120, 135, 143
    campaigning against, 110–111, 129–
    130, 131–133, 135–137, 143–144, 183
Communist Party USA, 110
Cone, John J., 39
Conference on Human Rights, 164
Confraternity Home Study Service, 142
Congregation for the Causes of Saints, 204
Congregationalist Church, 8
Conley, Charles, 19
Connecticut Catholic Temperance
    Society, 15
Connolly, Myles E., 103
Conrad, Michael, 257
Convention, "Klanbake," 80
Convention, 1924 Democratic National,
    80
Coolidge, Calvin, 87, 88, 100
Count Enrico Galeazzi Fund, 179
Coyle, James Edwin, 78
Creatore, Donald, 198
Crèches. *See* Nativity scenes.
Cristero War, 86, 88, 105
Cristeros, 84
Cristo Rey Assembly, 155
Cronin, Daniel A., 35, 203, 204
Cross, Wilbur L., 96
Cross, World Youth Day, 240
Crusade for Life campaign, 188
Crusade for Social Justice, 111
Crusade for the Preservation and
    Promotion of American Ideals, 132
Cuba, establishment in, 44, 45
Cuban Missile Crisis, 157
Cummings, Thomas A., 21, 29, 36, 37

Daily, Thomas, 200
*Daily Worker,* 110
Daly, Joseph Gordian, 12, 17
Daniel, Dan, 144
Darr, Charles W., 100
Davitt, William F., 64
De la Mora, Miguel de la Mora, 86
De Valera, Eamon, 155
Death March, Bataan. *See* Bataan.
Dechant, Virgil C., 170, 172, 173, 177,
    178, 179, 184, 188, 190, 192, 200,
    201, 202, 205, 224
Degree, Fourth. *See* Fourth Degree.
Degrees, the four, 24–25. *See also* Fourth
    Degree.
Delaney, Carol, 20
Democratic National Convention, 1924,
    80
Denton, Jeremiah, 161
Depression, Great. *See* Great
    Depression and the Knights.
Derry, George Hermann, 110–111, 132
Diamond Jubilee, 145–146
Diego, Juan, 209, 239, 242, 243
*Dignitatis Humanae,* 160
Dinkeloo, John, 166
Divine Mercy, 231, 232, 235
*Divini Illius Magistri,* 79
*Divini Redemptoris,* 110
Dome, Incarnation. *See* Incarnation
    Dome.
Domestic Church initiative, 72
Donahue, John, 131
Donovan, "Wild Bill," 62
Downes, Alfred, 16–17, 35
Downes, Edward, 35
Dr. John G. Coyle Council 163, 80
Draft, military. *See* Selective Service
    Act.
Driscoll, Cornelius T., 15
Du Bois, W.E.B., 81, 83, 162, 239
Duluth Circle 1, 71
Durán, Yocundo, 87
Dziwisz, Stanisław, 227, 234

Earthquake, Haitian. *See* Haitian
    earthquake.
Earthquake, San Francisco. *See* San
    Francisco Earthquake of 1906,
    Great.
Ecclesia in America conference. *See*
    Church in America conference.
Economic Opportunity's War on
    Poverty, Office of. *See* War on
    Poverty.
*Ed Sullivan Show,* 144

Edralin, Isaias X., 128

Educational Trust Fund. *See* Matthews
& Swift Educational Trust
Scholarships.

Eisenhower, Dwight D., 140, 143, 144

Ely, Joseph P., 96

Emblem of Columbian Squires, 72

Emblem of the Fourth Degree, Triad,
42–43

Emblem of the Knights of Columbus,
21

e-membership, 212

Employment Bureau. *See* Bureau of
Employment, New Haven.

Employment program, post WWI, 64–
65

Escoda, Antonio, 125

Eszer, Ambrose, 204

Ethisphere® Institute, 212

Evangelization, new. *See* New
evangelization.

Evers, Johnny, 57

*Everson v. Board of Education,* 130

Expansion into Europe, 227–229

Fabbrica di San Pietro, 181, 182

*Face of Mercy, The,* 239

Fagan, Chas, 193

*Faith and Fraternalism* (Kauffman), 187

Faith in Action, 208, 244–247

*Faith of Our Fathers, The* (Gibbons), 138

Fallon, Lester, 142

Family Life Bureau, K of C, 189

Fascism, 120

Father McGivney Guild, 203, 205

"Father McGivney of the Philippines."
*See* Willmann, George J.

Father Michael J. McGivney Gallery,
194, 197

Fathers for Good, 242–243

Fenster, Julie, 16

Finn, Leo, 145

Fitzgerald, Christopher I., 29

Fitzsimmons, William, 57

Five Points Program to Progress, 104,
105

Flaherty, James A., 51, 53, 54, 55, 62,
63, 67, 69, 79, 87, 89

Foch, Ferdinand, 229

Foik, Paul Joseph, 83

Food for Families, 246

*Fortnightly Review,* 53

*Foundations of our American Ideals,* 132

Fourth Degree, 24, 40–43

Francis, Pope, 221, 224, 230, 231, 241

*Francis: The Pope from the New World,* 239

Franklin, Benjamin, 7

*Fraternalist, The* (Dechant), 178

Frisbie, John B., Jr., 44–45

Fuentes, Alfredo "Al," 213

Fumasoni-Bondi, Pietro, 100

*Future of America, The,* 132

Gaggawala, Paul, 245

Galeazzi, Enrico Pietro, 69, 107, 122, 182

Galeazzi Fund. *See* Count Enrico
Galeazzi Fund.

Gallagher & Associates design firm, 232

Gary Sinese Foundation, 251

*Gaudium et Spes,* 160

Gaudium et Spes Award, 191, 193, 205

Genocide, acts of against Christians,
252–255

George W. Hudson Council 3701, 213

Georgetown University, 7

*Germans in the Making of America, The*
(Shrader), 81

Gettysburg Address, 139

Gibbons, James, 16, 51, 98, 100

Gibbons Institute, 165

Gibbons Memorial, James Cardinal,
98, 100

*Gift of Black Folk, The* (Du Bois), 81,
162, 239

Gift of Love: The Life of Saint John
Paul II, 232, 236–238

Glemp, Józef, 227, 228

Glennon, John J., 47

Global Wheelchair Mission, 247

Golden Anniversary of the Knights,
95–97

Goldstein, David, 54

Grady, Thomas J., 149

Graham, Robert, 199

Granados, Jose, 239

Grand Rapids Council 389, 89

Great Depression and the Knights'
charitable efforts, 101
efforts to boost membership, 96–
97, 101–104, 101–103
helping the unemployed, 92–93,
impact on, 91–92, 101–104

Great Famine, the, 8

Great Jubilee Year 2000, 182, 207

Griffin, John H., 155

Griffith, D.W., 74, 106

Grušas, Gintaras, 227

Guadalupe, Our Lady of. *See* Our
Lady of Guadalupe.

*Guadalupe, The Miracle and the Message,*
239

Guadalupe Council 1050, 45

Guadalupe Festival, 242

Guerin, James J., 44

Guilday, Peter, 7

Gulf States Hurricane Relief Fund. *See*
Hurricane Relief Fund, Gulf
States.

Gussman, Pedro, 78

Habash, Barnaba Yousif Benham, 257

Habitat for Humanity, 246

Hackett, John F., 166

Haitian earthquake, 219–220

Haiyan, Typhoon. *See* Typhoon
Haiyan, Super.

Happy Warrior. *See* Smith, Alfred E. "Al."

Harrison, Benjamin, 49

Hart, Luke E., 116, 129, 137, 142, 143,
145, 149, 150, 153, 155, 158, 162,
164

Hasson, Kevin "Seamus," 198

Hayes, James A., 39

Head Start, 168

Headquarters, seventh, 166

Healing Haiti's Children project, 219, 220

Hearn, Edward L., 24, 25, 39–40, 45, 51,
69, 97

Heroes Fund, $1 million, 215

Hickey, James, 190

Hill Military Academy, 79

Historical Commission, K of C, 81, 83, 110

Historical Commission, Texas K of C, 83

Historical Series, K of C., 82

*History of the Knights of Columbus in
Illinois,* 47

Hitler, Adolph, 107, 111, 113, 114

Holliday, Robert Cortes, 62

Holocaust, 107, 113, 120, 121

Holy Cross Family Ministries, 240

Holy Door, 182, 207

Holy Family Chapel, 212, 235

Holy Names of Jesus and Mary, Sisters
of the, 79

Holy Trinity Church, 8

Home Study Service. *See* Confraternity
Home Study Service.

Hoover, Herbert, 93, 100, 101

H.R. 390. *See* Iraq and Syria Genocide
Relief and Accountability Act.

Hungarian Revolution, 143

Hurricane Harvey, 217

Hurricane Katrina, 216–217

Hurricane Relief Fund, Gulf States, 217

Hurricane Sandy, 217

Hurtado, José Maria Robles, 86

Husar, Lubomyr, 227

Huts, Army. *See* Army hut program.

Immaculate Conception Church, 16
Immigration, early in the United States, 6, 8–9
Imperial Japanese Army, 125
In Defense of Christians, 253
Incarnation Dome, 150
Insurance program, 25–26, 31
International Congress for Vocations, 179
International Development, Agency for. *See* US Agency for International Development.
International Marian Congress festivals, 242
Invisible Empire. *See* Ku Klux Klan.
Iraq and Syria Genocide Relief and Accountability Act, 255, 256
ISIS. *See* Islamic State of Iraq and Syria.
Islamic State of Iraq and Syria (ISIS) and acts of genocide, 252–255. *See also* Middle East, aiding Christians in.

Jabbour, Gabriel, 257
*Jay's Treaty: A Study in Commerce and Diplomacy* (Bemis), 82
Jeanbart, Jean Clement, 256
Jersey City Council 137, 39
Jewish refugees, defense of, 109, 113
Jewish War Veterans, 109
*Jews in the Making of America, The* (Cohen), 81
Job Corps, 168
John Paul II, Pope, 88, 141, 177, 179, 183, 190, 191, 207, 227, 230, 235, 240, 241, 242
    and Mass at Aqueduct Racetrack, 200–201
    *See also* Saint John Paul II National Shrine.
John Paul II Council 14000, 227
John Paul II Cultural Center, 232
*John Paul II in America: Uniting a Continent,* 239
John Paul II Institute for Studies on Marriage and Family, 211
John Paul II National Shrine. *See* Saint John Paul II National Shrine.
John XXIII, Pope, 158
Johnson, Arnold, 136
Joseph P. Kennedy Jr. Foundation, 171
Juan XXIII Council 2033, 141
Jubilee of Mercy conference, 231
Jubilee Year. *See* Great Jubilee Year 2000.

Kansas Flood of 1903, 46
Karamles, Iraq, 252, 256, 257

Katrina, Hurricane. *See* Hurricane Katrina.
Kauffman, Christopher J., 187, 204
Kavanaugh, J. P., 44
Kelly, Patrick, 226, 232,
Kennan, George, 132
Kennedy, John B., 102
Kennedy, John F., 151, 152, 153, 155, 160, 168, 171
Kennedy, Joseph P., 168
Kennedy Foundation. *See* Joseph P. Kennedy Jr. Foundation.
Kerry, John, 253
Kilmer, Joyce, 62
King, Martin Luther, Jr., 162, 163
KKK. *See* Ku Klux Klan.
Klan. *See* Ku Klux Klan.
"Klanbake Convention," 80
Knecht, Marcel, 62
Knighthood, 18, 21, 25
*Knightline,* 192
Knights of Columbus
    Asset Advisors, 249
    and formation of insurance program, 25–26
    and the four degrees, 24–25
    charter of, 18
    early expansion of, 30, 36–37, 44–45
    emblem of, 21
    establishment of, 15, 18–19, 21, 23, 24–26
    museum. *See* Museum, Knights of Columbus.
    officers of, 23
    reasons for forming, 12–13
Knights of Columbus Museum. *See* Museum, Knights of Columbus.
Knights of Manila Council 1000. *See* Manila Council 1000.
Knights of Saint Patrick, 31
Knights' Tower, 149–150
Koehler, John, 199
Ku Klux Klan (KKK), 20, 49, 74–77, 78, 79–80, 106, 239

La Cristiada. *See* Cristero War.
*La Cristiada: The Mexican People's War for Religious Liberty* (Meyer), 239
LaCrosse Council 2970, 175
LaFarge, John, 164–165
LaFarge Institute, 164, 165
Lafayette, statue of, 67, 68
Lamboley, Harold J., 155
Larios, Leonardo Pérez, 86
Larkin, William P., 101–102
*Lawrence Welk Show,* 144

Lay trusteeism, 222
Lay vocation, call for, 159
Lee, Richard C., 166
Lentelli, Leo, 100
Leo XIII, Pope, 47
*Letter to Artists* (John Paul II), 235
Lewis, Chris, 247
*Liberating a Continent: John Paul II and the Fall of Communism,* 239
*Life and Times of John Carroll, The* (Guilday), 7
*Life* magazine, 144
Lincoln, Abraham, 139
Lindsay, John, 136
*Liturgy and Christian Culture,* 141
Lombardi, Vince, 174
*Long Telegram,* 132
Lori, William, 222, 231, 243
Los Baños, internment camp at, 127
Lourdes, Knights' involvement in, 250–251
Lourdes pilgrimage. *See* Military Pilgrimage, International.
Lucero, Pedro de Jesús Maldonado, 86
Lull, Blessed Raymon, 25
Lum, Brady, 168
Luminous Mysteries Chapel, 232, 234–235
*Lusitania,* RMS, sinking of, 55
Luther, Hans, 113

MacArthur, Douglas, 126
Macena, Wilfrid, 221
Macharski, Franciszek, 227
Mack, Connie, 48
Maderno, Carlo. 182
Maderno Atrium, 182, 207
Magallanes, Mateo Correa, 86
Mahoney, Thomas F., 94
Mahorner, M., Jr., 45
"Malice in Naziland," 107, 108, 109
Manila, Knights of, in World War I, 124, 125, 126, 127–128
Manila Council 1000, 125, 126, 128, 129
*Manual for Discussion Groups* (Derry), 132
Mar Addai Church, 252
March for Life, 173, 226
March on Washington for Jobs and Freedom, 162
Martyred knights. *See* Mexican persecution, martyred knights of.
Maryland Act of Toleration, 6
Mater Dei Council 9774, 168
Matthews, Francis P., 111, 114, 115, 116, 118

Matthews & Swift Educational Trust
    Scholarships, 118.
Matthias, Brother, 73
McCarthyism, 135
McCormack, John W., 144
McDevitt, John W., 157, 158, 159, 160,
    162, 164, 165, 166, 172, 175, 224
McDonald, Barnabas, 71
McGarry, Garry, 57
McGinley, William, 69
McGivney, Michael Joseph
    background of, 16–17, 98
    and cause for canonization, 35,
        203–205
    death of, 17, 32, 35
    and formation of Knights of
        Columbus, 11, 12, 13, 15
    Pope Benedict XVI's statement on,
        208
    reinterment of, 186
McGivney, Patrick J., 45, 69
McGivney House (Iraq), 254
McGivney Memorial, 145–146
McGuire, John V., 166, 179
McGuire, Paul, 111
McNamara, John M., 100
McSweeney, Edward F., 81, 82
Menace, The, 53
Mexican constitution, 1917, 84
Mexican Fund, 87
Mexican persecution, martyred
    knights of, 86, 207, 209
Mexican Pontifical College, 179
Mexican Revolution, 84, 88
Mexican Welfare Committee, 94
Mexico
    fighting religious persecution in,
        84, 85, 87–89, 105, 107
    Order's establishment in, 44
    Order's expansion in, 229
Meyer, Jean, 239
Middle East, aiding Christians in, 48,
    209, 252–257
Military Chaplain Scholarship, Father
    McGivney, 250
Military Pilgrimage, International, 250
Mindzensky, Josef, 143
Minerva, Hotel, 68
Missionaries of Charity, 192
Mobile Council 666, 78
Mobilization for Catholic Action,
    101–104
Mokryzcki, Mieczsław, 227
Molist, Andrés Solá, 86
Monroe Council 1337, 72
Monsignor Basche Council 4505, 174

Monsignor John T. Dwyer Council
    9851, 199
Montaño, José Trinidad Rangel, 86
Montreal Council 284, 44
Morrow, Dwight W., 88
Mother Teresa of Kolkata
    canonization of, 193
    Knights' support of, 189, 191,
        192–193
Moure, Emilio, 219
Moynihan, Patrick Edward, 45
Mr. Blue (Connolly), 103
Mt. Pleasant Council 98, 54
Muldoon, P. J., 47
Mullen, James T., 18, 19, 21, 24, 30
Multimedia Archives at K of C
    Museum, 194
Murphy, Robert, 144
Museum, Knights of Columbus, 187,
    194–197
Myon, John Chang, 138, 229

Narragansett Council 21, 36
Nation, The, 107
National Broadcasting Company
    (NBC), 102
National Catholic Community Service
    (NCCS), 116, 119, 126
National Catholic Welfare Conference
    (NCWC), 116
National Education Association, 139
National League for Defense of
    Religious Liberty, 84, 87
National Shrine of the Immaculate
    Conception. See Basilica of the
    National Shrine of the
    Immaculate Conception.
Nativity scenes
    at Knights of Columbus Museum,
        194, 197
    in Trumbull, Connecticut, 198
Natural Choice is Life campaign, 188
Natural Family Planning initiatives, 189
Nazism, rise of, 107, 108, 109, 120, 135
NCCS. See National Catholic
    Community Service.
NCWC. See National Catholic Welfare
    Conference.
Near East Relief Foundation, 48
Neighbors Helping Neighbors, 245–246
Nevins, Allan, 82
New evangelization, 242
New Rochelle Council 339, 62
New York Times, The, 12
Newton Council 167, 54
Nilan, John J., 96

Niland, Frederick "Fritz," 199
9/11 terrorist attacks. See Terrorist
    attacks, 9/11.
Nixon, Richard M., 151
North American College (Rome), 179
North Carolina Catholic Laymen's
    Association, 163
Nostra Aetate, 160
Notre Dame, University of, 72
Notre Dame Council 1477, 46, 248

O'Boyle, Patrick, 149
O'Brien, Henry, 145
O'Brien, Hugh, 39
O'Connell, William Henry, 96
O'Connor, John, 189, 224
O'Donnell, Camp. See Camp
    O'Donnell.
O'Donnell, Gabriel B., 203–204, 205
Office of Economic Opportunity's War
    on Poverty. See War on Poverty.
Officers, Knights of Columbus, 23
Olcott, Benjamin W., 79
Olympics, Special. See Special
    Olympics.
Operation Lamb, 163
Operation Share, 192
Origins of the Propoganda Movement, The
    (Russell), 82
Our Catholic Heritage in Texas, 1519–
    1936, 83
Our Lady of Angels Seminary, 16
Our Lady of Charity Council 5110, 147
Our Lady of Guadalupe, 210, 211, 229,
    230, 231, 242
Our Lady of Guadalupe, Basilica of. See
    Basilica of Our Lady of
    Guadalupe.
Our Lady of Guadalupe Fund, 179
Our Lady of Guadalupe: Mother of the
    Civilization of Love (Anderson,
    Chavez), 239
Pacelli, Eugenio, 103. See also Pius XII,
    Pope.
Papal Gallery at K of C Museum, 194, 196
Parish Priest: Father Michael McGivney
    and American Catholicism
    (Brinkley, Fenster), 239
Park City Council 16, 30
Parochial schools. See Religious schools,
    fight for, 79–80
Pastor Angelicus Playground, 70
Patriotism and Fraternalism in the Knights
    of Columbus (Kauffman), 187
Patterson, Floyd, 163
Paul VI, Pope, 70, 158, 165, 178

Paul VI Audience Hall, Pope, 70
Peace Corps, 168, 171
Peace Program, 120–121
Pearl Harbor, bombing of, 114
Pegram, Thomas, 76
Pence, Mike, 253
People's Republic of China, 135
Perry, Harold R., 164
Pershing, John J., 62
Phelan, John J., 30, 36, 37
Phelps, William Franklin, 53
Philip Sheridan Council 119, 27
Philippines and the Knights
    establishment in, 44
    expansion in, 129
    involvement during World War II,
      124–129
*Pierce v. Society of Sisters*, 79
Pius VI, Pope, 7
Pius X, Pope, 149
Pius XI, Pope, 69, 105, 110, 111
Pius XI Playground, 69, 79
Pius XII, Pope, 29, 111, 120, 122, 199
Pius XII Memorial Library, 143
Pius XII Playground, 70
Playgrounds, Knights' in Rome, 69–70,
    97, 122, 123, 133
Pledge of Allegiance, Knights' role in,
    139–140, 155
POAU. *See* Protestants and Other
    Americans United for the
    Separation of Church and State.
Polverini Playground, 69–70
Pontifical College Josephinum
    seminary, 178
Pontifical John Paul II Institute for
    Studies on Marriage and Family,
    179, 189, 190
*Pope and Poland During World War II,
    The* (Graham), 199
Pope Paul VI Audience Hall, 70
Positio, 204
Postulator, 204
Potomac Council 433, 210
Prayer for Peace, World Day of. *See*
    World Day of Prayer for Peace.
President's Organization on
    Unemployment Relief, 93
Preuss, Arthur, 53
*Proclaim Liberty: Notes on the Next Great
    Awakening in America* (Anderson),
    239
Project Medishare, 219, 220
Project of Equality, 164
Pro-life initiatives, 172–173, 178, 188–
    189, 224, 225, 226

Protestants and Other Americans
    United for the Separation of
    Church and State (POAU), 130, 131
Puritans. *See* Congregationalist Church.

Quinn, Rose J., 46

Rabaut, Louis C., 140
Racial Contribution Series, 81
Racial equality, support of, 27, 63, 160,
    162–165
Ratzinger, Joseph, 230. *See also* Benedict
    XVI, Pope.
Reagan, John Edward "Jack," 106
Reagan, Ronald, 106, 177–178, 183, 184,
    185
Rebuilding the Cradle of Christianity,
    257
Reconstruction Finance Corporation
    (RFC), 111
Recreation centers in Rome. *See*
    Playgrounds, Knights' in Rome.
Red Cross, American, 117, 119
Red Knights, 15, 31
Reddin, John H., 42, 81, 82, 94
Redemptor Hominis (Redeemer of
    Man) Church, 232, 234
Redemptoris Mater Chapel, 235
Redinger, Matthew, 107
Refund Support Vocations Program
    (RSVP), 179
Religious Information Bureau, 142,
    155, 166
Religious schools, fight for, 79–80,
    130–131
Rest House, K of C, 125
Ribicoff, Abraham A., 145, 146
Ricky, Michael, 249
Right-to-life initiatives. *See* Pro-life
    initiatives.
Ritual for the Patriotic Degree, 42
Roche, Dinkeloo, and Associates, 167
Roche, Kevin, 166, 186
Rodriguez, Carlos M., 141
*Roe v. Wade*, 172, 188
Roos, Lee R., 236
Roosevelt, Franklin D., 80, 101, 107,
    109, 111, 122
Roosevelt, Theodore, 98
Roosevelt Hotel, 164
Rosary Rally, 173
Round Table Program, Parish, 202
RSVP. *See* Refund Support Vocations
    Program.
Rupnik, Marko, 212, 235
Russell, Charles Edward, 82

Ruth, George Herman "Babe," 73

*Safeguards of America*, 132
Saint John Paul II National Shrine,
    193, 208, 232–238, 241
Sainted Knights, 86, 88, 209
Sáinz, Luis Batis, 86
Salvation Army, The, 114
San Agustín Council 1390, 45
San Francisco Earthquake of 1906,
    Great, 46, 215
San Giovanni Rotondo, 235
San Salvador Council, 19, 30
Sarsfield Guard, 15
Satolli, Francesco, 37
Saul, Nigel, 25
Save the Baby campaign, 188
Scott, Emmet J., 63
Second Vatican Council. *See* Vatican II.
Secretaries, K of C. *See* Caseys.
Selective Service Act, 116
Serra, Junipero, 231
Service Department, 104, 111
Sheen, Archbishop Fulton, 159
Shevchuk, Sviatoslav, 227, 228
Shrader, Frederick Franklin, 81
Shrine of Christ the King, 229
Shrine of the Immaculate Conception. *See*
    Basilica of the National Shrine of
    the Immaculate Conception.
Shriver, Camp. *See* Camp Shriver.
Shriver, Eunice Kennedy, 155, 168, 170,
    171
Shriver, Sargent, 155, 168, 170, 171
Silver City Council, 19
Simmons, William J., 74, 75
Sisters of Life, 224, 240, 241
Sisters of Our Lady of Mercy, 241
Sisters of the Holy Names of Jesus and
    Mary, 79
Sisters of the Sacred Heart of
    Guadalajara, 86
Smith, Alfred E. "Al," 80, 102
Smith, Charles F., 44
Smith, Chip, 17, 31, 203
Smith, Chris, 256
Soliven, Benito, 126
Special Olympics, 168, 170, 171, 189, 246
Spellman, Francis Cardinal, 143, 145, 150
*Spies in the Vatican* (Koehler), 199
Squires. *See* Columbian Squires.
St. Andrew Kim Taegon Council
    16000, 229
St. Augustine Council 2340, 175
St. Hyacinthe, College of, 16, 44
St. John the Baptist Council 10305, 257

St. Laurent, Louis, 147
St. Mary's Church, 8, 11, 13, 16
    renovation of, 186
St. Mary's College, 16, 44
St. Mary's Industrial School for Boys, 73
St. Mary's Seminary, 16
St. Paul, Cathedral of, 78
St. Paul Council 397, 117
St. Peter Council 16252, 227
St. Peter's Basilica (Rome), Knight's
    projects at, 181–182
"St. Peter's front door." *See* Maderno
    Atrium.
St. Peter's Oratory, 69, 70
St. Theresa Council 2961, 198
St. Thomas Church, 16, 32
St. Thomas the Apostle Church, 163
St. Vladimir Council 15800, 228
Stephenson, Edward, 78
Stephenson, Ruth, 78
Step-In clinics, 254
Stritch, Samuel, 116
Sullivan, D. Francis, 175
Sullivan, Ed, 144
Super Typhoon Haiyan. *See* Typhoon
    Haiyan, Super,
Supreme Council Archives at K of C
    Museum, 194, 197
Swift, John E., 118, 120, 129, 130, 131,
    135, 136, 145

Taft, William Howard, 49, 51, 98
Tank Pull, Knights of Columbus
    Annual, 250
Team Zaryen. 221
Teresa, Mother. *See* Mother Teresa of
    Kolkata.
Terrorist Attacks, 9/11, 213, 214, 215
Texas, Catholic history of. *See*
    Historical Commission, Texas K
    of C.
Textbooks, fight for historical accuracy
    of, 81–83
Thatcher, Margaret, 183
Third World Congress of the Lay
    Apostolate in Rome, 159
Thompson, Joseph J., 39
Three Saints Chapel, 181
Tito, Josip Broz, 143
Tobin, Daniel A., 71
Toleration, 1649 Act of, 6
Tomb memorials for the unborn, 189
Toomey, Daniel, 29
Tower, Knights. *See* Knights' Tower.
Track Meet, Annual Indoor. *See*

    Annual Indoor Track Meet of the
    NY Chapter.
Treaty of Versailles, 62
Triad Emblem of the Fourth Degree,
    42–43
Truman Doctrine, 133
Trumbull, Connecticut nativity scene,
    198
Trump, Donald, 255, 256
Trump Administration, and aid to
    Christians in the Middle East,
    253, 255, 256
Tsukomoto, Gregorio, 127
Tyler, Elizabeth, 75
Typhoon Haiyan, Super, 218

Ultrasound Initiative, 225, 226
*Unbreakable: A Story of Hope and
    Healing in Haiti*, 220, 239
United Nations Relief and
    Rehabilitation Agency, 123
United Service Organization (USO),
    116, 117, 133
US Agency for International
    Development, 245, 256
USO. *See* United Service
    Organization.
USS *Dwight Eisenhower*, 249

Valencia, Rafael Guízar, 88
Valencia Council 80, 129
Valle Giulia Playground, 70
*Vallejo Daily Times*, 46
Vatican, Knights' initiatives at the,
    181–182
Vatican, Knights' support of, 37
Vatican Council, Second. *See* Vatican II.
*Vatican Diplomacy* (Graham), 199
Vatican Film Library, 143, 165
Vatican Radio, 165
Vatican Transmitting Center, 165
Vatican II, 158, 160
    Knights' response to, 159,
    160
Venerable Knights, 209
Versailles, Treaty of, 120
Vicarius Christi Fund, 184–185
Vietnam War, 157
    and Knights of Columbus, 167
Villa Maria Guadalupe, 224
Visayas State Council, 218
VISTA, 168
Vocations, support of, 178–179
Vocations Program, 179
Volunteerism, 189

Wall of History, at K of C Museum, 194,
    196, 197
Walsh, John William, 145
Walters, Vincent S., 163
War Activities Committee, 55
War bonds, sale of, 117–118, 119
War Camp Fund, 61
War on Poverty, 168
Warda, Bashar, 254, 256–257
Washington Council 224, 138
Watson, Thomas Edward, 53
*Watson's Magazine*, 53
Welcome Home Program, 96–97
Welk, Lawrence, 144
Wheelchair mission. *See* Global
    Wheelchair Mission.
*William Tyler*, 118
Williams, Samuel F., 27
Willmann, George J., 124, 125, 126, 127,
    129
Wilson, Edith, 59
Wilson, Woodrow, 55, 59
Wojtyła, Karol, 183, 232, 236. *See also*
    John Paul II, Pope.
Work Projects Administration, 101
Works Progress Administration. *See*
    Work Projects Administration.
World Day of Prayer for Peace, 215
World Meeting of Families, 230, 231
World War I, Knights' involvement in,
    55–65
World War II
    Canadian Knights' involvement in,
    114–115
    and effect on Rome, 122–123
    and Peace Program, 120–121
    US Knights' involvement in, 116–
    119, 133
World Youth Day, 240–241
World Youth Day Cross, 240
"World's Most Ethical Company," 212
Wright, John, 172
Wuerl, Donald, 150

Yale University, 164
Yankee Staadium purchase, 136
YMCA, 114
Younan, Ignatius Joseph III, 256
*Young Catholics in the United States and
    Canada*, 179
*Youth's Companion, The*, 139
Yu Soo-il, Francis Xavier, 229

Zaryen, Team. *See* Team Zaryen.

# Image Permissions and Credits

Many of the published images are from the Knights' own multimedia archives; some of these were previously used in *The Columbiad, Columbia, Knightline,* and kofc.org. The provenance of certain photographs from the holdings is unknown despite the resources invested to identify the photographer and holder of copyright. Artwork and paintings are generally from the Knights of Columbus Museum; most images of Knights' documents and publications are from the Supreme Council Archives and other Knights of Columbus departments.

Special thanks to the Library of Congress, the National Archives, Catholic Research Resources Alliance, and other organizations making rights-free images readily available. The following organizations were particularly helpful in providing use of just the right image: Chaldean Catholic Archdiocese of Erbil, Iraq; Catholic News Service; College of the Holy Cross; Museum of New York City; The Near East Foundation. Square One supplied public domain images.

Credit for images from organizations that provide a unique identifier include that unique control or object number. Abbreviations are used for Multimedia Archives (KCMA), Knights of Columbus Museum (KCM), Supreme Council Archives (KCSCA), and Knights of Columbus (KC). Unless otherwise noted, images are identified in sequence of left-to-right and then top-to-bottom.

## Cover

Discussion of the persecution of Catholics in Mexico with President Coolidge, Paul Smiths in the Adirondacks, N.Y., 1 September 1926 [edited image]. KCMA 20130705amo011.

Columbia, August 1925. KC.

Signal Corps. KC secretary passing cup to soldier from rolling kitchen, Juvigny, France, 1918. National Archives 111-SC-21372.

Richard Whitney, artist. Father Michael J. McGivney, 1989. Photograph of painting copyright by the Knights of Columbus Supreme Council. Painting: KCM.

De Silva, New Haven. St. Mary's Church. 1880-1890 approximate. KCMA kc20120417lj12.

United States flag, on loan from the K of C Museum, displayed on the Knights Tower at the Basilica of the National Shrine of the Immaculate Conception, 11 September 2011. KCMA 20110911kc004.

L'Osservatore Romano. Pope John Paul II offers Mass at Aqueduct Raceway, 6 October 1995. Courtesy of L'Osservatore Romano. KCMA 201309027amo011.

Caulfield & Shook. Field secretaries posed casually in front of a recreation building, 1918. Forms part of T.D. Clines photograph album. KCMA 20130207amo021.

Percy Wenrich. John B. Kennedy. Casey: (K.C.), 1919. Collection 0008, World War I Collection, KCSCA.

Omar Alhayali. People from Mosul, Iraq, raise a wooden cross near St. Georges Monastery, 2017 Apr 24. EPA via Catholic News Service.

## Chapter 1. In the Beginning

**4.** Jose Maria Obregon. *Inspiration of Christopher Columbus,* 1856. Museo Nacional de Arte, INBA Acervo Constitutivo, 1982. Wikimedia File: Inspiracion de Cristobal Colon by Jose Maria Obregon, 1856.jpg.

**5.** Department of Planning Maryland. Maryland's Historical Markers. https://mht.maryland.gov/historicalmarkers/DetailsDirect.aspx?Marker_ID=RM-467 (accessed 5 September 2019).

J.G. Heinsch, engraver. *Andrew White, the Apostle to Maryland, baptizing the Indian chief Chitomachon,* 1694. In Mathias Tanner: Societas Jesu apostolorum imitatrix. Typis Universitatis Carolo-Ferdinandeae: Prague. Wikimedia: http://commons.wikimedia.org/wiki/File:Andreas_Vitus.jpg (accessed 5 September 2019).

**6.** James Barry. *Religious & civil liberty established in Maryland in 1649.* Library of Congress: 00650587.

Father Junipero Serra, 1700 approximate. Wikipedia File:Junipero Serra.jpg.

Michael Laty. Charles Carroll. 1846 approximate. Wikipedia File:Charles Carroll of Carrollton - Michael Laty.jpg.

**7.** Gilbert Stuart. Portrait of Archbishop John Carroll. Georgetown University Library; Gift of Judge Pacificus Ord, 1894. Wikipedia File:John_Carroll_Gilbert_Stuart.jpg.

**8.** Holy Trinity Church [sketch]. Courtesy St. Patrick-St. Anthony Church, Hartford, Connecticut.

De Silva, New Haven. St. Mary's Church. 1880-1890 approximate. KCMA kc20120417lj12.

John B. Perry. The destruction of Philadelphia's Church of St. Augustine in the 1844 Nativist Riots. Historical Society of Pennsylvania.Wikipedia File:Philadelphia1844riot.jpg.

**9.** Charles Jospeh Staniland. *On Board an Emigrant Ship–The Breakfast Bell* [engraving]. Source: The Graphic, v. 30, 1884, pp. 272-273. Library of Congress cph 3b08053.

## Chapter 2. The Early Years—1881 to 1896

**10.** Antonella Cappuccio. Father Michael J. McGivney, 2003. KCM. cAntonella Cappuccio.

**11.** *Daily Journal and Courier.* Wednesday Morning, Feb. 8, 1882. [Nameplate and article merged, 1982 approximate.] Courtesy Hearst Connecticut Media New Haven Group. KCMA kc20120412lj18.

Underwood & Underwood. Immigrants just arrived, awaiting examination, Ellis Island, New York harbor, 1870-1920 approximate. Library of Congress 2017660810.

William Thomas Minor, 1889 approximate. Stamford Historical Society. Wikipedia File:William T. Minor.jpg.

**12.** An Unprofitable Church. *New York Times,* 28 Jul 1870 [photocopy]. Collection 0003, St.

Mary's Church Collection, KCSCA. [Scanned and laid out by the Knights of Columbus, 1982 approximate.] KCMA kc20120417lj10.

Mother Seton. Library of Congress. https://lccn.loc.gov/2003677120 (accessed 16 September 2019).

R.T. Sperry. *Homeless and Friendless*, 1891. Library of Congress 2012647169.

13. De Silva, New Haven. St. Mary's Church, 1880-1890 approximate. [Color added, 1982 approximate.] KCMA kc20120417lj12.

*The Freethinker's Magazine*, Vol. IX, No. 6, June E.M. 291. Frederick Douglass Papers at the Library of Congress. https://www.loc.gov/item/mfd.41008/ (accessed 10 September 2019).

James Mahony. *The scene at Skibbereen, west Cork, in 1847*. Commissioned by *Illustrated London News*, 1847. Wikipedia File:Skibbereen_by_James_Mahony,_1847.JPG (accessed 10 September 2019).

14. Collection 0005, Bogus Oath Collection, KCSCA.

"No Irish need apply." Written by John F. Poole. Library of Congress, Rare Books and Special Collections Division, America Singing: Nineteenth-Century Song Sheets. https://www.loc.gov/item/amss.as109730 (accessed 25 September 2019).

Thomas Nast. *The American River Ganges*, 1871. Library of Congress 2004670394.

Thomas Nast. *Fact and Fiction*. Catholic League for Religious and Civil Rights. https://www.catholicleague.org/thomas-nast-cartoons/ (accessed 25 September 2019).

Thomas Nast. "The Promised land," as seen from the dome of Saint Peter's Rome, Harper's Weekly, 1 October 1870. Library of Congress 2010644044.

Grant E. Hamilton. *Where the Blame Lies*, 4 April 1891. Sackett & Wilhelms Litho. Co. Library of Congress 97515495.

15. Cornelius T. Driscoll, 1890-1899 approximate. KCMA kc20120412lj02.

Archbishop John McCloskey. Library of Congress pnp/cwpbh/01600/01643v.jpg (accessed 9/10/19).

J.J. Barralet, delineator; Geo. S. Lang engraver. *The First Landing of Columbus in the New World*, 1876. Library of Congress 2006678646.

16. McGivney homestead, Waterbury, Conn, 1960-1969 approximate. KCMA 20130703amo015.

Young Michael McGivney graduation, with classmates, 1870-1879 approximate. [Color added at unknown date.] KCMA kc20120410lj12.

17. John J. Tierney. Father Michael McGivney with fellow priests, 1870-1879 approximate. KCMA kc20120410lj16.

John J. Tierney. Father Michael McGivney, 1870-1879 approximate. KCMA kc20120410lj04.

18. Charter. San Salvador Council No. 1, 1882. KCM. KCMA kc20120412lj20.

Charter of the Knights of Columbus Granted by the General Assembly of the State of Connecticut, 29 Mar 1882. [Believed to be copied in 1982.] Collection 0001, Early History of the Knights of Columbus Collection, KCSCA. KCMA kc20120412lj19.

1897 Supreme Council meeting. KCMA kc20120222ts06.

19. James T. Mullen. [Color added, 1982 approximate.] KCMA kc20120417lj05.

Lewis Wickes Hine. Mrs. Streety (a widow) and her family, West Point, Mississippi, May 1911. Library of Congress 2018676469.

Guilimus Peraldus. Detail of Harleian ms. 3244, folios 27-28, allegorical knight. Wikimedia File:Peraldus Knight.jpg.

20. Sebastiano del Piombo. Portrait of a Man, Said to be Christopher Columbus (born about 1446, died 1506). 1519. Wikipedia File:Portrait of a Man, Said to be Christopher Columbus.jpg.

Rafael Monleon y Torres. *The three caravels of Christopher Columbus*, 1885. DEA/G.Dagli Orti. GettyImages-1056684480.

21. Knights of Columbus emblem.

Father Michael McGivney. Ledger of parish duties. SCA.

Scott Funk Hershey, et al. "Romanism at Washington." *Errors of the Roman Catholic Church: And Its Insidious Influence in the United States and Other Countries by the Most Profound Thinkers of the Present Day, and the History and Progress of the American Protective Association (A.P.A.)*. St. Louis: J.H. Chambers, 1894; photo plate between pp. x and xi.[cartoon]. Wikipedia https://en.wikipedia.org/wiki/File:94-RomanismAtWashington.jpg (accessed 19 September 2019).

22. J. M. Vickroy. Membership record [lithograph]. Courtesy of Rudy Shur.

23. Delegates to the 24th National Convention pause for a rest stop aboard the train, 1905 [cropped]. KCMA kc20120222lj04.

24. Andrew Walther. Knights of Columbus rosary. Courtesy the Walther family.

State of Rhode Island Seal. Wikipedia https://commons.wikimedia.org/wiki/File:Seal_of_Rhode_Island.svg (accessed 11 November 2019).

Francesca Cabrini. Wikimedia File:Francesca Cabrini.

25. *Columbia*, August 1925. KC.

26. Knights of Columbus. James McMullen Death Benefit Payment Receipt, [sic] Oct 1891. Record Group 0020, Office of Supreme Knight Records, KCSCA. KCMA kc20120417lj25.

St. Francis Orphanage. Courtesy the New Haven Museum. Dana Coll., v. 44, p. 57.

Pope Leo XIII. Wikipedia File:PapaleoXIII.jpg.

27. Caulfield & Shook. Knights of Columbus Secretaries Camp Zachary Taylor, Ky., October 8, 1918. KCMA 20130207amo021.

28. *The Columbiad*, November 1883. The Columbiad Publishing Company.

*The Columbiad*, October 1893; April 1894; May 1917. The Columbiad Publishing Company.

29. *The Columbiad*, August 1921. The Columbiad Publishing Company.

*Columbia*, December 1924; June, 1944; January 1968; September 2018. KC.

30. John T. Phelan, 1890-1899 approximate. KCMA kc20120417lj28.

Columbus Day badge, 1892 [cropped image]. National Museum of American History 2006.0098.0705. https://americanhistory.si.edu/collections/search/object/nmah_1325875 (accessed 10 September 2019).

U.S. Flag, 1891-1896. Wikipedia File:Flag of the United States (1891Г̧ô1896).svg.

31. Knights of Columbus Insurance Record, 1882-1901, Council Nos. 1 - 127, ledger. Collection 0001, Early History of the Knights of Columbus Collection, KCSCA.

Daniel Colwell, 1890-1899 approximate. KCMA kc20120412lj01.

22. E. J. Kilmer. St. Thomas Church [Thomaston, Connecticut], 1890-1899 approximate, KCMA, kc20120413lj25.

M. Warner. Hospital ward, 9 November 1898. Library of Congress 2016697221.

33, 34. Father Michael J. McGivney memorial card, 1982 [recto, verso]. KC.

35. J. M. Vickroy. Membership record [lithograph]. Courtesy of Rudy Shur.

*Columbia*, July 1932. KC.

36. Thomas Cummings, 1900-1910 approximate. KCMA 20130726amo012.

El Paso Council degree team, May 1903. KCMA 20130725amo001.

Knights of Columbus emblem.

## Chapter 3. Taking Root, Expansion, and the War Effort—1897 to 1919

38. Mole & Thomas. K of C formed by officers, men & camp activity workers at Camp Wheeler, Ga., [K of C Every Body Welcome]

1918. KCMA 20130717amo014.

**39.** James E. Hayes, 1890-1899 approximate. KCMA kc20120417lj32.

John Cone, 1890-1899 approximate. KCMA kc20120417lj40.

**40.** Edward L. Hearn, 1900-1910 approximate. KCMA kc20120417lj42.

Grand exemplification of the Fourth Degree, 22 February 1900, New York City. KCMA kc20120302lj01.

**41.** Fourth Degree, port swords, 1906. KCMA 20140612AAM021.

Fourth Degree. KC.

Fourth Degree uniform, 2017. [Edited image.] KCMA 20170807kc001.

Montreal coat of arms. Wikipedia File:Coat_of_arms_of_Montreal.svg.

David Parks Fackler. Sourced from "Empire State Notables, 1914" p. 344. https://www.flickr.com/photos/internetarchivebookimages/14596842820/in/photostream (accessed 5 September 2019).

**42.** John H. Reddin, 1910-1919 approximate. KCMA 20130705amo001.

La séparation. Allegory of the French Law of Separation of Church and State (1905). Wikimedia File:La séparation.jpg.

San Xavier Mission, Tucson, Arizona [postcard]. Courtesy the Walther family.

**43.** Fourth Degree Knights of Columbus emblem.

United States Geological Survey. Downtown North Topeka, Kansas, flood, 1903. https://www.usgs.gov/media/images/north-topeka-ks-down-town-flooded-street-and-buildings-1903 (accessed 5 September 2019).

G.V. Buck. Presentation of $50,000 check to The Catholic University of America, Washington, D.C., for the establishment of a chair in American history at the university, 1904. KCMA kc20120224ts29.

**44.** Star Photo Co. Supreme Council, St. Louis, Mo., 1908 [cropped]. KCMA kc20150416ts17.

Nevada. Public domain, Square One Publishers.

Fourth Supreme Headquarters, Chapel Street, New Haven, 1900-1910 approximate [cropped]. KCMA kc20120215ts11.

**45.** Father Patrick J. McGivney, 1900-1910 approximate. KCMA kc20120405lj05.

Mexico flag. Public domain, Square One Publishers.

Degree team for Havana, 1909. KCMA 20130703amo001.

**46.** Arnold Genthe. Sacramento Street, San Francisco, earthquake damage and fire, 1906.

Wikipedia File:San Francisco Fire Sacramento Street 1906-04-18.jpg.

William Howard Taft. Library of Congress 2001698190.

Notre Dame Council No. 1477, 1910. Courtesy of the University of Notre Dame Archives. KCMA 20100311ndu05.

**47.** Christmas tree in post gym, Fort Sheridan, Ill., 1918 [cropped]. KCMA 20130717amo016.

San Antonio Council baseball team, 1916. KCMA 20130712amo005.

**48.** Rochester Council clothes collection for Near East Relief, 1923. Near East Relief Historical Society, Near East Foundation Archives, Rockefeller Archive Center. KCMA 19230606nehs.

Connie Mack, 1911. Bain News Service, Library of Congress 2014689847.

**49.** *The Columbiad,* May 1907. The Columbiad Publishing Company.

**50.** Carol Highsmith. Christopher Columbus statue and fountain outside the entrance to the Union Station train terminal, Washington, D.C., 2011. Carol M. Highsmith Archive. Library of Congress 2011633286.

Columbus Memorial unveiling, 8 June 1912. KCMA 20140124amo005.

**51.** Grand Banquet Commemorating the Unveiling of the Christopher Columbus Memorial, Convention Hall, Washington, D.C., Saturday, June the Eighth, 1912, program [image cropped]. Collection 0103,Christopher Columbus Collection, KCSCA.

Unveiling of the Columbus Memorial, Saturday, June 8, 1912, Washington, D.C., 1912, program. Collection 0103, Christopher Columbus Collection, KCSCA.

*The Columbiad,* July 1912. The Columbiad Publishing Company.

**52.** Liberty Printing Company, Shall Romanism Control Us?

An Alledged [sic] Oath Taken by Knights of Columbus

Liberty Printing Company, Dying Like Christ

William Lloyd Clark, When Al Smith is President

William Lloyd Clark, Genuine Roman Catholicism

William Lloyd Clark, The Coils are Tightening, undated. Collection 0005, Bogus Oath Collection, KCSCA.

**53.** Donnelly Studio. James A. Flaherty, 1910-1919 approximate. [Color added at an unknown date.] KCMA 20130726amo019.

*The Menace* [newspaper]. KCMA 20130703amo007.

*The Birth of a Nation* [poster]. Courtesy Rudy Shur.

**54.** Knights of Columbus Commission on Religious Prejudices, Report of Commission on Religious Prejudices, Aug 1916. Collection 0108, Supreme Convention Collection, KCSCA.

John Singer Sargent. Theodore Roosevelt, 1903. The White House Historical Association (White House Collection). Wikipedia File: Troosevelt.jpeg.

Travelling card, Edward J. Youngfleisch, 27 Aug 1921. Collection 0111, Membership Collection, KCSCA.

**55.** Knights of Columbus hut, Laredo, Texas,1916 approximate. KCMA 20130729amo012.

**56.** J.C. Hemment. K of C and guests, Notre Dame Cathedral, Paris. 1918-1919 approximate. Knights of Columbus War Activities in France and Belgium [photo album], 1918-1919 approximate. KCMA 20121102amo076.

Pvt. John "Jack" Quinn letter to Margaret Biwer, 1 Apr 1918; Pvt. John "Jack" Quinn letter to Margaret Biwer, 1 May 1919; Knights of Columbus, Writing to the Folks at Home, postcard, undated. Collection 0008, World War I Collection, KCSCA.

**57.** *Columbia,* September 1917.

*New York Herald* [cropped], 2 July 1918. Courtesy of the LA84 Foundation Library. KCMA 20121102amo076.

**58.** Frank Goodman, Arthur & Lawrence Franklin, The Hut of the K. of C., 1918. Collection 0008, World War I Collection, KCSCA.

John Plunkett. Longacre Hut, 1918. Courtesy of the Museum of the City of New York X2010.11.3985. KCMA 20130729amo014.

Camp Gordon clubhouse, writing room, 1918-1919 approximate. KCMA 20130717amo012.

Military Park, Indianapolis, Welcome Home Day. 1919 approximate. Courtesy Indiana State Library. KCMA 20130717amo017.

An early Sunday Mass, 1918 [postcard]. KCMA 20130729amo011.

E.S. Brooke. Soldiers outside K of C hut, Andernach, Germany, 1919. Knights of Columbus war activities with the Army of Occupation, Germany [photo album], 1919. KCMA kc20110715lj31.

**59.** Campbell, J.S., Private. Servicemen waiting in line for free cigarettes and sweets from the K of C, 1919 Nov 9. National Archives and Records Administration 111-SC-32925. KCMA 20130725amo024.

Percy Wenrich. John B. Kennedy. Casey : (K.C.), 1919. Collection 0008, World War I Collection, KCSCA.

Signal Corps. K of C canteen travels with troops, Juvigny, France, 1918. National Archives and Records Administration 111-SC-21372. KCMA 20130725amo027.

Sears, R.W., Lieutenant. Secretary J.F. ["Uncle Joe"] Kernan giving wounded refugee some chocolate, Saint-Pierre, France, 7 November 1918. National Archives and Records Administration 111-SC-153601. KCMA 20130725amo020.

J.C. Hemment. During Argonne drives hundreds of wounded were men brought to K of C relief station furnished with soup, hot chocolate by Secretaries Le Sage, Oates, Tone and Lennon, 1918. Knights of Columbus War Activities in France and Belgium [photo album], 1918-1919 approximate. KCMA 20121102amo065.

**60.** William Balfour Ker for the Division of Pictorial Publicity. Knights of Columbus Three Million War Fund [poster], 1917. KCM.

**61.** Sweeney Sign Painting Co., New York City, for the Division of Pictorial Publicity. New York Catholic War Camp Fund and the Knights of Columbus [poster], 1918. KCM.

**62.** Joyce Kilmer. Wikimedia File:Joyce_Kilmer.jpg.

J. C. Hemment. K of C "Happy Family," Cora Youngblood Corson Instrumentalists, Bourg, 1919. Knights of Columbus War Activities in France and Belgium [photo album], 1918-1919 approximate. KCMA 20121107amo206.

E. S. Brooks. Cooks prepare doughnuts in K of C bakery, 1919, Koblenz, Germany. KCMA kc20110718lj56.

**63.** SK Flaherty was decorated by Secretary of War Newton D. Baker with the Distinguished Service Medal in recognition of the war work undertaken by the K of C in WWI, 1919. KCMA 20130422amo009.

J.C. Hemment. Mass at the Lourdes Grotto, 1918-1919 approximate. Knights of Columbus War Activities in France and Belgium [photo album], 1918-1919 approximate. KCMA 20121106amo137.

Company A, 31st Infantry, A.E.F. Siberian Expedition, on a practice hike near Vladivostok-Siberia. Note the K of C "rolling kitchen" pulled by a four-line American mule team. 1919 approximate. National Archives and Records Administration. KCMA 20130422amo002.

**64.** Father William Davitt. Courtesy of the College of the Holy Cross Archives. KCMA 20151021chc001.

J. C. Hemment. Cardinal Mercier and William Mulligan, 1918. Knights of Columbus War Activities in France and Belgium [photo album],

1918-1919 approximate. KCMA 20121106amo184. Knights of Columbus emblem.

**65.** Knights of Columbus emblem [1918]. Western Union Telegram. Longacre employment bureau, 1919 approximate. KCMA 20130729amo015.

**66.** Schoolroom, 1920-1929 approximate. Public domain, Square One Publishers.

**Chapter 4. In Search of Liberty—1920 to 1929**

**67.** J. C. Hemment. Old English tank Benbow [Edward Hearn, William Larkin], 1918. Knights of Columbus War Activities in France and Belgium [photo album], 1918-1919 approximate. KCMA 20121102amo010.

Poland. Bookkeeping Class, Knights of Columbus Free Night School, Memphis, Tennessee, 1919. KCMA 20130207amo003.

**68.** M. Branger, Photographie Paris. General Lafayette equestrian statue unveiling, Metz, France, 21 August 1920. Pilgrimage to Metz and Rome Photographs, 1920. KCMA 20130620gew008.

**22.** Count Enrico Galeazzi. [Cropped image.] KCMA 20130723amo013.

Felici. Pope Pius XI. KCMA 20130508amo007.

Felici. Mass in the Vatican Gardens, August 1920. Pilgrimage to Metz and Rome Photographs, 1920. KCMA 20170721amo021.

Fabbri. St. Peter's Oratory with view of the dome, 1925. KCMA 20130819amo002.

**70.** Boys playing [soccer] on Valle Giulia field that is ringed with spectators, 1927 approx. KCMA 20130819amo010.

**71.** Brother Barnabus. KCMA 20130705amo006.

Columbian Squires Circle No. 1, 1925, Duluth, Minnesota. KCMA 20130705amo002.

John H. Reddin. KCMA 20130705amo001.

Boy Scout emblem. Public domain, Square One Publishers.

**72.** Brother Florence. Boy Leadership Training Class, 1925, South Bend, Indiana. KCMA 20130729amo028.

Boy Leadership Class, 1924. KCMA 0140130amo008.

National Photo Company Collection. Ku Klux Klan Parade, Northern Virginia, 1922. Library of Congress File:Ku_Klux_Klan_Virgina_1922_Parade.jpg.

**73.** Irwin, La Broad, & Pudlin. Babe Ruth, 23 July 1920. Library of Congress. Wikipedia File:Babe_Ruth2.jpg.

Ernest Bihler, Co. Lou Gehrig and Babe Ruth visit Father Flanagan's Boys Town, 1927. KCMA 20150826gew001.

**74.** *The Birth of a Nation* [poster]. Courtesy Rudy Shur.

Arthur H. Bell, The Ku Klux Klan or The Knights of Columbus Klan, [1921]. Collection 0005, Bogus Oath Collection, KCSCA. Rail Splitter Press. KCMA 20130703amo009.

**75.** K of K vs K of C: Knights of the Klan versus Knights of Columbus, [1924]. Collection 0004, Anti-Catholicism, KCSCA.

Pope Pius XI. Wikimedia. https://upload.wikimedia.org/wikipedia/commons/0/04/Pius_XI_after_Coronation.jpg (accessed 9 September 2019).

Cardinal Gibbons Institute students, 1920-1929 approximate. Courtesy St. Mary's County (Maryland) Historical Society.

**76.** Carol M. Highsmith (photographer). Painting: *Columbus Coming Ashore* at the University of Notre Dame, a Catholic research university located in Notre Dame, an unincorporated community north of the city of South Bend, in St. Joseph County, Indiana. October 2012. Photographs in the Carol M. Highsmith Archive, Library of Congress, Prints and Photographs Division. Library of Congress 2013650754.

United Newspapers. Presenting a check for $25,000 for Japanese relief, 17 September 1923. KCMA 20130715amo041.

**77.** Knights of Columbus. Bogus Oath reward [working draft], 1928. Collection 0005, Bogus Oath Collection, KCSCA.

**78.** Father James Edwin Coyle. Wikipedia File:Father-coyle.jpg.

Texas Catholic Historical Society. Texas Knights of Columbus Historical Commission. Preliminary Studies of the Texas Catholic Historical Society, Mar 1930. Record Group 0003, Historical Commission (1916-1925) Collection, KCSCA.

Columbian Squires emblem.

**79.** Classroom. Public domain, Square One Publishers.

The U.S. Supreme Court in 1925. Library of Congress 2008675031.

**80.** Harris & Ewing. Alfred E. Smith. Library of Congress digital ID hec.21487. Wikimedia File:AlfredSmith.jpg.

Acme Newspapers, Inc. Supreme Knight James Flaherty and Supreme Treasurer Daniel Callahan present resolutions to Secretary of State Frank Kellogg, 1926. KCMA 20130715amo038.

Babe Ruth. Library of Congress 2017657369.

**81.** Edward McSweeney. Public domain, Square One Publishers.

Edward F. McSweeney. Knights of Columbus Historical Commission. The Racial Contribution to the United States, booklet, circa 1923. Record Group 0003, Historical Commission (1916-1925) Collection, KCSCA.

Addison N. Scurlock. W.E.B. Du Bois, 1911 approximate. National Portrait Gallery. Wikipedia File:Motto_web_dubois_original.jpg.

Jim Thorpe, New York, 1913. Bain Collection. Library of Congress 2014692176.

**82.** Racial Contributions Series. KCMA 20130207amo004.

Yale University. Samuel Bemis. 1970 approximate. KCMA 20150828gew003.

Fabbria. Classroom, St. Peter's Oratory, 1924 approximate. KCMA 20121231amo001.

M. Branger Photographie Paris. Supreme Knight Flaherty lays a wreath at the memorial cross, Chambierer Cemetery, Metz, France, August 1920. Pilgrimage to Metz and Rome Photographs, 1920. KCMA 20130612gew004.

**83.** Carlos E. Castañeda. Paul J. Folk. Texas Knights of Columbus Historical Commission. Our Catholic Heritage in Texas, 1519-1936, 1936. General Library Collection, KCSCA.

**84.** Margaret Sanger. Bain Collection. Library of Congress 2014703841.

**85.** International News Reel. San Francisco Avenue, Mexico City scene of strife between State and Church, 1926. KCMA 20130627amo003.

**86.** Martha Orozco, painter. Knights of Columbus Martyrs of Mexico, 2005. KCM. © Martha Orozoco.

Father Francisco Vera, shot by Mexico Army soldiers, 1927. KCMA 20181012amo077.

**87.** Carmen Quintanilla Vertiz. Virgin of Guadalupe, late 20th century. On loan courtesy of the Knights of Columbus in Mexico. KCM.

Discussion of the persecution of Catholics in Mexico with President Coolidge, Paul Smiths in the Adirondacks, N.Y., 1 September 1926 [edited image]. KCMA 20130705amo011.

**88.** Saint Rafael Guizar Valencia. http://www.vatican.va/news_services/liturgy/saints/ns_lit_doc_20061015_valencia_photo.html (accessed 10 September 2019).

Acme Newspapers. Supreme Knight Flaherty, 1926 [cropped]. KCMA 20130715amo043

Knights of Columbus emblem.

**89.** Harris & Ewing. Martin H. Carmody. KCMA 201309010amo003.

**Chapter 5. Helping Our Neighbors, The Great Depression—1930 to 1939**

**90.** Unemployed men queued outside a depression soup kitchen opened in Chicago by Al Capone, February 1931. Rolls Press/Popperfoto via Getty Images. https://www.gettyimages.com/detail/news-photo/unemployed-men-line-up-outside-a-great-depression-era-soup-news-photo/615307766 (accessed 22 October 2019).

**91.** Wall Street, 1929. Public domain, Square One Publishers.

Casti Connubi. Public domain, Square One Publishers.

**92.** Bowery men waiting for bread in breadline, New York City. Bain Collection. Library of Congress. Wikimedia https://commons.wikimedia.org/wiki/File:Bowery_men_waiting_for_bread_in_bread_line,_New_York_City,_Bain_Collection.jpg (accessed 9 September 2019).

**93.** Unemployment benefit aid begins. Farm Security Administration, Office of War Information Photograph Collection. Library of Congress 2017770698.

Knights of Columbus. Charity Football Game, 25 January 1931[program cover]. Courtesy of the Walther family.

International Newsreel. K of C Correspondence School. KCMA 20130726amo001.

Dorothea Lange. Son of depression refugee from Oklahoma now in California. Farm Security Administration, Office of War Information Photograph Collection. Library of Congress 2017763222.

**94.** Russell Lee. Mexican beet workers, near Fisher, Minnesota. Farm Security Administration, Office of War Information Photograph Collection. Library of Congress 2017736253.

**95.** Robinson Studio. Supreme Knight Martin Carmody with past supreme knights, 1932, Washington, D.C. KCMA 20130815amo009.

**96.** SK Carmody receives high honors from the Pope, 1931. KCMA 20130718amo004.

**97.** Advertisement for Golden Anniversary radio address [cropped]. Columbia, July 1932, p. 26. KC.

Kurz & Allison. *George Washington at Mt. Vernon* [lithograph]. Library of Congress 97503087.

**98.** Cardinal James Gibbons. Wikipedia File:James_Gibbons.jpg.

Unveiling of the Cardinal Gibbons Memorial, 1932. KCMA 20130717amo033.

Pay bonus stamp, 1932. Wikipedia File:USA-Cinderella-Stamp-1932_Pay_the_Bonus.jpg.

**99.** Cardinal James Gibbons statue, 1990-1999 approximate. KCMA 20130717amo034.

**100.** Unveiling of the Cardinal Gibbons Memorial, Invitation, 14 Aug 1932. Record Group 0008, James Cardinal Gibbons Memorial Statue Records, KCSCA.

Unveiling of Memorial to the late James Cardinal Gibbons, Program, 14 Aug 1932. Record Group 0008, James Cardinal Gibbons Memorial Statue Records, KCSCA.

**101.** N.C.W.C. News Service. Bishops Advance Crusade against Indecent Movies. 19 April 1934, *Catholic Transcript* (Hartford, Connecticut), Volume XXXVI, Number 46. [Cropped image.] Catholic Research Resources Alliance, The Catholic News Archive (accessed 25 September 2019).

Franklin Delano Roosevelt. Wikipedia File:FDR_in_1933.jpg.

**102.** Empire State Building. Public domain, Square One Publishers.

Arthur Rothstein. Wheat field Maryland. Farm Security Agency, Office of War Information. Library of Congress 2017776026.

**103.** Film Booking Company. Myles Connolly. Wikipedia File:Myles_Connolly.jpg.

**104.** Cardinal Eugenio Pacelli is welcomed to the Knights of Columbus office, New Haven, Connecticut, 1936. KCMA 20130705amo013.

**105.** Secretary of State Hull meets with the Knights of Columbus, 21 January 1935. AP Images 542113167238. KCMA 20130705amo014.

Nogales, Arizona, Knights bring Christmas necessities to families across the border, 1936. KCMA kc20120229lj21.

**106.** Ronald Reagan with family, 1916-1997. Ronald Reagan Library. Wikimedia File:Ronald_Reagan_with_family_1916-17.jpg.

**107.** Departure of Columbus, 1883. Library of Congress 2003679746.

Pope Pius XI. Wikipedia File:Pope_Pius_XI.jpg.

**108.** *Columbia*, July 1936, p. 3. KC.

**109.** Aubin's Photos. Blood drive, Hibbing, Minnesota [cropped]. KCMA 20130827amo022

German troops. Public domain, Square One Publishers.

**110.** *Encyclical letter of His Holiness Pius XI (Divini Redemptoris) Atheistic Communism*, Issued March 19, 1937, 1937. Collection 0007, Anti-Communism, KCSCA. Atheistic Communism [cover]. KCMA 20130703amo022.

Anderson Photo Company. Prayer for Peace broadcast, 11 November 1939. KCMA 20130705amo021.

Knights of Columbus emblem.

**111.** Francis P. Matthews. KCMA 20140812aam022.

**Chapter 6. War and Peace—1940 to 1950**

**112.** World War II soldier. Public domain, Square One Publishers.

113. *Columbia,* December 1939. KC.

C. V. Maxwell. K of C hostel, Halifax, Nova Scotia, 1939-1945 approximate. KCMA 20130701amo011

Ozone Park (N.Y.) Council No. 197 member donating blood to Red Cross blood bank, 1940-1949 approximate. KCMA 20130708amo010.

114. Claude Brown. *Columbia,* August 1930, p. 22. KC.

Ewing Galloway. Our Lady of Guadalupe Shrine, 1941, Mexico City, Mexico. KCMA 20180410amo024.

USS Shaw exploding in Pearl Harbor, 7 December 1941. National Archives and Records Administration. Wikipedia File:USS_SHAW_exploding_Pearl_Harbor_N ara_80-G-16871_2.jpg.

115. Jeanne-Mance clubhouse, Montreal, Quebec, June 1941. KCMA 20130709amo010.

Knights of Columbus canteen serving headquarters, 1st Canadian Army, 23 September 1943. Public Archives Canada/DND No. 24316. KCMA 20130701amo031.

Canadian Legion erected this replica of the Canadian Army Hut, Flin Flon, Manitoba, 1940. KCMA 20130708amo014.

*La Crosse Tribune.* (Wisconsin). Lending a hand at the USO center Sunday was Francis Matthews, chairman of NCCS, 21 February 1944. Courtesy the LaCrosse Tribune. KCMA 20130909amo003.

Winchester (Massachusetts) Council No. 210 work in their Victory Garden for the Sisters of St. Joseph, 1939-1945 approximate. KCMA 20130827amo038.

116. United Service Organizations campaign for $10,765,000 fund, 1941. KCMA 20130701amo007.

This picture, captured from the Japanese, shows American prisoners using improvised litters to carry those of their comrades who, from the lack of food or water on the march from Bataan, fell along the road. Philippines, May 1942. https://en.wikipedia.org/wiki/ Bataan_Death_March#/media/File:Ww2_131 .jpg (accessed 9 September 2019).

23-year-old Czech victim of dysentery in Nazi camp at Flossenburg, Germany, 4 May 1945. Signal Corps, U.S. Army. Library of Congress 2001696922.

117. Bishop Malloy Council No. 1874 hosts a blood donation event, 1947. KCMA 20130708amo002.

Blood bank collection, 29 May 1943, Dearborn, Mich. KCMA 20130725amo006.

Mass kit for the Naval Hospital at Oakland, California, from Council No. 784, 1939-1945 approx. KCMA 20130826amo010.

Christmas gifts for Council No. 733 members who are serving in the armed forces, 18 November 1942. KCMA 20130708amo019.

118. Knights of Columbus War Bond Headquarters, 1940 approximate, Rochester, N.Y. KCMA 20130701amo012.

"He won't dodge this ..." [war bonds advertisement]. *Columbia,* June 1944, p. 23. KC.

Verkin Studio. K of C class dedicated to men in Armed Forces, Galveston, Texas, 1943 approximate. KCMA 20130909amo023.

Office of War Information, Overseas Picture Division. Washington Division. Construction of a Liberty ship at Bethlehem-Fairfield Shipyards Inc., 1944, Baltimore, Maryland. Library of Congress File:Liberty_ship_construction_03_keel_plates.jpg.

22. Buy War Bonds [poster]. Courtesy of Rudy Shur.

120. Drucker-Hilbert Co. Knights of Columbus Peace Program committee meeting with clergy, 1943, New York, N.Y. KCMA 20130701amo029.

Andrzej Pitynski, sculptor; Eleanor Lang, photographer. Katyn Memorial. Wikimedia File:This_is_a_memorial,_located_in_Jersey_C ity,_New_Jersey,_commemorating_the_Katyn_ massacre_of_1940-_Eleanor_Lang_is_the_photographer-_2013-11-11_14-15.jpg.

John Vachon. Bob Aden and his wife, Marion, on graduation day, May 1942, University of Nebraska, Lincoln. Farm Security Administration, Office of War Information Collection. Library of Congress. https://www.loc.gov/ item/2017831532/ (accessed 9 September 2019).

121. *Columbia,* June 1942. KC.

*Columbia,* October 1945. KC.

122. Luce. Pope Pius XII leads the San Lorenzo district in prayer, 1943. KC.

L'Osservatore Romano. Pope Pius XII, Count Galeazzi and unidentified cardinal at Board meeting, 1961. Courtesy L'Osservatore Romano. KCMA 201309010amo011.

Artillery shell fragments. KCM. Gift of the Knights of Columbus Rome Office.

123. Georges Dimitri Boria. Food distribution in Rome, 1947. United Nations Relief and Rehabilitation Agency.

Pope Pius XII, To His Excellency Franklin Delano Roosevelt, 30 Aug 1943. Courtesy of the Count Enrico Galeazzi Papers [sic], KCSCA.

124. Father George Willmann. KCMA 20130726amo006.

Greta Kempton, painter. Presidential portrait of Harry S. Truman. Harry S. Truman Library. Wikipedia File:HarryTruman.jpg.

Manila Council No. 1000 Third Degree initiation, 27 April 1947, Cebu Center, Philippines. KCMA 201309011amo005

125. Ben Steele, artist. Giving a sick man a drink as U.S. P.O.W.s of Japanese, Philippine Islands, Cabanatuan prison camp [sketch]. © 1946. Library of Congress 98501808.

126. U.S. Navy. Navy Secretary Francis P. Matthews Inspects Treasure Island in California, 17 May 1951. 70-3358. Harry S. Truman Library.

Pope Pius XII, 1939 [sketch]. Ambrosius007 contribution to Wikipedia. https://commons.wikimedia.org/wiki/File:Pope_Pius_XI I_-_unwanted_portrait_1939.jpg (accessed 9 September 2019).

United Nations emblem. Public domain, Square One Publishers.

127. Father George Willmann, SJ, 1950-1959 approximate. KCMA 20151028amo006.

128. Vince Natale, painter. Father Isaias X. Edralin, SJ. Courtesy of Vince Natale.

129. Winston Churchill, 1945 approximate. Public domain, Square One Publishers.

St. Peter's Excavations [graphic created using Eternal Film Corporation film screen shots, 2019]. Knights of Columbus.

130. John E. Swift. KCMA 20130708amo032.

President Truman signs the Truman Doctrine, 1947. Public domain, SquareOne Publishers.

Arthur S. Siegel. Royal Oak, Michigan. A family listening to the radio and reading Father Coughlin's newspaper *Social Justice,* December, 1939. Library of Congress https://www.loc.gov/item/2017844938/ (accessed 9 September 2019).

131. Bob Sandberg. Jackie Robinson at bat, 1954. *LOOK* magazine Photograph Collection. Library of Congress. https://www.loc.gov/ pictures/item/97518921/ (accessed 9 September 2019).

Gerry Kisters, Congressional Medal of Honor and Distinguished Service Cross recipient, joins Council No. 1096, Bloomington, Indiana. KCMA 20130823amo001.

132. Abbie Rowe. President Truman signs the North Atlantic Treaty Organization, 24 August 1949. Harry S. Truman Library, National Archives and Records Administration and Records Administration (200163). Wikipedia File:Truman_ signing_the_North_Atlantic_Treaty.gif.

Knights of Columbus emblem.

## Chapter 7. "One Nation Under God"—1951 to 1964

134. American flag. Public domain, Square One Publishers.

**135.** F-86 Sabre. Wikipedia https://commons.wikimedia.org/wiki/File:F86F_Sabres_-Chino_Airshow_2014_(cropped).jpg (accessed 19 November 2019).

U.S. Army Signal Corps. General Mark Clark, 1943. Library of Congress cph.3a49989.

**136.** Walter Sanders. Luke Hart in Yankee Stadium, 1953. *LIFE* magazine/Getty Images. KCMA kc20120227ts12.

Aerial view of Yankee baseball stadium. https://www.123rf.com/stock-photo/yankee_stadium.html?oriSearch=yankee+syadium&imgtype=1&sti=o0i0c8l29heh99ihlf%7C&mediapopup=1826967 (accessed 18 September 2019).

Dwight D. Eisenhower, official photo portrait, 29 May 1959. Eisenhower Presidential Library. Wikipedia File:Dwight_D._Eisenhower,_official_photo_portrait,_May_29,_1959.jpg.

Paul R. Cramer. Cardinal Spellman luncheon, Supreme Convention, Los Angeles, California, 1952 [cropped]. KCMA kc20120221lj28.

**137.** Edwin St. Louis. Luke E. Hart. KCMA 20130806amo004.

Columbus School of Law (Dulles Mansion). The American Catholic History Research Center and University Archives, The Catholic University of America, Washington, D.C.

Exemplification of the 4th Degree under the direction of Master John McDevitt, May 1954. KCMA 20130729amo001.

**138.** Supreme Knight John Swift checks the membership pin of Dr. John Chang Myon, Supreme Convention. 17 August 1950, New York, N.Y. KCMA 20130729amo034.

Gatso. Supreme Knight Hart celebrates the Philippines fiftieth anniversary with the Knights in Manila, 1955. KCMA 20130809amo030.

Gift to the Catholic Hierarchy of Bolivia, December, 1956. KCMA 20130709amo001.

**139.** Vincent A. Finnigan. Supreme Knight Luke Hart visits President Eisenhower after a Columbus Day ceremony at the Columbus Memorial, 1953. White House photograph. KCMA 20130709amo009.

In God We Trust plaque. Public domain, Square One Publishers.

*Columbia,* January 1951. KC.

**140.** States Dinner, Supreme Council, 1955. KCMA 20130603amo001.

Jim Phelan. Supreme Knight Hart meets some of the children at the Knights of Columbus Research Center at the Joseph P. Kennedy Memorial Hospital, 1958. KCMA 20130809amo021.

Build an Estate [advertisement]. *Columbia,* July 1958, p. 49. KC.

**141.** Blessed Carlos M. Rodriguez. Wikipedia File:CarlosRodriguezSantiago1.jpg.

Franco Origlia/Getty Images. Beatification ceremony in St. Peter's Square. https://www.gettyimages.com/detail/news-photo/vatican-april-29-2001-beatification-ceremony-in-st-peters-news-photo/1174120548?adppopup=true (accessed 19 September 2019).

**142.** Workers at the Knights of Columbus Religious Information Bureau. KCMA 20130709amo011.

Foto Attualita Giordani. Visit of His Holiness Pope John XXIII to [St. Peter's] Oratory, 10 May 1959. Courtesy of L'Osservatore Romano. KCMA 20130111amo010.

Knights of Columbus, Religious Information Bureau, Why Catholics Believe as They Do, 1955. Collection 0021, Religious Information Bureau/Catholic Information Service Collection, KCSCA.

**143.** Artega Photos. Reverend Lowrie Daly and Charles Ermatinger study one of the new rolls of film, 1956. Courtesy of Artega Photos. KCMA 20130628amo001.

Hungarian uprising: Cardinal Mindszenty after his liberation. https://www.gettyimages.com/detail/news-photo/kardinal-mindszenty-nach-seinerbefreiung-aus-8j%C3%A4hriger-news-photo/542356951?adppopup=true (accessed 5 December 2019).

Logo. Hawaii State Knights of Columbus.

Andrew Walther. Plaque commemorating Knights of Columbus' gift of altar to St. Mary's Church. Courtesy of the Walther family.

**144.** *LIFE* magazine. 27 May 1957. *LIFE* magazine/Getty Images.

Catholic News. Procession at Auriesville Shrine, 1950-1959 approximate. KCMA 2013-0903amo012.

National Shrine of the Immaculate Conception. KCMA 20130621amo035.

**145.** Unveiling the Father McGivney Memorial, 31 March 1957. KCMA 2013-0628amo041.

High Mass for Cuban war dead, 26 January 1959. KCMA 20130709amo005.

Edmund S. Veltman. Fidel Castro, 1960 [cartoon]. Library of Congress cph 3c30441.

**146.** Father Michael J. McGiveny statue, 18 April 2004. KCMA 20040418kc07.

Silver Rose run, 1960. KCMA 20141223amo003.

Victor Lallier. John McCormack, 1966. Wikipedia File:Speaker John McCormack.jpg.

**147.** National Film Board. Louis St. Laurent. KCMA 20130709amo006.

**148.** Basilica of the National Shrine of the Immaculate Conception, 4 April 2009. KCMA 20090404kc03.

**149.** Jack Sleeper. Plaque commemorating the Knights of Columbus' gift of the Knights' Tower. Kay's Photo Service. KCMA 20130621amo003.

Building the wall in East Berlin, 20 November 1961. National Archives and Records Administration. Wikipedia File:Berlin_Wall_1961-11-20.jpg.

**150.** Crane hoisting the Mary bell, largest of the 56-bell carillon, 1956. Reni Photos. KCMA 20130621amo018.

The Christopher bell and others awaiting their placement in the Knights Tower, 1956. Reni Photos. KCMA 20130621amo023.

Luthar Wolley. Concilium Oecumenicum Vaticanum II, 1965 [cover]. Wikimedia https://commons.wikimedia.org/wiki/File:Wolleh_Das_Konzil.jpg (accessed 30 September 2019).

**151.** President Kennedy delivers his inaugural address, 1961, Washington, D.C. John F. Kennedy Presidential Library and Museum, Boston. Wikipedia File:President_Kennedy_inaugural_address_(color).jpg.

**152.** President John F. Kennedy. White House photograph. John F. Kennedy Presidential Library and Museum, Boston. Wikipedia File:John_F._Kennedy,_White_House_photo_portrait,_looking_up.jpg.

President Kennedy. Public domain, Square One Publishers.

**153.** Supreme Knight Hart presents President Kennedy with the Pledge of Allegiance, 1961. [White House photograph.] KCMA 20130709amo014.

Pope Paul VI, 1963. Wikipedia File:Paolovi.jpg.

Knights of Columbus emblem.

**154.** Abbie Rowe. Kennedy family leaves the Capitol after the ceremony, 24 November 1963. John F. Kennedy Presidential Library and Museum, JFKWHP-1963-11-24-B, National Archives and Records Administration.

**155.** Supreme Knight [sic] Luke E. Hart, Funeral of President John F. Kennedy [transcribed notes], 25 Nov 1963. Record Group 0027, Supreme Knight Luke E. Hart Records, KCSCA.

## Chapter 8. Balancing Modernization with Preservation—1964 to 1977

**156.** L'Osservatore Romano. Opening of Vatican II. Courtesy L'Osservatore Romano. KCMA 20171016gws010.

**157.** *Columbia,* November 1970. KC.

Cecil Stoughton. [Lyndon B.] Johnson taking oath [of office], 22 November 1963. *New York*

*World-Telegram and Sun* Newspaper Photograph Collection, Library of Congress cph 3c26329.

Child kissing Bishop Greco's ring. KCMA 20140619AAM025.

**158.** John W. McDevitt. KCMA 20130829amo023.

L'Osservatore Romano. Pope John XXIII. Courtesy L'Osservatore Romano. KCMA 20171120gws011.

L'Osservatore Romano. Pope Paul VI. Courtesy L'Osservatore Romano. KCMA 20180314amo029.

Ron White. 1964 World's Fair. Wikipedia File:1965_new_york_world_fair.jpg.

Pope Paul VI gives blessing before leaving for Istanbul in 1967. CNS file photo. Courtesy Pan American Historical Foundation.

**159.** S. Appetite. Third World Congress of the Lay Apostolate, 1967, Vatican City. KCMA 20130207amo030.

Catholic News Service. Pope Paul VI makes his way past bishops during session of Second Vatican Council. CNS file photo. Courtesy Catholic News Service.

Father Patrick Peyton. Courtesy Family Theater Productions. KCMA 20171221amo001.

**160.** Knights of Columbus, Religious Information Bureau, Humanae Vitae, 1968. Collection 0021, Religious Information Bureau/Catholic Information Service Collection, KCSCA.

Pollack and Daly Photography. Council No. 6847, East Columbia, South Carolina, donated sets of the Catholic Encyclopedia to local parishes and schools. Courtesy of Daly and Salter Photography. KCMA 20140806at007

**161.** Jeremiah Denton. Official U.S. Navy photograph by E. Dael, Atlantic Fleet Photographic Center. KCMA 20160425amo002.

**162.** Dr. Martin Luther King, March on Washington, 28 August 1963. Public domain, Square One Publishers.

Ernest I. King. KC.

James Heffernan. Supreme Knight McDevitt was present at the inauguration of the new Dr. Martin Luther King Council No. 6135, New York, New York. KCMA 20130207amo016.

**163.** Transcendental Graphics. Jackie Robinson and Floyd Patterson. Getty https://www.gettyimages.com/detail/news-photo/jackie-robinson-left-and-heavyweight-champion-floyd-news-photo/113464410?adppopup=true [cropped] (accessed 19 September 2019).

Watergate Complex, Washington, D.C. Public domain, Square One Publishers.

NASA's Manned Spacecraft Center, Houston,

May 1965. NASA S68-18785 008. KCMA 20171106nasa001.

**164.** I.A. Sneiderman. Professor Arthur Wright addresses the Conference on Human Rights, 3 April 1965, Yale University, New Haven, Connecticut. KCMA 20130207amo033.

Conference with La Farge Institute, 27 March 1968. KCMA 20130207amo035.

Our Lady of Czestochowa. Wikipedia File:Nuestra_Se%C3%B1ora_de_Czestochowa .jpg.

Council No. 4268, Nueva Ecija, Luzon, distributes piglets to area farmers, 1971. KCMA 201309012amo048.

**165.** Bartoni & Giuliani. Pope Pius VI blesses the newly donated radio transmitters, Vatican Radio, 1966. KCMA 20130709amo027.

Auxiliary Bishop Francis T. Hurley of Juneau, Alaska, poses with the amphibious plane, 1971. KCMA 20140812at019.

Maine Knights celebrate Mass on the shores of the St. Croix River where the first Mass in New England was offered, 1972. KCMA 20140815at005.

**166.** Seventh Supreme Headquarters, 2007. KCMA 20070929kc09.

President Nixon with Supreme Knight McDevitt at States Dinner, 1971 [cropped]. KCMA 20130711amo002.

Stone house of the Virgin Mary. Getty https://www.gettyimages.com/detail/news-photo/the-exterior-view-of-the-restored-house-now-serving-as-a-news-photo/864884 426?adppopup=true (accessed 19 September 2019).

**167.** Colorado Knights collect signatures for a petition calling for humane treatment of American prisoners of war in North Vietnam, 1971. KCMA 20140808at009.

Employees at Supreme Council headquarters and management collect gifts for American servicemen in Vietnam, 1967. KCMA 20180411amo034.

Cardinal Cooke blesses rosaries for Americans serving in Vietnam. New York councils made the program possible. 1970. KCMA 20131115amo022.

Council No. 612, Hutchinson, Kansas, has "adopted" a family of Vietnamese refugees, 1976. KCMA 20151021gew012.

Chaplain (MAJ) Charles J. Watters conducting a field Mass, Republic of Vietnam, 1967. Courtesy of the Army Historical Collection, U.S. Army Center of Military History.

**168.** Reni Photos. Robert Sargent Shriver. KCMA 20130709amo017.

Marion S. Trikosko, photographer. U.S. Supreme Court crowds, 8 July 1974. Library of Congress 2019630937.

American military in Vietnam. Public domain, Square One Publishers.

**169.** 39th Annual Indoor Athletic Meet, 5 March 1948, Madison Square Garden [program]. KC.

Council No. 5478, Caubig, Philippines, built a reservoir for the town, 1975. KCMA 20150805gew004.

James Heffernan. Supreme Knight McDevitt and Archbishop Sheen at the Supreme Convention, 1975. KCMA 20130726amo021.

**170.** Supreme Knight Dechant with athletes at the 1987 Special Olympics Opening Ceremony. KCMA 20130711amo013.

The University of Notre Dame hosted the first International Special Olympics, 21 July 1987. KCMA 20131206amo037.

A volunteer from Council No. 2883, Danielson, Connecticut, assists an athlete at the Connecticut Summer Games, 12 June 2010, New Haven, Connecticut. KCMA 20100612kc12.

Supreme Knight Carl Anderson is welcomed by Sargent Shriver, 2003. KCMA 2003kc05.

Supreme Knight Dechant and Eunice Shriver at the 1991 Special Olympics, St. Paul, Minnesota. KCMA 20131209amo021.

**171.** Michael O'Connor Council No. 5026, Beaufort, South Carolina, provides support to Camp Dynamite. KCMA 20160121gws011.

Protect Religious Freedom [poster]. KC.

**172.** First March for Life, 22 January 1974. Courtesy the March for Life Education and Defense Fund. KCMA 201801kcc029.

**173.** First March for Life, 22 January 1974. Courtesy the March for Life Education and Defense Fund. KCMA 201801kcc030.

Nellie Gray displays the Life Principles, 1974, New Haven, Connecticut. KCMA 20190708amo017.

Spaulding Council No. 417, Washington, D.C., essay contest winners are students at St. Francis de Sales Catholic School, 1976. KCMA 20151130gew003.

**174.** Tony Tomsic. Green Bay Packers Hall of Fame head coach Vince Lombardi is carried off the field by his players, 1 January 1967. Getty https://www.gettyimages.com/detail/news-photo/green-bay-packers-hall-of-fame-head-coach-vince-lombardi-is-news-photo/75890595?adppopup=true (accessed 25 September 2019).

1976 Guatemala earthquake damage. U.S. Department of the Interior, U.S. Geological Survey.

Wikipedia File:GuateQuake1976Patzicia.jpg.

Knights of Columbus emblem.

**175.** Bachrach. Virgil C. Dechant. KCMA 20131118amo039.

## Chapter 9. One Christian Family—1978 to 1999

**176.** L'Osservatore Romano. A portable organ, gift from the order, designed for use in the Sistine Chapel, 7 November 1995. Courtesy L'Osservatore Romano. KCMA 20131202amo013.

**177.** Felici. The Dechants in private audience with Pope John Paul, 1 September 1978. KCMA 20131120amo050.

Felici. Pope John Paul II speaks to the K of C, 1979. KCMA 201309018amo043.

**178.** Council No. 999 joined in the vocations program by erecting a billboard, 1978. KCMA 20150701MH019.

Cardinal Ratzinger was keynote speaker at the Pope John XXIII Medical-Moral Research and Education Center, 1984. KCMA 20160217gws001.

Jack Sleeper. Marian Hour of Prayer, Supreme Convention, Washington, D.C., 1986. KCMA 20160725gws009.

**179.** Thomas Serafin. Tim Hickey ordination, 2013. KCMA 20130611kcts003.

President Reagan inaugural address, 20 January 1982. Public domain, SquareOne Publishers.

Mother Angelica. KCMA 20170816amo002.

**180.** Andrew Walther. St. Peter [statue]. Courtesy Andrew Walther.

**22.** Felici. Dedication and blessing of Three Saints Chapel in Vatican Grottoes, 1981. KCMA 20130711amo029.

Pat Korten. Our Lady of Czestochowa Chapel. KCMA (Rome-0578.jpg).

Pope John Paul II meets with Mehmet Ali Agca, 1982. Public domain, Square One Publishers.

**182.** L'Osservatore Romano. Board of Directors meeting, October 1988. Courtesy L'Osservatore Romano KCMA 201309018amo048.

Fabbrica di San Pietro in Vaticano. Moderno Atrium. Courtesy of Fabbrica di San Pietro in Vaticano.

Pope John Paul II visiting the children. Photo by Grzegorz Galazka\Archivio Grzegorz Galazka\Mondadori via Getty Images. https://www.gettyimages.com/detail/news-photo/pope-john-paul-ii-visiting-the-children-at-sandro-pertini-news-photo/471623124?adp-popup=true (accessed 19 September 2019).

The Common Christian roots of the European nations. 1. General sessions, 1982. [sic] General

Library Collection, KCSCA.

**183.** Rusty Kennedy/AP. Pope John Paul II gestures to a huge crowd attending an outdoor mass at Logan Circle in Philadelphia, Pa., Oct. 3, 1979. AP 258051351546.

**184.** John Cummings. Reinterment of Fr. McGivney remains in St. Mary's Church, 29 March 1982. KCMA 20131114amo030.

Jack Sleeper. President Reagan speaks privately with Cardinal Casaroli after the President's address, 3 August 1982. KCMA kc20120326lj01.

**185.** Jack Sleeper. President of the United States, Ronald Reagan, speaking at K of C Centennial Convention, 3 August 1982. KCMA 20130814amo018.

Council No. 6603, Cagayan de Oro City, Philippines sponsored a marriage validation ceremony, 1987. KCMA 20160920gws010.

Order of Pius IX [medal]. Order of Pius IX - Grade of Knight. Wikimedia https://commons.wikimedia.org/wiki/File:3%C2%B0_Conde_de_ParatyDSC02687.JPG (accessed 17 September 2019).

**186.** John Cummings. St. Mary's Church restoration, choir and organ loft, 1981. KCMA 20131120amo004.

Jack Sleeper. 1982 Mass in St. Mary's Church, New Haven, CT, dozens of bishops and priests joined Cardinal Agiostino Casaroli. KCMA 20170515gws006.

**187.** Christopher Kauffman. KCMA 20160425-amo014.

Knights of Columbus Museum. KC.

Tuition tax credit bill meeting with President Reagan, 1982. White House Photo. KCMA 20131120amo061.

John Whitman. Honorable Hilario G. Davide Jr., Guadalupe Festival, 2009. KCMA 20090808kcjw71.

**188.** March for Life, 1987. KCMA 2016-0906gws001.

Chief Justice William Rehnquist administering the oath of office to George Bush on the west front of the U.S. Capitol, with Dan Quayle and Barbara Bush looking on, January 20, 1989. Photograph from Architect of the Capitol, AOC no. 73009-24. Library of Congress 00652329.

SSgt. F. Lee Corkran. East and West Germans converge at the newly created opening in the Berlin Wall after a crane removed a section of the structure beside the Brandenburg Gate. Department of Defense, Air Force. Wikimedia File:Crane removed part of Wall Brandenburg Gate.jpg.

**189.** Charles Lindberg. Ninth Special Olympics, New Haven, Conn., 1995. KCMA 20150610amo010.

Council No. 3768, Kansas City, Kans., erected this monument, 1989. KCMA 20170619gws007.

Susan Johann. Bud Jetty, 2005. Courtesy of Susan Johann.

**190.** John Whitman. John Paul II Institute for Studies on Marriage and Family commencement, 12 May 2010. KCMA 20140513kcjw026.

4th June 1989 by Sean O'Sullivan, Creative Commons. https://search.creativecommons.org/photos/8276e4e7-a67d-4d7b-a5e3-eff0fe3dd03a (accessed 15 November 2019).

Supreme Knight Dechant's visit to the Philippines, 1989. KCMA 20131206amo020.

**191.** President George Bush. Public domain, Square One Publishers.

Shutterstock. Shutterstock_27273565.

**192.** Visit by Mother Teresa to the Supreme Office, 16 June 1988. KCMA 20130711amo009.

**193.** Chas Fagan, artist. David Ramsey, photographer. Mother Teresa portrait, 2016. KCMA 20160630dr001.

Supreme Knight Dechant presents the first Gaudium et Spes Award to Mother Teresa at the States Dinner, 1992. KCMA 20160309amo001.

**194.** Knights of Columbus Museum. KCMA (Original ExtMuseum.jpg).

**195.** Peter Aaron/Esto. Wall of History gallery [cropped]. © Peter Aaron/OTTO. KCMA 20130430amo005.

**196.** Peter Aaron/Esto. Wall of History gallery [cropped]. © Peter Aaron/OTTO. KCMA 20130430amo004.

Peter Aaron/Esto. Wall of History gallery. © Peter Aaron/OTTO. KCMA 20130430amo006.

Peter Aaron/Esto. Wall of History gallery. © Peter Aaron/OTTO. KCMA 20130430amo010.

**197.** Peter Aaron/Esto. Father McGivney gallery. © Peter Aaron/OTTO. KCMA 2013-0430amo003.

Thomas Serafin. World War I: Beyond the Front Lines exhibit. KCMA (DSC_2142.JPG).

Bottega D'Arte Presepiale Cantone & Costabile (Naples, Italy); Thomas Serafin, photographer. Neapolitan creche, 2014 [edited]. KCM.

**198.** Council No. 2961 at the creche blessing, 2015, Trumbull, Conn. Courtesy of Anthony J. Mancini.

**199.** Agostina Bono. Father Robert Graham, 1992. Courtesy of Catholic News Service.

**200.** Giansanti Artistic Jewelers, Rome, Italy. Father Michael J. McGivney Memorial Chalice, 1990. KCM.

President Bill Clinton inauguration. Public domain, Square One Publishers.

World Trade Center bombing aftermath, 1993. Public domain, Square One Publishers.

201. L'Osservatore Romano. Pope John Paul II offers Mass at Aqueduct Raceway, 6 October 1995. Courtesy of L'Osservatore Romano. KCMA 201309027amo011.

202. James Heffernan. Supreme Convention, Miami Beach, Florida, 1975. KCMA 20150928gew009.

American, Mexican, Canadian flags. Public domain, Square One Publishers.

Gaudium et Spes medal. KCMA 2016-0718amo020.

203. Opening of cause for sainthood for Fr. McGivney, 18 December 1997. KCMA 2017-1204amo006.

Ron Hoerth. Council No. 710 mans video cameras for a televised daily Mass at Holy Family Medical Center in Manitowoc, Wisconsin, 1986. KCMA 20160829gws012.

L'Osservatore Romano. Pope John Paul II blesses television production van, 6 November 1995. Courtesy of L'Osservatore Romano. KCMA 20131202amo010.

204. Prayer to Father McGivney [holy card]. KC.

Permanent Observer of the Holy See [emblem]. Public domain, Square One Publishers.

Knights of Columbus emblem.

## Chapter 10. Into the New Millennium– 2000 to Present

206. Omar Alhayali. People from Mosul, Iraq, raise a wooden cross near St. Georges Monastery, 2017 Apr 24. EPA via Catholic News Service.

207. Supreme Knight Anderson signs his first charter for Padre Miguel Agustin Pro Juarez Council No. 12789, McAllen Texas, 2000. KCMA 20131219amo010.

Eric Draper. George W. Bush. White House Photo. Wikipedia File:George-W-Bush.jpeg.

208. 9/11 attack on the Twin Towers, New York City. Public domain, Square One Publishers.

Pacem in Terris coat of arms.

209. John Cummings. Javier Najera Cabrales carried the Mexican priest-martyrs reliquary at the Memorial Mass procession, 3 August 2006. KCMA 20060803kcjc01.

Cardinal George led a program of adoration and benediction, 2002 Eucharistic Congress, Chicago, Illinois. KCMA 20050805kc07.

Miguel Cabrera, artist. Juan Diego unveiling his cloak to Bishop Juan de Zumarraga. KCMA 20160404gws007.

210. Carl A. Anderson. Knights of Columbus.

Andrew Walther. Wheelchair recipient in Afghanistan, 2003. KCMA 200309001kc003.

Max Rossi. Concert of Reconciliation, 17 January 2004. CNS/Reuters. KCMA 20040117cns04.

211. Carl Anderson supreme knight installation at the Basilica of Our Lady of Guadalupe, 2000. KCMA 20000203kc01.

212. Archbishop Lori celebrates Mass in the Holy Family Chapel, 10 July 2013. KCMA 20130710kcts003.

*He Was Our Father* by Father Peter John Cameron [performance], 2005. KCMA 20050801kc10.

Joe Raedle/Getty Images. German Cardinal Ratzinger presides over the funeral Mass for Pope John Paul II, 8 April 2005. Getty https://www.gettyimages.com/detail/news-photo/cardinal-joseph-ratzinger-sprinkles-holy-water-over-the-news-photo/52603369 (accessed 19 September 2019).

213. Captain Al Fuentes addresses the College Councils Conference, 10 September 2004. KCMA 20040918kc014.

214. *Columbia*, January 2002. KC.

215. World Day Prayer for Peace, 2004 [poster]. KC.

Steel girders from the World Trade Center. KCM / Gift of the City of New York. KCMA 20171019kcts001.

216. Statue at St. Michael's Catholic Church, Biloxi, Mississippi, after Hurricane Katrina, 2005. KCMA 20050914kc11.

125 Years of Faith in Action [logo]. KC.

Kevin Manning. "Journey for Charity" Missouri councils food collection tractor parade, 2012. KCMA 20120907kcts014.

217. Hurricane Katrina damage, 2005. Federal Emergency Management Administration. Wikipedia File:Katrina-14588.jpg.

Pope Benedict meets with non-Christian leaders, Pope John Paul II Shrine, 17 Apr 2008, Washington, D.C. L'Osservatore Romano. KCMA 20080417lor27.

Marist Poll. Americans Opinions on Abortion, January 2018. KC.

218. Knights in Leyte deliver needed assistance after Typhoon Haiyan, 2013 [cropped image]. KCMA 201312kc005.

Ronalyn Ramos Regino. Livelihood Project brought 40 new boats to fishermen in Western Samar, 2014. KCMA 20140602rrr002.

219. More than 100 children have been fitted with prosthetics, Healing Haiti's Children, 5 March 2011. KCMA 20110305kc001.

220. SK Anderson and earthquake victims

share the joy a wheelchair can bring, Haiti. KCMA 20100427kc10.

Thomas Serafin. Evening Vespers, Year for Priests, 6 October 2009, St. John Lateran. KCMA 20100608kcts12.

221. Team Zaryen logo. Public domain, Square One Publishers.

Thomas Serafin. Team Zaryen vs. U.S. National Amputee Soccer Team, 18 October 2011, Bethesda, Maryland. KCMA 20111018kc020.

222. Pat Korten. Bishop Lori addresses the religious freedom rally in Hartford, 11 March 2009. KCMA 20090311kcpk03.

Minnie Garcia/Stringer. Demonstrations Planned Pro And Anti-Pledge Of Allegiance In Schools. Getty https://www.gettyimages.com/detail/news-photo/protestors-carry-signs-outside-the-supreme-court-in-favor-news-photo/3127472?adppopup=true.

Barack Obama, 2009. Official White House Photo by Pete Souza. Wikipedia File: President_Barack_Obama.jpg.

223. Blessing and dedication of San Carlos y San Ambrosio Seminary, Cuba, 4 October 2010. KCMA 20101104kc020.

"Big Mountain Jesus" statue, 2011, Whitefish Mountain Resort, Montana, 2011. KCMA 20111215kc003.

224. Supreme Knight Anderson and Archbishop Lori visit the Sisters of Life, Stamford, Conn. KC (IMG_0014).

Oil on the Wounds conference, jointly sponsored by the Knights and the Pontifical John Paul II Institute Marriage and the Family Rome Session at Lateran University, 2008. KCMA 20080404kc05.

Knights of Columbus provides relief after Pakistan flooding, 2010. KCMA 20100915kc03.

225 *Columbia*, January 2015. KC.

226. Roy Lagarde. March for Life, 2018, Manila, Philippines. KCMA 201801kcc021.

Pu Ying Huang. March for Religious Freedom, 22 November 2015. KCMA 20151122kcphu002.

L'Osservatore Romano. Pope Benedict blesses the high-definition television truck, 2010, Vatican City. Courtesy L'Osservatore Romano. KCMA 20101117or003.

227. Cardinal Lubomyr Husar addresses the Knights of Columbus at the 2005 Supreme Convention, 2005. KCMA 20050803kc04.

St. Peter Council No. 16252, Melitopol, Ukraine, support a recreational and spiritual formation camp for 7 to 12 year olds. KCMA 2018kc002.

Supreme Knight and Mrs. Anderson tour the 90 Years in Rome exhibit, Capitoline Museum, 9 June 2010, Rome, Italy. KCMA 20100609kcts44.

Christian Rizzo. Largo Cavalieri di Colombo sign, 2013. KCMA 20131009kccr010.

**228.** Third National Eucharistic Congress procession, 18 June 2005, Warsaw, Poland. KCMA 20050618kc03.

Slav Pavliuk. St. Vladimir Council No. 15800 with His Beatitude Sviatoslav Shevchuk, 2013, Kyiv, Ukraine. KCMA 2013116yp002.

First Degree class formation Cathedral of St. Ignatius of Loyola, 9 March 2017, Vilnius, Lithuania. KCMA 20170309kc002.

Matt Barrick. Supreme Knight Anderson announces the formation of five new councils in France, Supreme Convention, 4 August 2016. KCMA 20160804kcmb046.

Stephen Feiler. Fourth Degree exemplification, Seoul, South Korea, 18 April 2017. KCMA 20170418kcsf010.

**229.** Hector Segovia. Pilgrimage to Christ the King shrine, Cubilete, Mexico, 27 March 2011. KCMA (_HSF4369.JPG).

Ecclesia in America conference, 10 December 2012, Vatican City. KCMA 20121210kcts013.

Euromaidan. Wikipedia File:Euromaidan_2013_Mstyslav_Chernov-14.jpg.

**230.** Adolf Hyła. Divine Mercy [edited image]. Our Lady of Mercy. KC.

Thomas Serafin. Ecclesia in America conference, 10 December 2012, Vatican City. KCMA 20121210kcts006.

M. Falconi. Dr. Lorenza D'Alessandro works on the restoration of the *Madonna della Colonna*. 2013. Courtesy Fabbrica di San Pietro in Vaticano. KCMA 201302fdsp004.

Antonella Cappuccio. Pope Francis, 2017 [detail of painting]. KCM. © Antonella Cappucio.

**231.** L'Osservatore Romano. Private audience with Pope John Paul II. Supreme Knight Carl Anderson, Clare Anderson, Katherine Anderson, Dorian Anderson, 26 November 2004. Courtesy L'Osservatore Romano. KCMA kc20120327lj01.

L'Osservatore Romano. Private audience with Pope Benedict XVI, 2009, Vatican City. Courtesy L'Osservatore Romano. KCMA 20091210or05.

L'Osservatore Romano. Private audience with Pope Francis, 2019. Courtesy L'Osservatore Romano. KCMA 20190228lor001.

L'Osservatore Romano. Fourth Degree Honor Guard processes through Vatican Square on

Marian Day, Vatican City, 13 October 2013. Courtesy L'Osservatore Romano. KCMA 20140224amo012.

*Dabiq* (magazine). Screenshot (2019).

**232–233.** Matthew Barrick. Saint John Paul II Shrine, 2017. KCMA 20170622kcmb003.

**234.** Peter Skrlep & Tamino Petelinsek. Entrance to Redemptor Hominis Church, 2016. KCMA 201601kcpstp021.

**235.** Thomas Serafin. St John Paul II mosaic installation, 10 September 2015. KCMA (20150910kcts001).

Peter Skrlep & Tamino Petelinsek. Luminous Mysteries Chapel altar and reliquary, 2016. KCMA 201601kcpstp003.

**236.** Matthew Barrick. John Paul II Shrine: Gallery 1 Beginning. KCMA 201409kcmb001.

Matthew Barrick. John Paul II Shrine: Gallery 2 Light in the Darkness. KCMA 201409kcmb002.

**237.** Matthew Barrick. John Paul II Shrine: Gallery 3 Election to the Papacy. KCMA 201409kcmb003.

Matthew Barrick. John Paul II Shrine: Gallery 4 Man, the Way of the Church. KCMA 201409kcmb004.

Matthew Barrick. John Paul II Shrine: Holy Door replica. KCMA 201409kcmb005.

**238.** Matthew Barrick. John Paul II Shrine: Gallery 5 Totus Tuus. KCMA 201409kcmb006.

Matthew Barrick. John Paul II Shrine: Gallery 6 The Dignity of the Human Person. KCMA 201409kcmb007.

Matthew Barrick. John Paul II Shrine: Gallery 7 The Mysteries of the Light. KCMA 201409kcmb008.

Matthew Barrick. John Paul II Shrine: Gallery 8 A Great Gift. KCMA 201409kcmb009.

Matthew Barrick. John Paul II Shrine: Gallery 9 The Communion of Saints. KCMA 201409kcmb010.

Matthew Barrick. John Paul II Shrine: Gallery 10 The Life of Saint John Paul II. KC.

**239.** HarperCollins. *A Civilization of Love* [cover]. Knights of Columbus Charities, Inc. Courtesy HarperCollins.

*La Cristiada* [cover]. Courtesy of SquareOne Publishers.

*Francis* [cover]. KC.

Random House. *Beyond a House Divided* [cover]. Courtesy of Penguin Random House.

*Unbreakable: A Story of Hope and Healing in Haiti* [cover]. KC.

*Liberating a Continent: John Paul II and the Fall of Communism* [cover]. KC.

Random House. *Our Lady of Guadalupe* [cover]. Courtesy of Penguin Random House.

HarperCollins. *Parish Priest* [cover]. Courtesy of HarperCollins.

**240.** College Knights at the "Boat-a-cade" welcome Pope Benedict XVI, 17 August 2008, Sydney, Australia. KCMA 20080817kc03.

Thomas Serafin. Our Lady of Guadalupe: Star of the New Evangelization conference, 2013. KCMA 20131116kcts008.

St. Paul Council No. 10775 display mangrove seedlings. The council planted close to 600 bags of the seedlings along the coastal area of Ondol, Inabanga Bohol. KCMA 201806kckia006.

**241.** Pope Francis meets World Youth Day volunteers, Tauron Arena, 31 July 2016, Krakow, Poland. KCMA 20160731kc002.

Andy Fowler. World Youth Day FIAT Eucharistic adoration, 23 January 2019, Panama City, Panama. KCMA 20190123kcaf006.

Paul Haring. Pope John Paul II banner, St. Peter's Square, 27 April 2014. Catholic News Service 20140427cnsbr5137.

**242.** Thomas Serafin. Marian Congress on Our Lady of Guadalupe and Festival, 8 August 2009. KCMA 20090808kcts41.

Thomas Serafin. Veneration at the Saint Juan Diego's tilma relic during the Marian Congress, 6 August 2009. KCMA 20090806kcts10.

Building the Domestic Church [cover]. KC.

**243.** John Whitman. Archbishop Lori processes with the tilma relic of Saint Juan Diego at the Guadalupe Festival, 5 August 2012, Los Angeles, California. KCMA 20120805kcjw023.

**244.** Thomas Serafin. Coats for Kids, 28 January 2014, Jersey City, New Jersey. KCMA 20140128kcts005.

Cia Pak. Pope Francis addresses the United Nations, 20 September 2015. United Nations https://www.unmultimedia.org/s/photo/detail/644/0644169.html (accessed 8 September 2019).

Council No 8785 holds a diaper drive to support families. KCMA 201803kckia44.

**245.** Apostles of Jesus Father Paul Gaggawala and AIDS orphans school, 2015, Uganda. KCMA 20150313aj02.

Council No.11475 supports clean water in Uganda, 2019. KCMA 20190119kc004.

Ken Rohling. Shrine of Our Lady of Martyrs, Auriesville, New York, 13 June 2015. KCMA 20150613kckr001.

**246.** Corky Miller. Council No. 2171, Tillamook, Oregon, harvests cabbages to support area food banks, 2013. KCMA 20130807kccm001.

Woodie Williams. Georgia Knights support Special Olympics teen athletes at Camp Inspire, 2010. KCMA 20100713kc03.

Tamino Petelinsek. Eagle dancers of the Pueblo of Laguna, N.M., lead a procession of a relic of St. Kateri Tekakwitha, 7 August 2019, at the 137th Supreme Convention. KCMA 2019087kctp008.

**247.** Council No. 8489 assists in a wheelchair distribution, 14 October 2011, Mexico. KCMA 20111014kc001.

Thom Wolf. Knights of Columbus and religious leaders urge embrace of Rev. Martin Luther King's principles of non-violence, 2 October 2017, Washington, D.C. KCMA 20171002kc002.

*Columbia*, July / August 2019. KC.

**248.** College Knights and chaplains hiked the Tatra Mountains in Poland on their way to the 2016 World Youth Day in Poland. KCMA 20160721kc036

College Councils Conference 50th Anniversary. KC.

Council No. 64 in Putnam, Connecticut, makes visits to the families of deceased members. KCMA 201901kckia022.

**249.** Asset Advisors [logo]. KC.

Troops in Bagdad show their "Armed with Faith" Prayer book. KCMA 20040427kc01.

Pascal LeMaitre, Cailloux-et-Cie, for Lux Fiat. The Lady of the Hearts, Notre Dame Cathedral, Paris, France, 7 November 2017. Courtesy Pascal LeMaitre – Lux Fiat. KCMA (P_L_7489).

*Genocide against Christians in the Middle East* [cover]. KC.

**250.** Knights of Columbus tank pull, Clifton, N.J., 23 June 2019. Courtesy John Hughes, Founder & Chairman, State Tank Pull Committee.

Shealah Craighead, White House portrait. Donald J. Trump. Wikipedia File:Donald_

Trump_official_portrait.jpg.

Aaron Joseph. The Order of St. Martin of Tours medal. KCM. KCMA 20181101kcaj007.

**251.** Tamino Petelinsek. Mass for English-speaking military in the Grotto, 20 May 2017. Warriors to Lourdes pilgrimage. KCMA 20170520kctp012.

**252.** Mar Addai Church after ISIS, Karmales, Iraq. Courtesy of the Chaldean Catholic Archdiocese of Erbil, Iraq. KCMA 201708ccea001.

Chas Fagan, artist; David Ramsey, photographer. Mother Teresa. KCMA 20160630dr001.

Martyn Aim. Christians rebuilding in Karamles, Iraq. 2017. KCMA 20170916ma008.

**253.** Stivay Shany. Christian refugees in the Kurdish region, 2014. KCMA (E73A3948).

Jeffrey Bruno. Fourth Degree Honor Guard leads the entrance procession for Sunday Mass at St. Patrick's Cathedral, 7 April 2019. KCMA 2019007kcjb004.

Knights from Puerto Rico assist with the Hurricane Irma recovery, 2017. KCMA 201710kc006.

**254.** Tamino Petelinsek. Supreme Knight Anderson and Archbishop Warda in front of the newly-built McGivney House, 1 March 2019. KCMA 20190301kctp012.

Warehouse of K of C food for ISIS-displaced families, 2015. Courtesy Chaldean Catholic Archdiocese of Erbil, Iraq. KCMA 20150907ccae002.

Stivan Shany. Food packages from the Knights of Columbus for ISIS-displaced families, 2015. KCMA 20150912ss001.

Duda Matus. STEP-IN mobile clinic, 2018. Courtesy of STEP-IN. KCMA 201704md001.

**255.** Coptic Orthodox Archbishop Angaelos speaks on the Report on Christian Genocide, 10 March 2016, National Press Club, Washington, D.C. KCMA 20160310kc009.

Charles Votaw. Carl Anderson addresses the Congressional Subcommittee on Africa, Global

Health, Global Human Rights, and International Organizations, 26 May 2016. Courtesy Charles Votaw. KCMA 20160526cv004.

Sheala Craighead. H.R. 390: The Iraq and Syria Genocide Relief and Accountability Act signing, 11 December 2018. Official White House Photo.

**256.** Matthew Barrick. Syrian Patriarch Ignatius Joseph III Younan addresses the 2016 Supreme Convention. KCMA 20160802kcmb073.

Nick Crettier. Archbishop Jeanbart of Aleppo, Syria, blesses the icon of Our Lady Help of Persecuted Christians, Supreme Convention, 9 August 2018, Baltimore, Maryland. KCMA 20180809kcnc024.

Matthew Barrick. Saint Jean Marie Vianney relic, 9 August 2018, Baltimore, Maryland. KCMA 20180809kcmb021.

Knights of Columbus emblem.

**257.** Matthew Barrick. Bishop Yousif Habash, "Cradle of Christianity," 10 March 2018, Fort Calhoun, Nebraska. KCMA 20180310kcjc002.

**Back Cover**

Richard Whitney, artist. Father Michael J. McGivney, 1989. Photograph of painting copyright by the Knights of Columbus Supreme Council. Painting: KCM.

Babe Ruth, 23 July 1920. Library of Congress Prints and Photographs Division (cph.3g07246).

Cecil Stoughton, White House. John F. Kennedy portrait photograph, 11 July 1963. National Archives and Records Administration. National Archives Identifier (NAID)194255.

Chas Fagan, artist. David Ramsey, photographer. Mother Teresa portrait, 2016. KCMA 20160630dr001.

Floyd Patterson, 7 February 1961. Associated Press. http://www.apimages.com/metadata/Index/Watchf-AP-S-NY-USA-APHS330916-Floyd-Patterson/0ce84c2c9d144c5894f6961eea9e1a3d/228/0 (accessed 5 November 2019).